COLIN GUNTON'S TRINITARIAN
THEOLOGY OF CULTURE

T&T Clark Studies in English Theology

Series editors
Karen Kilby
Mike Higton
Stephen R. Holmes

COLIN GUNTON'S TRINITARIAN THEOLOGY OF CULTURE

Towards a Living Sacrifice of Praise

Andrew Picard

LONDON • NEW YORK • OXFORD • NEW DELHI • SYDNEY

T&T CLARK
Bloomsbury Publishing Plc, 50 Bedford Square, London, WC1B 3DP, UK
Bloomsbury Publishing Inc, 1359 Broadway, New York, NY 10018, USA
Bloomsbury Publishing Ireland, 29 Earlsfort Terrace, Dublin 2, D02 AY28, Ireland

BLOOMSBURY, T&T CLARK and the T&T Clark logo are trademarks
of Bloomsbury Publishing Plc

First published in Great Britain 2024
Paperback edition published 2026

Copyright © Andrew Picard, 2024

Andrew Picard has asserted his right under the Copyright,
Designs and Patents Act, 1988, to be identified as Author of this work.

For legal purposes the Acknowledgments on pp. ix–x constitute an
extension of this copyright page.

Cover image: clairevis/iStock

All rights reserved. No part of this publication may be: i) reproduced or transmitted in
any form, electronic or mechanical, including photocopying, recording or by means of
any information storage or retrieval system without prior permission in writing from the
publishers; or ii) used or reproduced in any way for the training, development or operation
of artificial intelligence (AI) technologies, including generative AI technologies. The rights
holders expressly reserve this publication from the text and data mining exception as per
Article 4(3) of the Digital Single Market Directive (EU) 2019/790.

Bloomsbury Publishing Plc does not have any control over, or responsibility for,
any third-party websites referred to or in this book. All internet addresses given
in this book were correct at the time of going to press. The author and publisher
regret any inconvenience caused if addresses have changed or sites have ceased
to exist, but can accept no responsibility for any such changes.

A catalogue record for this book is available from the British Library.

Library of Congress Cataloging-in-Publication Data
Names: Picard, Andrew, author.
Title: Colin Gunton's Trinitarian theology of culture : towards a living
sacrifice of praise / Andrew Picard.
Description: 1. | London : T&T Clark, 2024. | Series: T&T Clark studies in
English theology | Includes bibliographical references and index.
Identifiers: LCCN 2023052908 (print) | LCCN 2023052909 (ebook) |
ISBN 9780567712295 (hardback) | ISBN 9780567712349 (paperback) |
ISBN 9780567712301 (pdf) | ISBN 9780567712332 (ebook)
Subjects: LCSH: Gunton, Colin E. | Trinity. | Christianity and culture.
Classification: LCC BX4827.G86 P53 2024 (print) | LCC BX4827.G86 (ebook) |
DDC 231/.044092–dc23/eng/20240430
LC record available at https://lccn.loc.gov/2023052908
LC ebook record available at https://lccn.loc.gov/2023052909

ISBN: HB: 978-0-5677-1229-5
PB: 978-0-5677-1234-9
ePDF: 978-0-5677-1230-1
eBook: 978-0-5677-1233-2

Series: T&T Clark New Studies in English Theology

Typeset by Integra Software Services Pvt. Ltd.

For product safety related questions contact productsafety@bloomsbury.com.

To find out more about our authors and books visit www.bloomsbury.com
and sign up for our newsletters.

For Margaret, Olivia, and Amy

CONTENTS

Acknowledgments ix

INTRODUCTION 1

Part I: COLIN GUNTON'S EARLY TRINITARIAN THEOLOGY OF CULTURE AND ITS CRITICS

Chapter 1
THE ONE, THE THREE AND THE MANY AND COLIN GUNTON'S EARLY
WRITINGS ON A TRINITARIAN THEOLOGY OF CULTURE 17
    A: The One and the Many 19
    D/D': Creation, Truth, and Open Transcendentals 23
    C/C': Christology, Economy, and *Perichoresis* 34
    B/B': Pneumatology, Particularity, and Hypostasis 45
    A': Trinity, Relationality, and Ecclesiology 58
    Conclusion 64

Chapter 2
GUNTON'S LAUDABLE TRINITARIAN PROJECT AND ITS CRITICS 68
    A Critical Engagement with Gunton's Trinitarian Theology 71
    Social Trinitarianism 87
    The *Hauptbriefe* in Gunton Reception 106
    Conclusion 117

Part II: TOWARDS A TRINITARIAN THEOLOGY OF CULTURE

Chapter 3
THE MEDIATION OF THE FATHER: CREATION AND HUMAN CULTURE 121
    Gunton's Trinitarian Theology of Mediation, Creation, and Culture 123
    The Doctrine of Creation and God's Creative Action 140
    Conclusion 160

Chapter 4
THE MEDIATION OF THE SON: HUMANITY AND HUMAN CULTURE 161
    The Mediation of the Son: Jesus Christ as Lord of Creation and
        Redemption 161
    The Crucified and Risen Son and Human Culture 178
    Pneumatological Christology: The Action of the Son in the Spirit 194
    Conclusion 201

Chapter 5
THE MEDIATION OF THE SPIRIT: THE CHURCH AND HUMAN CULTURE   202
    The Spirit, Human Culture, and the Perfecting of Creation   202
    Gunton's Early Ecclesiology: The Being of God and
        the Being of the Church   209
    Gunton's Later Ecclesiology: The Church and Eschatological Culture   227
    Conclusion   246

Chapter 6
THE CHURCH, THE LORD'S SUPPER, AND HUMAN CULTURE AS
A LIVING SACRIFICE OF PRAISE   247
    Theology and the Rise of the Cultural Sciences   248
    The Church at Corinth in Light of the Roman Associations   252
    Paul's Theology of Foolishness as Social and Political
        Counter-Testimony   263
    Implications for the Church's Culture Today: Disability, Ecclesiology,
        and the Politics of Belonging in Community   268
    Conclusion: The Church's Sociological Politics as Her Sacrifice of
        Praise   279

Chapter 7
CONCLUSION   280

Bibliography   286
Index   309

ACKNOWLEDGMENTS

Among the many things I have learnt from studying Colin Gunton's theology is the conviction that theology is best done in conversation and community. Gunton's works are regularly marked by acknowledgments to those who he owes a debt of gratitude for insights that have shaped his thinking. It takes a village to write a book, and this book is the result of some important conversations and communities that have shaped me over many years. I offer my thanks with deep gratitude for all the support and encouragement I have received over these years.

I would like to thank Professor Murray Rae who supervised my doctoral thesis, which is the basis of this book. I am grateful for Murray's gentleness, patience, perseverance, and kindness over many years. I could not have asked for a better supervisor, and the litany of references to Murray's work testify to his enduring influence on me. His academic and personal knowledge of Colin Gunton, coupled with his scholarly acumen, has been an incalculable gift that has deepened my understanding of Gunton's theology and theology in general. Murray's friendship has been a grace to me, and conversations on Gunton's theology naturally segued into equally important conversations about the Blackcaps. I would also like to thank Dr. Martin Sutherland who was secondary supervisor in my doctoral project. Martin's friendship has shaped me, personally and academically, in innumerable ways over the last twenty years. He first introduced me to Colin Gunton's theology in his class on Mission and the Western Mind, and this book is in no small part a result of Martin's friendship and influence as my lecturer, supervisor, colleague, and friend. I am also deeply indebted to Brian Smith who, like Martin, has had a significant impact on me for many years as a lecturer, mentor, and friend. The fact that Brian has been willing to proofread this book, with his famous attention to detail, whilst juggling ministry, student support, ESOL teaching, and much more in his ninth decade of life, displays the extent of his graciousness, brilliance, and care. You are right, Brian: arrow down.

I would like to thank the remarkable community that is Carey Baptist College. This book is in large part the result of the love, support, and encouragement of the staff, students, management team, board, alumni, and stakeholders of Carey. I am indebted to the Carey team for all their support over many years, and I am humbled by their friendship, love, and care. The staffroom conversations, hallway chats, and kind deeds have helped me persist during the times when I felt least able to finish the work. I am likewise grateful to the students of Carey who have journeyed with my journey with Colin Gunton's theology and sharpened my work along the way. Thanks are due to the two principals of Carey, Charles Hewlett and Dr. John Tucker, who invested in me, believed in me, and encouraged me throughout this time. You are both dear friends, and your goodness and kindness have made working at Carey a joy. To the faculty at Carey, past and present, thank you for your kindness as colleagues, and thank you for contributing to this work in so many ways. Particular thanks are due to Dr. Myk Habets, *Doctor Serviens Ecclesiae*, for his kind friendship and investment in me. I would also like to thank the Heretics writing group whose comradery, support, and encouragement made the completion of this book much easier, and much more fun. Thanks are also due to Siong Ng for building a substantial holding of Gunton's works in the Carey Library and, with the University of Otago Library, supplying me with many of the more obscure Gunton references.

Finally, I would like to express my gratitude to my family. Thank you for your interest in my book and your support for its completion. To Mum and Dad, this may be a far cry from the more familiar mechanic's workshop in which I began my career, but I want to thank you for your relentless love and support in all avenues of my life. Finally, I want to thank Margaret, Olivia, and Amy. Without your love, support, and forgiveness throughout these years, I doubt this book would have been completed. You have sacrificed much to allow me time to complete this book, which has spanned much of Olivia and Amy's lives. You are my greatest work, not this book, and you have taught me what it means to live in a community of love. If Colin Gunton is correct that being is communion, and I think he is correct, then I am who I am because of who we are.

The author and publisher gratefully acknowledge the permission granted to reproduce the copyright material in this book. Some of the material in Chapter 6, Section 4, is adapted and revised from previous publications. Copyright (© 2023) From *Theology and the Experience of Disability: Interdisciplinary Perspectives from Voices Down Under* by Andrew Picard and Myk Habets. Reproduced by permission of Taylor and Francis Group, LLC, a division of Informa plc. This permission does not cover any third-party copyrighted work which may appear in the material requested. User is responsible for obtaining permission for such material separately from this grant. Also Paul Louis Metzger, "Beyond Ableism: A Politics of Belonging in Trinitarian Community. An Interview with Andrew Picard, PhD," *Cultural Encounters: A Journal for the Theology of Culture*, 16 no. 2 (2021): 63–72 (www.culturalencounters.org).

INTRODUCTION

Colin Gunton is, among other things, a theologian of culture. All of human culture is, as Murray Rae proposes, theologically interesting to Gunton.[1] Whether gardening, sport, politics, art, or science, human culture is interesting to Gunton because God affirms the significance of human culture and desires human contributions to the redemption and perfection of creation. Theology for Gunton is an engagement with the triune God and all things in relation to God. Therefore, theology must engage with life, and the intellectual and cultural challenges of its day. In his context, this meant confronting the abstract and dualistic forces of Western culture that undermine the goodness of creation and the realities of embodied life. Whilst Gunton's theological *analysis* of culture is the subject of much critical reception, his constructive trinitarian *theology* of culture has not been adequately examined to this point.[2]

---

1. Murray A. Rae, "Introduction," in *T&T Clark Handbook of Colin Gunton*, ed. Andrew Picard, Myk Habets, and Murray Rae (London: T&T Clark, 2021), 2.

2. William Whitney provides a helpful chapter on Gunton's theology of culture, and rightly sets it in the context of the doctrine of creation. However, this chapter contrasts Gunton's and Barth's theology of culture in service of renewing American Christian engagements with culture. As a result, Whitney highlights many important aspects of Gunton's theology of culture but does not delineate its systematic relations with Christology, pneumatology, eschatology, or ecclesiology. As I will argue, Whitney's conclusion that Gunton holds to a creational soteriology overwhelms the analysis. See William B. Whitney, *Problem and Promise in Colin E. Gunton's Doctrine of Creation* (Leiden: Brill, 2013), 146-93. Stephen Holmes utilizes Gunton's trinitarian theology of culture to develop his own insights, but the focus of his work is a constructive theology of culture rather than a sustained analysis of Gunton's trinitarian theology of culture. See Stephen R. Holmes, "Can Theology Engage with Culture?," in *Public Theology in Cultural Engagement*, ed. Stephen R. Holmes (Milton Keynes: Paternoster, 2008), 1-19; and Stephen R. Holmes, "Triune Creativity: Trinity, Creation, Art and Science," in *Trinitarian Soundings in Systematic Theology*, ed. Paul Louis Metzger (London: T&T Clark, 2005), 73-86.

This book examines Colin Gunton's trinitarian theology of culture and enquires into its ongoing fruitfulness for today. Gunton's trinitarian theology of culture finds its richest expression in his later writings. I argue that there is a progression in Gunton's articulation of trinitarian theology from analogical deployments of trinitarian theology to a trinitarian theology of mediation focused upon divine action in the economy and its creaturely fruit. The progression in Gunton's theology is not widely acknowledged or outlined. Stephen Holmes provides a very detailed and insightful analysis of the developments in Gunton's conception and use of trinitarian theology. He notes an initial shift from a simple acceptance of Barth's trinitarian theology to a Zizioulian account of persons in relation and the hermeneutical deployment of the doctrine of the Trinity to explore trinitarian analogies between divine and human personhood. In the early 1990s, Gunton's theology shifts from an exploration of trinitarian analogies to a trinitarian theology of mediation.[3] Since Holmes' important analysis, others have also begun to observe the shifts in Gunton's definition and use of trinitarian theology.[4] This book attempts to extend these analyses and fill them with further detail.

A major claim of this book is that there is a *Hauptbriefe* in Gunton reception that deems *The One, the Three and the Many* and the first edition of *The Promise of Trinitarian Theology* to be definitive of his trinitarianism, which results in a lack of

---

3. Stephen R. Holmes, "Towards the *Analogia Personae et Relationis*: Developments in Gunton's Trinitarian Thinking," in *The Theology of Colin Gunton*, ed. Lincoln Harvey (London: T&T Clark, 2010), 32–48. See also Stephen R. Holmes, "Gunton and Coleridge," in *T&T Clark Handbook of Colin Gunton*, ed. Andrew Picard, Myk Habets, and Murray Rae (London: T&T Clark, 2021), 315–16, 324–6.

4. Others who note the progression from trinitarian analogies of divine and human being to a trinitarian theology of mediation are: Michael D. Stringer, "The Lord and Giver of Life: The Person and Work of the Holy Spirit in the Trinitarian Theology of Colin E. Gunton" (PhD diss., University of Notre Dame, Australia, 2008), 46; Christoph Schwöbel, "Gunton on Creation," in *T&T Clark Handbook of Colin Gunton*, ed. Andrew Picard, Myk Habets, and Murray Rae (London: T&T Clark, 2021), 63; Myk Habets, "Gunton on Pneumatology," in *T&T Clark Handbook of Colin Gunton*, ed. Andrew Picard, Myk Habets, and Murray Rae (London: T&T Clark, 2021), 121–2; Uche Anizor, "Gunton on Ecclesiology," in *T&T Clark Handbook of Colin Gunton*, ed. Andrew Picard, Myk Habets, and Murray Rae (London: T&T Clark, 2021), 151; Picard, "Gunton on Culture"; Holmes, "Gunton and Coleridge," 315–16, 324–6; and Ivor Davidson, "Gunton and Jüngel," in *T&T Clark Handbook of Colin Gunton*, ed. Andrew Picard, Myk Habets, and Murray Rae (London: T&T Clark, 2021), 412.

adequate engagement with the progressions in his thought.⁵ Bernhard Nausner's claim that Gunton's laudable trinitarian project has failed remains influential in Gunton reception. However, this book disputes his definition of Gunton's project and argues that a sustained engagement with Gunton's full corpus presents a richer account of Gunton's theology and its developments. Nausner's assumption that the open transcendentals are the valves that make the trinitarian heart of Gunton's project beat fails to observe that Gunton never employs the concept of open transcendentals in any later writings.⁶ Such an analysis assumes the *Hauptbriefe* in Gunton writings that does not adequately engage with Gunton's full corpus. This book instead examines Gunton's trinitarian theology of culture as it is developed throughout his full corpus, and prioritizes his later constructive trinitarian articulations of culture.

Particular care needs to be taken with the chronology of Gunton's publications. A sustained engagement with Gunton's full corpus is essential, taking special note of the chronological order of his publications. Some of Gunton's most important books are collections of previously published essays, rather than monographs, and the original publication date of some material differs substantially from its republication in a later book. Most of these essays had little revision when they were republished, so the chronology observed in this book is that of original publication.⁷ Because the argument about progression in Gunton's work is vital to

---

5. My usage of the German term *Hauptbriefe* ("main letters") is drawn from debates in New Testament scholarship regarding the authenticity of the Pauline letters. Philip Towner observes that the authenticity of the disputed Pauline letters is determined by how closely they adhere to the undisputed Pauline letters. The outcome of this argumentation is that there are concentric circles of validity and importance attributed to the Pauline letters, and the disputed letters are often relegated in terms of importance. Towner suggests this approach imposes a pre-determined caricature of what is genuinely Pauline theology that overwhelms the reception of the disputed letters. Whatever the merits of Towner's assessment of Pauline theology, the term *Hauptbriefe* is employed here to indicate the tendency in Gunton scholarship to elevate Gunton's writings in the early 1990s, especially *The Promise of Trinitarian Theology* and *The One, the Three and the Many*, as the main letters and assume these are definitive of Gunton's theology. The *Hauptbriefe* creates a canon within the canon of Gunton's writings which shapes the critical reception of his work. When the earlier writings are assumed to be definitive, Gunton's full corpus, especially his later writings, is not adequately engaged, and the progressions in his thought often remain unrecognized. For Towner's account of the *Hauptbriefe* in Pauline theology, see Philip H. Towner, "Pauline Theology or Pauline Tradition in the Pastoral Epistles: The Question of Method," *Tyndale Bulletin*, 46 (1995): 303–4.

6. Bernhard Nausner, "The Failure of a Laudable Project: Gunton, the Trinity and Human Self-Understanding," *Scottish Journal of Theology*, 62 (2009): 403–20.

7. For instance, the essays in Colin E. Gunton, *Father, Son and Holy Spirit: Toward a Fully Trinitarian Theology* (London: T&T Clark, 2003) range from 1989 to 2002.

this book, it is important that essays are set in their original chronological context instead of the date of later republication.

In his later writings, Gunton offers a highly developed theological account of human culture in which humanity's cultural contributions are understood as an exercise in divinely appointed stewardship of creation. We can ascribe theological meaning and value to created creativity because the triune God calls and enables humanity to participate as sub-agents in the divine redemption and perfection of the project of creation. Delighting in the goodness of creation and createdness is a form of embodied worship—a living sacrifice of praise which is offered to the Father through Christ and in the Spirit.

Colin Gunton and His Historical and Theological Context

Gunton is a corrective and constructive trinitarian theologian who seeks to critique and correct dualistic influences in theology in order that he might construct a "more concrete" trinitarianism.[8] By more concrete, Gunton means a theology that takes greater account of God's declaration of the goodness of creation and embrace of materiality. This quest for a more concrete trinitarianism is both corrective and constructive. Working in the wake of Karl Barth, Gunton shares the theological mood of his time that seeks to engage the intellectual challenges inherited from the Enlightenment and its discarnate legacy. There are persistent tendencies in Western culture and theology that Gunton believes undermine the importance of materiality and embodiment. The roots of the Enlightenment's dualisms are found in various shortcomings in Western philosophical and theological traditions and Gunton's work seeks to correct these trajectories and construct an alternative trinitarian theology that upholds the goodness of creation and createdness.

Gunton's concern about the deleterious effects of dualistic and abstractive tendencies in philosophy and theology is best understood in the historical

---

8. Gunton regularly uses the phrase "more concrete" as an alternative to the disembodied tendencies in the theological and philosophical traditions and their impact upon subsequent theological developments. See especially Gunton, *Father, Son and Holy Spirit*, 6–11. Gunton seeks a more concrete *persona* for the Holy Spirit; a more concrete Christology that is rooted in the historical realities of Jesus Christ's human life; an account of mediation that offers a concrete human relationship with God in Christ; a more concrete doctrine of election and its temporal exigencies; and a more concrete ecclesiology. The quest for a more concrete trinitarianism must begin with an exploration of divine action in the economy in order to garner a more concrete knowledge of God. On pneumatology see Gunton, *Father, Son and Holy Spirit*, 72–3; on Christology see Gunton, *Father, Son and Holy Spirit*, 94; on mediation see Gunton, *Father, Son and Holy Spirit*, 179; on election and ecclesiology see Gunton, *Father, Son and Holy Spirit*, 148–54.

contingencies of the cultural context that he inhabited.⁹ Following his BA in classics and MA in theology, ordination in the United Reformed Church and two years into his doctoral research at Oxford, Gunton took up a post as Lecturer in the Philosophy of Religion at King's College, London. The landscape of British theology at that time was, in Gunton's reflections, largely devoid of a passion for systematic theology, and King's College was "then doctrinally in the grip of a kind of modernist high Anglicanism."¹⁰ Whilst Gunton's assessment of British theology can be disputed, he was not alone in holding this view. John Webster suggests that it is best to view Gunton's trinitarian theology "against the background of the instinctive deism of the leading British theologians from the 1950s on."¹¹ Rae observes that the preceding generation of English theologians had "largely capitulated to the insistence that the biblical world view is no longer tenable and that the task of modern theology was to identify and articulate that slim residue of the biblical proclamation that can still be believed."¹² The dominance of the natural sciences cultivated epistemic ideals of a detached human observer whose rational inquiry into, and separation from, the world produced objective knowledge. In this setting, faith was relegated to the realm of subjective private opinion which had little bearing on the truth.¹³ It is against these perceived problems that Gunton's corrective and constructive trinitarian project is best understood.

These currents of thought were highly influential in Gunton's career, and he consciously swam against them to engage the intellectual challenges of his day and construct a theological alternative. Gunton was not alone in this endeavour, and he joined a cadre of English-speaking theologians consciously working in the wake of Karl Barth to counter the Enlightenment's resistance to theological metaphysics and its elevation of the rootless individual subject.¹⁴ The British Council of Churches Study Commission on Trinitarian Doctrine, which ran from 1983 to

---

9. Colin E. Gunton, "Theology in Communion," in *Shaping a Theological Mind: Theological Context and Methodology*, ed. Darren C. Marks (Aldershot: Ashgate, 2002), 31.

10. Gunton, "Theology in Communion," 33.

11. John Webster, "Systematic Theology after Barth: Jüngel, Jenson, and Gunton," in *The Modern Theologians: An Introduction to Christian Theology Since 1918*, 3rd ed., ed. David F. Ford (Malden, Oxford and Victoria: Blackwell, 2005), 261.

12. Rae, "Introduction," 2.

13. Rae, "Introduction," 3.

14. For indicative examples of theological analyses of modernity and Western dualisms and trinitarian alternatives, see the essays in Alasdair I. C. Heron, ed., *The Forgotten Trinity: A Selection of Papers Presented to the BCC Study Commission on Trinitarian Doctrine Today* (London: BCC/CCBI, 1991). See also British Council of Churches Study Commission on Trinitarian Doctrine Today, *The Forgotten Trinity: 1. The Report of the BCC Study Commission on Trinitarian Doctrine Today* (London: British Council of Churches [BCC], 1989); British Council of Churches Study Commission on Trinitarian Doctrine Today, *The Forgotten Trinity: 2. A Study Guide on Issues Contained in the Report of the BCC Study Commission on Trinitarian Doctrine Today* (London: BCC, 1989).

1988, was especially formative for Gunton. His encounter with Eastern theology, particularly as it was represented by John Zizioulas, convinced him that the Trinity is "the heart of Christian living and thought."[15] In place of Western individualism, theologians, such as Gunton, explored the resources of trinitarian theology and discovered alternative insights about the nature of being in communion. It was common in this period to speak of a revival in trinitarian theology, even though such assessments are now subject to historical and theological critiques.[16] Whatever the merits of the critiques, which I assess in Chapter 2, Gunton is credited as a major figure in the restoration of trinitarian theology from the periphery to the centre of British theology.[17] In place of the relegation of theology to private subjective opinion, Gunton worked to restore a proper confidence in the Christian gospel and the basis of its authority that is found in God's self-revelation and self-interpretation in Jesus Christ.[18] For those who worked with Gunton as colleagues, friends, or students, "Colin helped a great many people to recover confidence in the intellectual coherence and explanatory power of the Christian faith, at a time when it has been under siege."[19]

Doing Theology in Conversation and Community

Theology, for Gunton, is conversational and best done in community.[20] This is not a subjective experiential preference for Gunton, but the essential nature of the theological enterprise. Christoph Schwöbel, Gunton's colleague at King's, notes that Gunton is a theologian in communion, and for Gunton that meant "to be a theologian in conversation."[21] At King's, Gunton and Schwöbel founded the Research Institute in Systematic Theology which became internationally renowned and drew students and faculty from around the world. Many of the graduates of the Institute have gone on to establish leading roles in contemporary theology around the world, and "the 'King's approach' has become one of the most

---

15. Gunton, "Theology in Communion," 34–5.
16. Sarah Coakley, "Afterword: 'Relational Ontology,' Trinity, and Science," in *The Trinity and an Entangled World: Relationality in Physical Science and Theology*, ed. John Polkinghorne (Grand Rapids: Eerdmans, 2010), 188. Chapter two employs Sarah Coakley's taxonomies of three waves of trinitarian renewal to assess the criticisms of Gunton's work.
17. Webster, "Systematic Theology after Barth," 259.
18. Rae, "Introduction," 2.
19. Murray A. Rae, "Introduction," in *The Person of Christ*, ed. Stephen R. Holmes and Murray A. Rae (London: T&T Clark, 2005), 12.
20. Christoph Schwöbel states that he "knows of no other leading academic who attributed so many significant points to conversations with students and colleagues." Christoph Schwöbel, "A Tribute to Colin Gunton," in *The Person of Christ*, ed. Stephen R. Holmes and Murray A. Rae (London: T&T Clark, 2005), 15.
21. Schwöbel, "A Tribute to Colin Gunton," 14–15.

respected species in the garden of theology."[22] Bruce McCormack holds that under Gunton's leadership, "King's became one of the most vibrant and exciting centres of theology to be found anywhere."[23] Gunton's service and contribution to the guild of academic theology were recognized by the various honorary doctorates and awards he received in his lifetime and following his untimely death.[24] Two important honours from communities where he made significant contributions are the bi-annual Colin Gunton Memorial Lecture at King's College,[25] and the Colin Gunton Memorial Essay Prize awarded by the *International Journal of Systematic Theology*, which he founded with John Webster, and *The Society for the Study of Theology*, which he served as secretary for ten years and later as president.[26]

Theology, however, is not only done in community and conversation with the academy, but also with, from, and for the Church. Before theology is an academic discipline it is a gift to, for, and from the Church. Gunton understood that his work in the university "was that to which I had been called as an ordained minister."[27] In parallel with his thirty-four-year career at King's College, Gunton was also Associate Minister at Brentwood United Reformed Church for twenty-eight years. Theology, for Gunton, must be done in communion and conversation with the Church. The Church in this case is not "some vague metaphysical ecclesial identity," but *this* particular local Church and *these* particular brothers and sisters in Christ.[28] As Holmes observes, to the people of Brentwood, he was simply Colin: the man

---

22. Schwöbel, "A Tribute to Colin Gunton," 17. Holmes suggests that the students Gunton inspired might well be, in final analysis, a greater legacy than his writings. See Stephen R. Holmes, "In Memoriam: Colin Gunton," *Shored Fragments*, May 6, 2013. http://steverholmes.org.uk/blog/?p=6973. See also the tributes to Gunton and recognition of the importance of the Research Institute in Systematic Theology from former students and colleagues in their respective chapters in Andrew Picard, Myk Habets, and Murray Rae, eds., *T&T Handbook of Colin Gunton* (London: T&T Clark, 2021).

23. Bruce L. McCormack, "Foreword," in *Trinitarian Soundings in Systematic Theology*, ed. Paul Louis Metzger (London: T&T Clark, 2005), 2. Jenson holds that Gunton's former students and colleagues are now spread throughout the world and make up "a sort of 'Who's Who' of Protestant theology." Robert Jenson, "Afterword," in *Trinitarian Soundings in Systematic Theology*, ed. Paul Louis Metzger (London: T&T Clark, 2005), 217.

24. Schwöbel, "A Tribute to Colin Gunton," 17.

25. "The Colin Gunton Memorial Lecture," https://www.kcl.ac.uk/events/the-colin-gunton-memorial-lecture.

26. "SST/IJST Colin Gunton Memorial Essay Prize," https://www.theologysociety.org.uk/postgraduates/gunton-prize/. On Gunton's service to these communities, see Schwöbel, "A Tribute to Colin Gunton," 15–17. The SST and IJST memorial essay prize is now, following the death of John Webster, given in memory of Colin Gunton and John Webster.

27. Gunton, "Theology in Communion," 35–6.

28. Stephen R. Holmes, "Introduction: The Theologian as Preacher, the Preacher as Theologian," in Colin E. Gunton, *The Theologian as Preacher: Further Sermons from Colin E. Gunton*, ed. Sarah J. Gunton and John E. Colwell (London: T&T Clark, 2007), xi.

who chaired Church meetings, stepped in during interregnums, sang in the choir, preached in the pulpit, washed dishes in the kitchen, and journeyed together in the ways of the gospel.[29] For his part, Gunton viewed Brentwood as a very ordinary Church, which is nonetheless "generous and loving, and has taught the lesson that right theology begins here, where the Gospel is proclaimed by word and sacrament and lived out in the company of others."[30]

Doing theology in communion and conversation provides important shape and method for interpreting Gunton's work. His writings and sermons are regularly punctuated with acknowledgements to an array of people to whom he owes a debt of gratitude for various insights. These are not paternalistic academic platitudes inserted into texts to signal Gunton's virtues, but a genuine acknowledgement of the way that thinking together in community transforms and enriches his work. Christoph Schwöbel maintains that he "knows of no other leading academic who attributed so many significant points to conversations with students and colleagues."[31] Theology is a collaborative exercise and Gunton welcomed genuine critiques of his own work in the spirit of shared inquiry in pursuit of greater truth. Whilst some describe him as "the most intellectually able British theologian of his generation by some distance,"[32] Gunton was no theological virtuoso. He regarded everyone involved, staff and students, as equals who collaborate together in the shared work of theology. Moreover, Gunton welcomed genuine critiques of his own work that were offered in the spirit of collaborative inquiry, and he did not, Rae stresses, engage in professional rivalries or attempt to show off his own intellectual prowess. "Gunton had not time for such nonsense. He welcomed genuine critical engagement, however, precisely because he knew none of us are masters of truth."[33] Instead, the faithful pursuit of God and God's truth in a spirit of collaborative inquiry shapes his work and his legacy, and he contributes his voice to extend the conversation, "rather than have the last word."[34]

---

29. See the tribute to Rev Professor Colin Gunton on the Brentwood United Reformed Church website: "Rev Professor Colin Gunton," http://www.brentwood-urc.org.uk/Colin.html. See also the reflections of members of Brentwood United Reformed Church that Gunton was as much a learner as a teacher in the church who took seriously the insights of other church members. "Having argued vehemently, he would, on many occasions, then grant the point and return to the discussion at a later date having thought further." Tony Cheer, Sheila Maxey, and Charles Steynor, "Foreword," in Colin E. Gunton, *The Theologian as Preacher: Further Sermons from Colin E. Gunton*, ed. Sarah J. Gunton and John E. Colwell (London: T&T Clark, 2007), x.

30. Gunton, "Theology in Communion," 36.

31. Schwöbel, "A Tribute to Colin Gunton," 15.

32. Holmes, "In Memoriam".

33. Rae, "Introduction," 3.

34. Rae, "Introduction," 3.

Gunton's collaborative approach is illustrated by his encouragement of his students to publish work that criticizes his theology, even though he sometimes disagreed with their criticisms.[35] With the progression of time, many of Gunton's former students have come to disagree with him; some on minor details of historiography and doctrine, and others quite substantially. Yet, as Rae explains, this is precisely the kind of collaborative and searching theological inquiry that Gunton promotes, as no one has exclusive claims on truth and all stand in need of correction, critique, and refinement from others who are committed to the prayerful task of theological attentiveness to God's address.[36] It is striking to observe in the edited *T&T Clark Handbook of Colin Gunton* that many of Gunton's former colleagues and students offer him warm tribute as well as careful critique in equal measure.[37] This only highlights Rae's point about the way Gunton understood the nature of collaborative theological inquiry.

At points, Gunton undoubtedly overstates some of his historical claims and misrepresents some aspects of the tradition. As a dissenting theologian, he is restless with the great tradition and theologies that support what he perceives to be institutional Christianity. Dissenters are often controversialists who are prone

---

35. See, for example, Richard M. Fermer, "The Limits of Trinitarian Theology as a Methodological Paradigm," *Neue Zeitschrift für Systematische Theologie aund Religionsphilosophie*, 41 (1999): 160. In the first footnote, Fermer thanks Schwöbel and Gunton for their scholarly integrity and generosity in encouraging him to publish the paper, despite their disagreements with his view.

36. Rae, "Introduction," 3.

37. For the tributes and careful criticisms of Gunton's former students and colleagues on Gunton's reading of historical figures, see Paul Molnar, "Gunton on the Trinity," in *T&T Clark Handbook of Colin Gunton*, 42; Oliver Crisp, "Gunton on Christology," in *T&T Clark Handbook of Colin Gunton*, ed. Andrew Picard, Myk Habets, and Murray Rae (London: T&T Clark, 2021), 86-9; Douglas Farrow, "Gunton and Irenaeus," in *T&T Clark Handbook of Colin Gunton*, ed. Andrew Picard, Myk Habets, and Murray Rae (London: T&T Clark, 2021), 245-8; Demetrios Bathrellos, "Gunton and the Cappadocians," in *T&T Clark Handbook of Colin Gunton*, ed. Andrew Picard, Myk Habets, and Murray Rae (London: T&T Clark, 2021), 260-2; Kelly Kapic, "Gunton and Owen," in *T&T Clark Handbook of Colin Gunton*, ed. Andrew Picard, Myk Habets, and Murray Rae (London: T&T Clark, 2021), 342-3; and Stephen R. Holmes, "Gunton and Coleridge," in *T&T Clark Handbook of Colin Gunton*, ed. Andrew Picard, Myk Habets, and Murray Rae (London: T&T Clark, 2021), 315-26. Holmes has written extensively on Gunton's theology and legacy. His work is marked by warm tributes to his doktorvater, colleague, and friend, as well as careful critical appreciation. Even where he now differs substantially from Gunton, his critiques remain warmly appreciative of Gunton's theology, legacy, and personal influence.

to overstatement and stark contrasts to establish constructive points.[38] Critique of Gunton's work may well be warranted, but Rae reminds us that his work should not be read as a complete and definitive systematic theology that addresses each theological *datum* according to established systematic practices. Communal and conversational theology does not unfurl itself in such ways. Therefore, instead of picking holes or pointing out lacunae, Rae suggests that we honour the spirit of Gunton's theological endeavours by listening "carefully first and then, in response, join Gunton in seeking to reach more deeply into the subject matter with which he was concerned."[39] This book attempts to follow such a method and think with and from Gunton's constructive trinitarian theology of culture and the fruitfulness of his work today.

Gunton is a systematic theologian from the dissenting tradition who resists attempts at tightly ordered doctrinal systems.[40] Christianity is gospel before it is a system, and while Gunton is certainly a theologian of the great tradition, he is not beholden to it. The dissenting tradition shapes Gunton's instincts and sources in some important ways. Much of Gunton's theology is restless with the established tradition, especially any hints of quick recourses to abstract metaphysics that sponsor institutional and ecclesial power. Theology, for Gunton, does not begin with *a priori* determinations of God's being in abstraction from divine action, but emerges *a posteriori* from God's self-revelation and self-interpretation in the economy. "Faith has its own logic," and strict adherence to systematic conventions risks masking the good news that is revealed through divine action in the economy.[41]

---

38. Gunton was proud of his dissenting tradition and remained unashamed of drawing from its resources. Robert Jenson recounts an evening conversation at which Blanche Jenson asked Gunton if, for the sake of the unity of the Church, he could belong to a church that was governed by bishops. Gunton replied, "I am a dissenter!" See Robert W. Jenson, "A Decision Tree of Colin Gunton's Thinking," in *The Theology of Colin Gunton*, ed. Lincoln Harvey (London: T&T Clark, 2010), 9. Oliver Crisp holds that in order to understand Gunton's theology, "one must grasp the fact that he was a contrarian and a dissenter, in the English ecclesiastical sense of that term." See Crisp, "Gunton on Christology," 77.

39. Rae, "Introduction," 3.

40. Colin E. Gunton, *Intellect and Action: Christian Theology and the Life of Faith* (Edinburgh: T&T Clark, 2000), 21.

41. Gunton, *Intellect and Action*, 13. This method becomes increasingly central to Gunton's theology, and his proposed multi-volume *A Christian Dogmatic Theology*, which he did not complete before his untimely death, begins with sections titled "The Economy of the Spirit," "The Economy of the Father," and "The Economy of the Son". See Robert Jenson, "Afterword," 219. This work remains unpublished, but some scholars have early drafts which Gunton shared at King's College. For various citations, see especially Jenson, "A Decision Tree of Colin Gunton's Thinking," 1–7; Paul Cumin, "The Taste of Cake: Relation and Otherness with Colin Gunton and the Strong Second Hand of God," in *The Theology of Colin Gunton*, 65–85; and Paul Cumin, *Christ at the Crux: The Mediation of God and Creation in Christological Perspective* (Eugene: Wipf and Stock, 2014), 169–95.

If theology is to avoid manufacturing an idol, Gunton believes it must go where the action is: in the economy and God's self-identification in Jesus Christ.[42] This central theological conviction guides Gunton's theology and leads him to search for alternative methods and voices in the tradition that provide resources for a more concrete trinitarianism that engages life within creation.

The proper starting point for theology, Gunton believes, is scripture's witness to the act and being of the triune God. Under Robert Jenson, Gunton pursued his doctoral studies on Karl Barth and found in him an approach to theology that prioritizes divine revelation: God is known because God makes Godself known in saving history through the action of the Son and the Spirit. This results in an emphasis upon divine action within the economy and the scriptural witness to that revelation. Methodological approaches that stress divine revelation and the action of the divine persons in the economy as the beginning point in theology are now questioned. Rather than engage in debates about theological method, this book follows Gunton's methodology as the basis to interpret his constructive work.[43] Gunton indwells this method most fully in his later writings. An important argument of this book is that there is a progression in Gunton's trinitarian theology from analogical deployments of trinitarian doctrine for insight into the nature of divine and created being to a trinitarian theology of mediation centred on divine action in the economy and its creaturely fruit. It is Gunton's later writings on a trinitarian theology of mediation that provide his most rigorous account of a trinitarian theology of culture.

Structure

This book is divided into two parts: Part I examines Gunton's trinitarian theology of culture in his early writings that offer an analysis of Western culture and his constructive exploration of trinitarian theology for insights into divine and human being. Part II acknowledges the development in Gunton's later writings and investigates his doctrine of creation, Christology, pneumatology, and ecclesiology as they relate to his trinitarian theology of culture.

Chapter 1 offers a patient delineation of *The One, the Three and the Many* and engages its critical reception. Gunton's early writings are marked by an engagement with trinitarian theology, buttressed by insights from non-theological sources such as philosophy, science, sociology, and political theory, to provide suggestive analogical accounts of divine and human relational ontology: being

---

42. Gunton, *Father, Son and Holy Spirit*, 26.

43. Katherine Sonderegger provides an insightful critique of those who stress the need to begin with the economy, and thus commandeer the immanent Trinity to Christology. In place, she outlines an account of the Trinity that begins with the inner life of God. See Katherine Sonderegger, *Systematic Theology: Volume 2, The Doctrine of the Holy Trinity: Processions and Persons* (Minneapolis: Fortress Press, 2020), 11–21.

in communion.⁴⁴ This work, with its use of philosophical history to buttress theological insights, largely coincides with Gunton's time as a lecturer in the philosophy of religion, and culminates in his widely acclaimed book *The One, the Three and the Many*.

Chapter 2 situates Gunton's trinitarian theology in the historical context of post-Barth Protestant theology and engages the critiques of Gunton's supposed social trinitarianism. This chapter argues that despite the many important critiques of Gunton's work, a chastened version of his relational trinitarian ontology remains fruitful for a theology of culture. Moreover, I argue that many of the criticisms of Gunton's work are based upon his earlier writings and do not adequately engage his later writings. The *Hauptbriefe* in Gunton reception results in the assumption that *The One, the Three and the Many* and the first edition of *The Promise of Trinitarian Theology* are his main writings, and the developments in his thought are not fully appreciated. In a telling addition to the preface of the second edition of *The Promise of Trinitarian Theology*, Gunton states that the two new chapters "demonstrate the impact of not so much arguing from the Trinity to the world by analogy as thinking trinitarianly through the focus provided by the action of God in the world mediated by his 'two hands.'"⁴⁵ Gunton's statement in the revised edition mirrors the argument of this book that there is a progression in Gunton's trinitarian theology from analogical uses of trinitarian doctrine to a trinitarian theology of mediation focused upon divine action in the economy.⁴⁶

Part II of this book details the progressions in Gunton's trinitarian theology and critically examines the way in which he extends his insights for contemporary

---

44. See, for example, Colin E. Gunton, *Enlightenment and Alienation: An Essay Toward a Trinitarian Theology* (London: Harper Collins, 1985); Colin E. Gunton, "Barth and the Western Intellectual Tradition: Towards a Theology After Christendom," in *Theology Beyond Christendom: Essays on the Centenary of the Birth of Karl Barth, May 10, 1886*, ed. John Thompson (Allison Park, PA: Pickwick Press, 1986), 285–301; Colin E. Gunton, "Knowledge and Culture: Towards an Epistemology of the Concrete," in *The Gospel and Contemporary Culture*, ed. Hugh Montefiore (London: Mowbray, 1992), 84–102; Colin E. Gunton, "Trinity, Ontology and Anthropology: Towards a Renewal of the Doctrine of the Imago Dei," in *Persons, Divine and Human: King's College Essays in Theological Anthropology*, ed. Christoph Schwöbel and Colin E. Gunton (Edinburgh: T&T Clark, 1992), 47–61; and Colin E. Gunton, *The One, the Three and the Many: God, Creation and the Culture of Modernity. The 1992 Bampton Lectures* (Cambridge: Cambridge University Press, 1993).

45. Colin E. Gunton, *The Promise of Trinitarian Theology*, 2nd ed. (London and New York: T&T Clark, 1997), xxix–xxx.

46. It is the Son and the Spirit, the Father's "two hands," who mediate God's purposes in the created order, and theology must be faithful to the scriptural revelation of "the works and relations of Father, Son and Spirit as they appear in saving history." Colin E. Gunton. *A Christian Dogmatic Theology. Volume One: The Triune God. A Doctrine of the Trinity as Though Jesus Makes a Difference*, 2003, unpublished typescript, Ch. 5. Cited in Jenson, "A Decision Tree of Colin Gunton's Thinking," 8–16, 10.

theological engagement with culture. Gunton's later writings progress to a trinitarian theology of mediation and this results in some important re-articulations as well as new developments in his trinitarian theology.⁴⁷ Previous conceptions, such as the open transcendentals and ubiquitous uses of *perichoresis*, recede from his work or are revised. What remains from *The One, the Three and the Many* is his analysis of Western culture and the theological *foci* he explores to construct a trinitarian alternative to the ailments of Western culture—creation, Christology, pneumatology, and ecclesiology. Whilst these *foci* remain, they undergo important internal developments in the light of his later theology of mediation. Part II examines each of these theological *foci*, and their progression under Gunton's trinitarian theology of mediation, in relation to his trinitarian theology of culture.

Chapter 3 explores Gunton's theology of mediation and the doctrine of creation, as the mediation of the Father, in relation to human culture. It begins by outlining Gunton's theology of mediation which is the basis of the theological method he employs in his later writings. This then gives way to an exploration of Gunton's doctrine of creation, and his account of creation as a project, in relation to his theology of culture.⁴⁸ Chapter 4 examines Gunton's account of the mediation of the Son in relation to human culture. The *imago Dei* and humanity's cultural calling faithfully subsist in Jesus Christ, and his life recapitulates Adam's and Israel's calling in such a way that the project of creation is restored towards its divinely intended end.⁴⁹ Christ's self-offering of faithful humanity and human culture is a living sacrifice of praise that is offered to the Father in the Spirit in praise of God's wise purposes in the beginning.

Chapter 5 examines the mediation of the Spirit in relation to human culture in general and the Church in particular. The Spirit is the perfecting cause who enables eschatological anticipations of God's universal purposes through all right forms of human culture and created creativity.⁵⁰ The Spirit's work is universal, but is particularly concentrated in Christ's body. For Gunton, the Church's common life is an embodiment of the gospel, a form of redeemed human culture, which the Spirit, from time to time, enables to be offered, through Christ, as a sacrifice

---

47. See Gunton's description of his theological method in Colin E. Gunton, *The Christian Faith: An Introduction to Christian Doctrine* (Oxford: Blackwell, 2002), xi, and 180.

48. Gunton utilizes Francis Watson's exegesis of Genesis to detail his understanding of God's project of creation. See Colin E. Gunton, *The Triune Creator: A Historical and Systematic Study* (Grand Rapids: Eerdmans, 1998), 61-2; Gunton, *The Christian Faith*, 5-8; Gunton, *Father, Son and Holy Spirit*, 138-9; Colin E. Gunton, *Theology Through the Theologians: Selected Essays, 1972-1995* (London and New York: T&T Clark, 1996), 134, 138; Colin E. Gunton, *The Barth Lectures*, ed. P. H. Brazier (London: T&T Clark, 2007), 248; and Gunton, *Revelation and Reason*, 80-1.

49. Gunton, *The Christian Faith*, 122. See also Gunton, *The Triune Creator*, 196.

50. Colin E. Gunton, "Reformation Accounts of the Church's Response to Human Culture," in *Public Theology in Cultural Engagement*, ed. Stephen Holmes (Milton Keynes: Paternoster, 2008), 93.

of praise.[51] Chapter 6 thinks with and from Gunton's work and explores the ongoing fruitfulness of his trinitarian theology of culture and its potential for engaging some of the key cultural currents of our day. This chapter utilizes the resources Gunton provides in his trinitarian theology of culture to build upon his work by considering the politics of the Church's belonging together at the Lord's Supper. The chapter and the book close with an exploration of the horizons Paul's alternative body politic, and Gunton's trinitarian theology of culture, offer in relation to the contemporary issues related to disability and the dominance of ableism in the Church.

Gunton provides an analysis of culture that serves as a foil for his search for a more concrete trinitarianism to overcome the abstractive and dualistic tendencies he perceives in Western culture. Initially, this takes the form of his trinitarian analogies of being in which divine ontology informs our understanding of the nature of what it is to be human. With the progression in his thought, Gunton's theology develops into a trinitarian theology of mediation that offers a more sustained account of divine action in the economy and its creaturely fruit. It is from this exploration of divine action in the economy that Gunton establishes his theological account of culture and humanity's calling to participate in the divine redemption and perfection of God's creation project. This book examines Gunton's trinitarian theology of culture and shows its ongoing fruitfulness for today.

---

51. Gunton, *The Christian Faith*, 127.

Part I

COLIN GUNTON'S EARLY TRINITARIAN THEOLOGY OF
CULTURE AND ITS CRITICS

Chapter 1

THE ONE, THE THREE AND THE MANY AND COLIN GUNTON'S EARLY WRITINGS ON A TRINITARIAN THEOLOGY OF CULTURE

Colin Gunton offers a theological assessment of modern Western culture, suggests correctives for imbalances and shortcomings, and proposes constructive remedies from the foundation of trinitarian theology. Modern Western culture is indelibly marked by its relationship to, and denial and rejection of, the Christian gospel, which formed much of its life and culture.[1] The Church's successes in Christendom came at great cost. The Church's vision of the heteronomous God was seen as an enslavement in which human diversity was subsumed under divine rule. Modernity is to some extent a rejection of Christendom's heteronomous God. Yet, Gunton believes this understandable reaction bequeaths new distortions that contribute to the confusions of modern life within the world. Rather than renouncing the cultural rejection of the heteronomous God, Gunton probes the narrative of how Christianity became offensive for the wrong reasons and proposes a trinitarian alternative.[2]

The One, the Three and the Many is a theological assessment of modernity that is widely regarded as Gunton's greatest work and a classic in the theological analysis of culture.[3] The wide critical acclaim for *The One, the Three and the Many* underlines its significance for a late twentieth-, and early twenty-first-, century theological analysis of culture. Equally, however, there are strong critiques of

---

1. Gunton, *The One, the Three and the Many*, 1.
2. Gunton, *The One, the Three and the Many*, 1.
3. Christoph Schwöbel proclaims *The One, the Three and the Many* as Gunton's most elegant book and a classic. Christoph Schwöbel, "The Shape of Colin Gunton's Theology: On the Way Towards a Fully Trinitarian Theology," in *The Theology of Colin Gunton*, ed. Lincoln Harvey (London: T&T Clark, 2010), 199 and Schwöbel, "A Tribute to Colin Gunton," 15. For other acclamations of the book see Bruce McCormack, "*The One, the Three and the Many*," 7; Webster, "Systematic Theology after Barth," 261; David A. Höhne, *Spirit and Sonship: Colin Gunton's Theology of Particularity and the Holy Spirit* (Farnham, UK and Burlington, VT: Ashgate, 2010), 2; and Stephen R. Holmes, "Obituary: Rev. Professor Colin E. Gunton," *Guardian*, June 3, 2003. http://www.theguardian.com/news/2003/jun/03/guardianobituaries.highereducation.

Gunton's work that question his historical genealogies and social trinitarian tendencies. I maintain that the critical acclaim of *The One, the Three and the Many* elevates its significance in Gunton's corpus to an extent that overlooks the later progressions and internal strengthening of his work. With Holmes, I contend that *The One, the Three and the Many* represents the end of one trajectory of Gunton's thought.[4] Much of the scholarly reception of Gunton's work fails to notice the progressions in his thinking and focuses criticism on material that Gunton develops and strengthens in his later writings. In order therefore to understand Gunton's work and the progressions in his thought, there is a need for a sustained and careful exploration of his claims in *The One, the Three and the Many*.

This chapter outlines *The One, the Three and the Many*, and Gunton's theological assessment of the ailments of Western culture, along with his alternative trinitarian proposals. The first four chapters of *The One, the Three and the Many* are a critical examination of modernity's ailments that seeks the roots of the modern crisis of culture.[5] These four chapters are then paired as a chiasm with a corresponding constructive chapter that offers a trinitarian remedy which emerges from a relevant theological focus and an open transcendental.[6] However, instead of following Gunton's chiastic structure, this chapter takes the first chiasm as an *inclusio*, and then combines the other chiastic pairs to examine his analysis with its trinitarian remedy. This approach enables Gunton's use of the one and the many as a heuristic device to remain the framework through which he asserts trinitarian theology as the mediating concept. Each section examines Gunton's critical diagnosis of modernity's ailments, tracing its ancient roots and theological distortions, before outlining his trinitarian remedy through a theological focus, a Coleridgean *idea*, and an open transcendental. The structure of this chapter, which is a revision of the structure of *The One, the Three and the Many*, is as follows:

- A: The One and the Many
    - D/D': Creation/Truth and Open Transcendentals
    - C/C': Christology/Economy and *Perichoresis*
    - B/B': Pneumatology/Particularity and *Hypostasis*
- A': Trinity, Relationality and Ecclesiology
- Conclusion: The One, *the Three* and the Many

---

4. Holmes, "Towards the *Analogia Personae et Relationis*," 39.
5. Gunton, *The One, the Three and the Many*, 4.
6. Gunton, *The One, the Three and the Many*, 4–5. Craig Bartholomew uses the same structure of diagnosis and remedy to analyse *The One, the Three and the Many*. See Craig Bartholomew, "The Healing of Modernity: A Trinitarian Remedy? A Critical Dialogue with Colin Gunton's *The One, the Three and the Many: God, Creation and the Culture of Modernity*," *European Journal of Theology*, 6 (1997): 112.

A detailed analysis of *The One, the Three and the Many* lays the necessary foundation for a critical examination of Gunton's theology of culture, and its progression in Gunton's thought.

A: *The One and the Many*

Modernity is a complex phenomenon. Instead of a singular reductive explanation there is a common mood that glorifies progress and denigrates the past, which, in Gunton's analysis, results in "grievous intellectual and moral problems."[7] Far from being anything particularly new, postmodernism brings the spirit of modernity home to roost and is best considered late modernity. Modernity, and late modernity, seeks individualized freedom from divine and ecclesial heteronomies but breeds unrecognized homogeneities and totalitarianisms. This section examines Gunton's assessment of modernity and its ethic of disengagement that plagues modern life and fails to recognize the nature of human embodiment within the material world. Gunton traces the roots of disengagement to the ancient world to show that the modern manifestations are part of a common Western lineage that attempts to achieve rational mastery over the external world through the disengagement of the sovereign human subject. The relation of the one and the many is used as a heuristic device to reveal the tendencies of Western culture towards abstraction and homogeneity that undermine the goodness of creation and human flourishing within it.

Modern Sounding: An Ethic of Disengagement

Modernity is the realm of paradoxes. Amidst the undoubted advances, Gunton is concerned by the endemic epistemological and ethical problems that Modernity bequeathed to Western culture. While seeking freedom, progress, and rationalization, Modernity bred totalitarianism, alienation, and cultural fragmentation.[8] The displacement of Christendom's heteronomous God may have secured greater freedom for the individual, but, as Vaclav Hável argues, it also resulted in a loss of co-ordinates for human life together in the world. Behind Modernity's drive towards individual freedom lies pressure towards an oppressive form of homogeneity that continues to manifest itself in consumerism's herd society.[9]

Modernity is marked by an impulse to disengage from the material world in order to achieve the rational mastery of the unencumbered subject over the external world. Drawing from Charles Taylor's assessment, Gunton argues that the Cartesian *cogito* is characteristic of modernity's ethic of disengagement and its

---

7. Gunton, *The One, the Three and the Many*, 12–13.
8. Gunton, *The One, the Three and the Many*, 13.
9. Gunton, *The One, the Three and the Many*, 13.

instrumental and objective stance towards external otherness.[10] Taylor maintains, "Descartes' ethic, just as much as his epistemology, calls for disengagement from the world and body and the assumption of an instrumental stance towards them. It is of the essence of reason, both speculative and practical, that it push us to disengage."[11] The sovereign subject turns inwards, instead of outwards towards the world, to create its own truth and values and this ethic of disengagement severs the historical relationship between the social order and its metaphysical basis in God's unifying function. The result is a culture of alienation from God, one another, and the created world.[12] There is, Gunton argues, an urgent requirement for a renewed philosophy or theology of how we belong together in the world, which he develops through his trinitarian open transcendentals.

Historical Antecedents: A Lineage of Disengagement

Western antiquity and Modernity share a strong family resemblance and many of the same kinds of questions arise in different eras. In Gunton's analysis, metaphysics are organically related to social order. Modernity's ethic of disengagement has its roots in antiquity, and Gunton maintains that the rationalistic demythologization of deities and their unifying agency, whether ancient or modern, is the beginning of disengagement. In the ancient world, the first Sophists' rationalistic demythologization of the Greek gods created a world empty of personal meaning because it abstracted knowledge of the world from its personal and relational context.[13] However, there are also alternative traces of an engaged philosophy in antiquity that provide the unified account of cosmology, metaphysics, and social order that Gunton seeks. Although critical of much of Plato's work, Gunton celebrates his engaged philosophy which upholds the unifying function of the anthropomorphic Greek gods and brings cosmology and social order into a single whole. Plato's emphasis on the whole provides the context for human self-knowledge and personal being that enables human habitation of the world to conform itself to reality.[14] It is the right human habitation of reality that Gunton seeks, an engaged and embodied existence within the richness of the given world.

In order to assess the tendencies and ailments of Western culture, Gunton employs a heuristic device, namely, the question of the relationship of the one and the many. The question is an ancient one, and emerges at the beginning

---

10. Gunton, *The One, the Three and the Many*, 13–14.
11. Charles Taylor, *Sources of the Self: The Making of Modern Identity* (Harvard: Harvard University Press, 1989), 155.
12. Gunton, *The One, the Three and the Many*, 14–15.
13. Gunton, *The One, the Three and the Many*, 15–16.
14. Gunton, *The One, the Three and the Many*, 15.

of philosophical discussions of the meaning of reality.[15] Is reality a Heraclitean dynamic state of flux, change, and difference where the many is prior to the one, or is it a Parmenidean stable state that is undergirded by an unchanging and timeless metaphysic where the one is prior to the many? Put differently, if cosmology and social order are organically related, in what sense is our universe a unity or a plurality? Is human society a totality or a loosely connected set of individuals?[16]

Independently, the Parmenidean and Heraclitean impulses fail for the lack of a mediating concept between the one and the many.[17] Gunton's quest is therefore for a mediating cosmological concept that holds the unity and diversity of all things in right relation for the sake of social flourishing. This mediating concept, he thinks, is a rightly conceived trinitarian theology, in which God's otherness-in-relation places stress upon the personal otherness and relatedness of the Trinity, and all being.

In Western thought, the concept of God (or the gods) provides a focus for the unity of all things. Differing conceptions of the deities establish differing understandings of unified social reality. The Pre-Socratic philosophers were the first demythologizers who sought to use reason to overcome the pluralistic and chaotic theology of the traditional warring Greek gods. Their rational attempt to make overall sense of being provided a basis for unified thought and behaviour.[18] Gunton traces this drive to find a basis for thought about the totality of the meaningful whole in the Christian theological tradition and Enlightenment thought.[19] The Western philosophical and theological tradition is dominated by the Parmenidean drive to unity in such a way that the many are often subsumed into the one. Christendom's conception of God as a single, changeless divine monad colluded with the Parmenidean impulse and created many forms of ecclesiastical and political totalitarianisms and repressions from which humanity sought liberty.[20]

---

15. See Plato's discussion on the abstract and unchanging form of the table which underlies the physical manifestations of a table. Plato, *The Republic*, trans. A. D. Lindsay (London: J. M. Dent, 1907), Book X, 596. See also Aristotle's discussion of the one and many as well as his twenty-three objections to Plato's forms in Aristotle, *Metaphysics*, ed. and trans. John Warrington (London and New York: Everyman's Library, 1961), 12-15; 75-83. For contemporary examples of the ongoing significance of the one and the many for philosophical discussion, see Gareth B. Matthews and S. Marc Cohen, "The One and the Many," *The Review of Metaphysics*, 21 (1968): 630-55 and Alain Badiou, "The One and the Multiple: *A Priori* Conditions of any Possible Ontology," in *Being and Event*, trans. Oliver Feltham (London and New York: Continuum, 2005), 23-30.

16. Gunton, *The One, the Three and the Many*, 18-19.
17. Gunton, *The One, the Three and the Many*, 18-19.
18. Gunton, *The One, the Three and the Many*, 22-3.
19. Gunton, *The One, the Three and the Many*, 23.
20. Gunton, *The One, the Three and the Many*, 25.

The distinct nature and shape of modernity come, in Gunton's analysis, from its rejection of Christendom's divine monad, who was worthy of rejection. In reaction to Christendom's heteronomous God, the thinkers of modernity sought freedom from the Parmenidean one by asserting the rights of the Heraclitean many. A radicalized account of the Heraclitean revolt against God pits humanity against divinity because the worship of God is seen as a diminishment of humanity. When God is no longer required to account for the coherence and meaning of the world, "the focus of the unity of things becomes the unifying rational mind."[21] However, Gunton suggests that deism's alternative is equally totalitarian and repressive, and results in absolutist forms of social and political order.

Despite modernity's legitimate attempts at emancipation from the heteronomous God of Christendom, it only manages to replace subservience to one oppressive universal with others.[22] The displacement of God as the source of unity for all things results in other impersonal sources of unity, such as technology, the public, or the market, rushing to fill the void. Underlying modern individualism, and its much-vaunted freedom, is a drive to homogeneity that denies plurality and breeds new and unrecognized forms of slavery.[23] Such impersonal universals fail to offer the personal and relational context necessary for diverse forms of human being in the world, and, instead, suppress, objectify, and instrumentalize the other.[24] The result of the new forms of bondage is the continued disengagement and alienation of the individual from their embodied context of relatedness to others and the world.

Theological Distortions: Reactionary Immanentism

Gunton argues that Christian theology often colludes with the impersonal and homogenizing forces of modernity and postmodernity and fails to offer a vision of God that mediates between the one and the many. In reaction to the displacement of Christendom's transcendent overlord, there is a fashionable rise of theologies of immanence that mistake the real enemy. Transcendence is not the problem, but the loss of personal space that is necessary for divine and human being. With the rejection of Christendom's heteronomous God, various surrogate immanent and impersonal divinities arise. The state, the market, and other totalitarian institutions of unitary order mercilessly devour devotees because there is no space between persons, and persons and world. Modernity's quest for freedom results in new forms of slavery because it is not transcendence that is the enemy, but forms of the one that fail to give space to the many.[25]

---

21. Gunton, *The One, the Three and the Many*, 27.
22. Gunton, *The One, the Three and the Many*, 28.
23. Gunton, *The One, the Three and the Many*, 31.
24. Gunton, *The One, the Three and the Many*, 31–2.
25. Gunton, *The One, the Three and the Many*, 38–9.

At root, Gunton's critiques of modernity are ontological, a failure to conceive and practice relationality. The loss of God's transcendence leads to immanentism at the expense of the necessary space for being.[26] Without the necessary space between God and the world there is no human or divine freedom, and divine and creaturely ontologies are collapsed and confused to the detriment of personal being. True freedom for personal being requires otherness, but the immanent divinities of modernity strip otherness bare in their quest to depose the heteronomous God. What is needed is not a revised immanentist deity, but the upholding of the relationship of the many to the one in such a way that a plurality of being flourishes in the context of the unity of all things.[27] According to Gunton, it is a trinitarian conception of God that provides the needed mediation between the one and the many: the one, *the three*, and the many. In the final section of this chapter, we will return to examine Gunton's constructive pairing with this critique, in which he develops his trinitarian account of relationality as an open transcendental that finds concrete expression in the Church. These two sections stand as an *inclusio* to Gunton's book and frame his argument for trinitarian theology as a mediating concept for the one and the many. However, in order to understand Gunton's positive proposals of trinitarian open transcendentals, we first need to comprehend his theological understanding of meaning and truth within the context of the doctrine of creation.

D/D': Creation, Truth, and Open Transcendentals

Modernity and postmodernity are marked by the loss of a coherent sense of meaning and truth. Gunton proposes an account of meaning and truth that attempts to avoid their perceived excesses.[28] This section firstly examines Gunton's criticisms of modernity's and postmodernity's epistemologies, and, secondly, his proposals of trinitarian open transcendentals. In place of what he perceives as modernity's proclamation of objective certainties and postmodernity's irrational anti-foundationalism, Gunton proposes a renewed account of theological rationality that is appropriate to created being. From this theological rationality, Gunton constructs his open transcendentals as non-foundationalist foundations that uphold the unity and diversity of knowledge and being within a unified created reality. Gunton's open transcendentals find inspiration in the work of Samuel Taylor Coleridge, who is the presiding genius of *The One, the Three and the Many*. Coleridge, on Gunton's account, sees things whole, and his work represents a dissenting voice to the trajectory of the Enlightenment and offers an alternative to its alienating and fragmenting forces.[29] What draws Gunton to Coleridge, apart

---

26. Gunton, *The One, the Three and the Many*, 36.
27. Gunton, *The One, the Three and the Many*, 38.
28. Gunton, *The One, the Three and the Many*, 129.
29. Gunton, *The One, the Three and Many*, 48–9.

from his British heritage,[30] is Coleridge's conception of the triune God as the one who unifies all things in their rich variety from his being that is marked by variety, richness, and complexity.[31]

Modern Sounding: Relativism and the Rootless Will

In his analysis of postmodernity, Gunton argues it is parasitically related to modernity and appears in reaction to the false objectivism of modernity's epistemological foundationalism. Against the false objectivity of modernity's rationalism, postmodern thinkers question, or deny, the possibility of objective meaning and truth.[32] Gunton detects a loss of confidence in creation as a unified reality, and notes that postmodernism's rupture between truth claims and reality results in a rise in emotivism, subjectivism, and the loss of a shared language for communication and a shared humanity. While postmodernism's deconstructive forces bring a necessary critique of modernity's falsely objective epistemology, Gunton views radical relativism as a siren song that has destructive effects upon our shared sense of human social living.[33] If individual cultures and judgements are so radically relative, there is no way of considering whether they truly represent reality. Across cultures, the celebration of value-free openness renders openness meaningless, and all truth claims are equally interesting and irrelevant. If all cultural values are equally significant and important, then the risk is a pluralism of indifference that homogenizes and undermines difference.[34]

Postmodernity's homogenizing pluralism does not necessarily breed polite acceptance of difference, but oftentimes a vigorous intolerance of any that opposes its totalitarian pluralism. The plurality of voices debating meaning and truth in modern culture is, in Gunton's assessment, evidence against the denial of

---

30. Stephen Holmes rightly observes that Gunton's interest in highlighting an English theological heritage is an important influence in what draws him to Coleridge. "[Whilst] the enthusiasm for Coleridge in the 1990 lecture seems genuine enough, Gunton needed an English theologian to admire for his argument, and having not to that point really explored John Owen, Coleridge, even if he now saw the flaws, was perhaps the best he had available." Stephen R. Holmes, "Gunton and Coleridge," 326.

31. Gunton, *The One, the Three and the Many*, 24. See also Gunton, *Theology Through the Theologians*, 10. Holmes rightly maintains, "Gunton used the doctrine [of the Trinity] as Coleridge had, as a way of establishing human freedom and the relative independence of the world; in that text [*A Brief Theology of Revelation*] and after it became a way of answering questions concerning mediation. This, I suggest, explains the fascination with Coleridge for a decade, and the relative lack of interest in him afterwards." Holmes, "Gunton and Coleridge," 316.

32. Gunton, *The One, the Three and the Many*, 102.

33. Gunton, *The One, the Three and the Many*, 102.

34. Gunton, *The One, the Three and the Many*, 103–4.

objective truth, as each voice is willing to contend rationally for its convictions.[35] Postmodernism's much-vaunted tolerance is highly selective and intolerant of any attempt to establish truth claims, to the point that varying views are undiscussable. The epistemological confusion of the West contributes to cultural fragmentation that renders distinct aspects unable to communicate together.[36] In many ways, Gunton maintains, postmodernity represents an extension of, as much as a rebellion against, modernity. Postmodernism's deconstructive force is an extension of modernity's reflexive turn to the emancipated sovereign subject whose rootless will extends back through modernity and into antiquity.[37]

Historical Antecedents: Displacement of Divinities and Relativism

There is an irony, Gunton notes, that a movement concerned with the priority of objective truth breeds a widespread suspicion of the existence of truth.[38] Yet this phenomenon is not new, and Gunton explores historical examples that share strong commonalities with postmodernism. The Sophists, especially Protagoras, show there is an inter-relationship of theological agnosticism towards divinities and epistemological and moral relativism. The displacement of divinities as the transcendent source of unity leads to the relocation of divinity in the unifying power of the human mind, and, whatever historical period, moral relativism is the inevitable outcome.[39]

Plato and Aristotle hold rational activity and contemplation as the highest of human values through which we share in the divine substance, aside from any relational context.[40] The Enlightenment replicates their divinization of the knowing human subject and defines the *imago Dei* in terms of free human thinking and action. The scientific quest for the certainty of rational foundations is cast as the emancipated individual's heroic struggle for truth, untrammelled by the burdens of history, tradition, or ecclesiastical oppression. In this setting, science

---

35. Gunton, *The One, the Three and the Many*, 105.
36. Gunton, *The One, the Three and the Many*, 106.
37. During this period, Gunton is not alone in recognizing the continuities as much as the discontinuities of modernity and postmodernity. Gunton makes significant use of Charles Taylor's work in his analysis of modernity and postmodernity. In his reading of Jacques Derrida's deconstruction, Taylor argues that Derrida's deconstructionism is an extension of the prodigious power of individual subjectivity to undo all allegiances that bind it—a pure form of untrammeled freedom. Taylor, *Sources of the Self*, 489. Ellen Charry suggests that emancipation, initially from external constraint and now from meaning itself, binds the narrative from Descartes to Derrida into a single tradition. Ellen Charry, "The Crisis of Modernity and the Christian Self," in *A Passion for God's Reign: Theology, Christian Learning and the Christian Self*, ed. Miroslav Volf (Grand Rapids: Eerdmans, 1998), 98.
38. Gunton, *The One, the Three and the Many*, 106.
39. Gunton, *The One, the Three and the Many*, 106–7.
40. Gunton, *The One, the Three and the Many*, 108.

is elevated as the source of verifiable objective truths and the humanities and the arts are relegated to the realm of subjective opinion.[41] However, the postmodern turn subjects science to the powers of radical Cartesian doubt, and posits it as a local social practice instead of a repository of objective truths. Postmodernism's attack on epistemology, and assertion of pragmatism, highlights the Western tendency, whether ancient, modern, or postmodern, to divinize the knowing human subject.[42] Far from being anything new or reactive, Gunton holds that postmodernism can be interpreted as most-modernism because it brings many of modernity's problems home to roost.

In the Enlightenment, criticisms of the assumed mythologies of theology give rise to new rational conceptualities tied especially to scientific methods of knowing. These new conceptualities, Gunton believes, find their leading proponent in Immanuel Kant who lays the basis for postmodern relativism by radicalizing the divinization of autonomous human rationality and will, while relegating God to the subjective realm.[43] In Kant's divided world there are two rigid forms of reality: the heteronomous world of the senses and the liberated inner world of autonomous human willing.[44] The objectivity of rational human thought, judgement, and will offers a God's-eye view of the world and stands in contrast to the subjectivity of sensate experience. Sensate experience is viewed as a form of heteronomy, because it is received passively, and is an influence from which the individual will and ethics need to be freed.[45] Practical reason, rather than divine will, determines ethics, while artistic judgement is relegated to the subjective, and inherently untrustworthy, category of feelings. The realms of truth, goodness, and beauty are fragmented and hierarchically ordered, and the possibility of making overall unified sense of the world is lost from view.[46] Instead, it is the rootless human will, which has no external reference but the self-imposed obligations that stem from autonomous human reason, that makes meaning of the world.[47]

The divinization of the rational individual results in, among other things, relativism and scepticism. Gunton examines the effect of these on culture. The displacement of divinities does not result in a vision of genuine human plurality of free people, but the fragmentation of culture and the self-assertion of multiple

---

41. Gunton, *The One, the Three and the Many*, 110.

42. Gunton, *The One, the Three and the Many*, 111. Alister McGrath describes the deconstructive attacks on the natural sciences as pseudo-scientific gibberish that are popular on account of their intellectual consequences more than the intellectual credentials. See Alister E. McGrath, *A Scientific Theology: Reality* (Grand Rapids: Eerdmans, 2002), 178.

43. Gunton, *The One, the Three and the Many*, 114.

44. Gunton, *Enlightenment and Alienation*, 58–60.

45. Gunton, *Enlightenment and Alienation*, 5–6 and 112.

46. Gunton, *The One, the Three and the Many*, 115–16.

47. Gunton, *The One, the Three and the Many*, 117. See also Gunton, *Enlightenment and Alienation*, 61.

unrelated and arbitrary human wills.[48] The outcome, Gunton suggests, is a new Babel. "'Postmodernism' represents that Babel perfectly, because when each speaks a language unrelated to that of the other – when language is not the basis of the communication that shapes our being – the only outcome can be fragmentation. In that sense, postmodernism is modernity come home to roost."[49]

Theological Distortions: An Inadequate Doctrine of Creation

For Gunton, the radical accounts of the rootless human have Christian theological provenance in the West's inadequate doctrine of creation. Comparing Irenaeus' doctrine of creation with later understandings in the West, Gunton observes the strength of Irenaeus' doctrine of creation that asserts the ontological distinction and freedom of creator and creation. Against Gnostic pantheism, Irenaeus holds that God alone exists in utter freedom *a se*, and creation exists in contingent relation to the creator. Nothing created is co-eternal with God, and everything derives from God's free and loving will, which is achieved through the personal action of the Son and the Spirit in creation. God's will for the creation is relational and purposeful, rather than unknown and arbitrary, and is mediated through the Son and in the Spirit to create, redeem, and perfect that which was created very good in the beginning.[50]

In contrast, later Western accounts of God and creation threaten the importance of materiality and its meaningfulness. Augustine is, in Gunton's infamous assessment, the fountainhead of the West's dualistic problems. In Augustine's formulation, creation's eschatological directedness and the mediation of the Son and the Spirit "play too limited a role."[51] Gunton firstly detects in Augustine a weakening in the link between material creation and immaterial redemption such that redemption is redemption from materiality. Secondly, Gunton holds that God's love becomes subordinate to God's will.[52] In the legacy of Augustine, creation becomes "the product of pure, unmotivated and therefore arbitrary will, a will that operates equally arbitrarily in the theology of double predestination that became after him so much a mark of the Western tradition."[53]

Later developments of the rootless will in Kant's thought arise, in Gunton's assessment, from theological provenance. One of the causes is the construal of God's will "in terms of arbitrariness rather than in terms of loving freedom." Another cause is "the unitary and restrictive conception of truth which is its correlative."[54] Whilst otherwise admirable, Anselm's conception of truth

48. Gunton, *The One, the Three and the Many*, 122–3.
49. Gunton, *The One, the Three and the Many*, 124.
50. Gunton, *The One, the Three and the Many*, 119–20.
51. Gunton, *The One, the Three and the Many*, 120. For Gunton's claim that Augustine is the fountainhead of the West's dualistic problems, see Gunton, *The Barth Lectures*, 96.
52. Gunton, *The One, the Three and the Many*, 120.
53. Gunton, *The One, the Three and the Many*, 120–1.
54. Gunton, *The One, the Three and the Many*, 121.

is highly unitary and restrictive and derives from a single, transcendent, and undifferentiated source. As a result, unity and plurality are deemed incompatible. According to Gunton, the christological and trinitarian determinants that are so central to Irenaeus are missing in Anselm's account of truth.[55] If meaning is founded upon an arbitrary will, whether human or divine, the result is irrationality and instability that subvert meaning. At issue is not merely God's relation to meaning, but the way that different views of God, and God's relation to the world, develop distinct understandings of the meaning of finite realities. Metaphysics, of whatever stripe, shape social reality, and the issues with modern relativism and scepticism are, Gunton concludes, partly the result of a failure in the doctrines of God and creation.[56]

Gunton argues that modernity is parasitic upon Christendom and emerges from a rejection of Christendom's heteronomous God and ecclesial institutions. While the displacement of Christendom's God is understandable, modernity's assertion of the rational individual willing agent has "serious deficiencies in thought about and practice of relationality, particularity, temporality and truth."[57] Most seriously, modernity produces a fragmentation of culture and social order that results from interpreting freedom as an individualistic escape from relations. Without the transcendent coordinates for life that are so central to the doctrine of creation, there is a weakening of the fundamental ontology in which created life exists in relation to its creator and the rest of creation. In the wake of his analysis, Gunton seeks a way to comprehend the world, culture, and social order that enables us to understand reality "as both one and many, unified and diverse, particular and in relation."[58] For this, he turns to trinitarian doctrine as a basis for theology to contribute towards the healing of modern fragmentation, and develops his account of creation, truth, and the open transcendentals.

Trinitarian Remedy: Creation, Truth, and the Open Transcendentals

In light of his analysis of modernity and postmodernity, Gunton sees his task as reinvigorating the concept of truth, whilst at the same time taking into account their reaction to the weaknesses of the theological tradition.[59] Given that the problems are theological, Gunton proposes that the solution must be a revised theological account of truth and a trinitarian theology of creation. This section explores Gunton's theological development of open transcendentals as forms of non-foundationalist foundations that uphold the richness and diversity of truth and being within the goodness of God's unified creation.

---

55. Gunton, *The One, the Three and the Many*, 122–3.
56. Gunton, *The One, the Three and the Many*, 122.
57. Gunton, *The One, the Three and the Many*, 123.
58. Gunton, *The One, the Three and the Many*, 124.
59. Gunton, *The One, the Three and the Many*, 129.

The Enlightenment quest for absolute rational truth morphed into the postmodern suspicion of the very idea of objective truth as something that is humanly realizable. This leaves the question as to whether any quest to account for meaning and truth is futile, or whether there can be a theory of meaning in which the rights of the universal and the particular are preserved. Any quest for universal meaning and truth must happily acknowledge the limits of human knowing and of the universals that it attempts to know.[60] There are no indubitable universal convictions on reality, and Gunton's quest is for non-foundationalist rationalities.

As Barth, Wittgenstein, and Polanyi show, epistemological methodologies need to conform to the subject they seek to know. Theological rationality does not easily conform to scientific methods of knowing because its subject, the living God, dictates the knowing process. God is not an inanimate object over which we can gain epistemic mastery. Rather, our knowledge of God begins with God's self-revelation that reshapes our ways of knowing. Moreover, the reality of human sin limits confidence in the knowing enterprise, and this non-foundationalist account of knowing allows historical and cultural particularity an important place in rationality.[61] However, the answer is not, in Gunton's assessment, found in the siren song of anti-foundationalism that evades the demands of invoking the name of God. God is the universal source of being, meaning, and truth, and theologians must take responsibility for theology's universal demands.

Instead of foundationalism or anti-foundationalism, Gunton proposes a quest for non-foundationalist foundations that seeks "to find moments of truth in both of the contentions, namely that particularity and universality each have their place in a reasoned approach to truth."[62] Rather than foundationalism's impossible search for indubitable universal truths, or anti-foundationalism's capitulation to subjectivities, Gunton seeks truth engaged by fallible, finite, and fallen human minds. Postmodernism's reaction against the failure of foundationalism's certainties is necessary, and reminds us that human quests for truth must be appropriate to their limits. But that does not mean there is a failure to find any truth at all. The ancient quest for foundations, which is not to be confused with foundationalism, is right and proper because God has created the world as a singular coherent reality.[63] If there are to be foundations, they need to be non-foundationalist foundations, or fallibilist foundations that are appropriate to the rationality of created knowers.[64] Gunton's search for non-foundationalist foundations culminates in his proposal for trinitarian open transcendentals.

---

60. Gunton, *The One, the Three and the Many*, 132.
61. Gunton, *The One, the Three and the Many*, 133.
62. Gunton, *The One, the Three and the Many*, 134.
63. Gunton, *The One, the Three and the Many*, 135.
64. Gunton, *The One, the Three and the Many*, 135–6. See also Colin E. Gunton, "Universal and Particular in Atonement Theology," *Religious Studies*, 28 (1992): 461.

An open transcendental is a notion, in some way basic to the human thinking process, which empowers a continuing and in principle unfinished exploration of the universal marks of being. The quest is indeed a universal one, to find concepts which do succeed in some way or other in representing or echoing the universal marks of being. But it is also to find concepts whose value will be found not primarily in their clarity and certainty, but in their suggestiveness and potentiality for being deepened and enriched, during the continuing process of thought, from a wide range of sources in human life and culture.[65]

The quest for transcendentals is an ancient one and seeks to find notions that embody "the necessary notes of being."[66] Transcendentals are notions that provide thought with a way of upholding the unity and diversity of being, and comprehending "what reality truly is, everywhere and always."[67] While supplying understanding of the unity of being, the transcendentals also uphold the necessary diversity, complexity, and richness of being. The traditional definition of transcendentals, however, tends to give being precedence over God. Gunton, by contrast, seeks to develop the transcendentals theologically.[68] Gunton's attempt to find transcendentals is set in a theological context that holds God as the source and ground of true being. "If there are transcendentals, they have their being in the fact that God has created the world in such a way that it bears the marks of its maker …. They are … notions which can be predicated of all being by virtue of the fact that God is creator and the world is creation."[69] Yet, not any notion of God will do. In place of the perceived dominance of monadic views of God, Gunton asserts an alternative that stresses God's triunity.

Historical approaches to transcendentals are marked by the dominance of the one at the expense of the many, which brings immaterial tendencies in its wake. The search for transcendentals is dominated by timeless, unchanging, and unitary accounts of ultimate being that hold plurality as only an appearance that is not part of true being itself. Plato's immaterial accounts of abstract forms are highly influential in Gnostic tendencies found in some theologies that devalue the plural and material as inferior.[70] According to Gunton, these discarnate trajectories are especially pronounced in Origen and Augustine, and their work tends to undermine the goodness of material creation.[71] The "Origenist-Augustinian

65. Gunton, *The One, the Three and the Many*, 142–3. See also Gunton, "Trinity, Ontology and Anthropology," 53–6; and Gunton, *Father, Son and Holy Spirit*, 185–7.

66. Daniel W. Hardy, "Created and Redeemed Sociality," in *On Being the Church: Essays on the Christian Community*, ed. Colin E. Gunton and Daniel W. Hardy (Edinburgh: T&T Clark, 1989), 24–5.

67. Gunton, *The One, the Three and the Many*, 136.

68. Gunton, *The One, the Three and the Many*, 136. See also Craig Bartholomew, "The Healing of Modernity," 119.

69. Gunton, *The One, the Three and the Many*, 136.

70. Gunton, *The One, the Three and the Many*, 137–8.

71. Gunton, *The One, the Three and the Many*, 137.

tradition" elevates the oneness of God over the plurality and richness of God's triunity, and unity, rather than plurality, is deemed transcendental.[72] The legacy of this unitary inheritance is, in Gunton's view, exemplified in Aquinas' qualified account of the analogy of being between God and the world. While upholding the otherness of God and the world, Aquinas' analogical approach assumes an abstract notion of God independent of God's trinitarian action in the economy. God is defined instead through the *via negativa* that projects a conception of God by negating the marks of created being. Temporal reality is, therefore, negated in preference to timelessness, while eternality and materiality are negated in favour of immateriality.[73]

Gunton's concern is the tendency to downgrade materiality in general and "materially embodied beauty" in particular.[74] Like Aquinas and Barth, Gunton seeks to develop a theology of analogy, but one that is more focused on God's eternal being *and* action that is derived from God's economic involvement in the world of the many.[75] The Guntonian quest is for a trinitarian analogy of being and becoming: "a conception of the structures of the created world in the light of the triune creator and redeemer."[76]

The Open Transcendentals

In place of the Western tendency for the one to dominate the many, Gunton attempts, through the concept of open transcendentals, an alternative approach that upholds the unity and plurality of being, reality, human experience, and culture.[77] The quest for open transcendentals, while rational, is also provisional, finite, and limited because of the impact that human sin has upon knowledge.[78] Before examining Gunton's proposed open transcendentals, it is necessary to explore Gunton's use of Samuel Taylor Coleridge's account of an *idea*, from which the open transcendentals develop.[79]

Coleridge's notion of *idea* is instructive for Gunton's quest for open transcendentals because *ideas* are dynamic rational concepts that are inexhaustible in nature. Coleridge's *ideas* are open and suggestive, rather than abstract and

---

72. Gunton, *The One, the Three and the Many*, 138.
73. Gunton, *The One, the Three and the Many*, 139–40.
74. Gunton, *The One, the Three and the Many*, 140.
75. Gunton, *The One, the Three and the Many*, 140.
76. Gunton, *The One, the Three and the Many*, 141.
77. Gunton, *The One, the Three and the Many*, 142.
78. Gunton, *The One, the Three and the Many*, 142–3.
79. For a helpful delineation of Coleridge's account of *idea* and Gunton's use of it, see Holmes, "Gunton and Coleridge," 321, 323–4. See also Sue Patterson, "Gunton on Theological Language," in *T&T Clark Handbook of Colin Gunton*, ed. Andrew Picard, Myk Habets, and Murray Rae (London: T&T Clark, 2021), 32–4.

static, and "'given by the knowledge of [the] ultimate aim' of something."[80] They are fathomless ontological notions that are marked by their inexhaustibility and give rise to "ever deeper involvement in the truth of things."[81] In the context of fallibilist rationality, *ideas* mediate between the universal and particular in such ways that each is given its proper weight. Importantly, Coleridge roots *ideas* in the triune God who, as the *Idea Idearum*, is the source of all being, truth, goodness, and beauty.[82]

Ideas, while relentlessly generative, are not transcendentals that give insight into all being. Gunton makes an important distinction between an *idea* and a transcendental. For instance, while the Trinity is the primary *idea* that makes known the character of the source of all being, the Trinity is not a transcendental. Divinity is not a mark of all being; rather, there is a fundamental ontological difference between creator and creation. Gunton's constructive proposal for transcendentals is that if the Trinity is the source of all being, meaning, and truth, we can expect that all being will reflect the being of the God who creates and upholds it in being.[83] The method employed here, as Bruce McCormack observes, moves from God's economic revelation to God's eternal triunity and returns to examine created being as a creation of the triune creator. This enables Gunton to highlight features of the created world that stand in analogical relation to the relational structures of the triune being of God.[84]

As with Aquinas' and Barth's analogical projects, the open transcendentals maintain the classic preservation of the otherness of God and the world and protect God's aseity and creation's createdness. At the same time, though, Gunton's transcendentals seek to give a more adequate account of the interrelation of truth, goodness, and beauty and the place of plurality.[85] This method requires, in Gunton's opinion, a stronger account of God's triunity than the monadic tendencies of the tradition. Coleridge's approach encourages a movement beyond the opposition of objectivism and subjectivism, and of absolutism and relativism to explore the universal directionality of creation that takes various and particular form in different times and places.[86] This requires that the celebration of the goodness and rational knowability of God's creation is held in creative tension with the universal effects of sin that mar all humanity's thoughts and actions, and limit our ability to comprehend the transcendentals. Although the meaning and import of the open transcendentals remain provisional within the fallen human mind, human

---

80. Gunton, *The One, the Three and the Many*, 143. Citing Samuel Taylor Coleridge, *On the Constitution of the Church and State According to the Idea of Each*, 3rd ed. (London: William Pickering, 1839), 11.
81. Gunton, *The One, the Three and the Many*, 144.
82. Gunton, *The One, the Three and the Many*, 144.
83. Gunton, *The One, the Three and the Many*, 145.
84. McCormack, "*The One, the Three and the Many*," 9.
85. Gunton, *The One, the Three and the Many*, 145.
86. Gunton, *The One, the Three and the Many*, 146.

thought and action take place in the light of Christ's redemption and the promised perfection of all things. Between these poles, Gunton's theology enquires into the kind of world we inhabit.[87]

The quest for open transcendentals welcomes the dynamism of creative thought, as well as being an objective and metaphysical quest that accepts the temporal, historical, and cultural locatedness of rational enquiries. The transcendentals are, therefore, provisional and open in ways that resist reductive searches for timeless universal foundations. In place of static fixities, Gunton seeks "an inner dynamic and direction within human thought."[88] Such an approach upholds Hegel's belief that truth comes to be within the historicity of human culture, as Gunton is especially interested in God's presence and action within human cultural agency and action. Cultural phenomena are relative to their context, but their contextual conditioning does not limit their ability to attain truth. Through his development of the concept of *Geist*, Hegel attempts to articulate a theological basis for renewed cultural unity. Whatever the limitations of Hegel's *Geist*, and there are limitations, Hegel rightly attempts to comprehend "how far God can be said to be present in and as culture."[89] Hegel's downfall, however, is his immanentism that undermines the ontological distinction between creator and created, and displaces the Father and the Son from the Spirit in a modalism of the Spirit (*Geist*). In place of Hegel's misconception of the being and nature of the Trinity, Gunton explores how an adequately trinitarian account of God might develop an account of God's presence in culture and fund trinitarian transcendentals. "Much, indeed everything, depends on the way that that particular doctrine [the Trinity] is articulated."[90]

In his development of the trinitarian transcendentals, Gunton turns to Gregory of Nazianzus' famous formulation of the oneness and threeness of God: "No sooner do I conceive of the One than I am illumined by the Splendour of the Three; no sooner do I distinguish Them than I am carried back to the One."[91] According to Gunton, Nazianzus' formulation upholds a dynamic dialectic that gives equal weight to the Parmenidean one and the Heraclitean many.[92] What are the transcendental possibilities for concrete thought about human life in the world, asks Gunton, if we explore the concepts the Church Fathers used to hold the one and the three together in their doctrine of God? The open transcendentals are not mere solutions to abstract problems, but draw from trinitarian conceptualities to shed light on contested questions and ailments of concrete human life and culture—specifically, relationality, particularity, and temporality, as well as truth, goodness, and beauty (culture).[93] This focuses thought upon the doctrine of

---

87. Gunton, *The One, the Three and the Many*, 146.
88. Gunton, *The One, the Three and the Many*, 146–7.
89. Gunton, *The One, the Three and the Many*, 147.
90. Gunton, *The One, the Three and the Many*, 149.
91. Gregory of Nazianzus, *Oration*, 40.41 (*NPNF* 3:375).
92. Gunton, *The One, the Three and the Many*, 149–50.
93. Gunton, *The One, the Three and the Many*, 150.

creation, and the light that the doctrine of God throws on created reality in the hope that the trinitarian transcendentals might enable new possibilities of thought about the created order and the plurality of its being.[94]

Gunton's open transcendentals face criticism from a variety of fronts, especially his historiographical tropes and his relational trinitarian ontology, which we will examine in detail in Chapter 2. A pressing concern for some is that Gunton's use of analogy in his open transcendentals turns creation into "a single massive vestige of the Trinity."[95] However, as Schwöbel rightly notes, Gunton's open transcendentals are not a simple account of trinitarian traces within creation. The open transcendentals, which Gunton develops from his trinitarian analogy of being, are rooted in the way that God's being-in-relation is actualized in the economy to constitute creation's structures as many-in-relation. Schwöbel explains, "If one can speak of an analogy between God and the world it is an *analogia transcendentalis* which is realised in the economy of creation and salvation."[96] For Gunton, the world is a revelatory kind of place, because it bears the marks of its creator, and the open transcendentals attempt to capture the inner logic of the divine economy.[97] The following sections examine Gunton's chiastic couplets and his constructive trinitarian transcendentals which try to understand the inner logic of the created order as a creation that bears the marks of the triune God.

C/C': Christology, Economy, and Perichoresis

This section examines Gunton's analysis of the rise of modern immanentism and the resultant cultural fragmentation, and his Christologically conditioned account of the relational unity of creation. Creation is unified by someone, not something. Jesus Christ is the mediator of creation and as the eternal Word incarnate he unites the eternal God and contingent creation in relationship. In the modern world, God is given a protracted leave of absence and it is assumed that human agency is responsible for progress and the world's future. Christendom's radical transcendence is replaced with modernity's radical immanentism and the dominance of science and technology as the gateway to progress. The passion for progress idealizes the future and problematizes the past in ways that fragment culture and undermine a happy indwelling of concrete life in the present. What is

---

94. Gunton, *The One, the Three and the Many*, 151.
95. McCormack, "*The One, the Three and the Many*," 9–10.
96. Christoph Schwöbel, "Radical Monotheism and the Trinity," *Neue Zeitschrift für Systematische Theologie und Religionsphilosophie*, 43 (2001): 73. See also Gunton, *The One, the Three and the Many*, 151.
97. Schwöbel, "The Shape of Colin Gunton's Theology," 201. On the world as a revelatory kind of place, see Colin E. Gunton, *A Brief Theology of Revelation: The 1993 Warfield Lectures* (London: T&T Clark, 1995), 39; and Colin E. Gunton, "Universal and Particular in Atonement Theology," 461–2.

required, Gunton proposes, is a theological account of time and reality as unified in and through Jesus Christ who holds all creation together in relation.

Modern Sounding: Immanentism

Modernity's displacement of God is a reaction to the other-worldly culture of medieval Christendom which prioritizes infinity over space and eternity over time. Modernity's response, as an alternative to the co-ordinating reality of a distant heaven, is to promote a this-worldly culture that realigns our time and space.[98] The resulting this-worldly orientation casts off the shackles of tradition in order that the present may be liberated for freedom of thought, rational enquiry, and creativity.[99] It is human agency, not transcendent agency or fate, that is efficacious in determining the course of events in time. Science is understood as the triumph of rationalism over superstition, and its gaze is fixed upon studies of the spatial and temporal world rather than a distant eternity. Meaning-making is ordered to that which is spatially and temporally observable and verifiable by the techniques of rationality and reason.[100] While this is, of course, an oversimplification, Gunton's interests lie in capturing the mood of modernity's relation to time and the nature and effects of its this-worldliness.[101]

Despite advances in our comprehension of time and space, modern people are less at home in the world than their historic predecessors. For all the utopian dreams of increased leisure as a result of technological advances, modern life is marked by hurry and the tyranny of time. These nowist proclivities negate "a serene dwelling in the body and on the good earth."[102] For Gunton, our conception of time and relationality is the issue at stake: how is the universe held together in relation, and how do we belong together with one another and the world? To discern the lineage of distortions in modern relationality, Gunton explores the ancient roots of this-worldliness and its interrelations with history, tradition, human agency, and science.[103]

Historical Antecedents: Atemporality

Ancient views of time hold reality to be of secondary significance to that of eternity, and believe that time is a path, not fully real, that leads towards eternity. Without succumbing to the simplistic binary of Hebrew and Greek thinking, there is, in Gunton's mind, a contrast. There remains in Greek thought, especially in Parmenides and Plato, a drive to find reality in timeless forms that transcend

---

98. Gunton, *The One, the Three and the Many*, 74–5.
99. Gunton, *The One, the Three and the Many*, 75.
100. Gunton, *The One, the Three and the Many*, 75.
101. Gunton, *The One, the Three and the Many*, 76.
102. Gunton, *The One, the Three and the Many*, 77.
103. Gunton, *The One, the Three and the Many*, 78.

temporality and underlie or overlie materiality's change and decay. Theirs, Gunton suggests, is a theology of escape from time that finds redemption outside the realm of temporality.[104]

The atemporal tendencies of Hellenistic thought are heavily influential in the development of theology. While Irenaeus' theology of recapitulation offers a positive affirmation of creation's history as the domain in which God redeems and perfects through the incarnate Son's faithful humanity and the eschatological Spirit's perfecting action, the tradition is more commonly marked by atemporal tendencies.[105] In Irenaeus, there is no contrast between timeless eternity and temporal imperfection. Although fallen, the creation's temporality and createdness are its glory. God respects creation's temporality, and, rather than abolishing it, takes time to redeem and perfect the creation by ordering it to its proper end in Christ by the Spirit.[106] As we will see in Part II, Gunton develops these Irenaean insights further through the progression to a trinitarian theology of mediation, from which he develops his trinitarian theology of culture.

Irenaeus' positive affirmation of creation stands in contrast with the atemporal and immaterial tendencies in Origen's and Augustine's theologies of creation. The Platonic influences in their work deem materiality to be ontologically inferior to immateriality and risk denial of creation's temporal goodness. Origen's theology of creation has overtones of the Gnostic denial of materiality that views creation as a training ground for correcting fallen spirits. Creation's plurality is a problem in Origen, a sign of its inferiority to immateriality.[107] Similar tendencies, though less pronounced, are also detectable in Augustine. Instead of Irenaeus' theology of God's economic action, Augustine views God's action as a timeless presence inserted into time, and ponders whether time is a human projection. The present is submerged between the past and the future in such a way that time is not integral to creation. To what extent, Gunton asks, does Augustine "conceive the order of time to be inherently and essentially the place of disorder rather than – say – of a fallenness whose redemption is the hope of the Christian gospel?"[108] The end is not anticipated in time, and between the incarnation and the end all history is equally fallen. The result is a homogeneity of history that pits divine action over and against temporal creation in such a way that it evacuates history of its meaning.[109] In Gunton's view, there is the lack of Christological and pneumatological determinants in Augustine's legacy, which are required for a theology of creation. This enables a Gnostic view of redemption from creation into an immaterial eternity.[110] Christianity's false eternity is divorced from the divine economy and

---

104. Gunton, *The One, the Three and the Many*, 79–80.
105. Gunton, *The One, the Three and the Many*, 80–1.
106. Gunton, *The One, the Three and the Many*, 81.
107. Gunton, *The One, the Three and the Many*, 81.
108. Gunton, *The One, the Three and the Many*, 82–3.
109. Gunton, *The One, the Three and the Many*, 83.
110. Gunton, *The One, the Three and the Many*, 84.

establishes the seedbed for the natural sciences to supply meaning to temporal and spatial reality apart from Christianity.[111]

The rise of modern science owes much to Christianity's belief in a meaningful universe, but science too has several features that mitigate against the importance of time and temporality. There are, in Gunton's estimation, Platonic overtones in Newton's idea that absolute time and space underlies our experience of relative time and space. Our experience of time and space is, therefore, relegated in its significance, and time is understood as not fully real or part of the inner being of things.[112] Kant, like Augustine, appeals to a timeless substratum. He differs from Newton, however, in following Augustine's contention that time is a projection of the mind. Hegel offers an important corrective to the trajectories of Newton and Kant, and holds that time is the realm of divine action. However, his immanentism involves a pantheistic divinization of the finite in which temporal time is the realm of divine self-realization through human cultural achievement.[113] Hegel's divinization of the finite results in time losing its proper being and reduces it to the site for the ubiquitous activity of *Geist*. Reactions to Hegel manifest in Marxism and historical relativism, which reduce time to the outworking of fate, or homogenize all times to an indistinguishable whole. The central issue at stake, in Gunton's assessment, is Václav Havel's diagnosis of the loss of transcendent coordinates for human living, and modernity's smothering immanentism.[114]

Gunton believes that the theological root of the problem is a displaced eschatology. The meaning and purpose of creation are displaced from divine to human agency, and humankind, rather than Christ and the Spirit, is understood to be responsible for the redemption and eschatological perfection of the creation.[115] "One revealing symptom of the displacement of eschatology is to be found in the modern obsession with the future."[116] Modernity's displaced eschatology averts humanity's gaze from the present to the future as "the place where it all happens."[117] The modern world is marked by an obsession about the future, and we discard the past by fleeing into the future. The future becomes another false abstraction that shapes our inability to live happily in the present. Without proposing a wholesale return to ancient other-worldliness, Gunton maintains that a divinely promised

---

111. Gunton, *The One, the Three and the Many*, 84–5.
112. Gunton, *The One, the Three and the Many*, 85–6.
113. Gunton, *The One, the Three and the Many*, 87.
114. Gunton, *The One, the Three and the Many*, 88–9. Gunton's repeated use of the phrase "transcendent coordinates" for human living is drawn from the work of Václav Havel, whose analysis accords with Gunton's conclusion regarding the impact of the displacement of God in Western culture. Havel holds that the displacement and loss of God result in the loss of universal coordinates for human living, See Gunton, *The One, the Three and the Many*, 71, 74.
115. Gunton, *The One, the Three and the Many*, 89.
116. Gunton, *The One, the Three and the Many*, 90.
117. Gunton, *The One, the Three and the Many*, 90.

future gives a context for life in the present. In place of radical transcendence or radical immanentism, Gunton proposes the need for an interweaving of the times in which the Spirit enables anticipations of the future in the present.[118] This requires an upholding of the delicate balance between creation and redemption, and divine action and human response.

The inbreaking kingdom of God requires obedient human action and response, but we cannot conceive of human action that brings about God's future without reference to past creation and present redemption. Modernity tends to overlook human fallenness and sin, and divinizes the finite agent, often with disastrous results.[119] Instead, Gunton argues that an account of the future requires a reaffirmation of the present as the context for human action. "It is the present that must be understood as that which, through Christ and the Spirit, is given from the past and redirected to its true end by the one God, creator and redeemer."[120] There is a balance between past creation and present redemption that needs to be upheld if we are to avoid the excesses of modernity's alienation from the world.

The distinctive character of modernity's alienation is displayed in its neurotic attitude to time. Instead of realizing the much-vaunted freedom and openness of time, freedom is diminished in modernity. This is pronounced in modernity's rejection of past traditions as that from which human freedom requires liberation to begin again. For Gunton, our relation to tradition includes our personal relatedness to others in the past and the present.[121] Modernity's highly individualized account of freedom deems the other, including the historical other, to be the source of unfreedom rather than relational freedom. Freedom on this account is freedom from the other, who must be suppressed, rather than freedom in and for relationship with others. In this way, human endeavour, especially in the natural sciences, is commonly cast as *creatio ex nihilo*, even though there is a strong sense of tradition within the discipline.

Our inability to live in comfortable relation with time reveals a renewed form of Gnosticism that is antithetical to the material world of space and time.[122] There is a Gnostic loss of confidence in the logic of temporality that breeds meaninglessness and the loss of the present. In response, Gunton believes Christianity is called to offer a redemptive vision that centres on Christology: the life, death, and resurrection of the one through whom all things are created and in whom all things cohere. The incarnation of Jesus Christ to share our time and its fallenness is not merely an affirmation of created being; it is the coming of creation's Lord to redeem and perfect creation to the praise of its creator.[123]

---

118. Gunton, *The One, the Three and the Many*, 92.
119. Gunton, *The One, the Three and the Many*, 93.
120. Gunton, *The One, the Three and the Many*, 94.
121. Gunton, *The One, the Three and the Many*, 95.
122. Gunton, *The One, the Three and the Many*, 96–7.
123. Gunton, *The One, the Three and the Many*, 100.

Trinitarian Remedy: Christology, Economy, and Perichoresis

If the displacement of God alienates us from our past and disturbs our present as we flee into the future, Gunton proposes a search for the appropriate theological integration of eternity and time as part of the necessary coordinates for human flourishing. In place of the rationalistic spatializing of time and mechanizing of space, Gunton proffers a Christologically conditioned account of how things hold together in the world. A theological conception of time enables an account of creation as an ordered whole where the past and present offer a unity of experience in the world, and a theological conception of space enables a unified account of our experience of reality amidst its vast distinctives.[124] Gunton's quest is for a theology of creation that provides coordinates for living in the world in a way that appropriately integrates the finite and the infinite without threatening human freedom or openness to newness.[125] He offers the concept of economy as a Coleridgean *idea* that gives rise to a Christologically conditioned theology of *perichoresis* and the relation of all things.

Coleridgean Idea: Economy

In Gunton's theology of creation, the concept of the economy integrates the richness and plurality of the one God's action towards and in creation.[126] Biblically, economy (οἰκονομία) carries an understanding of household management that describes forms of God's dealings with the world (Lk 16:2-4; 1 Cor 9:17; Col 1:25; and especially Eph 1:10, 3:2, 3:9).[127] Gunton also notes that Paul, in 2 Corinthians,

---

124. Gunton, *The One, the Three and the Many*, 155–6.
125. Gunton, *The One, the Three and the Many*, 157.
126. Gunton, *The One, the Three and the Many*, 157.
127. Economy, in its Greek usage, includes financial meaning related to resources, work, money production, and exchange, as well as the processes and relationships these involve. See Frances Young and David F. Ford, *Meaning and Truth in 2 Corinthians* (London: SPCK, 1987), 170–5. The meaning extends, though, to embrace God's plan of salvation, or God's world administration. Elizabeth Schüssler Fiorenza notes that the traditional translation of οἰκονομία as plan assumes household management consists in a variety of action plans. However, in ancient political discourse household management was the role of the matron while the role of statecraft was that of the master. Fiorenza argues οἰκονομία is a female image of God as the one who takes care of the whole cosmos and its members in and through Jesus Christ, the beloved. God's world-household management is realized in Christ and anticipated in the bringing together of Jews and Gentiles, and men and women, in the *ekklēsia*. See Elizabeth Schüssler Fiorenza, *Ephesians*. Wisdom Commentary (Collegeville: Liturgical Press, 2017), lxxiv–lxxvi, 9–10, and 37–8. In his work on imperial iconography, Harry Maier helpfully shows the importance of concord discourse, or ὁμόνοια, in Roman ideology, and suggests the unity rhetoric in Ephesians draws from the concord discourse. It is God's unifying action in Christ, rather than the emperor's, that unifies the church, and this results in a different body politic and peace than that which exists in the empire. See Harry O. Maier, *Picturing Paul in Empire: Imperial Image, Text and Persuasion in Colossians, Ephesians and the Pastoral Epistles* (London: T&T Clark, 2013), 107–18.

while not referring directly to economy, utilizes a range of financial metaphors to describe the divine generosity of Christ's exchange and reconciliation. Christ's generosity conditions all relationships in God's new economy and enables a new way of being human in the world.[128] In later developments, theologians, such as Irenaeus, began to make use of the term "economy" to express aspects of God's involvement in the creation. "'Economy' embraces the being of the world in its relations to God and the action of God in relation to the world."[129]

In his resistance to the Gnostics, Irenaeus develops the concept of economy to encompass the distinct, yet united, action of the Son and the Spirit to bring about God's purposes in the creation.[130] In contrast to modernity's tyranny of time, Irenaeus' notion of recapitulation allows for a positive account of creation's temporal and spatial structures and God's creating, sustaining, redeeming, and perfecting action within the economy.[131] God's structured embrace of time through the Son and in the Spirit maintains the important link between creation and redemption that stresses the redemption of creation through time rather than a timeless redemption from creation. A trinitarian conception of the divine economy enables temporal and spatial history to have its own dynamic of interrelatedness by virtue of God's economic action. Economy maintains the diversity of God's action in the world within a coherent unity, and the richness and variety of created being as that which God embraces in its createdness.

Despite its theological richness, a trinitarian account of the economy is not, in Gunton's assessment, a transcendental because God's being cannot be reduced to God's economic action. While God's economic actions reveal God's being, they do not exhaust it as God's immanent being is not dependent on the creation. An account of the immanent Trinity preserves God's aseity as well as the relative freedom required to maintain creation's distinct and proper being in its createdness. At the same time, the immanent Trinity enables a celebration of God's structured embrace of contingent creation.[132] The economy is an endlessly fruitful Coleridgean *idea*, a rational human concept developed under the impact of inspiration and revelation, but it is not an open transcendental.[133] Instead, the fruitfulness of economy spawns a discovery of "the universal dynamic and interrelatedness of everything in time and space."[134] Noting the conceptual insights of modern relativity physics, Gunton asks if this enables further exploration into the interconnectedness of all reality. He suggests that a Christologically conditioned understanding of the patristic trinitarian concept of *perichoresis* can be understood as an open transcendental.

---

128. Gunton, *The One, the Three and the Many*, 158.
129. Gunton, *The One, the Three and the Many*, 160.
130. Gunton, *The One, the Three and the Many*, 158.
131. Gunton, *The One, the Three and the Many*, 159.
132. Gunton, *The One, the Three and the Many*, 161.
133. Gunton, *The One, the Three and the Many*, 160–1.
134. Gunton, *The One, the Three and the Many*, 162.

Open Transcendental: Perichoresis

Perichoresis is an open transcendental that opens up possibilities for thought because it gives insight into God's eternal being from the various, yet united, economic activities of the one God in and towards the creation. Rather than a speculative doctrinal irrelevance, the concept of *perichoresis* is rooted in the revelation of divine action in the economy. God's diverse, yet united, action in the economy reveals that God's eternal nature exists in the mutual reciprocity, interpenetration, and inter-animation of Father, Son, and Spirit. The Father, Son, and Spirit are a mutually involved personal dynamic, and *perichoresis* is laden with spatial and temporal conceptualities that involve movement, recurrence, and interpenetration, as well as the unity-in-variety of divine economic action.[135]

Perichoresis is an open transcendental that opens up possibilities for thought. The doctrine of *perichoresis* holds that God is not the atemporal and shapeless Parmenidean monad of Christendom. Instead, God is an eternal personal being whose life exists in the way the Father, Son, and Spirit give to and receive from each other what they are in love.[136] At first glance the concept of *perichoresis* might seem to be nothing more than an irrelevant speculation. But for Gunton it is a vital concept that is rooted in God's action in the economy. It is the action of God in the creation through the Son and the Spirit that reveals God's eternal nature as existing in the mutual reciprocity, interpenetration, and inter-animation of the three trinitarian persons. And precisely because the *perichoretic* love of the Trinity extends outwards to the creation, it cannot be conceived as timeless and non-spatial. Therefore, Gunton proposes a dynamic understanding of the universe constituted by the triune God which bears the marks of its creator as a spatio-temporal relational order.[137]

All this leads Gunton to suggest that the concept of *perichoresis*, as the expression of the unity and plurality of God's triune nature, might extend beyond divine being and give insight into all reality as the creation of the God who exists in eternal dynamic relationship. This in turn invites consideration as to whether *perichoresis* may serve as an analogical and transcendental concept for all being.

Divine reality, however, cannot be directly read upon created reality, and Gunton is aware of the dangers of drawing analogical links between God and the creation. Finite being cannot completely share the being of other finite realities in the same way that the divine persons do. Sin and evil distort creation's dynamic of being, and it is only redirected towards perfection by the incarnation of the Son and the perfecting action of the Spirit. Yet created ontology is given particular shape as a result of its relation to the triune creator. So, Gunton asks, does the world, as a creation of the triune God who exists in eternal *perichoresis*, offer a temporal and spatial echo of God's relational being?[138] In response, he proposes an

---

135. Gunton, *The One, the Three and the Many*, 163.
136. Gunton, *The One, the Three and the Many*, 164.
137. Gunton, *The One, the Three and the Many*, 165.
138. Gunton, *The One, the Three and the Many*, 165–6.

apophatic analogical development of *perichoresis* that avoids the simple equation of divine and created being, and gives due allowance for the "distinction in relation between God and the world."[139] Against the disintegrating forces of modernity, *perichoresis* offers a dynamic unity of the one and the many that may provide the necessary coordinates for relational human being in the world.

If the world is an order of things dynamically related to each other, where everything contributes to the being of all else and enables everything to be what it is in relationship, the world may be conceived as *perichoretic*.[140] Gunton's analogical and transcendental exploration of *perichoresis* employs the concept developed from consideration of the economy to shed light on the being of creation through *perichoretic* analogies. Such an enquiry cannot be free speculation. Accordingly, Gunton maintains a strong awareness of the apophatic limitations necessary when employing concepts derived from examination of God's ineffable being to describe God's fallen creation.[141] However, scripture, Gunton believes, invites an exploration of the positive possibilities of creation displaying God's invisible nature (Rom 1:20). A quest for the marks of the creator must begin with God's triune nature and the *taxis* of divine relations that may be reflected in the world and generate some measure of understanding of creation's being.[142] In this regard, Gunton suggests three realms of being and meaning: Firstly, the personal world, and the being-in-relation of humans. Secondly, the material world, and the being-in-relation of the wider creation in itself and in relation to humanity. And, thirdly, culture and the being-in-relation of truth, goodness, and beauty. It is the third category that Gunton focuses upon in particular, because his interest is in the coordinates within which all created being makes sense. His interest is in an engaged theology that integrates the realms of the personal, the material, and the cultural, and celebrates their interrelationship in the face of modernity's disintegrating forces.[143]

In place of modernity's notion of individualized freedom from others, *perichoresis* invites an understanding of the mutual constitution of human beings in relationships. Human particularity is established in and through relationships, not apart or in abstraction from them. Our particularity is the fruit of a *perichoretic* being-in-relation together with one another and God's good creation.[144] Accepting the spatial and temporal limitations of created being means living in relationships in which we give and receive particularity. This includes relationship with the traditions and people of the past, which modernity dismisses as slavery and unfreedom. Life in the world is mediated through time and in space and our

---

139. Gunton, *The One, the Three and the Many*, 165.
140. Gunton, *The One, the Three and the Many*, 166.
141. Gunton, *The One, the Three and the Many*, 167.
142. Gunton, *The One, the Three and the Many*, 167–8.
143. Gunton, *The One, the Three and the Many*, 168.
144. Gunton, *The One, the Three and the Many*, 170.

positive relation to the past, without falling into romantic traditionalism, is part of contented life in the *perichoresis* of the times.[145]

If *perichoresis* speaks meaningfully of our personal being in the material world, Gunton then considers whether it may provide insight into non-personal being. In place of modernity's mechanistic view of the universe, Gunton proposes a *perichoretic* understanding of the universe which offers a different understanding of human being, especially in relation to the environment. Insights from Michael Faraday and modern relativity physics suggest an implicit *perichoretic* conception of reality in which the nature of material being derives from their relations.[146] The Butterfly Effect indicates a universe whose inscape is *perichoretic*, such that an electron on one side of the world can affect the behaviour of gas on the other side of the world.[147] As the divine persons are distinct and constituted by their relatedness, so the various relations of created being constitute particularity without descending into a smothering homogeneity. There is an array of relations and our temporal and spatial situatedness means that our closest relations shape us most deeply.[148] We live, Gunton concludes, in a *perichoretic* universe, such that "everything may be what it is and not another thing, but it is also what it uniquely is by virtue of its relation to everything else."[149]

If people and the material universe are a *perichoretic* unity, there is a contrasting vision of human culture over against the fragmenting forces that beset modernity. Modernity is marked by the hierarchical separation of rational, ethical, and aesthetic thought from each other that alienates humanity from the world and the meaningful universe. The dominance of scientific enquiry and objectivist epistemologies elevates a mechanistic world at the expense of ethics and aesthetics. Alternatively, the reflexive rebellion of postmodernism celebrates subjectivity and meaninglessness at the expense of rationality and unified meaning. In place of these twin poles of fragmentation, Gunton proposes a *perichoresis* of culture and meaning.[150] Science uses aesthetic criteria to develop theories about the beautiful and complex world revealed by the microscope and mathematics. The insights from science and mathematics should encourage the artist to express the deeper truth of the world instead of social alienation and cosmic disillusionment.[151] Likewise, art and aesthetics can offer a vision of human moral and ethical

---

145. Gunton, *The One, the Three and the Many*, 171.
146. Gunton, *The One, the Three and the Many*, 172.
147. Gunton, *The One, the Three and the Many*, 172. See also Gunton, *The Promise of Trinitarian Theology*, 151; Gunton, "Knowledge and Culture," 89; and Colin E. Gunton, "Proteus and Procrustes: A Study in the Dialectic of Language in Disagreement with Sally McFague," in *Speaking the Christian God: The Holy Trinity and the Challenge of Feminism*, ed. Alvin F. Kimel (Grand Rapids: Eerdmans, 1992), 70.
148. Gunton, *The One, the Three and the Many*, 172–3.
149. Gunton, *The One, the Three and the Many*, 173.
150. Gunton, *The One, the Three and the Many*, 174.
151. Gunton, *The One, the Three and the Many*, 175.

reality. There needs to be an integration of all three realms of meaning (science, ethics, and aesthetics) with each upholding their distinct contribution. Gunton's suggestion is that this integrative vision needs to be rooted in an account of God that provides the unifying coordinates for human cultural flourishing. It is the Christian understanding of the triune God who exists in the richness of God's tri-personal being as one God that provides the conceptual clarity needed for the unity and variety of human culture.[152]

The triune God is the source of all being, meaning, and truth, and, therefore, we can develop an integrated theology of culture, while at the same time upholding the validity of distinctions within it. In creation, there is a *perichoresis* of all things; Gunton cites the motor car as a suggestive example of the reciprocal entanglements of social and personal ethics, culture, and the environment.[153] Cars shape human relations with each other and the environment, as well as shaping our institutions, city geographies, and sociality. Cars can also be the source of disrupted human relations, even to the extent of verbal and physical abuse. The motorcar, Gunton suggests, is a symbol of the mutual constitutiveness of all things in relation to all else.[154] For Gunton's critics, however, this stretches *perichoresis* far beyond its intended meaning and risks a form of reverse projection that images God in the light of the most pleasing human ideals.[155] We will examine these criticisms in detail in Chapter 2, but it is important to note that *perichoresis* is not a general concept of relatedness, but a Christologically conditioned concept defined by the triune relations. Gunton's account of *perichoresis* is conditioned by an understanding of Christ as the mediator of creation and its relational inscape.

Trinitarian Foci: Christology

Gunton's account of the *perichoretic* universe is concentrated in and through Christology, as it is in and through Jesus Christ that all things cohere. Some attempts to articulate the relation of the incarnate Jesus Christ with the eternal *Logos* root the relation in an underlying structure of material being, rather than embodied rationality. Gunton opposes any suspicion of abstraction, and detects a tendency to account for the coherence of the world through abstract rational structures that are de-personalized from the one in whom all things are held together. God comes into personal relation with the creation through Jesus Christ, the mediator between God and creation. As the eternal Word who spoke creation into being, Jesus Christ is also the one who holds time and space together and provides it with its dynamic and meaning. It is not a principle of unity that holds the world together, but the triune God who lives in a *perichoretic* unity of love. God creates and redeems a world that reflects God's being within its temporal

---

152. Gunton, *The One, the Three and the Many*, 177.
153. Gunton, *The One, the Three and the Many*, 177.
154. Gunton, *The One, the Three and the Many*, 178.
155. See especially Kilby, "Perichoresis and Projection," 437–8.

and spatial structures. "It is not therefore some*thing* which holds things together, but some*one*: the one through whom, in the unity of the Father and the Spirit, all things have their being."[156]

As we will see in Chapter 2, Gunton's deployment of *perichoresis* in *The One, the Three and the Many* is not without its critics. With Holmes, I argue that *The One, the Three and the Many* represents the end of one trajectory of Gunton's thought: the hermeneutical deployment of the doctrine of the Trinity.[157] Gunton's commitment to trinitarian theology does not change, but his trinitarian articulations do and these result in an internal strengthening of his work. As Gunton's thought progresses, he no longer deploys *perichoresis* as a ubiquitous general concept of relatedness, but instead strengthens the internal structuring of his work through a trinitarian theology of mediation that focuses on divine action in the economy.[158] As a result, his use of *perichoresis* is restricted to reflections on God's eternal being. Whilst Gunton's analysis of modernity and postmodernity does not change, what does change is his use of trinitarian formulae, buttressed by philosophical insights, to provide insights into all created being.

B/B': Pneumatology, Particularity, and Hypostasis

All created being is a substantial particular and made to be so by the particularizing action of the Holy Spirit. This section examines Gunton's analysis of modern homogeneity, and his pneumatologically conditioned account of substantiality and particularity. After exploring the unity of the many in the context of cultural fragmentation, Gunton turns to examine the many and establish an appropriate theological account of individuality and substantial particularity. Attempts to assert the rights of the many over the one have resulted not in new freedoms but in new cosmic heteronomies and forms of slavery to secular homogenizing forces that deny the particularity of the many. Gunton holds that homogeneity is a key sounding in modernity. He thus develops his second open transcendental, substantiality, to address modern enslavement to deities of immanence that subsume the many to the one.[159] Modernity, he argues, is unable to do justice to the one or the many, and struggles to happily affirm "the people and things which make up the manyness of reality."[160] In contrast to the homogeneity of Western culture, Gunton seeks to develop a trinitarian ontology that establishes personal particularity in and through relationship to God and others by the Spirit's power.

156. Gunton, *The One, the Three and the Many*, 179.
157. Holmes, "Towards the *Analogia Personae et Relationis*," 39.
158. Christoph Schwöbel rightly argues that the progressions in Gunton's thought represent an internal strengthening of his work, rather than a significant shift. This book gives greater detail to the contours of the internal strengthening that Schwöbel notes. See Schwöbel, "The Shape of Colin Gunton's Theology," 202.
159. Gunton, *The One, the Three and the Many*, 41.
160. Gunton, *The One, the Three and the Many*, 42.

Modern Sounding: Homogeneity

The Western social order may assert the rights of the individual, but Gunton believes that the forces of homogeneity subsume their distinct particularities into a collective herd society. Without an appropriate account of the relational character of being human, individualism metamorphoses into its alter ego: collectivism.[161] The social disorder of the West's individualism emerges from its cosmology that undergirds the social realities. Social orders are the embodiment and expression of dominant cosmologies, and Gunton holds that it is cosmologies that need to be examined in order to diagnose the ailments of Western culture.

The objectivism of modern scientific thought promotes timeless universals and ideals, but it struggles to deal with temporal particularities. Science, in Gunton's reckoning, prefers to deal with abstractions and abstract Platonic universals and generalities rather than the messy, and often conflicting, realities of material particulars.[162] As Polanyi argues, valuable knowledge is reduced to knowledge of atomic data and this tendency remains with us today. Yet, knowledge is a form of embodied particularity amidst specific locations and relations with the world.[163]

---

161. Gunton, *The One, the Three and the Many*, 42.
162. Gunton, *The One, the Three and the Many*, 42–3.
163. Gunton, *The One, the Three and the Many*, 43. While it is beyond the scope of this book to examine Gunton's indebtedness to Polanyi, it is important to note Polanyi's influence. Gunton, along with a variety of other Christian theologians in the later twentieth century, draws upon Polanyi's work to develop both a critique of Enlightenment epistemology and open the way to a relational epistemology that is grounded in the personal actions of the triune God. Polanyi offers an alternative to the Enlightenment's objectivist epistemology and contends that all knowledge is limited and personal. Against the objectivism of Enlightenment epistemology, Polanyi shows that no knowledge is neutral, nor should it be, and all knowledge, including scientific knowledge, is constituted by the tacit knowledge and commitments of the knower because "*we can know more than we can tell.*" The distinction between focal awareness and subsidiary awareness stresses the significance of tacit knowledge and offers a broader conception of our cognitive powers than objectivist epistemologies. The knowing subject is not independent from external influences, and the ideals of discarnate knowledge must give way to an account of incarnate and indwelt personal knowledge which, Gunton says, accords with a trinitarian account of theological rationality. Polanyi's post-critical account of personal knowledge takes the risk of the personal commitment of the knower as the only possible route to discovery. No knowledge is neutral, Gunton argues, nor should it be, and all knowledge, including scientific knowledge, is constituted by the tacit knowledge and commitments of the knower. See Gunton, *Enlightenment and Alienation*, 38–41. For the influence of Polanyi on Gunton's theological epistemology, see Gunton, *Enlightenment and Alienation*, 37–44. For the influence of Barth's doctrine of revelation on Gunton, see Gunton, *Becoming and Being*, 119–37. For Polayni's account of tacit knowledge, focal and subsidiary awareness, and personal knowledge, see Michael Polanyi, *Personal Knowledge: Towards a Post-Critical Philosophy* (Chicago: Chicago University Press, 1962), 16–17; 55–65; and 261–342. See also Michael Polanyi, *Science, Faith and Society* (Chicago: Chicago University Press, 1946), 31–9; and Michael Polanyi, *The Tacit*

In practice, science operates in, and reveals, a world that is rich in particularities, unhomogeneities, happenings, and change. Such particularity is offensive to certain kinds of scientific and political theories as it is untidy and raises questions about realities that do not adhere to objectivist assumptions.[164] The Platonic drive to turn particularities into abstractions and variety into homogeneity dominates our assumptions about science and human being in the world.[165]

Modernity's conception of human personhood is related to its homogenizing cosmology which subordinates particularity to general theories.[166] Concern for the freedom of the individual *from* all else won freedom on the wrong terms because it abstracted the person from the particular relationships which constitute human being. Individualism defines freedom as freedom *from* relationship, and particularity is established through individual self-assertion. Gunton, however, holds that freedom and particularity are found *in* and *through* relationships, and our distinctiveness is by virtue of, not in spite of, these relations. He highlights Alistair McFadyen's suggestion that the link between individualism and social homogeneity is the result of Kantian ethical theory. The individual is defined through rational willing and universal dispositions which give an abstracted definition of universal individuality without personal or individual content.[167] Genuine difference and individuation are deemed an aberration in need of correcting or purifying because human personhood is rooted in a universal conception of being which underlies who we are in our concrete relationships.[168] The disorder of particularity in culture, both scientific and social, raises for Gunton theological issues related to the doctrine of creation. In Gunton's analysis, the roots of the disordered conception of human personhood can be traced to antiquity, especially Plato's problematic treatment of particularity.

Dimension (Chicago: Chicago University Press, 1966), 1–26. For helpful accounts of Gunton's use of Polanyi, see Lincoln Harvey, "The Theological Promise of Michael Polanyi's Project: An Examination within the Contemporary Context of Atheism and the Constructivist Critique of the Natural Sciences," in *Critical Conversations: Michael Polanyi and Christian Theology*, ed. Murray A. Rae (Eugene: Wipf and Stock, 2012), 56–73, and Rae, "Colin E. Gunton," 212–13.

164. Gunton, *The One, the Three and the Many*, 43–4. See also Stanley L. Jaki, *God and the Cosmologists* (Edinburgh: Scottish Academic Press, 1989), 37.

165. Gunton, *The One, the Three and the Many*, 44.

166. Gunton, *The One, the Three and the Many*, 44.

167. Gunton, *The One, the Three and the Many*, 45. "The person into whose position we are instructed by Kant to think ourselves is not a particular, but an abstract individual." See Alistair I. McFadyen, *The Call to Personhood: A Christian Theory of the Individual in Social Relationships* (Cambridge: CUP, 1990), 183–5, quote from 184.

168. Gunton, *The One, the Three and the Many*, 46.

Historical Antecedents: Immateriality

The drive to homogeneity and suppression of particularity are not new. Gunton takes soundings from the history of ideas to trace the roots of the disorder and shed light on contemporary realities.[169] Plato's attempts at an engaged philosophy emerge at a time of anti-institutionalism and the demythologization of the traditional Greek deities.[170] In the *Phaedo* and the *Symposium* Plato's attempts to counter these tendencies result in an anthropology that struggles to give full reality to material particulars. On Gunton's reading, human physicality and sexuality are downgraded in the *Symposium*. The notion of a person is primarily found in the non-bodily dimensions of the soul, because the material world of matter, plurality, and becoming is regarded with suspicion. It is the material body that divides and distinguishes humans, rather than relating them.[171] What we share is timeless soul-stuff, and our relations with each other are reduced to the rational at the expense of relational, aesthetic, or material realities.[172]

If who we particularly are is established through our concrete bodily life, relationships, and differences, there are a variety of problems that emerge from discarnate definitions of humanity. Firstly, there is a breach between appearance and reality, as essential being is abstracted from embodied being. Secondly, human ontology is intrinsic to the inward and rational aspects of the individual, not our encounter of extrinsic otherness-in-relation.[173] As immaterial souls encased in material bodies, engagement with the external material world and its pleasures is problematized. "We truly are when we think, but not when we love or make music."[174] Moreover, the eschatological hope is defined as escape from the world of materiality to the world of immateriality and abstract forms.

Plato's suspicion of matter, plurality, and material particulars, especially aesthetics and art, as bearers of truth creates shortcomings in the doctrine of creation and theology of culture, which Western theology did not entirely avoid.[175] In Gunton's judgement, Western theology made the wrong kind of compromise with Platonism in two important areas: anthropology and the doctrine of creation. Anthropologically, Plato's account of human being influenced Christian understandings of the *imago Dei* as fixed internal characteristics, such as human reason and will, that determine humanity in isolation from relationality. Gunton argues that Plato's legacy extends through Christian theological misconceptions of the human will and is exemplified in Augustine and William of Ockham. Human willing agency can give freedom to others in relation, or instrumentalize them as a

---

169. Gunton, *The One, the Three and the Many*, 46.
170. Gunton, *The One, the Three and the Many*, 47.
171. Gunton, *The One, the Three and the Many*, 48.
172. Gunton, *The One, the Three and the Many*, 48.
173. Gunton, *The One, the Three and the Many*, 49–50.
174. Gunton, *The One, the Three and the Many*, 50.
175. Gunton, *The One, the Three and the Many*, 50.

means to our end and deprive them of their particularity.[176] The misplaced will is at the heart of the problem of particularity.

The figurehead for Christian theology's collusion with Platonism, in Gunton's estimation, is Augustine. Where Irenaeus offers a particularizing account of God's willing of creation, Augustine views creation as the result of God's arbitrary will.[177] In the Irenaean approach, God's will is particularizing and the Son and the Spirit direct creation's particularities towards perfection, which gives purpose to embodiment in matter. Comparatively, Gunton holds that Augustine lacks the strength of Irenaeus' Christological and pneumatological determination in his doctrine of creation, and this opens the way to a theology of creation as the outcome of arbitrary will. In Irenaeus' work, creation's inscape is determined by the Son and the Spirit holding the world in relation to God, whereas after Augustine this function is increasingly achieved by Platonic universal archetypes that leave creation shapeless and ultimately meaningless.[178]

At the transition of the medieval period to modernity, William of Ockham attempts to assert the existence of only particulars, but in the process abolishes particularity by denying the necessary real relations between them.[179] Following Ockham, the tradition, in Gunton's reading, veers towards theological absolutism that results in a reflexive process. Responsibility for ordering the world is transferred from an abstract and unknown divine will to the individual human will that establishes freedom through self-assertion.[180] In modernity, the Platonic individual escape of embodiedness escalates to a freedom from the constraints of all external reality, especially God. The individual rational human mind and will is divinized, and the Platonic separation of the mind from materiality results in a multiplicity of wills competing for ascendency.[181]

Both antiquity and modernity suffer from an ability to provide conceptual clarity and meaning to material particularity. Where ancients tended to spiritualize humanity as souls encased in flesh, moderns appear to place high value on embodiment and materialism. Yet the materialism of modern technology and consumerism, displayed especially in the ecological crisis, continues to subsume the material world to the human will.[182] Moderns are no more at home in the world than ancients, and Gunton identifies two important issues that need attention: who we are as particular persons (anthropology) and the nature of the world in which we live our embodied lives (creation). Regarding anthropology and particularity,

---

176. Gunton, *The One, the Three and the Many*, 52.
177. Gunton, *The One, the Three and the Many*, 54.
178. Gunton, *The One, the Three and the Many*, 54–5.
179. Gunton, *The One, the Three and the Many*, 56.
180. Gunton, *The One, the Three and the Many*, 58.
181. Gunton, *The One, the Three and the Many*, 59.
182. Gunton, *The One, the Three and the Many*, 60–1.

Gunton explores the concept of freedom, as it is related to what we make of our particularity.[183]

In his first case study, Gunton examines modern accounts of freedom and draws from Isaiah Berlin to show that they are oftentimes sources of unfreedom. Modern freedom is the individual realization of one's being which is positively defined as the freedom to be one's own master, though this can easily morph into a negatively defined freedom as freedom *from* the other.[184] However, Gunton notes through Berlin that there is no finally satisfactory account of individualized freedom because we are social beings who shape one another. Aloneness and enforced communitarianism are both unfreedoms because they are non-relational, and individualism separates, rather than distinguishes, one from each other in relation.[185] Freedom is something exercised and received relationally. Accordingly, Gunton seeks to extend Berlin's work through an ontological account of freedom in which personal particularity is determined by relations.[186] Gunton detects similar weaknesses in some accounts of the *imago Dei* that posit an internal relation to God to the exclusion of neighbour and world. Modernity's displacement of the allegedly malevolent God results in a plurality of self-grounded wills competing for divinity. What is required is a doctrine of creation that celebrates the goodness of finite human beings who exist in mutually constitutive relations with God, one another, and the wider world.[187]

In his second case study, Gunton turns to the human shaping of art and aesthetics to engage the relation of subjective artistic endeavour and its objective meaning. Like the one and the many, there is a lack of a mediating concept and we are forced to choose between the subjective action and objective reality of the material piece produced.[188] If the meaning of art, and its use of materiality, is the beholder's subjective response, then art is reduced to pure subjectivity. Science is assumed to be the source of objective knowledge and material particulars are regarded as meaningless and insubstantial. Can art, and its use of material particulars, be the source of meaning and truth?[189] This question returns us to the relation of the one and the many. On the one hand, modernism cannot do justice to unity and multiplicity because it suppresses particularity and otherness. On the other hand, postmodernism cannot do justice to unity and multiplicity because it homogenizes otherness, making everything equally interesting and equally irrelevant.[190] What is required for particularity is an

---

183. Gunton, *The One, the Three and the Many*, 62.
184. Gunton, *The One, the Three and the Many*, 62–3.
185. Gunton, *The One, the Three and the Many*, 63–4.
186. Gunton, *The One, the Three and the Many*, 64.
187. Gunton, *The One, the Three and the Many*, 65–6.
188. Gunton, *The One, the Three and the Many*, 66–7.
189. Gunton, *The One, the Three and the Many*, 68–9.
190. Gunton, *The One, the Three and the Many*, 69.

account of otherness-in-relation in which people and things are what they distinctively are in their constitutive relatedness.[191]

The displacement of God has not resulted in many and varied forms of human particularity but in the loss of the unifying coordinates of reality. God's unifying role is displaced into individual human subjectivity that often views the other as one to escape or rule. Whatever the shortcomings, Gunton believes that the doctrine of God provides a system of coordinates that enables the necessary space for particulars to relate to one another in ways that do not threaten particularity.[192] Without an account of God who provides the space for personal being and relation, the space between one another and the world is lost along with particularity. Within aesthetics, the displacement of *creatio ex nihilo* from God to humanity results in an instrumental stance towards the created world.[193] Science and technology are fused with pure human will in abstraction from ethics and aesthetics to serve a naked public square. The loss of particularity and substantiality is an urgent issue in Gunton's analysis of culture. He suggests that the positive theological alternative lies in a pneumatologically conditioned account of created particularities that function as vehicles for the praise of God.[194]

Trinitarian Remedy: Pneumatology

In place of the Western drive to homogeneity, Gunton seeks a trinitarian ontology where substantiality and particularity bulk large. In the context of the modern drive to immateriality and abstraction, particularity is central to Gunton's theological project. If we still followed the ancient custom of venerating the great doctors of the Church by giving them a particular title, Schwöbel concludes that Gunton would be the Doctor of Particularity.[195] Schwöbel's suggestion captures the importance of particularity and pneumatology in Gunton's thoughts and contributions. Particularities lie at the heart of Christianity, according to Gunton, and its focus upon a particular historical human figure set in the context of a particular national story is precisely what is needed in an age marked by the drive to homogeneity.[196] It is the gift of the Spirit to establish all being in its particularity and relate them together in their substantial differences as otherness-in-relation.

---

191. Gunton, *The One, the Three and the Many*, 70.
192. Gunton, *The One, the Three and the Many*, 71.
193. Gunton, *The One, the Three and the Many*, 72.
194. Gunton, *The One, the Three and the Many*, 73.
195. Christoph Schwöbel, "A Tribute to Colin Gunton," 14. John Webster reminds us that Gunton's own consideration of his work was that it is a set of essays on Christian ontology—"an attempt to explicate the kind of being God is in order to explicate creaturely being." Webster, "Systematic Theology after Barth," 262.
196. Gunton, *The One, the Three and the Many*, 181.

In Gunton's view, there are two main aspects to the Spirit's work in scripture: crossing relational boundaries, and establishing and strengthening particularity.[197] Firstly, the Spirit crosses boundaries by relating opposed or separated beings and realms to one another, that they might be established in relation. The Spirit draws the world into creative and renewing relation with God, enabling dry bones to live, the Word to become flesh, and the Son to rise to new life. Likewise, in adoption (Rom 8:15-16), the Spirit's action is relational and enables finite creation to be open to the infinite God and all else.[198]

Secondly, the Spirit is God's particularizing action who establishes created being in its particularity as otherness-in-relation. The Spirit maintains and strengthens particularity without merging or assimilating otherness. As we see in Jesus' ministry, the Spirit is not Jesus' immanent possession but a personal other who relates him to the Father in his human, and Jewish, particularity. As the personal other, the Spirit forms Jesus in the womb, enables him to learn and grow, empowers him at baptism and renews his human relationship with the Father.[199] Following the ascension, it is the Spirit's particularizing action that guides the Church towards God's surprising purposes that set humans free and finds concentration in the Church's life of richness and variety in community.[200] As God's liberating Other, the Spirit respects the otherness and particularity of those he elects, and establishes them in their particular being.

Coleridgean Idea: Spirit

Without a conception of spirit, that includes boundary crossing and the preservation of particularity, we cannot conceive of vital aspects of our life in the world. In this sense, therefore, Gunton suggests that spirit is a candidate for being a Coleridgean *idea*.[201] One influential account of spirit as the transcendental of transcendentals is Hegel's *Geist*, translated as rational spirit. Positively, Hegel's account reinforces the Spirit's enabling of dynamism, openness, and interrelationship between mind and world. In contrast to mechanistic deism, Hegel's *Geist* stresses the personal and relational being of the world.[202] However, all is spirit in Hegel's view, and his modalism of the spirit overwhelms the plurality of the godhead. *Geist* etherealizes materiality as insubstantial, and matter, time, and space are subsumed into God. If all is spirit, materiality is no longer central to being, and *perichoresis* is stripped of its material particulars and replaced by unrelational homogeneity.[203] Yet, Hegel's

---

197. Gunton, *The One, the Three and the Many*, 181–2.
198. Gunton, *The One, the Three and the Many*, 182.
199. Gunton, *The One, the Three and the Many*, 182–3.
200. Gunton, *The One, the Three and the Many*, 183.
201. Gunton, *The One, the Three and the Many*, 184.
202. Gunton, *The One, the Three and the Many*, 185.
203. Gunton, *The One, the Three and the Many*, 186.

pneumatological emphasis remains important, and Gunton examines whether a theologically revised version of spirit may be a Coleridgean *idea*.[204]

The Spirit is central to a theology of personal and particular ontology and, understood analogically, gives rise to wide-ranging thought on different levels.[205] Gunton holds that the Spirit is of *ideal* status, but it is not a transcendental because it is not a universal mark of all being. Although human beings *have* spirit and can enter a variety of relations through their openness to God, each other and the world, God *is* spirit. God *is* spirit through the openness of the triune persons to each other in God's immanent being and God's ecstatic movement in creation and redemption. The openness and relatedness of the triune persons in God's immanent being, or ecstatic economic action in creation, are not, however, analogous or replicable to finite created realities. Furthermore, Gunton maintains that the non-personal world does not have spirit, and, therefore, spirit is not a universal mark of being.[206] Spirit is an *idea*, not a transcendental, that is limited to the world of persons and personal being, but this need not result in a mechanistic view of the non-personal world. In his quest for a transcendental notion, Gunton, as he did with Christology, turns to the economy to comprehend the activity of the Spirit and the universal features of our world.[207]

Gunton draws from Basil to extend his account of the Spirit as the perfecting cause in the economy and in the being of God. The Spirit realizes the true being of created reality by bringing it into saving relation with the Father through the action of the Son.[208] In the economy, the Spirit acts as God's eschatological perfecting cause of creation, and this suggests to Gunton that the Spirit performs a similar function in God's immanent being and life. Gunton notes that affirming the Spirit's distinct action in the Godhead requires careful nuance to avoid the tritheistic tendencies of social trinitarianism. Given the criticisms of Gunton's supposed social trinitarianism, which are explored in Chapter 2, it is important to note that he holds that revelation does not enable us to speak of God's social life.[209] However, if the Spirit acts as the perfecting cause in the economy, it is fair to assume the Spirit performs a similar function in the Godhead as divine action corresponds to divine being. The Spirit's action as the bond of love between the Father and the Son can be expanded to include the Spirit's action in establishing them as the particular persons they are in communion. The Spirit's distinctive mode of action within the heart of the being of God is the constitution and realization of particularity; a perfection of the Father's and the Son's particular and substantial being-in-relation.[210] The emphasis upon particularity draws Gunton to

---

204. Gunton, *The One, the Three and the Many*, 186.
205. Gunton, *The One, the Three and the Many*, 188.
206. Gunton, *The One, the Three and the Many*, 188.
207. Gunton, *The One, the Three and the Many*, 189.
208. Gunton, *The One, the Three and the Many*, 189.
209. Gunton, *The One, the Three and the Many*, 190.
210. Gunton, *The One, the Three and the Many*, 190.

consider the concept of *hypostasis* and its centrality for our understanding of the substantiality of being.

The Spirit's action as perfecting cause offers insights into the importance of substantiality for understanding particularity and relational being. At this stage of his career, Gunton is highly influenced by John Zizioulas' work, especially Zizioulas' understanding of substantiality and ontology. Gunton repeats Zizioulas' belief that the Cappadocians bequeathed a highly original understanding of personhood. The Cappadocian innovation, according to Gunton and Zizioulas, is the desynonymizing of *hypostasis* and *ousia*, and the assertion that God's being is constituted by who the particular persons are in what they receive and give to one another in communion.[211] God exists in the richness and plurality of God's being as a community of persons as Father, Son, and Spirit, each with their own distinct and particular way of being in and from their relations as one God.[212] The substantiality of God resides not in God's underlying substance that is anterior to who God is in the relations of Father, Son, and Spirit, but in the concrete particularities of the divine persons who exist in mutually constitutive relationship.

In Gunton's reading, the West failed to comprehend the Cappadocian ontological innovation and developed an abstract account of God that subsumes particularity into a blank monadic homogeneity. The Western tradition mistakenly interpreted *ousia* as *substantia* and stressed the underlying reality of God in such a way that the concept of the person is deprived of its due weight. As a result, person is defined through abstract generalities rather than concrete and particular being-in-relation. The Cappadocian approach, that Gunton affirms, holds that God is constituted without remainder by *perichoretic* communion, and prioritizes the particular over the universal.[213] Such particularity and substantiality at the heart of divine being are of transcendental significance because the particularity and substantiality of created beings are established from God's own substantial and particular being-in-relation.[214] Gunton goes on to develop his account of

---

211. Gunton, *The One, the Three and the Many*, 191. See also Gunton, *The Promise of Trinitarian Theology*, 8–10 and John D. Zizioulas, *Being as Communion: Studies in Personhood and the Church* (London: Darton, Longman and Todd, 1985), 16–17.

212. Gunton, *The One, the Three and the Many*, 191. While quoting from Barth's language of the divine persons as "mode of being," Gunton becomes highly critical of Barth's cautious delineation of divine personhood and suspects that Barth has succumbed to Western abstractions. See Coin E. Gunton, *Becoming and Being: The Doctrine of God in Charles Hartshorne and Karl Barth*, 2nd ed. (London: SCM, 2001), 228–30.

213. Gunton, *The One, the Three and the Many*, 191.

214. Gunton, *The One, the Three and the Many*, 191. This definition of personhood is vital to Gunton's work in *The One, the Three and the Many* and remains the centre of his constructive alternative to the homogenizing tendencies of the West. Later, while critiquing Barth's definition of the divine persons as "modes of being", he states, "For the fact is that the truly creative achievement of *all trinitarian thought* was that of the trinitarian ontology produced by the Cappadocians." See Gunton, *Becoming and Being*, 232. Italics mine.

substantiality as an open transcendental through a pneumatologically conditioned exploration of *hypostasis* and personhood.

Open Transcendental: Substantiality

Gunton argues that while the West misunderstood the Cappadocians' conceptual revolution, the East failed to capitalize upon it, and abstractness, rather than concreteness, dominated assumptions about divine and human being. The dominance of abstraction and indeterminacy in the understanding of divine being results in the loss of human substantiality and particularity. Western reactions to the abstract heteronomous God did not result in many and various accounts of human substantiality but the postmodern loss of substantiality in which each particular is rendered equally interesting and insignificant.[215] Gunton detects twin problems of substantiality in Western culture: particularity without relation and relationality without particularity. What is required is an account of created substantiality that emerges from God's substantial being in which particularity and relationality are held in unity.[216] In place of substantialist accounts of being, Gunton argues for an understanding of relational ontology as central to divine and created personhood.

At the heart of Gunton's understanding of particularity and substantiality is a trinitarian concept of the person. If persons, by virtue of being made in the image of the triune God, are concrete and particular *hypostases*, their particularity is central to their being.[217] Personal particularity is vital for a concrete account of the world within which personal life takes particular shape. Rethinking the Spirit's particularizing action of personal being involves rethinking the non-human creation as well. Creation's inscape is created in such a way that all created being is given its own proper and distinct being and the parts cannot be understood in abstraction from the concrete context of the whole.[218] A proper doctrine of creation and created being holds Scotus' concept of *haecceitas* ("thisness") at the heart of personal being. Each created thing is what it substantially is and not another thing by virtue of being held in being by constitutive relationship with God and all other being in time and space.[219]

Abstraction is a tendency that Gunton believes plagues Western theology and culture. The default to underlying generalities undermines an account of concrete createdness that proposes something is real by the way it is held in being by God *and* other things in its particular temporal and spatial configurations.[220] Our comprehension of createdness needs to understand created reality in the context

---

215. Gunton, *The One, the Three and the Many*, 193.
216. Gunton, *The One, the Three and the Many*, 194. Italics original.
217. Gunton, *The One, the Three and the Many*, 196.
218. Gunton, *The One, the Three and the Many*, 196.
219. Gunton, *The One, the Three and the Many*, 196–8.
220. Gunton, *The One, the Three and the Many*, 200.

of the whole. Even if reality is constituted of parts, the related whole is more than the sum of the parts. Abstract approaches to understanding material realities and their particularity are mirrored in the human realm. Without entirely rejecting the internality and introspection of Western notions of human personhood, Gunton argues that external relations are essential for the constitution of personal being through relation with God and the network of human and cosmic relatedness.[221]

Even with the qualitative distinction between personal and impersonal being, there is, Gunton suggests, an analogy between things and persons when it comes to particularity. Both persons and things are *hypostatic* in the sense of being substantial particulars, and they are rendered such by the patterns of relations with God and created being that constitute them what they distinctively are. "Everyone and every thing is what it uniquely is as a hypostatic being."[222] The notion of *hypostasis* can be understood as a substantial particular defined by the shape of its relations, which contributes to the transcendental significance of particularity. In place of postmodernity's pluralism that deems everything the same, Gunton promotes an exploration of the practical implications of *hypostasis*, understood as substantial particularity, as a transcendental.[223] Gunton's suggestive analogies attempt to tread a fine theological line at this point, but critics argue that his analogical deployment of *hypostasis* in such broad terms stretches its intended definition beyond breaking point. Chapter 2 examines these critiques in detail, but it is interesting to note at this point that his transcendental use of *hypostasis*, understood as substantial particularity, tends to homogenize its meaning and risks emptying it of its particular meaning that is restricted to the divine persons.

Trinitarian Foci: Pneumatological Particularity

A theology of the many in which particularity and substantiality bulk large needs to be founded in the being and action of God. With special reference to the account in John's gospel, Gunton holds that the incarnate Son's relation with the Father is a relation without absorption. The affirmation that the Son and the Father are one posits not a homogenous oneness, but a unity marked by a variety of relatedness. It is the Spirit who mediates the relation of the Father and the Son and constitutes the incarnate Son as the Son of the Father.[224] Likewise, the eschatological Spirit establishes Jesus in his particular Jewish humanity, and enables his faithful life, death, and resurrection. The Spirit's particularizing action is universal, and in Gunton's pneumatology the Spirit's distinctive work is to give direction to created being by relating it to the Father through the Son. Working in unison with the Son, the Spirit perfects created being by constituting it in its otherness and particularity. The Son, as creation's mediator, unifies creation, and

---

221. Gunton, *The One, the Three and the Many*, 202–3.
222. Gunton, *The One, the Three and the Many*, 203.
223. Gunton, *The One, the Three and the Many*, 204.
224. Gunton, *The One, the Three and the Many*, 205.

the Spirit constitutes and maintains the particularity and uniqueness of all things as otherness-in-relation.[225] "The mystery of existence is that everything is what it is and not another thing. That is the point of arguing for the transcendentality of *hypostasis* or substantiality."[226]

The perfecting action of the Spirit invites an understanding of creation as that which is destined to achieve finite perfection in and through time. In place of static understandings of eternal forms instantiated in time, Gunton promotes a dynamic account of the created order and its eschatological orientation to an end that is greater than its beginning. While creation will only achieve its completion through redemption, the Spirit sometimes enables the creation to realize finite anticipations of perfection, each in their own particular way.[227] Creation is the constitution of particulars, not static forms, that are ordered by the action of the Son and the Spirit towards perfection in their richness and variety. Created matter, whether persons or things, is not, therefore, a meaningless object of human instrumentality, but substantial particulars that are formed by the inseparable relations we have with God and all else in time and space.[228] "Their form is secondary to, because derivative of, their relation to the Other and to others."[229] Through this pneumatological account, Gunton holds that substantiality is an open transcendental. "'Substances', material particulars, are the most real things that there are, *because* the divine hypostases together constitute the being of God."[230] The God who exists as three *hypostases* in one *ousia* creates a world that reflects God's being. Just as a Christologically conditioned account of *perichoresis* offers insight into the relationality of the world, so too a pneumatologically conditioned account of *hypostasis* offers insight into the particularity and substantiality of the world as otherness-in-relation.[231]

Substantiality is given as a gift from God, and by the perfecting action of the Spirit achieves its particular eschatological perfection through time and in space. In Gunton's thought, creation's eschatological directedness towards perfection by divine and human agency provides important scope for human culture. At times, the Spirit enables concrete human activity in science, art, and morality to participate in the divine perfecting of creation that it may be offered to the Father in Christ and through the Spirit. Such openness to finite perfecting gives rise to vast possibilities for human cultural contributions to the perfecting of the personal and material creation. What Gunton establishes here through analogical insights from the Trinity for created being, he later establishes through a theology of

---

225. Gunton, *The One, the Three and the Many*, 205–6.
226. Gunton, *The One, the Three and the Many*, 206.
227. Gunton, *The One, the Three and the Many*, 206.
228. Gunton, *The One, the Three and the Many*, 207.
229. Gunton, *The One, the Three and the Many*, 207.
230. Gunton, *The One, the Three and the Many*, 207.
231. Gunton, *The One, the Three and the Many*, 207–8.

mediation that focuses upon the project of creation, pneumatology, Christology, ecclesiology, and human culture.

A': Trinity, Relationality, and Ecclesiology

In place of modernity's elevation of the one over the many and postmodernity's elevation of the many over the one, Gunton suggests a theology of the Trinity provides the necessary mediating concept that upholds the one and the many in relation. This section returns to the theme of the first—the one and the many—to complete Gunton's chiasm that asserts the need for the Trinity as a mediating concept: the one, *the three* and the many. Gunton proposes an ecclesiologically conditioned account of relationality in which the personal and non-personal worlds realize their true being in relationship to God and all else. God enables human cultural agency, from time to time, to contribute to the perfecting of God's creation, and participate in the offering of a sacrifice of praise to God for God's wise purposes in the beginning.

The open transcendentals emerge from Gunton's exploration of trinitarian concepts revealed through God's action in the economy, and understood apophatically of God's eternal being. Because creation reflects the being of its triune creator, the trinitarian concepts are echoed in some way within human thought and creation's structures.[232] This knowledge is not merely the result of human effort, but is primarily a revelation by the Holy Spirit. The revelation of God can be expanded, in Gunton's opinion, to draw links between the theological implications of revelation and all knowledge, ethics, and aesthetics. "Revelation speaks to and constitutes human reason, but in such a way as to liberate the energies that are inherent in created rationality."[233] Gunton's Christologically conditioned account of *perichoresis* offers insight into the unity of creation, and his pneumatologically conditioned account of substantiality offers insight into the particularity of creation. Through the unifying action of the Son and the particularizing action of the Spirit, God holds creation in being as being-in-communion.[234] Gunton's final open transcendental, relationality, develops a relational account of the one and the many from trinitarian insights that enable us to reconsider the world as a context where free personality and open society can develop.

Trinitarian Remedy: Ecclesiology, Koinōnia, and Relational Personhood

The two open transcendentals—*perichoresis* and substantiality—combine to offer a trinitarian conception of sociality. But Gunton maintains a trinitarian account of sociality need not assume a basis in social theories of the Trinity. There are

---

232. Gunton, *The One, the Three and the Many*, 211.
233. Gunton, *The One, the Three and the Many*, 212.
234. Gunton, *The One, the Three and the Many*, 213.

tritheistic tendencies in social theories of the Trinity that Gunton seeks to avoid, but he does want to affirm that persons, divine and human, are constituted by relations with one another.[235] It is important to note Gunton's distinction of his work from social theories of the Trinity because, as we will examine in Chapter 2, he is severely criticized for his social trinitarianism.[236] Gunton's broader constructive point is an affirmation of Zizioulas' argument that God is not a blank unity but a being in communion. This trinitarian conception of God invites an analogical exploration of human sociality that respects the necessary limitations of any analogy between divine and created persons.

Any analogy between divine and human persons must recognize their ontological unlikeness. Yet, Gunton suggests there is a likeness within the unlikeness as "we too are particulars in relation."[237] Human persons are constituted in being by our primary relation with God and our secondary relations in human society. The two poles of this analogy are concentrated in ecclesiology as ecclesiology is "concerned with human being together under God."[238] Where Christology and pneumatology condition Gunton's theological account of *perichoresis* and substantiality, ecclesiology conditions Gunton's theological account of community.

The first pole of the analogy of divine and human persons is the triune God whose being is communion. The central concept the New Testament uses to describe God's being and action in the world as well as the Church's life is *koinōnia*. According to New Testament authors, especially the author of John's gospel, God exists in inseparable communion and acts through the distinct functions of the divine persons without the loss of divine unity. John's gospel affirms the unity of the Father and the Son, as well as the Son's distinct role as the incarnate one who is sent to do the Father's will on earth. After his glorification, it is the Son who asks the Father to send the Spirit to empower the Church and bring about the Father's purposes on earth. The testimony of the New Testament is that there is a distinction within unity which points towards God's being as communion, "a unity of persons in relation."[239]

The second pole of the analogy is human being in communion, which Gunton develops by reference to the Genesis creation narratives. At the beginning of the book, Gunton holds that the doctrine of creation and the theology of culture belong together, and that the roots of the modern crisis of culture can be analysed as an inadequate exegesis of the opening chapters of Genesis.[240] At the end of the

---

235. Gunton, *The One, the Three and the Many*, 214.
236. Karen Kilby labels Gunton as one of the foremost social trinitarians in the English-speaking world. Karen Kilby, "Trinity, Tradition and Politics," in *Recent Developments in Trinitarian Theology: An International Symposium*, ed. Christophe Chalamet and Mark Vial (Minneapolis: Fortress Press, 2014), 76.
237. Gunton, *The One, the Three and the Many*, 214.
238. Gunton, *The One, the Three and the Many*, 215.
239. Gunton, *The One, the Three and the Many*, 215.
240. Gunton, *The One, the Three and the Many*, 2.

book, Gunton claims that *The One, the Three and the Many* can be understood as a summary of Genesis, and the creation narratives form the exegetical basis of the book as a whole.[241] Genesis affirms that creation is the creation of beings in relationship, which can be understood in three distinct yet related conceptions. Firstly, Creation's createdness is established by its otherness to and relation with the creator. Secondly, humans have their being in communion, and image God most fully in relations of communion-in-otherness, such as male and female. The fall is a form of uncreation that unfolds a cascading series of breaches of communion with God, one another and the creation.[242] The third conception, which is most central to Gunton's final chapter, is that the shape of the created world is largely the result of what humanity makes of it in and through relationship. This relation is often misconstrued as humanity's domination, rather than dominion, of creation. However, scripture affirms that the "created world is not truly itself without us, its most problematic inhabitants."[243] Without humanity there may be no pollution, moral evil, suffering, or death, but there is also no human cultural agency in science, ethics, or aesthetics that enables the creation to be itself.[244] The divine being-in-communion is analogically reflected in the relation of humans to God and one another. Furthermore, through divine agency and human sub-agency the created order, as a unified and diverse reality, is brought into the relation of the one and the many.

Human community is rooted within the context of the created order, and made concrete in the Church whose calling is to mediate and realize redeemed communion with God, one another, and the rest of creation.[245] This calling is not the Church's immanent institutional possession. Gunton's dissenting instincts contribute to his ambivalence about the historical manifestations of the Church.[246] The New Testament writers, Gunton maintains, are much more concerned with human communion and sociality than the institutionalism that has so often marked the Church in its history. The theme of communion dominates much of Paul's ecclesiological thought. The image of the Church as a body is a relational account of being in communion. To be brought through the Son to the Father in the power of the Spirit is to be simultaneously brought into the community of Christ's body, the Church. The fruit of Paul's theology of community results in a near identification of Christ with the Church, which Gunton believes reinforces Genesis' stress upon relational ontology. The New Testament does not rest with the Church's life in communion but envisions a cosmic account of redeemed human community in the context of a redeemed created material order (Rev 21–2). Such

---

241. Gunton, *The One, the Three and the Many*, 215–16.
242. Gunton, *The One, the Three and the Many*, 216.
243. Gunton, *The One, the Three and the Many*, 216.
244. Gunton, *The One, the Three and the Many*, 217.
245. Gunton, *The One, the Three and the Many*, 217.
246. Gunton, *The One, the Three and the Many*, 217. See also Gunton, *The Promise of Trinitarian Theology*, 58–60.

a vision returns to themes of the relation of the one and the many in the cosmic and social orders.[247]

Coleridgean Idea: Sociality

In a further exploration of open transcendentals, Gunton examines sociality to see if it qualifies as one. Sociality is not merely the joy of living life in community, but a metaphysic, or ontology, of persons in communion. Modern dogma gives primacy to human willing that is ontologically so separate from the world or so melded with it that humanity's posture is either dominance or resignation. Oftentimes, impulses in Western thought deem our being-in-relation to be an unfortunate necessity. Gunton proposes a theology and ontology of human community in the world that stands in contrast to these impulses.[248] In some accounts of social Darwinism and its antecedents, the idea of a social contract is necessary to protect the weak from the predations of the strong, and restrain our inherent human propensities to domination and violence. Others, such as Hobbes and Locke, are more optimistic, but they too assume that entry into social contracts comes by way of human willing agency rather than the result of human relationships. While social contracts offer safety and convenience, they reduce social being to collective agreements that risk the suppression of otherness.[249] Instead, Gunton turns to Coleridge's reformulation of the idea of a social contract by personalizing it. Social contracts are a continued way of determining human being-in-relation.[250] In place of the juridical views of social contract, Gunton suggests that the concept of covenant captures the nature of the Church's social being. Ecclesial being is the deepest expression of human reality, and it is in and through God's covenant, not individual choice or legal contracts, that humanity is called to free and joyful partnership with God and each other.[251]

Is sociality, asks Gunton, a transcendental whose significance extends beyond redeemed being to all created reality? Daniel Hardy argues it is, and that ecclesiology is sociality made explicit. Ecclesial being displays the true form of human being that the Son and the Spirit refine and realize in relationship with God and other human beings. Because it is constituted by the triune God, ecclesial being-in-communion gives due recognition to particularity and relationality.[252] For all the merit of Hardy's insights, Gunton holds that sociality is a Coleridgean *idea*, but it is not an open transcendental as it does not give due reference to the non-personal creation as humanity's shared context.[253] Human sociality is

---

247. Gunton, *The One, the Three and the Many*, 218–19.
248. Gunton, *The One, the Three and the Many*, 220.
249. Gunton, *The One, the Three and the Many*, 220.
250. Gunton, *The One, the Three and the Many*, 221–2.
251. Gunton, *The One, the Three and the Many*, 222.
252. Hardy, "Created and Redeemed Sociality," 34.
253. Gunton, *The One, the Three and the Many*, 223.

organically related to its material environment, and the interrelation of the two is central to the being of each.

Open Transcendental: Relationality

In place of sociality, Gunton proposes relationality as an open transcendental that gives insight into all being.[254] God exists as one God in a dynamic personal communion of giving and receiving whose relations are not merely reciprocal, but an asymmetrical diversity of relations. The asymmetrical diversity of relations, marked by gift and reception, is the key to the transcendentality Gunton seeks, as it provides universal analogies in which otherness and particularity bulk large in the context of relatedness.[255]

As a Coleridgean *idea*, sociality generates universal analogies, of which Gunton explores two: human relationality and human relation to the non-personal world. Gunton's first analogy of relationality is the relational determination of human action and being by gift and reception. The dynamic of gift and reception in human relationality is analogous to Christ's non-reciprocal ethic of sacrificial self-giving that Paul develops, especially in Rom 12:1. The ethic of sacrifice is an ecclesial form of social and communal life together that is manifest in praise and righteous action that creatively subordinates reality in the shape of Christ's kenotic manner of being towards others in the world.[256] Jesus' sacrificial recapitulation of faithful human being completes creation and liberates humanity for redeemed human life and action in the world that is an embodied offering of praise to God. While Christ's way of being in the world includes suffering, suffering need not be understood passively. The ethic of sacrifice is an ethic of transformation, not suffering, that offers the right human habitation of creation to God as praise for God's wise purposes for the creation.[257] In a fallen world, sacrificial human action is marked by suffering and cruciformity, but suffering is not the transcendental reference of sacrifice. The transcendental reference of sacrifice is a reference to a form of human living, concentrated in Jesus Christ's recapitulation of faithful humanity, that freely offers redeemed creation to God in worship: "a giving in praise of that which was given to be used for the praise of God."[258] The ethic of sacrifice stands in contrast to the Western myth of individual self-fulfilment that instrumentalizes people and creation as a means to the individual's will. Rather than excluding or trivializing the other, a theological understanding of sociality places relationality at the centre. It determines that our personal being is constituted by what we give to and receive from others because as humans we have our being in relationship.[259]

254. Gunton, *The One, the Three and the Many*, 224.
255. Gunton, *The One, the Three and the Many*, 225.
256. Gunton, *The One, the Three and the Many*, 225.
257. Gunton, *The One, the Three and the Many*, 226.
258. Gunton, *The One, the Three and the Many*, 226.
259. Gunton, *The One, the Three and the Many*, 227.

Gunton's second analogy of relationality is found in the diverse human actions and relations with the non-personal world in science, ethics, and art. The true end of faithful human cultural action is the praise of creation's creator in response to God's goodness. The sacrifice of praise is human action in the mode of gift and reception through which the Spirit enables the world to be itself before God, and offers humanity and creation in right relation to God and each other through Christ. Human culture is best understood as a sacrifice of praise, an emphasis that Gunton develops and strengthens throughout his writings. This understanding, however, does not prescribe the form of cultural enterprise. Instead, it places human cultural action in a transcendental framework.[260] The relatedness of everything to God, realized through faithful forms of human culture offered to God, is the basis for Gunton's universal and open transcendentality.

Human Culture and the Sacrifice of Praise

The sacrifice of praise that offers all creation in relation to God makes human cultural action in art, and faithful human dominion of creation, a theological imperative. The human dominion of creation is neither the pure action of mechanistic domination nor pure receptivity of New Age idolization of the creation, as each misconstrues humanity's relationality with creation and the centrality of otherness.[261] Modernity's denial of transcendence threatens the necessary otherness and space required for personal and cosmic relatedness. The trinitarian logic of gift and reception redeems the logic of the rootless individual will by setting human thought and action in a social metaphysic of gift and reception.[262] The doctrine of the Trinity enables us to understand the otherness of God and creation as ontologically distinct realities, and offers an account of God's relation to creation as otherness-in-relation that is personal, free, and liberating.[263] Creation is what it is by virtue of its relation to God who creates, sustains, and directs the creation to its intended end by the Son and the Spirit. Creation's inscape is formed by the Son, who takes up humanity's and creation's cause within the temporal and spatial structures he made. Through the particularizing and eschatological action of the Spirit, creation is enabled to become itself in relation to God and all else. Gunton concludes that a trinitarian theology of creation offers what neither antiquity or modernity could achieve: the right relation of the one and the many—the one, *the three* and the many.[264]

For all its explanatory power, however, sociality as personal relatedness is not a transcendental because it is not a mark of all creation. While sociality is appropriate for God and humanity, it is not so for non-personal being. The universe as a whole

---

260. Gunton, *The One, the Three and the Many*, 227.
261. Gunton, *The One, the Three and the Many*, 228.
262. Gunton, *The One, the Three and the Many*, 228.
263. Gunton, *The One, the Three and the Many*, 229.
264. Gunton, *The One, the Three and the Many*, 229.

is not marked by sociality but relationality, and the universality of relationality makes it Gunton's third open transcendental that enables us to learn something of all reality. "All things are what they are by being particulars constituted by many and various forms of relation ... all created people and things are marked by their coming from and returning to God who is himself, in his essential and inmost being, a being in relation."[265] This definition of relationality, Gunton reminds us, incorporates the two other open transcendentals—*perichoresis* and substantiality—into its meaning.

The open transcendentals are the result of the revelation of the general characteristic of God's eternal being as being in communion—a revelation that emerges from divine action in the economy. This account of God, derived from the economy, enables us to see the ways that creation bears the marks of the triune creator so that the open transcendentals tell us something about the nature of all being in its particularity. "In sum, the transcendentals are functions of the finitely free relations of persons and of the contingent relations of things."[266] The triune God orders creation with an eschatological directedness towards perfection that gives its dynamic. Sin can disorder and disorient this dynamic through relations that subvert its ontological integrity, but it cannot be deprived of its God-given being. Created ontology is given and directed by God towards an end in time and space, and redemption is the redirection, not re-creation, of the particular to its *telos* in Christ by the Spirit. Humanity is called to serve a mediating function through forms of culture (science, ethics, and art) that enable the rest of creation to achieve its perfection. Through the action of the Son and the Spirit, such human cultural agency enables a sacrifice of praise that freely offers all things, perfected, to God.[267] Gunton concludes with a theological account of his thesis:

> The created world becomes truly itself – moves towards its completion – when through Christ and the Spirit, it is presented perfect before the throne of the Father. The sacrifice of praise which is the due human response to both creation and redemption takes the form of that culture which enables both personal and non-personal worlds to realise their true being.[268]

Conclusion

This chapter lays the foundation for Gunton's analysis of Western culture and his trinitarian theology of culture by providing a detailed account of *The One, the Three and the Many*. Gunton's careful chiastic structuring of the book offers

265. Gunton, *The One, the Three and the Many*, 229.
266. Gunton, *The One, the Three and the Many*, 230.
267. Gunton, *The One, the Three and the Many*, 230.
268. Gunton, *The One, the Three and the Many*, 231.

a cultural analysis which traces modern soundings to their roots in antiquity to understand the common trajectories in Western culture and theology. These critical analyses of Western culture and theology are followed by constructive theological proposals that offer remedies developed from trinitarian theology to bring healing to cultural ailments. The healing remedies emerge from Gunton's exploration of trinitarian theology and of concepts derived from God's economic action which are set within the framework of a quest for open transcendentals. In this intricate argumentation, Gunton's theological proposals emerge from the inter-relationship of a Coleridgean *idea*, coupled with insights conditioned by relevant theological *foci* derived from the economy, which give way to open transcendentals that provide insight for all being. Gunton's conviction is that the world is a revelatory kind of place that bears the marks of its triune creator; the open transcendentals attempt to capture the inner logic of the divine economy.[269]

However, Gunton's proposals are not beyond critique. Gunton's account of intellectual and theological history is oftentimes impressionistic. Furthermore, he employs historiographical tropes to establish binary arguments that tend to essentialize variegated histories. John McDowell notes that while Gunton is cautious of reductive and essentializing accounts of modernity, he regularly transgresses his own cautions and defaults to shorthands that assume a singular monolithic account of modernity.[270] Others take issue with his doctrinal genealogies that risk misrepresenting the tradition through the use of meta-narrative strategies and simplistic ideal typologies.[271] When it comes to his constructive work, critics hold Gunton to be one of the foremost social trinitarian theologians who makes robust claims about the inner being of God and knowingly offers them as insights for human social, political, and ethical life.[272] As noted, Gunton, at times, employs trinitarian formulae as analogical bridge terms that traverse the passage between divine and created being too easily, and risk distorting the original meaning and nuance of those terms. Such charges, especially in relation to the open transcendentals, lead one Gunton critic to conclude that his laudable trinitarian project is a failure, and a defensible version awaits realization.[273] Chapter 2 examines these criticisms in detail and, whilst acknowledging the veracity of some critiques, argues that a patient reading of Gunton's full corpus offers its own defence.

269. Schwöbel, "The Shape of Colin Gunton's Theology," 201. On the world as a revelatory kind of place, see Gunton, *A Brief Theology of Revelation*, 39; and Gunton, "Universal and Particular in Atonement Theology," 461-2.

270. John C. McDowell, "Gunton on Modernity," in *T&T Clark Handbook of Colin Gunton*, ed. Andrew Picard, Myk Habets, and Murray Rae (London: T&T Clark, 2021), 69.

271. Lewis Ayres, *Nicaea and Its Legacy: An Approach to Fourth-Century Trinitarian Theology* (Oxford: OUP, 2004), 387-90. See also Lewis Ayres, "Recent Books in … Systematic Theology," *Reviews in Religion & Theology*, 4 (1997): 76-7.

272. Kilby, "Perichoresis and Projection," 438.

273. Nausner, "The Failure of a Laudable Project," 420.

Chapter 2 details the criticisms of Gunton's claims and engages them in the context of developments in trinitarian theology in the twentieth century. Gunton's work is best understood in the context of the post-Barth era of the second wave of trinitarian renewal. However, there are a range of criticisms of the second wave of trinitarian renewal, and Gunton's trinitarian theology faces critiques of his historiographical tropes and a perceived social trinitarianism. Given the importance of relational trinitarian ontology to Gunton's work, Chapter 2 argues that a chastened account of Gunton's relational trinitarian ontology, which takes account of the critiques, remains fruitful. Many of the criticisms of Gunton's work focus primarily on *The One, the Three and the Many* and the first edition of *The Promise of Trinitarian Theology*, and do not adequately observe the progressions in his thought. This results in the *Hauptbriefe* in Gunton reception that mistakenly assumes his work in the early 1990s to be definitive of his project.[274] As Holmes notes, *The One, the Three and the Many* marks the end of one trajectory of thought in Gunton's work. Gunton's own assessment of *The One, the Three and the Many*, despite its wide acclaim, is that "there was not much theology in it."[275] In his later writings, Gunton does not employ many of the central concepts of *The One, the Three and the Many*. Most tellingly, the open transcendentals and Coleridge's *idea* no longer feature in Gunton's writings after *The One, the Three and the Many*.

The One, the Three and the Many represents one stage in Gunton's career: the hermeneutical deployment of trinitarian theology to provide analogical insights for divine and created being.[276] This work is buttressed by insights from an array of philosophical and sociological sources to critique the Western drive towards disembodiment and abstraction and affirm concrete embodied life in a relational world. In his later writings, Gunton's analysis and criticisms of Western culture do not change, nor does his belief that trinitarian theology provides the resources needed for healing Western culture. What does change, though, is his articulation of trinitarian theology as it progresses to a trinitarian theology of mediation. This progression in Gunton's theological project mirrors the progression in his career from the philosophy of religion to Christian doctrine. As his career progresses, Gunton's use of philosophical and sociological sources to buttress theological insights recedes as he draws more often from theological and biblical sources to establish theological conclusions. Likewise, the deployment of theological formulae as analogical bridge terms to provide insight into divine and human being also recedes. Instead, Gunton focuses much more on a trinitarian theology of mediation and divine action in the economy and its creaturely fruit. What

---

274. For a definition of *Hauptbriefe* ("main letters"), see p. 3, fn 5.
275. Holmes, "Towards the *Analogia Personae et Relationis*," 39.
276. This definition is drawn from Holmes, "Towards the *Analogia Personae et Relationis*," 39. For a similar account of the developments in Gunton's theology, see Davidson, "Gunton and Jüngel," 412.

remains vital from *The One, the Three and the Many* in Gunton's later writings are the theological *foci* he examines: a trinitarian account of creation, Christology, pneumatology, and ecclesiology. These theological *foci* form the centre of his trinitarian theology of culture. Part II explores these four theological *foci*, and their internal strengthening as Gunton progresses his trinitarian theology of culture.

Chapter 2

GUNTON'S LAUDABLE TRINITARIAN PROJECT AND ITS CRITICS

Where it was once commonplace to speak of the revival of trinitarian theology or *The Forgotten Trinity* in the late twentieth century, recent developments in trinitarian theology question these robust claims.[1] There has been a sea change within the field of trinitarian theology, and what could once be assumed about a trinitarian revival is now questioned. Scholars have returned to the patristic texts and question the central assumptions about dogmatic history and its contemporary import that inform much of Gunton's writing. Gunton and many of his theological contemporaries had fears about the encroachment of modalism that risks abstract accounts of God's inner life detached from God's action in the economy. However, the theological mood has changed. Contemporary theologians are now concerned with the encroachment of tritheism and the historicizing tendencies that risk reducing God's eternal being to God's temporal acts.[2] Whilst debates remain, this book explores Gunton's theology according to his avowed method rather than subsequent developments.

Proclamations of a trinitarian revival are now in dispute and, as Lincoln Harvey observes, the trinitarian renaissance project "beats a retreat on a number of fronts."[3]

---

1. See, for example, British Council of Churches Study Commission on Trinitarian Doctrine Today, *The Forgotten Trinity: 1*; British Council of Churches Study Commission on Trinitarian Doctrine Today, *The Forgotten Trinity: 2*; Alasdair I. C. Heron, ed., *The Forgotten Trinity: A Selection of Papers Presented to the BCC Study Commission on Trinitarian Doctrine Today* (London: BCC/CCBI, 1991).

2. Sonderegger, *Systematic Theology*. John Webster also raises concerns that such approaches give first priority to history instead of God's eternal being *a se*. Whilst holding that God's economic acts play an important role in theology, he maintains that primacy must be given to God's inner works. "The material priority in systematic theology of God in himself is an acknowledgement of the unqualified priority of the creator over the creature; God is first in being, and so theology precedes economy." John Webster, "The Place of Christology in Systematic Theology," in *The Oxford Handbook of Christology*, ed. Francesca Aran Murphy (Oxford: OUP, 2015), 615.

3. Lincoln Harvey, "Essays on the Trinity: Introduction," in *Essays on the Trinity*, ed. Lincoln Harvey (Eugene: Wipf and Stock, 2018), 4.

2. Gunton's Laudable Trinitarian Project and Its Critics 69

In the second edition to *The Promise of Trinitarian Theology*, Gunton remarks on the developments in trinitarian theology in the intervening years between the first and second editions. "Suddenly we are all trinitarians, or so it would seem."[4] Gunton's hesitancy about some of the developments in the field has now turned on his own work. Recent accounts of trinitarian theology have assessed the developments in the twentieth century against the classical tradition and raised significant queries and debates. Some of those who were influenced by Gunton and his approach to trinitarian theology have departed from their former positions and directions. "As a result [of the changes in the field], leading theologians such as Stephen R. Holmes and Fred Sanders are repenting of their former ways, and now align their thinking to the classical tradition as they dismiss the renaissance as a mistaken dead-end."[5]

Amidst the changes, Gunton's work is regarded among the sources that are now in question. Jason Sexton traces Stanley Grenz's decreasing interest in Gunton's work. Despite Gunton appearing prominently in earlier drafts of *Rediscovering the Triune God: The Trinity in Contemporary Theology*, Grenz removes almost all references to Gunton in the final version. This removal of Gunton is likely the result of Grenz's attempts to distance himself from charges of social trinitarianism.[6] Many regard Gunton as a leading social trinitarian, a term, as Harvey notes, that now carries derogatory connotations in certain circles.[7]

In the wake of the changes, Holmes reflects on his time at King's College at the turn of the twenty-first century, where he studied and taught under Gunton's leadership, and holds that it was at the centre of social trinitarianism. Holmes is now critical of some of the formulations of the supposed trinitarian revival, in which he participated, and notes that at a historical level it represents a departure from classical doctrine. If social trinitarianism is right, Holmes argues, then Athanasius, the Cappadocian Fathers, Augustine, Aquinas, Calvin, and the creeds are wrong.[8] "We called what we were doing a 'Trinitarian Revival'; future historians might want to ask us why."[9] The shifts in trinitarian theology represent some important criticisms of Gunton's work, especially as it is presented in *The One, the Three and*

---

4. Gunton, *The Promise of Trinitarian Theology*, xv.

5. Harvey, "Essays on the Trinity: Introduction," 4.

6. Jason S. Sexton, *The Trinitarian Theology of Stanley J. Grenz* (London: T&T Clark, 2013), 100-2. See also Jason S. Sexton, "Beyond Social Trinitarianism: Stanley J. Grenz's Baptist, Trinitarian Innovation," *Baptist Quarterly*, 44 (2012): 479-81. Grenz's use of Gunton is limited to three pages in his chapter on "The Triumph of Relationality." See Stanley J. Grenz, *Rediscovering the Triune God: The Trinity in Contemporary Theology* (Minneapolis: Augsburg Press, 2014), 145-7.

7. Harvey, "Essays on the Trinity," 4.

8. Holmes, "The Rise and Fall of 'Social Trinitarianism,'" 6. See also Stephen R. Holmes, "Response: In Praise of Being Criticized," in *The Holy Trinity Revisited: Essays in Response to Stephen R. Holmes*, ed. Thomas A. Noble and Jason S. Sexton (Milton Keynes: Paternoster, 2015), 151-2.

9. Holmes, *The Quest for the Trinity*, 200.

the Many. The rise of these important critiques means that for those following Gunton and the King's College approach, "a lot feels at stake."[10]

This chapter examines the criticisms of Gunton's trinitarian theology and their implications for his theology of culture. I do this by setting Gunton's work in its historic context by utilizing Sarah Coakley's account of the three waves of trinitarian renewal in the twentieth century.[11] Given his untimely passing, Gunton did not get to reply to many of his critics, and his work needs to be assessed against the questions and issues of his own day rather than now. There was a common mood in second-wave trinitarian renewal which Gunton shared with other leading scholars of the time. This mood consisted in the belief that the work undertaken was a revival of trinitarian theology, and any "theologian worth their salt was talking about the Trinity."[12] However, the third wave of trinitarian theology now questions these claims and disputes the historiographical accounts of the tradition that the likes of Gunton employ to establish their constructive trinitarian proposals. Likewise, the stress upon recovering the divine threeness risks undermining God's oneness, and the utilization of trinitarian ontological proposals to give insights for human being in relation risks breaching the divine and human distinction.

It is necessary to examine the criticisms of Gunton's historiographical tropes to establish his trinitarian claims. Gunton is often cavalier in his reading of theological history and deploys impressionistic readings of the tradition that misrepresent some authors. Gunton's reading of the tradition is, however, best understood in light of the common mood of his time, and his critiques serve as foils for his constructive proposals rather than incontestable claims of historical theology. Moreover, the deployment of claims about the inner relations of the Trinity to provide a range of insights into social, political, or ecclesial issues is deemed to be a form of social trinitarianism that stretches trinitarian theology beyond its intended meaning. It is important to note Gunton's shift from these approaches and I argue that his later writings are marked by greater restraint and specificity that enable him to avoid some of the excesses of social trinitarianism. Finally, I conclude by showing that the *Hauptbriefe* in Gunton reception tends to focus upon his earlier works, and does not take adequate account of his full corpus or the developments in his thought.[13] Gunton's later writings go some way to addressing Bernhard Nausner's demand for a defensible version of Gunton's laudable project. I maintain that Nausner's demand for a defensible version is realized to some extent by a careful reading of Gunton's full corpus and its progressions.[14]

---

10. Harvey, "Essays on the Trinity," 5.
11. Coakley, "Afterword," 185–95.
12. Harvey, "Essays on the Trinity," 3.
13. For a definition of *Hauptbriefe* ("main letters"), see p. 3, fn 5.
14. Nausner, "The Failure of a Laudable Project," 420.

A Critical Engagement with Gunton's Trinitarian Theology

Bernhard Nausner reviews Gunton's trinitarian project and his critics, and concludes that Gunton's laudable trinitarian project is a failure. In Nausner's reading, Gunton's project is an attempt to show how everything looks different from a trinitarian perspective and that the doctrine of the Trinity has radical consequences for human living and the healing of modern culture.[15] The causes of the failure in Gunton's project are, in Nausner's analysis, the abstract open transcendentals which risk projectionism, and are a stumbling block to him "spelling out the practical implications" of trinitarian theology. Nausner concludes that a "defensible version of his project, therefore, still awaits adequate realisation."[16]

Nausner's analysis collates many of the existing criticisms of Gunton's work and it remains influential in the way Gunton's work is perceived.[17] To date, though, there has been little critical response to Nausner's claims or conclusions.[18] In the first section below, I engage the major critiques of Gunton's trinitarian theology as it relates to his theology of culture and argue that a chastened account remains fruitful even in the light of contemporary critiques.

Setting Gunton in Context: Three Waves of Trinitarian Renewal

Sarah Coakley provides a very helpful historical delineation of three waves of trinitarian renewal in her analysis of the developments in late twentieth and early twenty-first-century trinitarian theology. This section utilizes her taxonomy and

---

15. Nausner, "The Failure of a Laudable Project," 420.
16. Nausner, "The Failure of a Laudable Project," 420.
17. See Uche Anizor, *Trinity and Humanity: An Introduction to the Theology of Colin Gunton* (Milton Keynes: Paternoster, 2016), 187; Paul Molnar, "Classic Trinity: Catholic Perspective," in *Two Views on the Doctrine of the Trinity*, ed. Jason S. Sexton (Grand Rapids: Zondervan, 2014), 76; Michael A. Tapper, *Canadian Pentecostals, the Trinity and Contemporary Worship Music: The Things We Sing* (Leiden: Brill, 2017), 117; Arthur Gregory Daggett, "Metaphysicians of Modernity: Colin Gunton and George P. Grant Confront the Zeitgeist" (MA diss., Acadia University, 2013), 66; Naomi Noguchi Reese, "Seeking the Welfare of the City: Toward an Evangelical Appropriation of the Pneumatology of Colin Gunton for Public Theology with Special Reference to U.S.A Context" (PhD diss., Trinity Evangelical Divinity School, 2016), 61; and Joshua McNall, *A Free Corrector: Colin Gunton and the Legacy of Augustine* (Minneapolis: Fortress Press, 2015), 40–1.
18. For the most significant challenge to Nausner's claims, which seeks to affirm Gunton's reading of the tradition, see Youngsung Han, "Trinity and Ontology: Towards a Theology of Being as Space in Colin Gunton" (PhD diss., Middlesex University, 2017), 56–82. In an initial response to Nausner's article, Mark Thompson offers some critiques in a blog post which are not furthered elsewhere. See Mark Thompson, "Has Colin Gunton's Theological Project Really Failed?," *Theological Theology*, December 2, 2009, http://markdthompson.blogspot.com/2009/12/has-colin-guntons-theological-project.html.

supplements her analysis with Christoph Schwöbel's similar, yet distinct, account. Both scholars note three waves of trinitarian renewal in the late twentieth and early twenty-first-century, which attempt "to establish trinitarian theology as a field of theological reflection in the Churches and in academic theology."[19]

Coakley and Schwöbel are helpful conversation partners as they represent distinct positions within the contemporary debates. Coakley is a leading proponent of the third wave's critical ressourcement of trinitarian theology that is critical of Gunton and some of the instincts of second wave trinitarianism. Schwöbel, on the other hand, was a close friend and theological colleague of Gunton's, who worked closely with him at King's, and was the executor of Gunton's literary estate. Schwöbel is an important voice from the second wave of trinitarian revival who defends a revised version of its instincts in the face of third-wave criticisms. Together, their analyses of the three waves of trinitarian renewal help to situate Gunton in the context of historical developments in trinitarian theology and understand the influences upon his work. Importantly, their analyses also enable Gunton's work to be read in its own historical context rather than in the context of contemporary debates, in which he did not participate.

Coakley suggests that the first wave of trinitarian renewal comes from the creative rethinking of the Eastern Patristic heritage by Russian exiles in Paris following the Russian Revolution. Vladimir Lossky is a key figure in this group, and draws upon the work of Théodore de Régnon to create a disjunction between the mystical trinitarian theology of the Eastern Fathers and the rationalistic trinitarian theology of the Western Fathers.[20] In Lossky's use of de Régnon's thesis, the Western tradition is highly influenced by Hellenistic thought and stresses the abstract unity of God's being. Alternatively, the East begins from the concrete *hypostases* and stresses the relationality of the three persons in communion.[21] The result, Coakley argues, is a disjunction between Eastern and Western doctrines of the Trinity which becomes entrenched in the second wave of trinitarian renewal.

At the same time, there is a parallel renewal in the West through Karl Barth's and Karl Rahner's respective contributions to Protestant theology and Catholic theology. Among Barth's remarkable achievements is the placement of the doctrine of the Trinity as the *theologoumenon* of his *Church Dogmatics* in a turn away from rationality and experience and towards revelation as the ground of theology.[22] Barth

---

19. Schwöbel, "Where Do We Stand in Trinitarian Theology?" 36.

20. Vladimir Lossky, *The Mystical Theology of the Eastern Church* (London: James Clarke & Co. Ltd., 1957), 7–66. Kristen Hennessy argues that de Régnon's thesis did not create the disjunction between East and West that is supposed, and his work has been misunderstood and misappropriated in later trinitarian scholarship. See Kristen Hennessy, "An Answer to de Régnon's Accusers: Why We Should Not Speak of 'His' Paradigm," *Harvard Theological Review*, 100 (2007): 179–97.

21. Lossky, *The Mystical Theology of the Eastern Church*, 52. Sarah Coakley, "Afterword," 185–7.

22. Karl Barth, *Church Dogmatics* I/1: *The Doctrine of the Word of God*, ed. G. W. Bromiley and T. F. Torrance, trans. G. W. Bromiley (Edinburgh: T&T Clark, 1936), 295–489. Hereafter CD. See also Coakley, "Afterword," 187, and Holmes, *The Quest for the Trinity*, 3–9.

develops his doctrine of the Trinity in the face of secular philosophy and science and is concerned to overcome the metaphysical impasse regarding speculation about knowing God-in-Godself. Barth lays significant emphasis upon God's act within the economy being revelatory of God's immanent being, but not exhaustively so. Humanity has no inherent capacity to know God, and human knowledge of God is a miracle of revelation in which God gives Godself to be known as Lord.[23]

The other towering figure in the West during this time is the Jesuit theologian, Karl Rahner. Rahner is strongly influenced by Barth and seeks to restore the doctrine of the Trinity from the experiential and monistic trends in Western scholastic theology.[24] Barth's influence leads Rahner to enunciate his famous maxim: "The 'economic' Trinity *is* the 'immanent' Trinity and the 'immanent' Trinity *is* the 'economic' Trinity."[25] Without such a maxim, Rahner's concern is that the immanent Trinity is separated from the economic Trinity and it follows that trinitarian theology becomes a speculative enterprise that risks manufacturing an idol of human construction. Such speculative theology results in a marginalization of the Trinity and the entrenchment of monistic faith amongst Western Christians.[26]

What distinguishes the first wave of trinitarian renewal from the second, according to Coakley, is the caution over the use of the word person. In distinction from Lossky's insistence on the basicality of the "persons" of the Trinity, Barth and Rahner remain cautious about calling the *hypostases* "persons" because of the individualized and psychologized overtones that the word carries in the West. Where Barth and Rahner are cautious, their second-wave followers are deemed too robust and expansive.[27]

The second wave of trinitarian renewal is heavily indebted to the work of John Zizioulas and his reading of the Eastern Patristics. While the first wave attempts to counter the Enlightenment's resistance to theological metaphysics, the second wave attempts to counter the Enlightenment's turn to the subject and its influence on Western individualism.[28] Zizioulas' trinitarian theology stresses the distinction of the East's relational concept of the person from the West's individualized concept of the person, and argues that the relationality of the persons is more fundamental than, and even definitive of, their individualization.[29] High importance is placed

---

23. Barth, CD I/1, 168. See also Coakley, "Afterword," 187; Gunton, *The Barth Lectures*, 76–82; and Gunton, *Revelation and Reason*, 173–89.

24. Coakley, "Afterword," 187–8.

25. Karl Rahner, *The Trinity*, trans. Joseph Donceel (Tunbridge Wells: Burns & Oates, 1970), 22.

26. Rahner, *The Trinity*, 15–21. See also Christoph Schwöbel, "Introduction," in *Trinitarian Theology Today: Essays on Divine Being and Act*, ed. Christoph Schwöbel (Edinburgh: T&T Clark, 1995), 6. See also Holmes, *The Quest for the Trinity*, 10–11.

27. Coakley, "Afterword," 188.

28. Coakley, "Afterword," 188.

29. John D. Zizioulas, "On Being a Person: Towards an Ontology of Personhood," in *Persons, Divine and Human: King's College Essays in Theological Anthropology*, ed. Christoph Schwöbel and Colin E. Gunton (Edinburgh: T&T Clark, 1991), 37–44.

on the distinction between the Cappadocian prioritization of personhood, understood as being-in-relation, and the Western (and Augustinian) prioritization of the unified substance of the Trinity.[30] These proposals have not gone without critique. Third-wave scholars, such as Coakley, argue that Zizioulas, and those who utilize his work, fundamentally misreads fourth-century texts to construct his own version of relational trinitarian ontology. This relational trinitarian ontology is then uncritically predicated of human personhood and all created reality without the necessary distinctions between divine and human persons.[31]

Schwöbel is much more sympathetic to the developments in Zizioulas and the second wave, and adds some important texture to Coakley's critical analysis. In the British setting, to which Gunton belonged, developments in trinitarian theology were influenced by four key factors: ecumenical conversations in which Western theology encountered Eastern Orthodoxy; the marginalization of the doctrine of the Trinity; the influence of philosophical theism; and the realization that theology always has social effects.[32] Again, the perceived dominance of deism is important in order to understand what Gunton, Zizioulas, and others of the second wave are trying to correct. Interpreting Gunton requires an acknowledgement that his corrective impulses emerge from opposition to the dominance of liberalism that he deems too intellectually feeble and too accepting of the assumptions of Enlightenment culture.[33]

When Gunton began his career, his commitment to constructive trinitarian theology appeared as quaint. That by the end of his career it could be regarded as the mainstream of English-language theology is, Holmes suggests, due in large part to Gunton's influence.[34] This understanding of Gunton's context in British theology, which itself is open to debate, is important when it comes to understanding Gunton's sometimes over-zealous correctives. Whilst theologians of the second wave hold that trinitarian theology was never completely dead, they employ the metaphor of trinitarian revival to capture the spirit of a new way of doing theology that places the doctrine of the Trinity at the centre of theology.

---

30. Zizioulas, *Being as Communion*, 40–2. See also Sarah Coakley, "Afterword," 189.

31. Sarah Coakley, "'Persons' in the 'Social' Doctrine of the Trinity: A Critique of Current Analytical Discussion," in *The Trinity: An Interdisciplinary Symposium on the Trinity*, ed. Stephen Davis et al. (Oxford: OUP, 1999), 137. See also Lucian Turcescu, "'Person' Versus 'Individual', and Other Modern Misreadings of Gregory of Nyssa," *Modern Theology*, 18 (2002): 527–8; and Holmes, *The Quest for the Trinity*, 12–16.

32. Schwöbel, "Where Do We Stand in Trinitarian Theology?" 11.

33. For a brief discussion, see Gunton, "Theology in Communion," 32. See also "The Rev Professor Colin Gunton," https://www.telegraph.co.uk/news/obituaries/1430548/The-Rev-Professor-Colin-Gunton.html. On this topic, Kelly Kapic notes that whether one agrees with Gunton's assessment or solutions, his attempt at creative retrieval of trinitarian theology is laudable. Kapic, "Gunton and John Owen," 342–3.

34. Holmes, "The Rev Prof Colin Gunton." See also Christoph Schwöbel, "A Tribute to Colin Gunton," 16–17. Schwöbel suggests Gunton almost single-handedly established the discipline of systematic theology in English universities.

The British Council of Churches Study Commission on Trinitarian Doctrine Today is of particular significance to the British scene. The Commission's publications under the title *The Forgotten Trinity* attempt not merely to offer a trinitarian reorientation, but to reshape the life of the Churches from a trinitarian perspective.[35] Again, there is a need to interpret Gunton as one among many who imbibed and created a shared mood and conversation about the past and the possibilities of trinitarian theology.[36] It is in this context that the significance of the Research Institute of Systematic Theology (RIST), which Gunton and Schwöbel established and developed at King's College, is best considered. RIST became a highly influential centre that produced a vast amount of constructive trinitarian theology by an impressive array of faculty, associates, and students. Noting Gunton's immense influence upon systematic theology in England, Schwöbel suggests that "the 'King's approach' has become one of the most respected species in the garden of theology."[37] Some of Gunton's colleagues, students, and admirers note the legacy of his influence on a generation of theologians at King's, many of whom now occupy a variety of positions in international theology.[38] At a recent conference, Alan Torrance recounts the development of the Logos Institute at the University of St Andrews and traces its lineage, among other influences, through Gunton and the major role of the RIST at King's in redefining the thrust and direction of theology in Britain.[39]

The second wave's pursuit of the wide-ranging implications of trinitarian theology stems from the deep conviction that trinitarian theology is not merely *an* element of theology, but the ground and grammar of *all* theology. Schwöbel reinforces Robert Jenson's remarks that one can only understand the point of trinitarian theology once one has already understood that trinitarian theology is the point. In his eulogy to Gunton, Schwöbel states that he is a trinitarian theologian for whom the doctrine of the Trinity is "no optional extra to theology," as trinitarian theology is Christian theology.[40] Trinitarian theology is not one among many doctrinal *foci*, it encompasses all doctrinal *foci* and offers important enrichments to all.[41]

---

35. Schwöbel, "Where Do We Stand in Trinitarian Theology?" 13.

36. The publications of the commission show a shared conviction about the decline of trinitarian theology in Western churches, an East/West disjunction, and the rise of deism and rationalism in the West. See British Council of Churches Study Commission on Trinitarian Doctrine Today, *The Forgotten Trinity 1*, 5–7.

37. Schwöbel, "A Tribute to Colin Gunton," 16–17.

38. Jenson, "Afterword," 217. See also Harvey, "Essays on the Trinity: Introduction," 5.

39. Alan Torrance, "Welcome to Participants at the *Logos* Conference, 2019," https://soundcloud.com/user-931091141/eleonore-stump-on-aquinas-understanding-of-a-life-in-grace.

40. Schwöbel, "A Tribute to Colin Gunton," 14.

41. Schwöbel, "Where Do We Stand in Trinitarian Theology?" 16–17.

Following *The Forgotten Trinity*, trinitarian theology enters an explorative phase where the programmatic new orientations are explored and new possibilities opened up. Whilst it is now contentious to speak of the "forgotten" Trinity, Schwöbel reminds us that the interesting question is not about the appropriateness of the metaphor but whether the renaissance produces significant and fruitful theological developments.[42] Surveying the developments of the past twenty years, Schwöbel celebrates the lively flourishing of trinitarian approaches, developments, and constructive expositions across the theological disciplines and traditions. "It would be difficult to point to any other theological topic that has attracted so much scholarly attention in recent decades."[43]

Whilst there is an undoubted renaissance of trinitarian theology in the late twentieth century, not all of the developments in trinitarian theology are celebrated. The third wave of trinitarian renewal, Schwöbel's Critical Ressourcement Phase, is currently in progress and is somewhat of a reaction to the second wave.[44] This group of scholars, many of whom are patristic specialists, disputes the reading of theological history upon which much of the second wave is based. The third wave of trinitarian renewal is marked by a return to the fourth-century sources and a critical reassessment of the second wave's representation of patristic trinitarianism.

Lewis Ayres, a major figure in the critical ressourcement, maintains that much of the theology of the second wave is built upon assumptions about fourth-century theology that are historically indefensible.[45] Trinitarian revivalists engage classical trinitarianism from a different theological culture and fail to understand the wider theological matrices in which fourth-century theological terminologies are developed. Instead, Ayres argues, they employ a variety of "meta-narrative strategies" to account for pre-modern theology which in essence distort and obstruct pro-Nicene theology.[46] The third wave of trinitarian renewal has put many of the intuitions of the second wave to the test of historical scholarship and found them lacking in some vital areas. This is especially the case with its lack of pedigree regarding historical sources and the robust social consequences of trinitarian theology. The following section details the third wave's criticisms of the second wave's historiographical tropes and social trinitarianism, especially as they relate to Colin Gunton's work.

Gunton's Historiographical Tropes

In the critical ressourcement of contemporary theology, Gunton's universalizing and essentializing historiographical tropes are seen as emblematic examples of the second wave's meta-narrative strategies for reconstructing theological history.

---

42. Schwöbel, "Where Do We Stand in Trinitarian Theology?" 12.
43. Schwöbel, "Where Do We Stand in Trinitarian Theology?" 35.
44. Sarah Coakley, "Afterword," 191.
45. Ayres, *Nicaea and Its Legacy*, 1.
46. Ayres, *Nicaea and Its Legacy*, 387–90.

Ayres, along with many other third-wave scholars, critiques Gunton for his cavalier attitude towards doctrinal history and his lack of appropriate engagement with primary or secondary historical scholarship. "He prefers a simplistic narrative about ideal types – Aquinas is 'aristotelian', Augustine 'neoplatonic' or 'platonic', there is the 'Western' tradition and there is also something called a 'cappadocian approach'."[47] Gunton's historiographical tropes develop impressionistic understandings of variegated theological history and false syntheses that conceal historical nuances. This section examines the criticisms of three historiographical tropes that Gunton perpetuates: an East/West disjunction; the reconstruction of Augustinianism over Augustine; and the reconstruction of Cappadocianism over the Cappadocians.

Whether examining a theological friend or foe, Gunton's work is not best read as historical theology. Kelly Kapic, one of Gunton's former students, is emphatic on the question of whether Gunton is a good historical theologian: no.[48] His (mis)-reading of Augustine is infamous, and he is also known to quickly glean insight from historical figures he admires to construct his own ideas without taking time to qualify or nuance his claims. Not all of the faults Gunton accuses Augustine of are found in Augustine. Nor are all the insights Gunton attributes to the Cappadocians, Owen or Irving found in their works. Kapic warns that Gunton should not be relied upon as a primary source for an account of historical figures. But, Kapic reminds us, Gunton did not fashion himself as a historical theologian. "We must always keep in mind, even when he is speaking about historical theologians, his actual goal is not *historical reconstruction* (which he was relatively poor at) but *theological construction* (pointing to potential dangers and possibilities in our day)."[49] Gunton's interest is in constructive theology and past figures, whether friends or foes, serve as foils for his constructive work. This does not exonerate Gunton from some of his sweeping and inaccurate readings of doctrinal, social, and philosophical history, but it does ensure that his real interests remain the centre of critical reception. Gunton primarily seeks to make theological points, not historical points, and it is his positive trinitarian proposals, and his particular interest in a concrete trinitarian theology of culture, that are the focus of this book.

Gunton's East/West Disjunction

The de Régnon thesis alleges a disjunction between Eastern and Western trinitarian theologies. Gunton is a strong proponent of an East/West split, and many of his historical critiques, and constructive proposals, rely on a disjunctive reading of the tradition.[50] There is, in Gunton's mind, a monadic Western approach to the Trinity

---

47. Ayres, "Recent Books in ... Systematic Theology," 76–7.
48. Kapic, "Gunton and Owen," 342.
49. Kapic, "Gunton and Owen," 343.
50. Sarah Coakley, *God, Sexuality, and the Self: An Essay "On the Trinity"* (Cambridge: CUP, 2013), 301.

and a relational Eastern approach to the Trinity. He willingly speaks of a monolithic account of the West, whose roots are found in Augustine's Platonism. The West stresses the singular divine essence which subsumes the distinct particularity of the divine persons into a blank unity. In contrast, there is another monolithic entity called the East, whose theological roots are found in the Cappadocians and in their stress upon the distinction of the three persons of the Trinity and their mutually constitutive relations with one another. As is well known, Gunton favours the Cappadocian approach. His commitment to it is such that his intended title for *The Promise of Trinitarian Theology* was *Homage to Cappadocia*, and, according to Schwöbel, he could barely be persuaded to change his mind.[51] Yet, Gunton's account is not a flat binary, and he is quite willing to criticize the Cappadocians and acknowledge he is utilizing their work for his own purposes.[52]

The disjunction of Eastern and Western approaches to the Trinity has come under severe scrutiny, and its revision is among the most important critical ressourcements of the third wave of trinitarian renewal. Historical theologians of the third wave have returned to the Cappadocian Fathers, and their Western counterparts, to read their texts afresh. Rather than finding the established framework of distinct Eastern and Western theologies of the Trinity, they argue that there are remarkable continuities in fourth-century approaches to the Trinity—whether Greek, Latin or Syriac. Ayres proposes that there is a pro-Nicene theology in which all of the diverse theologies that evolve in the fourth century are logically compatible and precursors of later orthodoxy.[53] These pro-Nicene theologies have a shared set of strategies and arguments about the nature and enterprise of trinitarian theology that forms the basis of Nicene Christian belief on divine simplicity; the irreducibility of the divine nature, power, essence, and glory; the irreducibility of the divine *hypostases*; the inseparability of divine operations; and the traditional *taxis* of Father-Son and Spirit.[54] Because these strategies and arguments are shared by the evolving theologies in Greek, Latin, and Syriac speaking regions, the division into "relational" Eastern and "monadic" Western approaches to the Trinity is misleading. Third-wave scholars argue that not only is the disjunction of East from West misleading, so too are the critical accounts of Augustine and the constructive accounts of the Cappadocians.

---

51. On the title, see Gunton, *The Promise of Trinitarian Theology*, 204. For Schwöbel's account, see Schwöbel, "The Shape of Colin Gunton's Theology," 207 n. 59.

52. Gunton, *Father, Son and Holy Spirit*, 46–7. For a helpful summary of Gunton's critical appropriation of the Cappadocians, see Bathrellos, "Gunton and the Cappadocians," 259–62.

53. Ayres, *Nicaea and Its Legacy*, 239; 273–4.

54. Lewis Ayres, "*Nicaea and Its Legacy*: An Introduction," *Harvard Theological Review*, 100 (2007): 141–2.

Augustine or Augustinianism?

Colin Gunton's criticisms of Augustine are infamous.[55] In the later stages of his career, Gunton is aware his criticisms of Augustine are controversial, but he remains unrepentant in viewing Augustine as "the fountainhead of our troubles."[56] Gunton's Augustine is enraptured by Platonic thought and falls prey to substance metaphysics that envisages God to be a static monad, whose real being is abstracted from God's acts within the economy.[57] The proper principle of the inseparability of the divine operations develops in such a way in Augustine that Gunton believes they are indistinguishable. This separation of the distinct economic actions of the divine persons from knowledge of God *ad intra* subsumes the particularity of the divine persons into a homogenized unity.[58] These dualistic tendencies are further exacerbated in Augustine's conception of creation which elevates immateriality over materiality,[59] his docetic Christology,[60] his depersonalized pneumatology,[61] and his failure to comprehend the ontological revolution wrought by the Cappadocian Fathers.[62] Gunton's litany of alleged errors is now regarded as a fundamental misreading of Augustine. As Jenson wryly remarks, where it was once fashionable to bash Augustine, it is now more fashionable to bash the Augustine bashers, and Gunton is a prime target.[63]

---

55. Stephen Holmes contends that Augustine featured largely positively in Gunton's work until at least 1985. Whilst Holmes is correct that the definitive article that declares Gunton's unabated attack on Augustine is published in 1990, Gunton's negative analysis of Augustine is in seed form from his earliest works. For example, Gunton's 1980 article traces the roots of the Western tendency towards dualistic subjectivism in Christology to Augustine. See Colin E. Gunton, "The Truth of Christology," in *Belief in Science and in the Christian Life: The Relevance of Michael Polanyi's Thought for Christian Faith and Life*, ed. Thomas F. Torrance (Edinburgh: The Handsel Press, 1980), 93. See also Holmes, "Towards the *Analogia Personae et Relationis*," 39–40. On Jenson's admission of his influence on Gunton's reading of Augustine, see Jenson, "A Decision Tree of Colin Gunton's Thinking," 10–12.

56. In his 2002 publication *Act and Being*, Gunton notes the controversy that his article, "Augustine, the Trinity and the Theological Crisis of the West," *Scottish Journal of Theology*, 43 (1990): 33–58, has caused, but he refers back to it as a continuing account of his views on Augustine. See Colin E. Gunton, *Act and Being: Towards a Theology of the Divine Attributes* (London: SCM, 2002), 135 n. 3. See also Gunton's admission of his biased characterization of Augustine in *The Barth Lectures*: "I don't like Augustine, I think he is the fountainhead of our troubles … " Gunton, *The Barth Lectures*, 96.

57. Gunton, *The Promise of Trinitarian Theology*, 32.

58. Gunton, *The Promise of Trinitarian Theology*, 3–5.

59. Gunton, *The One, the Three and the Many*, 54.

60. Gunton, *The Promise of Trinitarian Theology*, 33–5.

61. Gunton, *The Promise of Trinitarian Theology*, 37.

62. Gunton, *The Promise of Trinitarian Theology*, 53.

63. Jenson, "A Decision Tree of Colin Gunton's Thinking," 11.

Augustine scholars deem such descriptions of Augustine's doctrine to be overly simplistic, or, more forcefully, dead wrong.[64] Richard Cross challenges the narrative of Augustine's miscomprehension of the Cappadocian ontological revolution and holds that this misconstrues Augustine's point regarding the Greek distinction of οὐσία and ὑπόστασις. Augustine does not fail to understand the Cappadocian ontological revolution; he utilizes Porphyry's "Tree" to traverse the differences in Latin and Greek trinitarian language and conceptuality regarding persons and essence.[65] Working from a doctrine of divine simplicity, Augustine shows that trinitarian logic and grammar defy Porphyry's logic of *genus* and *species*, and demands different patterns of speech which uphold the indivisibility of God's being.[66] His reluctant analogy of the singular divine essence to matter comes at the end of a long and carefully developed argument, which has strong qualifications and reservations. The singular divine essence is neither *genus* nor *species* but a common matter, understood as a mass noun rather than a count noun, which cannot be enumerated or divided. "The divine essence is fully real (as evidenced by the analogy to matter), and yet undivided—identically the same singular thing in each divine person."[67] Hence, Gunton's accusation that Augustine failed to understand the complexities of Cappadocian ontology results from Gunton's failure to understand the complexities of Augustine's argument—an argument that Augustine does not develop or utilize in his wider trinitarian discussions.[68]

The Cappadocians or Cappadocianism?

In Gunton's theology, what Augustine is not, the Cappadocians are. The Cappadocian ontological revolution asserts that the substance of God has no ontological content apart from communion.[69] The BCC Study Commission on Trinitarian Doctrine proved to be profoundly formative for Gunton, and is likely the environment where he first encountered the riches of patristic theology through his interaction with Zizioulas.[70] Gunton's reading of the Cappadocians owes much to Zizioulas and to his assertion that the Cappadocians developed a new concept of the person as being-in-relationship.

---

64. See Lewis Ayres, "Augustine, the Trinity and Modernity," *Augustinian Studies*, 26 (1995): 130 and Michel René Barnes, "Rereading Augustine's Theology of the Trinity," in *The Trinity: An Interdisciplinary Symposium on the Trinity*, ed. Stephen Davis et al. (Oxford: OUP, 1999), 145.

65. Richard Cross, "*Quid tres*? On What Precisely Augustine Professes Not to Understand in De Trinitate 5 and 7," *Harvard Theological Review*, 100 (2007): 216–29. See also Lewis Ayres, *Augustine and the Trinity* (Cambridge: CUP, 2010), 217–20.

66. Cross, "*Quid tres?*" 221–3.

67. Cross, "*Quid tres?*" 226–8.

68. Ayres, *Augustine and the Trinity*, 220.

69. Gunton, *The Promise of Trinitarian Theology*, 9. See also Gunton, *Father, Son and Holy Spirit*, 52–3 and Zizioulas, *Being as Communion*, 36–41.

70. See Gunton, "Theology in Communion," 34–5. See also Terry J. Wright, "Colin Gunton: An Introduction," https://www.theologyandreligiononline.com/article?docid=b-9781350996595&tocid=b-9781350996595-002.

However, third-wave scholars argue that claims of a Cappadocian ontological revolution have been read into, rather than out of, the Cappadocian Fathers. Richard Fermer, a student of Gunton's, critiques Gunton and Zizioulas' selective reading of the Cappadocians and their development of relational trinitarian ontology.[71] Fermer accuses them of elevating some Cappadocian concepts and strategies, relating to their relational ontology, over other, more apophatic, elements of Cappadocian thought.[72] The quest for a relational trinitarian ontology reduces *ousia* to *koinōnia*, supplants *hypostasis* with a modern human conception of "person," and fails to capture the stress of Gregory of Nyssa and Basil upon divine unity.[73] Fermer's early criticisms of Gunton and Zizioulas anticipate the later criticisms of third-wave scholarship, which have become more trenchant and detailed.

Ayres and Coakley believe that Gunton and Zizioulas' passion for relational ontology derives from an interest in combating modern individualism. As a result, they project the issues and instincts of modern personalism onto the Cappadocians' conceptions of divine *hypostases*.[74] Instead of a robust exploration of distinct persons and personhood, Ayres and Coakley offer alternative readings of Gregory of Nyssa that suggest his work is marked by an emphasis upon the unity of the divine nature, not relational ontology.[75] Whilst Gregory upholds the distinct *hypostatic* existence of the divine persons, he stresses the unity of one divine action rather than the distinct actions of the three.[76] In a similar vein, Holmes argues that much of the second-wave usage of fourth-century terms such as "person" and "relation" reads new meaning into old words in ways that conflate their meaning for divine and human realities.[77] Rather than finding an extensive exploration of the interanimation and mutual constitution of the three distinct persons who are united together in *perichoretic* relations, we discover a stress upon a simple divine essence and an apophatic modesty regarding God's inner being.[78] This lack of modesty in the face of divine immensity is regarded by Karen Kilby as a marker of social trinitarianism.

---

71. Fermer, "The Limits of Trinitarian Theology as a Methodological Paradigm," 160. In the first footnote, Fermer thanks Schwöbel and Gunton for their scholarly integrity and generosity in encouraging him to publish the paper, despite their disagreements with his view.

72. Fermer, "The Limits of Trinitarian Theology as a Methodological Paradigm," 164–5.

73. Fermer, "The Limits of Trinitarian Theology as a Methodological Paradigm," 166–7.

74. Lewis Ayres, "On Not Three People: The Fundamental Themes of Gregory of Nyssa's Trinitarian Theology as Seen in *To Ablabius: On Not Three Gods*," *Modern Theology*, 18 (2002): 446–7.

75. Sarah Coakley, "'Persons' in the 'Social' Doctrine of the Trinity," 131.

76. Ayres, "On Not Three People," 461.

77. Holmes, "Classical Trinity," 25–8.

78. Holmes, "Classical Trinity," 34–6.

Kilby holds that Gunton is one of the foremost social trinitarians in the English-speaking world.[79] Gunton's work, along with other social trinitarians, is believed to be too knowing and too robust in regard to God's inner being and in need of greater austerity and apophaticism regarding divine immensity and ineffability.[80] Such self-confident robustness regarding God's inner being, Kilby argues, is then offered as the basis for insights into a dazzling array of ethical, political, social, and ecclesial issues. These forms of trinitarian robustness are in danger of not only misrepresenting the tradition, but projecting our most pleasing ideas on to God and then, through reverse projection, offering them back as a model for human community.[81] Not only does this misrepresent the Fathers, it borders on a form of idolatry.[82]

By contrast, Kilby argues that the Cappadocians emphasize a lack of knowledge about God's inner being in response to God's superabundant richness; a trinitarian austerity rather than a trinitarian robustness.[83] Coakley observes similar criticisms of social trinitarianism, and she concludes her criticisms of Zizioulas' relational ontology by stating that "a more chastened, or at least more complicated, argument has to be mounted for the third-order relation of Trinitarian and physical relationality."[84] Coakley is correct that any form of relational trinitarian ontology will be more chastened and complicated than that which was common in the expansive second wave. However, it is the extent and significance of such complications and chastening which are still debated. Before examining the responses from those who continue to affirm a version of relational trinitarianism, there is a need to evaluate the criticisms of Gunton's reading of history.

A Free Corrector

The criticisms of the pedigree of Gunton's historical details are significant. Gunton undoubtedly perpetuates the East/West disjunction as a false binary. Whilst some still uphold a form of distinction between Eastern and Western trinitarian theologies, it is a distinction of degree not a disjunction. Similarly, the critical ressourcement of the third wave shows Gunton's reading of Augustine is highly impressionistic and in need of significant revision, if not outright rejection. There remains, however, some debate as to the contours of such a revision. Whilst many advocate a wholesale rejection of Gunton's account, some of Gunton's supporters, such as Jenson, believe that there are still questions over Augustine's bequest to subsequent theology.[85] Like Jenson, John Colwell is similarly reticent to absolve

---

79. Kilby, "Trinity, Tradition, and Politics," 76.
80. Kilby, "Is an Apophatic Trinitarianism Possible?" 66–7.
81. Kilby, "Perichoresis and Projection," 438.
82. Kilby, "Is an Apophatic Trinitarianism Possible?" 66.
83. Kilby, "Is an Apophatic Trinitarianism Possible?" 72.
84. Coakley, "Afterword," 193–4.
85. Jenson, "A Decision Tree of Colin Gunton's Thinking," 11–12.

Augustine of all his shortcomings, and catalogues a variety of ongoing concerns that remain from Gunton's analysis.[86] It is beyond the scope of this book to enter into a detailed critical evaluation of Gunton's reading of Augustine, or the Cappadocians, let alone other historical, philosophical or theological figures. Yet, there is a need to position this work within the debates.[87]

At the tenth anniversary of Gunton's death, Holmes wrote a moving memorial to his *Doktovartor*, mentor, colleague, and friend. Holmes concedes that despite Gunton being the most intellectually able British theologian of his generation, by some distance, he is prone to see the theological world in black and white.[88] Elsewhere, Holmes winces at Gunton's characterizations of the medieval period, Augustine, Descartes, and Locke, and notes that his telling of intellectual and theological history is often enough impressionistic. Whilst critical, Holmes' critiques are appreciative, and he likens Gunton's historical reconstructions to a great painting that offers heightened contrasts, bold colours, and stark lines. When Gunton distorts an individual or an element of reality, "it was only to reveal more clearly the essence of what was being looked at."[89] Holmes notes that for Gunton, "the big picture, the essential intellectual issue, was the thing, not nice historical details."[90]

Criticisms of Gunton's historiography are necessary, but they risk missing the theological point of what he is doing: highlighting what is at stake with discarnate trajectories in theology and the need for the theological affirmation of created life within God's good creation. His grand narratives may well be cavalier in detail, but they remind students that ideas matter and why studying these things is worthy of serious time and attention.[91] Criticisms of Gunton's historical reconstructions need to be placed in the context of the vast scope of his constructive work. Gunton is convinced that theology makes public truth claims about the way that reality is constituted and this demands a wide-ranging theological engagement with all forms of knowledge and inquiry. This vast scope adds to the complications as well as the impressiveness of his project. Schwöbel reminds us, whilst not all elements that Gunton attributes to Augustine can be found in him, nor can all the insights

---

86. John Colwell, "A Conversation Overheard: Reflecting on the Trinitarian Grammar of Intimacy and Substance," *Evangelical Quarterly*, 86 (2014): 68–72.

87. For critical book-length engagements on Gunton's reading of Augustine, see Bradley G. Green, *Colin Gunton and the Failure of Augustine: The Theology of Colin Gunton in Light of Augustine* (Eugene: Wipf and Stock, 2011); McNall, *A Free Corrector*; and Keith E. Johnson, *Rethinking the Trinity and Religious Pluralism: An Augustinian Assessment* (Downers Grove: IVP, 2011), 221–57. See also McNall, "Gunton and Augustine," in *T&T Clark Handbook of Colin Gunton*, ed. Andrew Picard, Myk Habets, and Murray Rae (London: T&T Clark, 2021), 269–84.

88. Holmes, "In Memoriam Colin Gunton."

89. Holmes, "Introduction," in Gunton, *Revelation and Reason*, 5.

90. Holmes, "Introduction," in Gunton, *Revelation and Reason*, 5.

91. Holmes, "Introduction," in Gunton, *Revelation and Reason*, 8.

he develops from the Cappadocians be traced to their writings, they serve as foils from which his positive theological constructions commence.[92]

Gunton's tendency to offer grand narratives of intellectual, social, and theological history matched the mood and methods of the second wave. Though he might be among the most fervent critics of Augustine, it needs to be remembered that Gunton is far from alone in his negative analysis. Barth's unflattering description of Augustine as "sweet poison" (*süßes Gift*) undoubtedly influenced Gunton's perspectives, even though he came to believe that Barth himself was too influenced by Augustine and the West.[93] More significant is the general mood of the second wave that is displayed in the various publications on *The Forgotten Trinity*.[94] Joshua McNall suggests critiques of Augustinian tendencies were almost a rite of passage in the trinitarian revival, and Gunton excelled at making Augustine the "whipping boy."[95]

Gunton's criticisms of Augustine, and the tradition, are best understood in the common mood of second-wave trinitarianism. Key figures and peers no doubt also influenced Gunton's assessments of the tradition. Jenson, for example, acknowledges that, like Gunton, he might have overdone his criticisms of Augustine.[96] Thomas Torrance, a contemporary of Gunton's, ranks Augustine, with Descartes and Newton, among those that sponsor "the Latin Heresy" and whose work is "inherently dualistic."[97] Gunton's reading of Augustine cannot be abstracted from this context, and it is unsurprising he exclaims to his students, despite evidence to the contrary, all the text books agree with an East/West disjunction.[98] Gunton's critics are right to argue that he did have secondary sources available that could have provided a different account. But in the context of the second wave, and their mutually reinforcing interpretation of Augustine, these accounts would be a minority report that did not demand Gunton's attention. This is, of course, no longer the case, and Augustine interpretation is much richer as a result.

In his important study of Gunton's engagement with Augustine, McNall acknowledges that Gunton's corrections are unfair and unnuanced. Gunton's

---

92. Schwöbel, "The Shape of Colin Gunton's Theology," 207–8 n. 59.

93. Gunton, *Becoming and Being*, 225–32. See also Gunton, *Father, Son and Holy Spirit*, 95. On Barth's description of Augustine as "sweet poison" see Gunton, *Father, Son and Holy Spirit*, 41 and Karl Barth, *The Holy Spirit and the Christian Life: The Theological Basis of Ethics*, trans. R. Birch Hoyle (Louisville: Westminster John Knox Press, 1993), 22.

94. British Council of Churches Study Commission on Trinitarian Doctrine Today.

95. McNall, "Gunton and Augustine," 270.

96. For Jenson's acknowledgement, see Jenson, "A Decision Tree of Colin Gunton's Thinking," 11.

97. Thomas F. Torrance, *Theology in Reconciliation: Essays Towards Evangelical and Catholic Unity in East and West* (Grand Rapids: Eerdmans, 1976), 285. I am grateful to Myk Habets for this reference.

98. Gunton, *The Barth Lectures*, 96.

impressionistic readings of Augustine make him a relatively easy target for those who want to criticize his work.⁹⁹ Gunton did elevate favourite texts from Augustine out of their wider context to emphasize his point, and this resulted in fundamental misreadings of Augustine's work. McNall catalogues a compelling array of Guntonian misreadings of Augustine, and acknowledges that "Gunton's critics have good reason to object."¹⁰⁰ However, McNall also notes that Gunton's interest is as much in Augustine's theological legacy as in Augustine himself. Later generations did appropriate Augustine's work in their own ways, and not all Gunton's claims about Augustine's heritage can be so easily dismissed. While Augustine has good reason to stress the unity of God to refute some Arian opponents, later generations did not always take account of these contextual factors.¹⁰¹ Later thinkers draw from Augustine to go far beyond him in their theological speculations and they exacerbate potential imbalances in the turn inwards. Still, attributing "all" these imbalances to Augustine is unrealistic.¹⁰² There may be moments of insight in Gunton's grand narratives, but turning past figures into caricatures that suit binary argumentation is too large a price to pay.¹⁰³ Whatever the final outcome of the third wave's historical ressourcements of trinitarian theology, Schwöbel is surely correct in stating that points which were made *against* parts of the tradition must now be made *with* the tradition.¹⁰⁴

Any assessment of Gunton's reading of theological history needs to remember that Gunton was not primarily attempting to make historical points but theological ones. More pointedly, Harvey observes that deficiencies in patristic studies do not, by consequence, mean a systematic project can be so easily dismissed. Misreadings of the tradition are serious, but the historical research can "only ever support constructive proposals, they don't constitute them in themselves."¹⁰⁵ Though it should be noted that Harvey's own appraisal of the issues has shifted as the third-wave criticisms have strengthened.

In his introduction to *The Theology of Colin Gunton*, Harvey suggests that Gunton captures a legitimate trajectory of thought that developed in the Western tradition, even if his historical details are somewhat scruffy.¹⁰⁶ Nearly ten years on, and the criticisms of the likes of Gunton and Zizioulas have forced Harvey to reassess whether his own studies under Gunton at King's may have been

---

99. McNall, "Gunton and Augustine," 269.

100. McNall, *A Free Corrector*, 80. Though McNall does suggest that certain elements in Augustine's treatment of creation can tend towards a limited dualism of time and eternity, mind and matter and Christ and creation. McNall, *A Free Corrector*, 129–30.

101. McNall, *A Free Corrector*, 92.

102. McNall, *A Free Corrector*, 213.

103. McNall, *A Free Corrector*, 295.

104. Christoph Schwöbel, "Where Do We Stand in Trinitarian Theology?" 42.

105. Harvey, "Essays on the Trinity," 6.

106. Lincoln Harvey, "Introduction," in *The Theology of Colin Gunton*, ed. Lincoln Harvey (London: T&T Clark, 2010), 7.

fundamentally misguided.[107] Yet, he rightly argues that the true test is not historical fundamentalism but whether the proposals accord with the biblical witness and the creedal confession of who God is eternally. Harvey's point is important, especially given the progression in Gunton's thought which results in a more sustained engagement with biblical scholarship and theological sources. Harvey concludes that the attacks on Zizioulas and Gunton are yet to disprove their readings of scripture which form the basis of their interpretations of the Trinity.[108]

Moreover, Harvey holds that the fundamental problem of the peripheral presence of the Trinity in the Church's life and worship remains. It is still the case that if the Trinity were to be disproven, little would change in the life of the Churches. Bald accounts of "God," no matter how much technical language it comes wrapped in, do not, in Harvey's experience, invigorate the Church or its leaders in the gospel in anywhere near the same way that Zizioulas' relational trinitarian ontology does. This does not prove second-wave trinitarianism is right, as all heresies are popular. But Harvey believes its fruitfulness in the Church's life should at least see it treated with some patience and given careful testing, refinement, and rejection where needed.[109] Turf wars in theology do not serve the gospel, theology, or the Church. Claiming grace for Gunton, given his tendency for absolutist and oppositional rhetoric, can seem like special pleading. However, Holmes' plea to Gunton and Torrance for greater generosity to the past than they at times give offers a helpful reminder to their contemporary critics. "Living in a context which is less inclined to assume the simple correctness of such ideas, I wonder if we should be more generous to our forebears?"[110]

Whilst the criticisms of Gunton's impressionistic reading of Augustine and of his perpetuation of the false disjunction of Eastern and Western trinitarian theologies can be accepted and his project chastened, criticisms of his relational trinitarian ontology strike at a vital aspect of Gunton's constructive work. If, as some third-wave scholars argue, Gunton's relational trinitarian ontology is entirely indefensible from the perspective of historic orthodoxy, then it is difficult to justify any attempt to engage his trinitarian theology of culture. However, there are contemporary scholars who remain committed to a chastened and nuanced form of relational trinitarian ontology. The following section examines the criticisms of Gunton's supposed social trinitarianism and draws from Gunton's own work, as well as relevant secondary literature, to suggest a chastened form of relational trinitarian ontology.

107. Harvey, "Essays on the Trinity," 5.
108. Harvey, "Essays on the Trinity," 6.
109. Harvey, "Essays on the Trinity," 7.
110. Holmes, "Introduction," in Gunton, *Revelation and Reason*, 4.

Social Trinitarianism

Social trinitarianism is a term used to define approaches to trinitarian theology that "draw ethical consequences for human society from the eternal triune life."[111] In his definition of social trinitarianism, Holmes summarizes Kilby's three indicative themes of social trinitarianism: "a celebration of the true personhood of the three divine hypostases; a particular account of the history of doctrine; and a belief in the ethical usefulness of trinitarian dogma."[112] As the criticisms of social trinitarianism have developed, it has become an umbrella term that carries derogatory connotations and is used to cluster a way of doing theology that is now considered passé. In this section, I examine the criticisms of social trinitarianism in general, and assess their import for Gunton's trinitarian theology. Whilst Gunton's construction and deployment of trinitarian theology tend to over-reach in some areas, this need not result in a retreat into trinitarian austerity. Instead, this section outlines a chastened version of Gunton's relational trinitarian ontology and its implications for created being that take account of the criticisms of third-wave scholarship without necessarily accepting their austere proposals. There are important criticisms of the kind of robust deployment of trinitarian doctrine that Gunton attempts in *The One, the Three and the Many*. Whilst the criticisms are important and convincing, Gunton remains unconvinced by recourses to apophaticism and the *via negativa* as the negative risks driving out the positive constructive affirmations of trinitarian theology.

Persons and Relational Trinitarian Ontology

Zizioulas' trinitarian ontology is highly influential amongst a generation of theologians, especially Gunton who was his close friend and theological colleague. However, his relational trinitarian ontology has come under increasing scrutiny.[113] Coakley and others muse whether Zizioulas' stress upon relational ontology owes as much to influences from modern Western philosophy and personalism as it does to the insights of the Cappadocian Fathers. The popularity of Zizioulas' work, especially among Western theologians, is, Coakley suggests, found less in his doctrine of the Trinity proper, and more in Western attempts to combat modernity's turn to the subject. Western attempts to combat individualism appear as "a form of self-flagellation" from Western theologians regarding their own heritage and only serve to fortify the East/West disjunction.[114]

---

111. Holmes, "The Rise and Fall of 'Social Trinitarianism,'" 4.

112. Stephen R. Holmes, "Three Versus One? Some Problems of Social Trinitarianism," *Journal of Reformed Theology*, 3 (2009): 78. Holmes' summary is drawn from Kilby, "Perichoresis and Projection," 432–45.

113. Coakley, "Afterword," 189–90.

114. Coakley, "Afterword," 189–90.

In the third wave of trinitarian renewal, central concepts in the second wave's relational ontology, such as person, relation, ontology, and *perichoresis*, are now thought to stem from a fundamental misunderstanding of the patristic sources. Holmes examines the etymology of the word "person" and argues that meaning changes through time, and contemporary uses of "person" assume it to mean something it did not mean in earlier formulations.[115] "Words like 'person' and 'relation' in particular have been redefined from their original, metaphysical meanings to some supposedly radical new ontological claims in the doctrine of the Trinity — the 'social Trinity.'"[116] Such etymological errors result in claims that the fourth century established a personalist or relational ontology and read new meanings into old words.[117] Holmes' bold conclusion summarizes many of the earlier criticisms third-wave scholars have of Zizioulas' reconstruction of the supposed Cappadocian relational trinitarian ontology. In an earlier work, Coakley maintains that Gregory of Nyssa does not conceive of divine persons in the personalist terms of contemporary conceptions, and he allows only "the minimally distinctive features of their [the divine 'persons'] different internal causal relations."[118] Gregory does not privilege person over substance in the way that Zizioulas and Gunton suppose, nor does he start with the three and their being in communion. Gregory's interest in the communion between the divine persons is centred in divine oneness, and is not immediately transferable to discussion of community or communitarianism beyond the divine essence.[119]

Similar issues arise regarding the individualistic notions of person that are employed in relational trinitarian ontology and the ubiquitous use of relation. The emphasis upon the distinct particularity of the persons is argued to border on tritheism, which is the very thing Cappadocian theology attempts to counter. Instead of robust accounts of God's eternal being as the interanimation and mutual constitution of the three distinct persons who are united together in *perichoretic* relation, we find a strong emphasis upon divine unity and an ontological modesty that is reticent to define God's ineffable essence.[120]

The stress upon the unity of God is expressed in terms of divine simplicity, and discussions of God's love, power, will, and mind are discussions of God's simple divine essence. Divine simplicity excludes any discussion of three centres of consciousness or, even worse, three wills.[121] In Holmes' account, the tradition

---

115. Holmes, "Classical Trinity," 27.
116. Holmes, "Classical Trinity," 28.
117. Holmes, "Classical Trinity," 28. Ayres, in a discussion of the concept of "person" in Cappadocians, "We do not find, then, the Cappadocians attempting to construct a Christian ontology based on the primary reality of person over against non-Christian ontologies." Ayres, *Nicaea and Its Legacy*, 313.
118. Coakley, "'Persons' in the 'Social' Doctrine of the Trinity," 137.
119. Coakley, "'Persons' in the 'Social' Doctrine of the Trinity," 134-7.
120. Holmes, "Classical Trinity," 36.
121. Holmes, "Classical Trinity," 37.

stresses the unity of the divine operations and attempts to speak of the immanent life of the Godhead. The distinctions of the divine persons are limited to the eternal generation of the Son and the eternal procession of the Spirit.[122] Aside from the language of the relations of origin (begotteness and spiration), all other language, Holmes maintains, refers to the unrepeatable divine essence. Kilby agrees with Holmes and writes,

> The three *hypostases*, according to the Fathers, are distinguished by their relations of origin—the Father begets the Son, the Spirit proceeds from Father or Father and Son—but not in any other way. One can speak of these relations of origin, and one can speak of a distinction between the persons that is tied to this, but that is all, according to the Fathers.[123]

In the excitement of robust accounts of God's triunity and the distinct, yet united, action of the divine persons, third-wave scholars sense an aversion to the biblical account of the One God. Such stress upon God's triunity results in God's oneness being muted, lost, or, in Gunton's case, it becomes a term of contempt.[124] Over and against the emphasis upon God's triunity, Katherine Sonderegger seeks to reclaim God's oneness as the beginning point of theology, and exclaims, "*monotheism* is not a shame word!"[125] Christian theology and worship emerge from worship of Israel's God and from the commitment to monotheism. Israel's *Shema* is, Holmes argues, central in declaring, against external pressures, the sole lordship of Israel's one God.[126] Sonderegger begins her *Systematic Theology* with an affirmation of the perfect oneness of God and states, "The Christian doctrine of God begins, is governed by, and finds its rest in the call to the One God, the One Lord of Israel."[127] Jesus' reply to the lawyer's question about the greatest commandment reasserts the *Shema* and the oneness of God, and the wider New Testament affirms God's oneness. The shift from second-wave trinitarianism to third-wave trinitarianism marks a shift from concerns about monadic tendencies, which require greater emphasis on the distinct, yet united, action of the three persons, to concerns about tritheism, which require greater emphasis upon divine oneness. Instead of robust

---

122. Stephen R. Holmes, "Trinitarian Action and Inseparable Operations: Some Historical and Dogmatic Reflections," in *Advancing Trinitarian Theology: Explorations in Constructive Dogmatics*, ed. Oliver D. Crisp and Fred Sanders (Grand Rapids: Zondervan, 2014), 67.

123. Kilby, "Trinity, Tradition, and Politics," 76.

124. Katherine Sonderegger, *Systematic Theology: Volume 1, The Doctrine of God* (Minneapolis: Fortress Press, 2015), 7. Sonderegger references Gunton's work in *The Triune Creator* as an example of such contempt.

125. Sonderegger, *Systematic Theology*, xiv.

126. Holmes, "Classical Trinity," 32.

127. Sonderegger, *Systematic Theology*, 3.

claims about God's triunity, Sonderegger advocates, with much of the tradition, that God's oneness is the proper starting point for theology.[128]

In a similar vein, Holmes proffers that the Cappadocian achievement has nothing to do with relational ontology and everything to do with a theory of language that attempts, through *epinoia*, to employ the least inadequate language to grasp the ineffable divine nature. Basil's rebuttal of Eunomius, for instance, is aimed at his exact logical formulations that presume too much for our language's ability to describe God.[129] The doctrine of the Trinity is not primarily an ontology, Holmes argues, but a formal conceptual framework that allows texts to be read adequately.[130] Such trinitarian austerity calls into question the trinitarian robustness of Gunton and other second-wave scholars as well as their relational trinitarian ontology.

Whilst the stress upon oneness is an important corrective to the excesses of some of Gunton's instincts to assert God's threeness, Gunton maintains that the New Testament does not simply restate Jewish monotheism. In his reading of 1 Corinthains, Gunton observes that the *Shema's* affirmations of the oneness of God cannot be read aside from Paul's reworking of it in the light of Jesus Christ (1 Cor 8:4-6).[131] Paul's restatement of the *Shema* (8:4) is given a Christological re-reading only two verses later (8:6). The placement of Christ alongside the Father, subtly differentiated in his relation to the world, "can scarcely be exaggerated."[132] In his extended examination of this passage, Erik Waaler observes that Paul's binitarian re-reading of the *Shema* is strikingly original in Jewish literature. Moreover, the binitarian affirmation is extended in 1 Cor 12:4-6 to affirm the triple basis of unity.[133]

Chris Tilling, a New Testament scholar who engages in the contemporary trinitarian debates, draws from contemporary biblical scholarship to argue that Jewish stress upon oneness is not primarily upon knowing that there is one God, but relating to the one God. The *Shema's* confession that YHWH is one is set in personal and relational terms. Affirmations of the *Shema* require a relational understanding, instead of abstract metaphysical accounts of oneness, because monotheism is not merely a truth to be comprehended, but also a relationship in which to be committed.[134] The conception of oneness in terms of relation need not

---

128. Sonderegger, *Systematic Theology*, 8–9.
129. Holmes, "Classical Trinity," 41.
130. Holmes, "Classical Trinity," 34–5.
131. Gunton, *The Christian Faith*, 83–4; 183–4.
132. Gunton, *The Christian Faith*, 83.
133. Erik Waaler, *The Shema and the First Commandment in First Corinthians: An Intertextual Approach to Paul's Re-Reading of Deuteronomy* (Tübingen: Mohr Siebeck, 2008), 439, 446. For his extended argument, see 262–439.
134. Chris Tilling, "Paul, the Trinity, and Contemporary Trinitarian Debates," *Pacific Journal of Baptist Research*, 11 (2016): 28. See also Chris Tilling, "Paul the Trinitarian," in *Essays on the Trinity*, 47–8.

mean unrestrained excesses that draw excited connections between divine and human being. But, it does mean that appeals to the *Shema* as a proof-text for divine oneness as a metaphysical predicate cannot be comprehended in distinction from God's covenantal and relational action within the world.

Tilling draws from Nathan MacDonald's detailed study of Deuteronomy and monotheism, in which MacDonald concludes that "Deuteronomy does not, at any point, present a doctrine of God that may be described as 'monotheism.'"[135] God is certainly one, but the affirmation of God as one is not an intellectual claim for knowledge; it is a relational claim for Israel's covenantal loyalty and love. The *Shema*'s stress upon a covenantal account of loyalty and love accords with Gunton and Schwöbel's point that oneness and divine simplicity is not an abstract metaphysical claim of divine unity and must include within it an account of divine complexity. The Trinity is not constituted of separable parts, but divine persons whose action is "distinguishable but not separable, and therefore constitute a 'simple' God."[136]

It is Gunton's persistent point that knowledge of God comes from action not contemplation. When it comes to examining the divine attributes, Gunton orients his interest to an exploration of divine action. They are attributes in action, and Gunton holds that we move from God's communicable attributes to God's incommunicable attributes.[137] Craig Bartholomew believes that Gunton's emphasis upon determining God's aseity through divine action in the economy, as opposed to abstract philosophy, captures an important trajectory in the Hebrew Bible. "In Scripture God is rendered truly to us narratively and credally; in the narratives of his action and in the creed-like summaries of those actions. Both need to be attended to closely. Neglect of the narratives neglects the historical contexts of God's actions; neglect of the creedal statements risks losing touch with the being of God."[138]

When it comes to Paul's reappropriation of the *Shema* in 1 Corinthians, we find his multivalent affirmation of oneness does not result merely in a focus upon metaphysical monotheism. Instead, the *Shema* is an important source for his accounts of internal unity and external distinctiveness that frame the letter. Andrew Byers examines Paul's use of the *Shema* in 1 Corinthians and holds that

---

135. Nathan MacDonald, *Deuteronomy and the Meaning of "Monotheism"*, 2nd ed. (Tübingen: Mohr Siebeck, 2012), 209. See also R. W. L. Moberly, *Old Testament Theology: Reading the Hebrew Bible as Christian Scripture* (Grand Rapids: Baker Academic, 2013), 7–40; and through a reading of Naaman in 2 Kings 5, R. W. L. Moberly, *The God of the Old Testament: Encountering the Divine in Christian Scripture* (Grand Rapids: Baker Academic, 2020), 165–202.

136. Gunton, *Act and Being*, 122. See also Schwöbel, "Where Do We Stand in Trinitarian Theology?" 59.

137. Gunton, *Act and Being*, 109–25.

138. Craig G. Bartholomew, *The God Who Acts in History: The Significance of Sinai* (Grand Rapids: Eerdmans, 2020), 154.

the oneness language of the *Shema* in Deut 6:4 serves two social functions: firstly, it promotes internal group unity which reflects the identity of the one God. Secondly, the *Shema* serves an external social function of communal distinctiveness. Rather than merely stressing internal oneness, the *Shema* promotes a "more elemental social function, that of *establishing and enforcing boundary demarcation lines that preserved the uniqueness of the people of the one and only Deity.*"[139]

Paul employs the *Shema* to identify the Church's "one God" and "one Lord" amidst many other Roman deities and lords, and "one bread" and "one body" amidst the many other cultic meals and associational communities in Corinth.[140] Whilst this is certainly a call to internal social harmony, it is also a call to external social distinctiveness. Paul's *Shema* affirmation of one God and one Lord in 8:6 provides the framework to understand one bread and one body (10:17), as "*a call to social distinctiveness* premised on Jewish theology *as well as* a call to internal social harmony premised on the rhetoric of *homonoia* discourse."[141] As we will see in Chapter 6, Paul addresses disunity at the Lord's Supper in 1 Cor 11, but Paul's application of oneness in 1 Cor 10 "is not the church's failure to be socially *unified* but its failure to be socially *unique*."[142] Paul's language of oneness is "grounded in the boundary-marking functionality of the Shema" and its import extends not only to Christology, pneumatology, and divine unity, but also to ecclesiology and the Church's social distinctiveness.[143] The *Shema* promotes loyalty and allegiance to God, not merely metaphysical oneness, and the disunity in the Corinthian Church is not only a failure of the Church's social unity, but also its social uniqueness.

This emphasis upon the Church's social distinctiveness and holy calling accords with Gunton's account of the Church's holiness and distinctive way of being as a finite expression of redeemed human culture, shaped by the Torah. Chapter 5 outlines the importance of the Torah and the Church's holiness for understanding Gunton's trinitarian ecclesiology and theology of culture.

Towards a Chastened Relational Trinitarian Ontology

Schwöbel welcomes the historical ressourcements as an important development in resourcing and revising trinitarian theology, but they do not necessarily spell the death knell of relational trinitarian theology or ontology. Instead, he sees the contrast between the third wave's return to divine simplicity and apophaticism and the uncritical excesses of the second wave's resurrection of old heresies as a simplistic contrast that creates its own disjunction.[144] Divine simplicity and divine complexity need not be regarded as opposites, as it is the desire to avoid speaking of

---

139. Andrew Byers, "The One Body of the Shema in 1 Corinthians: An Ecclesiology of Christological Monotheism," *NTS*, 62 (2016): 520. Italics original.
140. Byers, "The One Body of the Shema in 1 Corinthians," 525.
141. Byers, "The One Body of the Shema in 1 Corinthians," 525. Italics original.
142. Byers, "The One Body of the Shema in 1 Corinthians," 526.
143. Byers, "The One Body of the Shema in 1 Corinthians," 531.
144. Schwöbel, "Where Do We Stand in Trinitarian Theology?" 37.

a composite divine essence that motivates early developments. Schwöbel attempts to show that divine simplicity must also retain an appropriate acknowledgement of divine complexity because we know the triune God only as Father, Son, and Spirit. "On such an account, the trinitarian relationality of God is complex because of the constitutive internal relations of the three persons, but this complexity is exactly what constitutes God's simplicity that it cannot be divided into parts."[145] The quest for a middle way between arguments for greater apophaticism and austerity in trinitarian formulations and the analogical excesses of trinitarian robustness marks out an important group of scholars who are willing to uphold a chastened version of relational trinitarian ontology that also stresses divine simplicity.

Such a position is similar to what Gunton advances, just before his untimely death, in response to Holmes' early exploration of the importance of divine simplicity for trinitarian theology.[146] Divine simplicity cannot be denied, in Gunton's opinion, if we are to hold to accounts of divine unity and the coherence of the divine being.[147] However, always on the alert to abstraction, Gunton detects a recourse to the *via negativa* in some accounts of divine simplicity that seeks to define God's perfections by the negation of material being. Because material things have parts, it is argued, God, by a process of negation, must be simple. Instead, Gunton construes divine simplicity in terms of personal relations and actions.

> The being of Father, Son and Spirit constitute one God without remainder because their communion is perfect and unbroken. The being of Father, Son and Spirit is constituted entirely from being who they particularly are in their relations one to another. The Trinity is indeed not constituted of parts – which can be separated – but of persons, who are distinguishable but not separable, and therefore constitute a 'simple' God.[148]

However, as we have seen, Gunton's stress upon divine persons in relation comes in for serious criticism as a misunderstanding of the patristic concept of person and a conflation of divine and human persons. Yet, there are contemporary patristic scholars who are not willing to reject all suggestions of relational personhood.

Demetrios Bathrellos, an Eastern Orthodox scholar who studied under Gunton, still holds to the suggestion of a Cappadocian ontological revolution. He argues that the Nicene approach aligns mostly with the Western tradition "in whose theological vocabulary *hypostasis* (*substantia*, substance) and essence remain identical to this very day."[149] This limited the use of the term "person" to denote the distinction between the Father and the Son, while person, unlike *hypostasis* and essence, is not a strong ontological term.

145. Schwöbel, "Where Do We Stand in Trinitarian Theology?" 59.
146. See Stephen R. Holmes, "'Something Much Too Plain to Say': Towards a Defence of the Doctrine of Divine Simplicity," *Neue Zeitschrift für Systematicsche Theologie und Religionsphilosophie* 43.1 (2001): 137–54.
147. Gunton, *Act and Being*, 32.
148. Gunton, *Act and Being*, 122.
149. Bathrellos, "Gunton and the Cappadocians," 254.

Therefore, by identifying *hypostasis* with essence, by using the term '*homoousios*', by claiming that the Son was begotten of the *essence* of the Father, and by allowing only the ontologically weak term 'person' to signify the distinction between the Father, the Son, and the Holy Spirit, Nicene terminology emphasized the essential identity of the Father and the Son without being able to counterbalance this with an equally strong emphasis on their personal differentiation.[150]

Bathrellos observes that in Basil's attempts to defend Nicaea, his argument that the creed distinguishes between essence and *hypostasis* reveals his desire to reinterpret its terminology to safeguard the *hypostatic* distinction of the divine persons. To achieve this, "Basil drew a sharp terminological distinction between essence and *hypostasis* and identified the latter with person (*prosopon*)."[151] In his exegesis of Basil's *Letters*, Bathrellos argues there is a daring transition, which Basil shared with all the Cappadocian Fathers, from a terminology of "one essence, one *hypostasis*, three persons" to "one essence, three *hypostases*, three persons". This replaced the Nicaean terminology with an ontologically stronger terminology that also enabled a parallel between divine and human persons.

As in humanity we have a common essence and particular persons/*hypostases*, likewise in divinity we have one essence and three "*homoousia*" persons/*hypostases*. Although this by no means implies that there are no differences in the way the distinction between essence and *hypostasis* is applied to God and to humans, it offers some grounds for relevant parallelisms.[152]

While Bathrellos observes that Gunton's reception of Cappadocian trinitarianism is not always unproblematic, often stretching their trinitarian concepts beyond their intended usage, he affirms Gunton as a deeply trinitarian theologian whose trinitarianism is derived from the Cappadocians. And central to this is his appreciation of the Cappadocian ontological revolution, and his use of their theology "to rethink the whole range of theology."[153] Whatever the final debates about the East/West disjunction, this shows that some Eastern Orthodox theologians support a chastened version of the positions Gunton holds.

Khaled Anatolios, a patristics scholar, also welcomes the revisions of the third wave, but emphasizes his solidarity with Ayres is a critical solidarity.[154] Like Schwöbel, Anatolios does not see the problems with personalist trinitarianism to be as drastic as many third-wave scholars declare. He seeks to develop a middle path between dichotomous presumptions of uncritical continuity or radical discontinuity between patristic and modern views of relational trinitarian

---

150. Bathrellos, "Gunton and the Cappadocians," 255.
151. Bathrellos, "Gunton and the Cappadocians," 255.
152. Bathrellos, "Gunton and the Cappadocians," 256.
153. Bathrellos, "Gunton and the Cappadocians," 266.
154. Khaled Anatolios, "Yes and No: Reflections on Lewis Ayres, *Nicaea and Its Legacy*," *Harvard Theological Review*, 100 (2007): 154.

ontology.¹⁵⁵ Anatolios is wary of the reductive tendencies of some modern historical scholarship on the Trinity that reduce the focus of inquiry to a word study instead of a comprehensive analysis of the complex patristic reception of the biblical narrative. Similarly, he holds that the stress upon the radical discontinuity between patristic and modern notions of personhood has not been sufficiently demonstrated, and neither has a carefully argued theology of divine consciousness which encompasses both trinitarian unity and distinction. Finally, Anatolios argues, the analogical predication of language about God and creation does not fit into simplistic binaries of likeness and difference. Instead, there is likeness within difference. "Difference does not negate likeness, and likeness does not cancel out difference."¹⁵⁶

In his book *Retrieving Nicaea*, which is a foray into the modern debates about the fourth century, Anatolios concludes by stressing the appropriateness of speech about divine personhood. The biblical narrative presents Father, Son, and Spirit as persons who are each endowed with consciousness and intentionality. As such, they can be conceived as persons in a way that is not absolutely discontinuous from modern conceptions of personhood.¹⁵⁷ Citing Gregory of Nyssa, Anantolios notes that all contemporary ideas of personhood are distorted in comparison to the revelation of God as three *hypostases*. One of the tasks of modern trinitarian theology is to reveal them to be so in the light of the revelation of God as Father, Son, and Spirit.¹⁵⁸ Elsewhere, Anatolios contends that it is possible to develop a nuanced account of the analogy between God and creation and that an "analogy does not simply do away with the radical otherness between God and creation but functions to illuminate a certain likeness within that radical unlikeness."¹⁵⁹ There is continuity within discontinuity, but this is neither radical discontinuity nor radical continuity. Anatolios cites the example of Gregory's eschatological vision in *Homily 15 on the Song of Songs*, in which human action will be harmonized by the Spirit to cling to the good in such a way that it imitates the mutual indwelling of the Father and the Son.¹⁶⁰

Drawing from the work of Athanasius and Gregory of Nyssa, Anatolios argues we should not be afraid of claiming that the divine communion is willed by each of them and, therefore, is a genuinely interpersonal communion. At the same time, the Father, Son, and Spirit are consubstantially united and equally endowed with the divine perfection "such that the divine being is a single perfection. In

---

155. Khaled Anatolios, "Personhood, Communion, and the Trinity in Some Patristic Texts," in *The Holy Trinity in the Life of the Church*, ed. Khaled Anatolios (Grand Rapids: Baker, 2014), 150.

156. Anatolios, "Personhood, Communion, and the Trinity," 150.

157. Khaled Anatolios, *Retrieving Nicaea: The Development and Meaning of Trinitarian Doctrine* (Grand Rapids: Baker, 2011), 291.

158. Anatolios, *Retrieving Nicaea*, 291–2.

159. Anatolios, *Retrieving Nicaea*, 233.

160. Anatolios, *Retrieving Nicaea*, 233.

the last analysis, neither the unity nor the distinctions among the Trinity can be adequately expressed."¹⁶¹ Through a reading of Gregory of Nyssa and Augustine, Anatolios also reminds us that trinitarian faith is not human comprehension of a passive object, but stems from God's relation with us truly reflecting God's trinitarian being. "Trinitarian faith is ultimately the project of allowing ourselves to be determined by God's trinitarian being. To be so determined is to signify or mean the Trinity by our whole being without thereby encompassing the 'object' of our signification."¹⁶²

In his important chapter on trinitarian personhood and communion, Anatolios outlines an integrated approach to trinitarian personhood that draws together the biblical narrative, patristic doctrinal formulations, and contemporary understandings of personhood and communion.¹⁶³ He shows the positive possibilities of a nuanced approach to relational trinitarian ontology that upholds divine complexity within divine simplicity, as well as continuity within difference for human and divine personhood in a dialectic of difference and likeness. Such an integrated approach enables us to speak meaningfully about the Trinity as a community of persons. Whilst attempts to understand trinitarian persons and trinitarian communion as equivalent to their human counterparts lead to tritheism, the question is not one of equivalence. Instead, the question is whether there is continuity within difference that reveals who God is and how God is related to the world.¹⁶⁴

Anatolios helpfully suggests three ways to uphold analogical continuities between the biblical narrative, patristic trinitarian reflection, and modern conceptions of personhood and communion:

1. Father, Son, and Spirit are persons inasmuch as scripture presents them in conversation with each other in such a way that a mere monologue would betray the meaning of the biblical narrative;
2. Father, Son, and Spirit are persons inasmuch as the scriptures portray them as distinct agents whilst constituting a single unified agency in relation to creation;
3. Father, Son, and Spirit are persons in communion not only in the sense that they share the divine nature, but also inasmuch as the mutual relations by which they share in the divine substance can be characterized by the interpersonal categories of delight and mutual glorification.¹⁶⁵

---

161. Anatolios, *Retrieving Nicaea*, 292.
162. Anatolios, *Retrieving Nicaea*, 291.
163. Anatolios, "Personhood, Communion, and the Trinity," 147–64.
164. Anatolios, "Personhood, Communion, and the Trinity," 150–1. Gunton makes a similar point in the apophatic limitations he places on echo language when considering the church's ontology in the light of trinitarian ontology. See Gunton, *The Promise of Trinitarian Theology*, 73–4.
165. Anatolios, "Personhood, Communion, and the Trinity," 151.

Each of these three analogical continuities is then expanded by showing how the biblical narrative, patristic trinitarian reflection, and modern conceptions of personhood and communion can be woven together. Such an approach does not allow divine personhood to give univocal reference to human or creaturely personhood. Divine being cannot be univocally signified in created being, but the use of analogy allows the possibility of applying creaturely perfections to the divine and subtracting creaturely deficiencies to give a glimpse of the glory of God.[166]

Whilst Anatolios' defence of relational trinitarian ontology strengthens and reinforces some of Gunton's work, Gunton would not subscribe to the suggestion that creaturely perfections can be applied to God, even if deficiencies are subtracted. Analogous relations between God and humanity operate from the creator to the creature, but not in reverse. Gunton consistently upholds the ontological otherness of creator and creature to preserve the aseity and freedom of God, as well as the dignity and freedom of the creature in its createdness. For Gunton, and Zizioulas, creaturely personhood and communion are derived from the personal action of the Son and the Spirit who mediate the Father's presence in the world and set the creation free to be what God intends it to be in relationship.[167] It is through the divine action in the economy that God reveals God's being.

In his engagement with Holmes' criticisms of modern trinitarianism, Paul Molnar applauds Holmes' concern about projecting human concepts of personhood on to God, but sounds a note of caution, similar to Gunton, regarding revelation. Molnar is concerned that Holmes' conception of relation as primarily logical, not personal, assumes a form of metaphysics that risks supplanting the revelation of God's personal being-in-relation as Father, Son, and Holy Spirit.[168] In language reminiscent of Gunton's own claims, Molnar states that we are "talking about personal relations based on the scriptural witness to revelation. These are therefore uniquely divine personal relations into which we are drawn by the Holy Spirit of the risen Lord; they are not abstract metaphysical relations, but personal acts of God's free love in himself and toward and with us."[169] We undoubtedly should not attempt to imagine the Trinity as a model for human community, but this "hardly means that the relations of Father, Son and Spirit are not deeply personal relations."[170] Molnar's continued insistence on the significance of the personal relations of the triune God for created being, and Anatolios' defence of a chastened form of relational trinitarian ontology, offers possibilities for sustaining the intent of Gunton's relational trinitarian ontology. Given their closeness,

---

166. Anatolios, "Personhood, Communion, and the Trinity," 163.

167. Gunton, *Act and Being*, 104–8.

168. Paul D. Molnar, "Response to Stephen R. Holmes," in *Two Views on the Doctrine of the Trinity*, ed. Jason S. Sexton (Grand Rapids: Zondervan, 2014), 51.

169. Molnar, "Response to Stephen R. Holmes," 52. Gunton, *The Promise of Trinitarian Theology*, xxix.

170. Molnar, "Response to Stephen R. Holmes," 53. See also Gunton, *Father, Son and Holy Spirit*, 10–15.

Zizioulas on Relational Trinitarian Ontology

Not all contemporary theologians accept the criticisms of third-wave trinitarianism without response. Zizioulas's response to criticisms of his work, as well as those who defend his work against its critics, is among the most important in regard to Gunton's work. Zizioulas is criticized for distorting Gregory of Nyssa in his attempts to establish relational trinitarian ontology. However, Zizioulas responds that his work barely relies on Nyssa for its construction.[171] As Aristotle Papanikolaou notes, Gregory of Nazianzus is far more central to Zizioulas' project of relational trinitarian ontology, but Zizioulas' critics do not engage Nazianzus in their criticisms.[172] Further, attempts by the third wave to identify the subtle influence of modern questions and notions of relational personhood are pointless because Zizioulas and Gunton are explicit that they *are* doing this. Both theologians are attempting to relate questions of dogma to contemporary concerns, but both theologians attempt to show how relational trinitarian ontology differs from modern notions of personalism.[173]

Such superficial criticisms, Zizioulas argues, entirely miss the point that dialoguing with modern philosophy to find points of convergence and difference is not foreign to the approach of the patristics. The patristics themselves co-opted the contemporary Greek philosophical concepts to express the divine-human communion.[174] The alternative is a false objectivity that assumes ideas arise in a vacuum, or a form of patristic fundamentalism that baldly restates patristic texts in new contexts.[175] Whilst Zizioulas does draw from contemporary philosophy, he is clear that where contemporary philosophers draw their concepts of personalism from the study of human beings, he refuses to do this because personhood is derived from the Trinity, not the other way around.[176] If God were like the human conception of an individual, God would be an anthropomorphic monstrosity.[177]

Against the charge of the inappropriate use of analogies between divine and human persons, Zizioulas is firm that all language of human and divine persons is analogical. The Fathers have a strong awareness of the limitations and deficiencies of language. The limitations which the Cappadocians put on such language demand

---

171. Aristotle Papanikolaou, "Is John Zizioulas an Existentialist in Disguise? Response to Lucian Turcescu," *Modern Theology*, 20 (2004): 602.

172. Papanikolaou, "Is John Zizioulas an Existentialist in Disguise?" 602.

173. Papanikolaou, "Is John Zizioulas an Existentialist in Disguise?" 605.

174. John D. Zizioulas, *Communion and Otherness: Further Studies in Personhood and Church*, ed. Paul McPartlan (London: T&T Clark, 2006), 177.

175. Papanikolaou, "Is John Zizioulas an Existentialist in Disguise?" 605.

176. Zizioulas, *Communion and Otherness*, 177.

177. Zizioulas, *Communion and Otherness*, 171.

that the following be excluded: addition or diminution; alteration or change; more than one ontological cause; and any other properties or qualities except those of ontological relations.[178] The divine relations cannot be based on impersonal natural and moral qualities, because these are commonly possessed by all three persons and have nothing to do with divine personhood. Zizioulas therefore argues that "the concept of personhood, *if it is viewed in the image of divine personhood*, is, as I have insisted in my writings, *not* a 'collection of properties' of either a natural or moral kind. It is only a 'mode of being' comprising relations (σκέσις) of ontological constitutiveness."[179] Given the closeness of Gunton's personal and theological relationship with Zizioulas, Zizioulas' defence and clarification of his positions offer a response to the third-wave critiques that supports Gunton's quest for a relational trinitarian ontology.

Zizioulas is not alone in defending his work in the face of critics. Papanikolaou notes that whilst there is merit in the criticisms of Zizioulas reading too much into the patristic texts, there is not enough credit given to him for drawing out implications that were not previously noticed. Of particular importance is Zizioulas' claim that the category of *hypostasis* does not simply express the distinctive properties of the trinitarian persons. The reach of this insight, notes Papanikolaou, extends to rendering coherent the union between two ontological others, creator and creature, which is not possible in the ontology of essence.[180] Similarly, he defends Zizioulas' suggestion of an ontological revolution in the development of *hypostasis* to describe the divine-human communion because it attempts to think of God's free relationship with that which is not God. In other words, Zizioulas' relational ontology enables us "to think a God-world relation that is one of free loving communion in which the distinctive otherness of the created is not absorbed but the basis for such a loving communion."[181] Importantly for the study of Gunton, Papanikolaou, in a similar vein to Anatolios, goes on to state, "I must admit that although no thinker is ever above criticism, especially when writing about God, I simply cannot understand the attack by patristic and systematic theologians alike against what I cannot otherwise but see as very retrievable insights in Zizioulas' trinitarian theology."[182]

Whilst neither Zizioulas' defence and clarification of his own work, nor Papanikolaou's, Bathrellos', and Anatolios' defence of patristic trinitarian ontology is the final word on the subject, it at least shows that these positions remain fruitful according to some contemporary patristic and systematic theologians.

---

178. Zizioulas, *Communion and Otherness*, 172.
179. Zizioulas, *Communion and Otherness*, 173.
180. Aristotle Papanikolaou, "The Necessity for *Theologia*: Thinking the Immanent Trinity in Orthodox Theology," in *Recent Developments in Trinitarian Theology: An International Symposium*, ed. Christophe Chalamet and Marc Vial (Minneapolis: Fortress, 2014), 94.
181. Papanikolaou, "The Necessity for *Theologia*," 94.
182. Papanikolaou, "The Necessity for *Theologia*," 94.

Trinitarian Robustness or Trinitarian Austerity

In the current context of third-wave trinitarian theology, deployments of trinitarian doctrine to provide insights for created being are no longer a virtue, but a vice. In her influential article, Kilby argues that social trinitarians are drawn to the doctrine of *perichoresis* because it presents God's wonderfully attractive inner life and suggests that it has perceived implications for that which is not God.[183] The quest for *perichoretic* community begins by establishing the divine persons as distinct centres of consciousness, and sometimes will, and then seeks to develop a concept of *perichoresis* as that which binds the three together. In the hands of these theologians, Kilby maintains, *perichoresis* is developed by drawing from a wide array of non-theological sources that promote the latest ideas on communitarianism to infuse it with meaning from the best of human relationality—mutual giving, love and relatedness. "What binds God into one is then said to be like all the best that we know, only of course, unimaginably more so."[184]

In his early writings, Gunton uses non-theological sources on communitarianism, such as MacMurray, Faraday, and the Butterfly Effect, to elucidate the echoes of God's relational being in the relational structures of the created order—a *perichoretic* universe which bears the marks of its creator.[185] In this kind of approach, Kilby detects a dangerous form of projectionism in which ideas about the best of human togetherness are projected on to God. In turn, through reverse projection, these ideas are then offered as a healing remedy for contemporary individualism. Such expansive trinitarian claims stand in danger of projectionism and, ultimately, idolatry: we project our most pleasing ideas on to God and make them the object of our worship.[186] "In the hands of these thinkers, then, the claim that God though three is yet one becomes a source of metaphysical insight and a resource for combating individualism, patriarchy and oppressive forms of political and ecclesiastical organization. No wonder the enthusiasm."[187]

Kilby's critiques certainly capture a trajectory in Gunton's theology which typifies some of his earlier writings. However, Kilby's account of projectionism does not adequately capture the entirety of Gunton's approach. In his early writings, Gunton overtly opposes such projectionism, and instead seeks to understand how creation bears the marks of the triune creator in its created structures. The beginning point is not the most pleasing ideas of human together, but God's revelatory action in creation, which bears the marks of its triune creator.

The claims of social trinitarians that the Trinity provides insight into a wide array of social, political, and ecclesial issues are regarded as too knowing, and lack the necessary apophaticism that marks Cappadocian theology. In fact, the Cappadocians, if there is such a unified group, emphasize a lack of knowing

---

183. Kilby, "Perichoresis and Projection," 436.
184. Kilby, "Perichoresis and Projection," 441.
185. Gunton, *The One, the Three and the Many*, 165.
186. Kilby, "Is an Apophatic Trinitarianism Possible?" 66.
187. Kilby, "Perichoresis and Projection," 438.

of God's inner being in response to God's superabundant richness.[188] The Cappadocian apophaticism stands as a corrective to the excessive cataphatic knowingness of social trinitarianism and promotes trinitarian austerity in place of rampant trinitarian robustness.[189] Consistent attention to the Trinity, according to Kilby, should result in a greater sense of God's unknownness and highlight the necessity of apophaticism.[190]

In the face of trinitarian robustness, Kilby suggests a greater humility and willingness to accept that answers to questions about God's inner being are simply beyond us. Likewise, Holmes highlights the Cappadocians' reticence regarding language of divine person and personhood, and observes that there is an unwillingness to explore implications of God's being *a se* for any created being. Divine ineffability ensures that there is no claim to have a developed knowledge of the divine essence or even an account of divine ontology.[191] The usefulness of the doctrine of the Trinity is found in its uselessness because the Trinity is its own *telos*. Aside from clarifying errors of articulation and giving a glimpse of the glory and beauty of the divine life, "the doctrine serves no end."[192] The doctrine of the Trinity is our least inadequate, partial, and hesitant language that anticipates the eschatological end of glorifying God and enjoying God forever. Indeed, for Kilby, trinitarian formulations are our technical ways of formulating the inability to know God's unknowability.[193] Bafflement, unknowing, silence, and the importance of negative theology are marks of Kilby's approach.[194]

These calls to greater apophaticism are an important corrective to some of Gunton's excesses. However, there is also a need to uphold an appropriate balance in the apophatic/cataphatic dialectic. Anatolios observes that those who want to deny any form of "social analogy" in Gregory of Nyssa tend to resort to a misleading extreme apophaticism. Such misguided extreme apophaticism needs to be refreshed by Gregory's apophatic-cataphatic framework. Gregory's framework does not operate with a fundamental polarity of knowing-not knowing, "but the subtle distinctions between knowing and 'encompassing' the nature and knowing 'about' or 'around' (*peri*) the nature through that nature's self-prescencing

---

188. Kilby, "Is an Apophatic Trinitarianism Possible?" 72.
189. Kilby, "Trinity, Tradition, and Politics," 76.
190. Kilby, "Is an Apophatic Trinitarianism Possible?" 72–3.
191. Holmes, "Classical Trinity," 35–7.
192. Holmes, "Classical Trinity," 48.
193. Kilby, "Is an Apophatic Trinitarianism Possible?" 67.
194. Karen Kilby, "Theology and Meaningless Suffering," *Modern Theology* 30 (2020): 95–8. Kilby outlines a constructive definition of apophatic theology that is a helpful alternative to Gunton's more critical definition of apophaticism and the *via negativa*. "Apophatic theology is not all about having nothing to say about God. It is instead about the acknowledgement, the recognition, of the failure of all language, an acknowledgement and recognition that needs to be accomplished as much through a profusion and piling up of language about God as through its negation." See Kilby, "Theology and Meaningless Suffering," 99.

energia."¹⁹⁵ If these nuances and distinctions are ignored and a blanket extreme apophaticism is promoted, without intelligible content, there is a risk of returning to the notional trinitarianism that Rahner cited as the cause of the doctrine's decline in the lived experience of Christians.¹⁹⁶

There are conflicting theological methodologies and epistemologies that stand at the centre of modern debates. Kilby holds that the doctrine of the Trinity does not need to be understood as first-order teaching that gives insight into the nature of God. "It can instead be taken as grammatical, as a second order proposition, a rule, or perhaps a set of rules, for how to read the Biblical stories, how to speak about some of the characters we come across in these stories, how to think and talk about the experience of prayer, how to deploy the 'vocabulary' of Christianity in an appropriate way."¹⁹⁷ In this sense, it is a doctrine that develops only partially from biblical accounts of revelation, and the role of tradition is elevated to centrality in her methodology and epistemology. From a different methodological perspective, Gijsbert van den Brink argues that the charge of projectionism depends entirely on how the supposed social trinitarians utilize the sources of the Christian faith.¹⁹⁸

In van den Brink's analysis, Kilby is no longer simply criticizing social trinitarianism. The real issue is one of religious epistemology and the status we should give to doctrinal claims.¹⁹⁹ Perhaps even more crucially, the central questions surround theological epistemology and methodology. Claims about divine unknowability and hiddenness are themselves very knowing positions. This raises an important methodological distinction between Kilby's austere trinitarianism, which distinguishes between knowledge of God in revelation and God's immanent being, and those working in the wake of Barth's doctrine of revelation. For Kilby, trinitarian theology requires a rigorous restatement of the tradition, and she holds to a theological epistemology that emphasizes what we have received from tradition and reason. In contrast, Gunton, among many others, holds to Barth's doctrine of revelation that stresses the necessary, yet not exhaustive, link between knowledge of God in the economy and knowledge of God's immanent being. In freedom, God chooses to give Godself to be known as Lord through the Son and in the Spirit. This self-revelation and self-interpretation ensure that revelation shapes reason and tradition, and not the other way around.²⁰⁰ Many second-wave theologians are quite willing to go beyond the Cappadocians to expand insights or rectify shortcomings through appeals to the biblical witness of divine self-revelation in the economy.²⁰¹ Theological accounts of God cannot, in Gunton's mind, be determined by *a priori* assumptions of divine being, but

195. Anatolios, *Retrieving Nicaea*, 234.
196. Anatolios, *Retrieving Nicaea*, 234.
197. Kilby, "Perichoresis and Projection," 443.
198. Gijsbert van den Brink, "Social Trinitarianism: A Discussion of Some Recent Theological Criticisms," *International Journal of Systematic Theology* 16 (2014): 339.
199. van den Brink, "Social Trinitarianism," 344.
200. Gunton, *Becoming and Being*, 126.
201. van den Brink, "Social Trinitarianism," 341–3. On Gunton's critical appropriation of Cappadocian theology, see Bathrellos, "Gunton and the Cappadocians," 259–65.

must emerge *a posteriori* from God's self-revelation and self-interpretation in the economy.[202]

Gunton is alert to issues of projectionism when it comes to divine and human persons. In his later writings, such as *Act and Being*, there is a marked progression in his thought about analogical accounts of persons and a caution of the dangers of projectionism. But this does not mean an understanding of divine persons in abstraction from divine action. Gunton observes that the danger in analogical accounts of persons is that "we take what we believe to be characteristic of finite persons, and project this on to God by a process of denying what we take to be the marks of deficiency and elevating their supposedly positive features to infinity."[203] Methodologically, Gunton maintains that understanding the attributes of God, and the divine persons, is best understood in the closest possible relation to action.[204]

The common restriction of the being of the three persons to the relations of origin, Gunton argues through Pannenberg, "is simply inadequate."[205] Such limitation cannot distinguish between the different kinds of action of the three persons and risks a form of modalism. There is a need for an account of the kind of person the Father is in creating, redeeming, and sanctifying, and the kind of persons the Son and the Spirit are as the two hands who mediate the Father's will. The acts and mediation of the Trinity in the economy are undoubtedly undivided, but that does not mean they are homogenous.[206] Acknowledging his indebtedness to Gunton, John Colwell makes a similar point in response to Holmes' landmark book *The Holy Trinity*, and maintains that Holmes' stress upon the unity of divine action does not adequately represent the triune character of divine action.[207] Holmes accepts this as a valid criticism and acknowledges that in a controversial work, he "badly overstated the case."[208] Holmes clarifies his view that "in each single divine act, the Father initiates, the Son executes, the Spirit perfects."[209]

When it comes to more extreme versions of apophaticism, Gunton is cautious that they promote the prevalence of the *via negativa* in theology. Quick recourses to apophaticism, in fear of over-reaching, risk creating a gulf between the economic and immanent Trinity with the effect that there is an abstract and unknowable

---

202. For an extended account of the importance of revelation through divine action in the economy, see Gunton, *Act and Being*, 76–87. See also Gunton, *Revelation and Reason*; and Barth, CD I/1, 111–20.

203. Gunton, *Act and Being*, 137.

204. Gunton, *Act and Being*, 138.

205. Gunton, *Act and Being*, 137.

206. Gunton, *Act and Being*, 139–40.

207. John Colwell, "A Conversation Overheard: Reflecting on the Trinitarian Grammar of Intimacy and Substance," in *The Holy Trinity Revisited: Essays in Response to Stephen R. Holmes*, ed. Thomas A. Noble and Jason S. Sexton (Milton Keynes: Paternoster, 2015), 97–109.

208. Holmes, "Response," 148.

209. Holmes, "Response," 148.

God who exists outside of revelation. What appears as an act of proper human modesty before the divine can become a blasphemous denial of revelation.[210] As well as denying revelation, extreme forms of apophaticism define God's being by negating characteristics of the material world which Gunton fears undermine the goodness of material being. God's being is not abstracted from involvement in created being, and the biblical account of God is oriented to action rather than contemplation.[211] Without consistent engagement with divine revelation in the economy, the *via negativa* risks projecting attributes on to God; without the primacy of divine revelation, Gunton believes "there is no end to the demons which can be let loose."[212] The assumptions of a deity conceived in abstraction from revelation reveal an overconfidence in human rationality and in our ability to know in advance the concepts with which to speak of God.[213] With Barth, Gunton's concern is that "the negative theology has in effect driven out the positive, so that the God who makes himself known in scripture has been turned into one who cannot be known as he is."[214]

Others likewise note the significant implications radical apophaticism has for the doctrine of revelation. In his response to Holmes' argument for the unknowability of the divine essence, Paul Molnar wonders how, without the centrality of revelation, we can affirm that who God has revealed Godself to be in the economy is who God is in God's eternal being.[215] "Of course God's essence is and remains a mystery to us in that we do not know God as God knows himself, but in our knowledge of God as Father, Son, and Spirit, it must be true that we know God in his internal relations, or we don't have true knowledge of God's essence and existence."[216] If tradition determines the nature of God's being without due reflection on revelation, there is a risk of a disjunction between the economic and immanent Trinity. Such a disjunction, concludes van den Brink, means we have to remain agnostic about who God is in Godself, "or we have to live by our own ideas and intuitions (of whatever provenance, but probably not the New Testament) about what it means to be God."[217] Murray Rae reinforces the importance of Gunton's stress upon divine revelation. Criticisms of Gunton's reading of Augustine may well be legitimate, he observes, but they should not detract from what Gunton viewed to be the issues at stake.

> What mattered above all [to Gunton] was that Christian theology should be faithful to 'Scripture's portrayal of the works and relations of Father, Son and

---

210. Gunton, *Act and Being*, 36.
211. Gunton, *Act and Being*, 40–1.
212. Gunton, *Act and Being*, 93.
213. Gunton, *Act and Being*, 66–7.
214. Gunton, *Act and Being*, 17.
215. Molnar, "Response to Stephen R. Holmes," 50.
216. Molnar, "Response to Stephen R. Holmes," 50.
217. van den Brink, "Social Trinitarianism," 345.

Spirit as they appear in saving history'. Failure to treat Scripture's witness to the works of the Triune God as the proper starting point for theology is yet one more instance of the idolatry to which theologians are especially vulnerable, the idolatry in which a conceptual frame of our own devising is preferred to the Word addressed to us by God in person.[218]

Anatolios holds that Gunton's doctrine of revelation, in which God's trinitarian being is revealed by God's trinitarian action in the world, is perceptible with elements of the Cappadocian tradition. Anatolios cites Gunton's emphasis on rethinking the doctrine of the divine attributes in the light of the economic Trinity as a summary of the contents of Gregory of Nyssa's *Oration*, "which endeavours to present the divine attributes in light of the Christological narrative."[219] Likewise, the emphasis of a range of theologians upon the importance of the doctrine of revelation shows that Gunton's emphasis upon divine action in the economy as the site of God's self-revelation, albeit incompletely, stands in continuity with emphases in the Cappadocians and modern systematic theology. However, the stress upon the doctrine of revelation for trinitarian theology marks second-wave trinitarianism, and more recent developments argue instead for trinitarian theology to begin with God's perfect being. Where it was once commonplace to stress the threeness of God's being against modalistic tendencies by beginning with divine action in the economy, it is now more commonplace to stress the oneness of God against tritheistic tendencies by beginning with God's immanent perfection.[220]

This section acknowledges the shortcomings of Gunton's historiographical tropes and some of his expansive analogical connections between divine and human personhood. However, as argued, this need not drive us towards an austere trinitarianism but to a revised account of trinitarian theology that is derived from an emphasis upon divine action in the economy. This approach may no longer be in fashion, but Gunton's approach fits well within the context of the trinitarian theology of his day. Part II of this book observes that Gunton's later writings are marked by a more consistent adherence to this method and its creaturely fruit.

---

218. Rae, "Introduction," 4. Quoting from Colin E. Gunton. *A Christian Dogmatic Theology. Volume One: The Triune God. A Doctrine of the Trinity as Though Jesus Makes a Difference*, 2003, unpublished typescript, Ch. 5. Cited in Jenson, "A Decision Tree of Colin Gunton's Thinking," 8–16, 10. See also Paul Louis Metzger, "Gunton on Revelation," in *T&T Clark Handbook of Colin Gunton*, ed. Andrew Picard, Myk Habets, and Murray Rae (London: T&T Clark, 2021), 9–23.

219. Anatolios, *Retrieving Nicaea*, 198.

220. For an important recent account, see Sonderegger, *Systematic Theology: Volume 2*, Chs. 1 and 2.

The Hauptbriefe *in Gunton Reception*

The *Hauptbriefe* in Gunton reception assumes the centrality of his earlier writings and does not take adequate account of the progressions in his trinitarian articulations.[221] His early writings, *The One the Three and Many* and *The Promise of Trinitarian Theology*, are taken to be the epitome of his theology to the neglect of his later work. In fact, the final decade of Gunton's life was his most prolific period of publication. As a result of this neglect, criticisms of Gunton's project do not take adequate account of later developments in which he progresses from analogical accounts of the Trinity to a trinitarian theology of mediation. This section assesses these critical evaluations of Gunton's work and shows they are severely truncated and in need of substantial revision.

Which Project? Whose Failure?

According to Nausner, Gunton's trinitarian project outlines the difference the Trinity makes to theology, which also has radical consequences for human life. This is certainly not untrue, but it is, at best, only partially true. Gunton's project is much broader than Nausner allows, as displayed in his contributions to all major areas of doctrine. Definition of Gunton's project aside, it is Nausner's judgement that Gunton's laudable project is a failure and does not deliver on his promise to show the difference trinitarian theology makes for Christian doctrine and human living.[222] Whilst others might not share Nausner's assessment, the article loosely brings together the criticisms of Gunton's trinitarian project and is often cited as a useful critique of his work.[223] Yet, Nausner's assessment of Gunton's project assumes "[Gunton's] two most influential and acclaimed books, *The One, the Three and the Many* and *The Promise of Trinitarian Theology*, undoubtedly reveal and pursue the project."[224] This assumption leads Nausner to misunderstand the heart

---

221. Schwöbel, "The Shape of Colin Gunton's Theology," 202.
222. Nausner, "The Failure of a Laudable Project," 420.
223. Molnar, "Classical Trinity," 74–5. Drawing from Nausner, Molnar holds that "While Gunton asserted that everything looks different in light of the Trinity and while he clearly wanted to avoid individualism and collectivism as well as projectionism, in the end he was led to subvert the function of *ousia* within the being of God by elevating the concept of relationality to a position of dominance."
224. Nausner, "The Failure of a Laudable Project," 404.

and valves of Gunton's project, and fail to observe the progressions in Gunton's thought.

Nausner is not alone in prioritizing *The One, the Three and the Many* and the first edition of *The Promise of Trinitarian Theology*. It is commonplace for scholars, such as Kilby and Coakley, to base their critiques of Gunton's work on these two books.[225] Similarly, Brad Green's criticisms of Gunton's reading of Augustine, as well as his critiques of Gunton's supposed noetic and epistemic account of hamartiology, are primarily based upon his reading of *The One, the Three and the Many*. "Gunton's *The One, the Three and the Many: God, Creation and the Culture of Modernity* ... is the best work for understanding Gunton's thesis regarding the far-reaching effects of confusion relating to the doctrine of God."[226] In his three publications on Gunton's theology, Green primarily depends upon Gunton's work in *The One, the Three and the Many* and *The Promise of Trinitarian Theology* and does not adequately engage with Gunton's later writings. This does not affect Green's criticisms of Gunton's reading of Augustine, which do not change, but it does truncate his exposition of Gunton's doctrine of God and his criticisms of Gunton's hamartiology.

Even those who are critically appreciative of Gunton's work, such as Uche Anizor, Roland Chia, and Leon Harris, assume the open transcendentals are vital to

---

225. In her criticisms of Gunton's supposed social trinitarianism, Kilby focuses primarily upon Gunton's work in *The One, the Three and the Many* and *The Promise of Trinitarian Theology* and fails to engage his wider corpus in any sustained sense. In her major article on "Perichoresis and Projection," Kilby offers a single reference to Gunton's work which cites *The One, the Three and the Many* and a chapter on "Trinity, Ontology and Anthropology" from 1991. Similarly, whilst naming Gunton, alongside Jürgen Moltmann, as social trinitarians who are too robust in their theology, Kilby offers no reference or direct engagement with Gunton's work. Likewise, Sarah Coakley often labels Gunton among those who she regards as social trinitarians without offering careful engagement with the details of his work or the breadth of his corpus. Coakley judges Gunton to be a social trinitarian, and cites *The One, the Three and the Many* and *The Promise of Trinitarian Theology* (second edition) without any page references. Her only specific references are to Gunton's infamous 1990 article: Gunton, "Augustine, the Trinity and the Theological Crisis of the West." See Kilby, "Perichoresis and Projection," 437–8 and Kilby, "Trinity, Tradition, and Politics," 76. See also Coakley, *God, Sexuality, and the Self*, 28, 301, 304. Coakley is equally imprecise in her criticisms of Gunton in Sarah Coakley, "Afterword," 190–1.

226. Green, *Colin Gunton and the Failure of Augustine*, 2.

comprehending Gunton's theology and especially his ecclesiology.[227] It, therefore, comes as something of a surprise to find that Gunton does not employ the open transcendentals, or the related Coleridgean *ideas*, in any publications after *The One, the Three the Many*. As we will see in our examination of the progressions in Gunton's thought, Holmes is right to argue that *The One, the Three and the Many* marks the end of one trajectory in Gunton's thought.[228]

Nausner's assumption of the centrality of *The One, the Three and the Many* contributes to his mistaken assessment of Gunton's trinitarian project. He holds that whilst personhood and communion are the heart of Gunton's project, the open transcendentals are the valves that make the heart beat.[229] Yet, Nausner's attempt at establishing a complex argument reduces the nuances of Gunton's work into a metanarrative of personhood and communion.[230] Instead of following Gunton's chiastic structure in *The One, the Three and the Many*, Nausner establishes a three-levelled hermeneutical circle that abstracts broad ideas on personhood and communion. Nausner draws mostly from Gunton's section on *perichoresis* as an open transcendental, but does so in abstraction from Gunton's critiques of immanentism, the *idea* of the economy or its theological basis in Christology.[231] Nausner's account of Gunton's argumentation is overwhelmed by his predetermined conclusion that Gunton's work on personhood and communion emphasizes the relational constitution of human being in such a way that it sublates *ousia* into *hypostasis*. In Nausner's reading of Gunton, persons are constituted by relations

---

227. On the centrality of the open transcendentals to Gunton's ecclesiology, see Uche Anizor, "A Spirited Humanity: The Trinitarian Ecclesiology of Colin Gunton," *Themelios*, 36 (2011): 27. Anizor repeats this conclusion in Anizor, *Trinity and Humanity*, 150. Anizor assumes the legitimacy of Nausner's critique of Gunton and the centrality of the open transcendentals to Gunton's project, and references Nausner's work in his critiques of Gunton's ecclesiology. For Chia's suggestion that Gunton's communio-ecclesiology is based off his understanding of relationality as a transcendental, see Roland Chia, "Trinity and Ontology: Colin Gunton's Ecclesiology," *International Journal of Systematic Theology*, 9 (2007): 452. Harris suggests that Gunton's ecclesiology is built upon the idea of open transcendentals. See Leon L. Harris, "Holy Spirit as Communion: Colin Gunton's Pneumatology of Communion and Frank Macchia's Pneumatology of *Koinonia*" (PhD diss., University of Aberdeen, Scotland, 2014), 153.

228. Holmes, "Towards the *Analogia Personae et Relationis*," 38–9. Holmes provides a very helpful account of the rapid drop in Gunton's use of Coleridge in the context of the progressions in Gunton's work. See Holmes, "Gunton and Coleridge," 321–5.

229. Nausner, "The Failure of a Laudable Project," 406.

230. Nausner titles his section on Gunton's trinitarian theology "Establishing a Complex Argument." Nausner, "The Failure of a Laudable Project," 406–8.

231. Nausner's most common references to establish his argument come from *The One, the Three and the Many*, 163–79 without mention of the structure of Gunton's argument or acknowledgement that *perichoresis* is only *one* open transcendental.

to such an extent that the concept of *ousia* is abandoned and the substance of the person is reduced to relation.[232]

However, Gunton's opposition is not to conceptions of substance, but an excessive emphasis on the primacy of *ousia* to which the distinct *hypostases* are appended. Monistic tendencies determine an *a priori* account of God as an impersonal principle in abstraction from the concrete and particular ways the divine persons reveal themselves in the economy.[233] If divine personhood is determined aside from the closest possible relation to divine action, the emphasis upon the unity of divine action crowds out the distinct, yet inseparable, persons. This emphasis in Gunton, however, does not equate to reducing the concept of substance to communion, and it certainly does not result in Gunton reducing persons to relations.[234]

Gunton holds that the reduction of persons to relation is "baneful," and "particularly to be avoided," because it defines the personal through impersonal terms and undermines the significance of persons as concrete particulars in relation to each other.[235] Relatedness requires otherness and concreteness, and divine unity consists in the way the three persons are from and to one another in relations of love. Nausner is correct in observing that Gunton utilizes his relational conception of divine being to give analogical insights into created being. As we have seen, Gunton's ubiquitous analogical use of *perichoresis* in his early writings traverses the divide between divine and human being too quickly, and fails to attend to the necessary unlikeness in divine and human being.[236]

Nausner rightly critiques Gunton's robust analogical uses of *perichoresis*, and Gunton's exploration of a *perichoretic* universe, which he establishes through an amalgam of theological, sociological, scientific, and political sources. God's being-in-relation is not equivalent to created community, and relational accounts of the *imago Dei* cannot be developed so easily.[237] Yet, Nausner's readings of Gunton's doctrine of the *imago Dei* and *perichoresis*, along with many other Guntonian themes, are severely truncated because he engages primarily with Gunton's earlier

---

232. Nausner, "The Failure of a Laudable Project," 413–15.

233. Gunton, *Father, Son and Holy Spirit*, 55–6.

234. Nausner, "The Failure of a Laudable Project," 416–18.

235. See Gunton, *The Promise of Trinitarian Theology*, 39 and 200. In his later writings, see Gunton, *Becoming and Being*, 229 and Gunton, *Father, Son and Holy Spirit*, 53. See also Stringer, "The Lord and Giver of Life," 149 n. 71.

236. John Webster, "'In the Society of God': Some Principles of Ecclesiology," in *Perspectives on Ecclesiology and Ethnography*, ed. Pete Ward (Grand Rapids: Eerdmans, 2012), 206. Webster references Gunton's work as an example of this point. See also Tom Greggs, "Proportion and Topography in Ecclesiology: A Working Paper on the Dogmatic Location of the Doctrine of the Church," in *Theological Theology: Essays in Honour of John Webster*, ed. R. David Nelson, Darren Sarisky, and Justin Stratis (London: T&T Clark, 2015), 91, 98.

237. Nausner, "The Failure of a Laudable Project," 410.

writings. Gunton's later articulations of the *imago Dei* in relation to humanity's cultural mandate, and its concentration in Jesus Christ, are a vital aspect of Gunton's theological account of human culture. It is also important to note that Gunton's analogical explorations of the Church as an echo of the triune community are not without apophatic limitations in his early writing, and, as Chapter 5 will show, these limitations need to be acknowledged.[238] More significantly for the argument of this book, Gunton's use of trinitarian formulae as analogical bridges to affect the transition to divine and human persons significantly recedes in the progression of his thought towards a trinitarian theology of mediation. Without recognizing the developments in Gunton's trinitarian articulations, scholars risk reading previous conceptualities into later work.

An indicative example is Nausner's suggestion that in *Act and Being*, Gunton claims that person means the same at the levels of creator and creation.[239] This is a misapprehension that reads criticisms of Gunton's work into the text. Instead, Gunton explores the usefulness of Scotus' view of univocity and discusses the concept of person through a Christologically conditioned reading of Heb 1:3. The incarnate Jesus Christ is the exact representation of God's being, and, therefore, "what it is to be a person is *in this case* identical with what it is to be a divine person."[240] This is not a general claim about divine and human persons, but a strictly Christological claim that only "in this case," divine and human personhood means the same at the levels of creator and creation.[241] Conclusions formed from an analysis of Gunton's earlier writings should not overwhelm an interpretation of his later writings, especially given the shift from trinitarian analogies to a trinitarian theology of mediation. Given the misrepresentation of Gunton's work, Gunton's project has not failed, nor does a defensible version await realization. Instead, the progression in Gunton's trinitarian articulations is Gunton's own realization of a more defensible version of his project. What is required are a patient engagement with his full corpus and a careful delineation of its central claims.

Social Trinitarianism: The Need for Definition

Before outlining some of the progressions in Gunton's thought, there is a need to raise questions regarding the definition and genealogy of social trinitarianism. As noted, social trinitarianism is something of a derogatory term used to encompass a wide array of theologians from the second wave. However, the breadth of theologians clustered under the umbrella term "social trinitarianism" unites a variety of otherwise differing thinkers. In her doctoral study on Zizioulas and Gunton, Eve Tibbs defends Gunton against Randall Lyle's charges of social

---

238. Gunton, *The Promise of Trinitarian Theology*, 73–4, and 80.
239. Nausner, "The Failure of a Laudable Project," 411.
240. Gunton, *Act and Being*, 147. Italics mine.
241. See also Holmes, "Towards the *Analogia Personae et Relationis*," 43–4.

trinitarianism.[242] Lyle's definition of social trinitarianism is so broad as to include Leonardo Boff, Karl Rahner, Jürgen Moltmann, John Zizioulas, Thomas F. Torrance, Robert W. Jenson, Alan J. Torrance, Cornelius Plantinga Jr., Catherine Mowry LaCugna, Christoph Schwöbel, and Colin Gunton.[243] Rightly, Tibbs maintains that Lyle has by no means established Gunton as a social trinitarian, and there is a need to situate his work in the proper theological milieu.[244]

Whilst Lyle's work has not gained an audience in scholarship, it highlights the way a wide array of theologians who are conflated together under the umbrella term, social trinitarianism. As a taxonomy, social trinitarianism is stretched beyond its capacity, to the point of losing its usefulness, and needs redefinition to give account of the varying theologies it conflates into one essentialized category. Van den Brink, along with Paul Collins, observes that there is not a clear theological genealogy of social trinitarianism, and this is a significant disadvantage in its contemporary discussion.[245]

Gunton is well aware of the dangers of the tritheism that social analogies of the Trinity face, and he is overt in his attempt to avoid these tendencies.[246] Not only is Gunton critical of social doctrines of the Trinity, he is highly critical of those to whose family he is meant to belong. For example, he disputes LaCugna's rejection of the immanent Trinity, and he disagrees with Moltmann's theodicy and affirmation of the suffering God, and develops a different trinitarianism.[247] Equally odd is the combination of Gunton and Paul Fiddes into a singular category of social trinitarianism, or even relational trinitarianism.[248] Both theologians reject the idea of a social doctrine of the Trinity, but for different reasons. Fiddes denies he is a social trinitarian because his view that *hypostases* are relations means there are not three persons who are objectified or objectifiable, but three movements

---

242. Eve M. Tibbs, "East Meets West: Trinity, Truth and Communion in John Zizioulas and Colin Gunton" (PhD diss., Fuller Theological Seminary, 2006), 137–9. On her defence of Gunton against Lyle's charges of social trinitarianism, see 156–64.

243. Randal C. Lyle, "Social Trinitarianism as an Option for 21st Century Theology: A Systematic Analysis of Colin Gunton's Trinitarian Paradigm" (PhD diss., SouthWestern Baptist Theological Seminary, 2003), 2.

244. Tibbs, "East Meets West," 6.

245. van den Brink, "Social Trinitarianism," 332. See also Paul M. Collins, *The Trinity: A Guide for the Perplexed* (London: T&T Clark, 2008), 30–1.

246. Gunton, *The Promise of Trinitarian Theology*, 198.

247. On LaCugna see Colin E. Gunton, *The Promise of Trinitarian Theology*, xvii–xix. On Moltmann see Gunton, *The Promise of Trinitarian Theology*, 20–1; and Gunton, *Theology Through the Theologians*, 78–9.

248. Jason S. Sexton, "Introduction," in *Two Views on the Doctrine of the Trinity*, 14.

of love within God that have some resemblance with finite persons.[249] Such a position, Fiddes acknowledges, puts him at odds with Gunton on an issue that is fundamental to their distinct trinitarian theologies.[250] As Fiddes notes, and we have seen, Gunton views the suggestion of persons as relations as a baneful Western trend that he opposes, and instead advocates persons as concrete particulars.[251] Elsewhere, Gunton is critical of Fiddes' open theistic positions, and Fiddes is unconvinced by Gunton's theology of mediation. An analysis of their differences lies beyond this book. I cite these examples to highlight the contrast in their work. They are both aware that their work is very different from each other's on central issues of trinitarian theology, and this raises questions about how they can be clustered together.[252] The taxonomy of social trinitarianism requires greater nuance and specificity, especially in relation to Gunton's work, if it is not to be reduced to a mere term of abuse.

Progressions and Internal Strengthening in Gunton's Trinitarian Theology

Like many scholars who develop their writings over a career, Gunton's theology progresses with time and changes in its articulation. This is especially the case with his career progression from philosophy of religion to Christian dogmatics. There are important progressions in Gunton's later writings through which some theological conceptions recede, others remain, and are refined, and new concepts

---

249. Paul S. Fiddes, "Relational Trinity: Radical Perspective," in *Two Views on the Doctrine of the Trinity*, ed. Jason S. Sexton (Grand Rapids: Zondervan, 2014), 159. See also Paul S. Fiddes, *Participating in God: A Pastoral Doctrine of the Trinity* (Louisville: Westminster John Knox Press, 2000), 11–62.

250. "With Colin Gunton, who comes in for a good deal of criticism by Molnar, I want to affirm that the eternal relations of the persons constitute the 'substance' of God; at the same time I think that this makes most sense when the persons are identical with relations (a position which Gunton himself rejected)." Fiddes, "Response to Paul D. Molnar," in *Two Views on the Doctrine of the Trinity*, 108.

251. Gunton, *The Promise of Trinitarian Theology*, 39 and 200. In his later writings, see Gunton, *Becoming and Being*, 229 and Gunton, *Father, Son and Holy Spirit*, 53.

252. On Fiddes' view of passibility, Gunton writes, "That God achieves reconciliation by the actively accepted suffering of his Son is rather different from generalities like 'only a suffering God can help' or the contents of a book like Paul Fiddes' *The Creative Suffering of God*." Gunton, *Being and Becoming*, 244. See also Gunton's critical review of Fiddes' book *Past Event and Present Salvation*. Colin E. Gunton, review of Paul S. Fiddes, *Past Event and Present Salvation: The Christian Idea of Atonement*, New Blackfriars, 71 (1990): 209–10. On Gunton's view of mediation, Fiddes writes, "While releasing Christ from identity with a supreme intellectual idea, his [Gunton's] continued use of the paradigm of mediation means that he has still not escaped the trap of separating two orders of reality." Paul S. Fiddes, *Seeing the World and Knowing God: Hebrew Wisdom and Christian Doctrine in a Late-Modern Context* (Oxford: OUP, 2013), 210.

rise. This section examines these important progressions in Gunton's thought as they relate to his trinitarian theology of culture. The purpose of this examination is twofold: Firstly, to highlight the *Hauptbriefe* in Gunton reception which shapes much of the analysis of Gunton's work, and, secondly, to outline the many under-examined aspects of Gunton's theology that relate to his trinitarian theology of culture. Schwöbel rightly reminds us that the progressions in Gunton's thought are best understood as the development and strengthening of the internal structures of Gunton's trinitarian theology.[253] These important developments combine to form Gunton's distinctive, and under-examined, trinitarian theology of culture.

Ivor Davidson holds that in *The One, the Three and the Many*, Gunton's account of the Trinity produces a "non-competitive construal of God and the world." Following Holmes' analysis of the developments in Gunton's trinitarian theology, he notes the significance of the progression in Gunton's articulation of the doctrine of the Trinity.

> Gunton himself came to think – with some justice – that his argument in *The One, the Three and the Many* was theologically inadequate, an instance of a sort of tendency to treat trinitarian doctrine too much as hermeneutical instrument, almost a way of describing the world more than the character of the God who is present in action within it. The outline treatment of revelation in the 1993 Warfield Lectures began to consider a fuller exposition of mediation, somewhat less invested in analogical applications of sociality, concerned more with what it means that God the Father operates in the world of creaturely reality through the distinctive agencies of God the Son and God the Holy Spirit.[254]

Whilst some Gunton scholars suggest the open transcendentals are central to Gunton's trinitarian project, they do not appear in any of his later writings.[255] Holmes rightly maintains that *The One, the Three and the Many* marks the end of Gunton's hermeneutical deployment of trinitarian formulae. Gunton's own assessment of *The One, the Three, and the Many*, as Holmes recounts it, was that there was not much theology in it.[256] The incisive evaluation of Holmes and Davidson can be further substantiated by an examination of Gunton's later writings and an observation of the changes in his thought. Following *The One, the Three and the Many*, Gunton ceases to employ the open transcendentals, and

---

253. Schwöbel, "The Shape of Colin Gunton's Theology," 202.
254. Davidson, "Gunton and Jüngel," 412.
255. The concept of transcendentals does appear in a chapter in *Father, Son and Holy Spirit*, but this chapter was originally written in 1989. In the preface, Gunton notes that this chapter is written somewhat earlier than the others, and its exploration of metaphor, drawn from *The Actuality of Atonement*, indicates different interests from those at the centre of the book. The reason for its inclusion is the examination of sacrifice, which is important to Gunton's later work. Gunton, *Father, Son and Holy Spirit*, xvi–xvii.
256. Holmes, "Towards the *Analogia Personae et Relationis*," 39.

their supporting argumentation, as concepts that give insight into the necessary notes of all being. Not only do the open transcendentals recede from significance, so too does Gunton's use of Coleridge's *idea*. Whilst he does allude to the Trinity as the *Idea Idearum*, there is no development of Coleridge's notion of *idea* as fathomless ontological notions that give rise to deeper involvement in the truth of things. In his important analysis of Gunton's engagement with Coleridge, Holmes highlights that Coleridge was an alternative voice to the Enlightenment tradition in Gunton's earlier writings. But, in his later writings, Coleridge plays an increasingly insignificant role in Gunton's constructive theology.[257]

Not only do the open transcendentals and Coleridge's *idea* recede from usage, Gunton's use of *perichoresis* as a framework for a relational universe also declines. Following *The One, the Three and the Many*, discussion of *perichoretic* ecclesiology, a *perichoretic* universe, the *perichoresis* of time, the *perichoresis* of non-human and human persons, and the methodology which drew from a wide array of non-theological sources recedes in Gunton's work. After this time, Gunton does not deploy *perichoresis* as an expansive univocal bridge term to establish insights into personal and non-personal created being. Instead, Gunton only employs *perichoresis* to discuss the immanent Trinity, particularly in conversations about Thomas Torrance's view of the immanent Trinity (in which there are no connections made beyond the immanent Trinity).[258] Elsewhere, in a discussion of Christ's two natures, he stresses that the asymmetrical relation between creator and creature limits the use of perichoresis beyond divine being. "What is appropriate for the three persons of the Trinity is far less satisfactory when applied to the asymmetrical relation between God and man."[259] Similarly, we cannot, Gunton maintains, "develop a concept of *perichoresis* and use it to throw light from God's reality to ours. *Perichoresis* is not an analogy between divine and worldly being."[260]

This is a different emphasis from Gunton than we observe in *The One, the Three and the Many*, which is more cautious about the misuse of *perichoresis* in relation to human persons. *Perichoresis* undergoes an internal progression from his earlier use of the term as a general relational principle in which creation bears the marks of its creator. What was once central and transcendental in Gunton's trinitarian

---

257. Coleridge is a vital source in Gunton's fight against the mechanistic rationality of the Enlightenment, and his arguments for imagination mediate between passive sensory reception and active intellect. Gunton, *Enlightenment and Alienation*, 30–4; 48–9; and 85–8. In Gunton's later writings, Coleridge's work recedes from its importance to his systematic theology, and Gunton uses his work sparingly to highlight the relationship of words and things, and Coleridge's opium habit as an example of the habitual nature of human fallenness. Gunton, *Act and Being*, 71–2; and Gunton, *Intellect and Action*, 108–9. For a more detailed account, see Holmes, "Gunton and Coleridge," 321–5.

258. See especially Gunton, *Father, Son and Holy Spirit*, 23; 44–8; and Gunton, *Act and Being*, 107, 119–23, 129–31, 138, 143–5.

259. Gunton, *Father, Son and Holy Spirit*, 98 n. 13.

260. Gunton, *Father, Son and Holy Spirit*, 23.

theology acquires greater theological precision in Gunton's work towards a fully trinitarian theology. The relation between God and the creation is described not by the ubiquitous use of *perichoresis*, but as the personal action of the Son and the Spirit who mediate the Father's presence in creation.

Similarly, Gunton's use of the language of echo in relation to ecclesiology also recedes in its importance.[261] Citing Gunton, John Webster raises concerns about the deduction of ecclesiological doctrine from trinitarian doctrine which suggests the relations of the Trinity are echoed in the Church. "Deploying 'relation' (or, more abstractly, 'relationality') as a bridge term between God and creatures can prove precarious, effecting the passage from God to Church too comfortably, without securing an adequate sense of the unqualified gratuity of the Church's created existence and of its difference from God who is the uncreated source of its life."[262] Webster's critique is important, yet, as Chapter 5 delineates, Gunton's use of echo language in relation to ecclesiology recedes from prominence under the influence of his theology of mediation. Webster goes on to suggest instead that divine action, which is grounded in the immanent being of God, is the starting point for the connection of theology and ecclesiology. "The connection of theology proper and ecclesiology is best explicated not by setting out two terms of an analogy but by describing a sequence of divine acts both in terms of their ground in the immanent divine being and in terms of their creaturely fruit."[263] Webster's proposed ecclesiological method resonates strongly with Gunton's progression to a trinitarian theology of mediation, which results in an enriched account of the creaturely fruit of divine mediation and forms the basis of Gunton's theology of culture.

The sources Gunton employs in his later theology are more restrained. Like Gunton's analogical bridges, the use of various non-theological sources to establish theological insights also recedes from the centrality of Gunton's theological argumentation. In *The One, the Three and the Many*, Gunton utilizes a variety of philosophers, and social and political theorists, such as MacMurray, Faraday, McFadyen, Havel, Polanyi, and Jaki, to develop his assessment of Western culture and proposal of a relational trinitarian alternative. In place of these non-theological sources, Gunton's later writings are marked by a rise in sustained engagement with biblical texts and theological sources that focus upon God's economic action. Whilst Gunton's critiques of the Enlightenment remain, insights such as the Butterfly Effect recede from their prominence as evidence of the universal marks of being in a relational *perichoretic* universe. Instead of general conceptions of a relational

---

261. Gunton uses echo language in his 1997 chapter in *The Promise of Trinitarian Theology*, 176. However, as other ecclesiological conceptions rise, such as election, holiness, sociality, polity, and ethics, the language of echo recedes from usage.

262. John Webster, "'In the Society of God,'" 206. See also Greggs, "Proportion and Topography in Ecclesiology," 91, 98.

263. Webster, "'In the Society of God,'" 206.

universe, Gunton develops a Christological and pneumatological account of the relation of creator and creation, from which he develops his theology of culture.

With the recession of the open transcendentals and their associated analogical and philosophical structures, what remains is the theological heartbeat of Gunton's theology. Instead of modern soundings, historic antecedents, Coleridgean *ideas* or open transcendentals, it is the theological *foci* of creation, Christology, pneumatology, and ecclesiology, which remain. Together, these are the heartbeat of Gunton's trinitarian theology. The progression in Gunton's thought leads to an internal strengthening of earlier insights in these *foci* through a sustained exploration of divine action in the economy. Instead of a quest for the transcendental marks of the creator in the creation, Gunton pursues a trinitarian theology of mediation through the personal action of the two hands, the Son and the Spirit, who mediate the Father's will in creation.[264] Part II examines each of these *foci*, creation, Christology, pneumatology and ecclesiology, and their contribution to Gunton's trinitarian theology of culture.

As well as the recession of particular trajectories in Gunton's thought, there are refinements of existing trajectories and the rise of new conceptualities in his later writings. Part II explores these under-examined aspects of Gunton's trinitarian theology that shape his trinitarian theology of culture. For Gunton, Irenaeus rises as the vital source of a refined account of a trinitarian theology of mediation.[265] Whilst Irenaeus is important to Gunton's early writings, he becomes a central figure for Gunton's theology of mediation through the Father's two hands.[266] Chapter 3 examines Gunton's trinitarian theology of mediation and his account of the doctrine of creation and their relation to his trinitarian theology of culture. If there are to be found valves which make Gunton's trinitarian heart beat, they are the two hands of the Son and the Spirit who mediate the Father's presence, action, and will in creation. A theology of mediation maintains the ontological distinction of creator and creation, and celebrates God's free relatedness to creation in its createdness.[267] Createdness is a gift given from God, and God personally relates to creation through the redeeming and perfecting action of the Son and the Spirit.

The rise of the concept of creation as a project enables Gunton to further his account of creation's orientation towards an end that is greater than its beginning. Gunton's account of creation as a project opens horizons on a theological account of human culture in which God calls humanity to act as sub-agents in the divine redemption and perfection of creation.[268] The explorations of creation as a project arise from a sustained exegetical engagement with the opening chapters of Genesis. This exegesis is implied but unexamined in *The One, the Three and the Many*, but it is realized in his later writings. This leads to the refinement and

---

264. Gunton, *The Christian Faith*, 183.
265. Holmes, "Towards the *Analogia Personae et Relationis*," 38–9.
266. Gunton, *Father, Son and Holy Spirit*, 79–80.
267. Gunton, *The Barth Lectures*, 242. See also Gunton, *The Triune Creator*, 145, 178.
268. Gunton, "Reformation Accounts," 80.

internal strengthening of Gunton's understanding of creation, the *imago Dei*, and human culture.

Nausner holds that Gunton's relational understanding of the *imago Dei* is too dependent on conceptual similarities between divine and human being, yet he does not observe the progression in Gunton's theology of the *imago Dei* in his later writings.[269] The implications of a relational *imago Dei* are important meta-statements but, Nausner argues, "they still remain very abstract and are in need of a more concrete and relevant completion."[270] However, Gunton's later writings extend his earlier explorations in ontological relationality by a sustained examination of Jesus Christ's recapitulation of Adam and Israel, and humanity's ministerial calling as part of the *imago Dei*. The demand for a more concrete account of the *imago Dei* is realized in Gunton's later writings, which Nausner does not adequately engage. As we will see in subsequent chapters, Nausner is not alone in reducing Gunton's work to a canon within the canon of Gunton's writings.

Conclusion

This chapter has engaged the criticisms of Gunton's work and acknowledged the veracity of critiques of his historiographical tropes and analogical deployment of trinitarian formulae. However, these criticisms need to be set in the context of Gunton's opposition to the abstract tendencies of his day, and the mood of the trinitarian revival in which he worked. The excesses of robust trinitarian social analogies are rightly criticized, but these need not result in the excessive apophaticism of austere trinitarianism. There remain trinitarian theologians who are willing to affirm a version of relational trinitarian ontology, albeit chastened by the historical ressourcement that demands such affirmations be made *with* the tradition rather than *against* it.

The criticisms of Gunton's analogical deployment of trinitarian formulae for insights into divine and created being have overwhelmed Gunton reception. The second section of this chapter shows the *Hauptbriefe* in Gunton reception which assumes that *The One, the Three and the Many* and the first edition of *The Promise of Trinitarian Theology* are Gunton's "main writings" and definitive of his theology. This results in a failure to engage adequately with Gunton's full corpus or recognize the progressions in his thought. Many of the trinitarian articulations that are central to *The One, the Three and the Many* are no longer employed in his progression from trinitarian analogies to a trinitarian theology of mediation. Moreover, as Part II will examine in detail, Gunton's later writings strengthen earlier articulations through the revision of earlier claims and the rise of new trinitarian articulations.

---

269. Nausner, "The Failure of a Laudable Project," 409–10.
270. Nausner, "The Failure of a Laudable Project," 417.

When considered together, the recessions, refinements, and new articulations in Gunton's later writings highlight important progressions in his thought that internally strengthen his trinitarian theology of culture. Taken together they represent a much more *theological* account of culture than what Gunton attempts in *The One, the Three and the Many*. This accords with Gunton's concern to develop "a biblical and Trinitarian approach to culture" that grounds the theology of culture in a robust Christological pneumatology.[271] Nausner's suggestion that Gunton's project has failed and a defensible version awaits realization is therefore mistaken, in my view. Gunton's trinitarian theology of culture is not a laudable project that has failed, but a project which many have failed to adequately engage.

Part II critically examines Gunton's theology of the mediation of God the Father, God the Son, and God the Holy Spirit in creation, Christology, pneumatology, and ecclesiology, as they relate to Gunton's trinitarian theology of culture. The concern of these chapters is to examine Gunton's theological account of human culture that emerges from his constructive theology as it is found in his later writings. It is through his accounts of the project of creation, Christ's faithful humanity, the Spirit's eschatological action in creation, and the church's elect calling to a distinctive sociality, polity, and ethics that Gunton develops his theological account of culture. Gunton's constructive theology of culture is the outcome of his wider theological articulations, which culminate at the Church's celebration of Lord's Supper. In Chapter 6, I argue that far from being a failure, Gunton's trinitarian theology of culture remains a rich resource that can be extended to inform a contemporary theological account of culture that addresses contemporary cultural concerns.

---

271. Gunton, "Reformation Accounts," 91–2.

Part II

TOWARDS A TRINITARIAN THEOLOGY OF CULTURE

Chapter 3

THE MEDIATION OF THE FATHER: CREATION AND HUMAN CULTURE

Colin Gunton's account of the doctrine of creation is one of his most important theological legacies, and it is within his trinitarian account of creation that he develops his theology of culture.[1] Concern for the doctrine of creation runs throughout Gunton's writings and shapes his analysis of Western culture as well as his trinitarian theology of human culture. Gunton detects the persistent influence of Gnostic tendencies that undermine the happy indwelling of embodied life in the world, and seeks to develop a more concrete account of creation and material life within it.[2] At the heart of Gunton's doctrine of creation is an explication of the relation of the eternal God with temporal creation, and of the shape that divine action takes within it. Describing God's mediating action in the creation describes the act and being of God as well as the being and action of God's creation.[3] In order to understand Gunton's theology of culture, we must first understand his account of creation and createdness.

Human culture is not its own independent reality that is knowable aside from God. Instead, it is known through an exploration of God's establishing action that creates humanity and the created order, and God's providential action that redeems and reorients creation towards an eschatological perfection that is greater than its beginning. Creation is a project, and God calls humanity as God's representatives to a non-competitive participation in the divine redemption and perfection of creation.[4] Gunton establishes the trinitarian shape of this claim through a wide-ranging exploration of divine action in the economy in which the Father's loving purposes for creation are mediated by the Son and the Spirit.

Part II of this book explores Gunton's trinitarian theology of culture by examining his trinitarian theology of mediation. It is through the Father's

---

1. Murray Rae, "Colin E. Gunton (1941–2003): The Triune God, Scientific Endeavour, and God's Creation Project," in *Science and the Doctrine of Creation: The Approaches of Ten Modern Theologians*, ed. Geoffrey H. Fulkerson and Joel Thomas Chopp (Downers Grove: InterVarsity Press, 2021), 206.
2. Gunton, *The Christian Faith*, ix–x.
3. Gunton, *The Christian Faith*, 5. See also Schwöbel, "Gunton on Creation," 63.
4. Gunton, "Reformation Accounts," 80.

mediation of creation, the Son's mediation of redemption, and the Spirit's mediation of perfection that Gunton develops his theology of culture. Human culture is not knowable aside from Christ's incarnation and faithful humanity as he alone is the true human. Nor is human culture knowable aside from the Spirit's enabling of created reality to anticipate God's eschatological purposes as it is the Spirit who enables faithful human action rather than independent human agency. Whilst the Spirit is at work in all creation, because Christ's lordship is over all the earth, God chooses Israel and the Church as elect communities whose common life (culture) mediates God's mediation. In examining the differentiated unity of trinitarian mediation in the divine economy we gain insight into Gunton's positive trinitarian theology of human culture that emerges from God's persistent love for the creation.

This chapter examines creation as the work of the Father that is established through the loving action of the Son and the Spirit, the two hands who personally mediate the Father's will in creation. In relation to this, Gunton explores the actions of the triune creator in establishing, upholding, and orienting the creation to its intended end in loving communion with God. It also reveals the nature of contingent creation and the goodness of createdness. Gunton's persistent concern is to combat the discarnate tendencies he perceives in Western culture by developing a more concrete and embodied theology of creation and its goodness. This requires a greater unity between creation, salvation, and eschatological perfection, such that salvation is not understood to be redemption *from* materiality but the redemption and perfection *of* the material order. Whilst the New Testament christologically and pneumatologically fills out the accounts of creation in the Hebrew Bible, the Genesis accounts of creation form the basis of Gunton's understanding of God's establishing action in creation. Genesis 1 provides three models of God's pluriform creating action that progress Gunton's theology of creation and develop the foundation of his understanding of creation and humanity as *imago Dei*. Human beings are made in the image of God and called to be God's representatives who extend God's royal administration of the world. Such theological exegesis of scripture marks Gunton's later writings and, along with more sustained engagement with theological sources, shows his commitment to an examination of divine action in the economy and its creaturely fruit.

Before exploring the biblical and theological basis of Gunton's theology of culture, this chapter begins with an examination of Gunton's trinitarian theology of mediation. Mediation is, as Christoph Schwöbel suggests, the hinge on which Christian doctrine turns in Gunton's thought as it explains the relation of the immanent being of the triune God to the trinitarian economy.[5] The development of Gunton's trinitarian theology of mediation results in a number of important progressions in his trinitarian articulations that internally strengthen earlier claims and extend his theology of culture. Having established Gunton's trinitarian theology of mediation, the next section examines his theological method in

---

5. Schwöbel, "Gunton on Creation," 61–5.

relation to mediation. The progression towards a trinitarian theology of mediation results in a more sustained focus on divine action in the economy and its creaturely fruit, which Gunton establishes through biblical and theological reflections. The final section explores Gunton's theological exegesis of Genesis, which, interpreted in the light of the New Testament, forms the basis of his trinitarian theology of creation and human culture. Gunton's theology of culture is only comprehensible through his account of God, creation, humanity, and the project of creation.

Gunton's Trinitarian Theology of Mediation, Creation, and Culture

"The question of mediation," Gunton remarks, "is a central one for all theology."[6] If we hold that the eternal God is ontologically distinct from temporal creation, there is a need for some form of mediation. Mediation is the way in which we denote the form God's action takes in relation to that which is not God, "the way, that is, by which the actions of one who is creator take form in a world that is of an entirely different order from God because he made it so."[7] It is important to note the emphasis mediation places upon the distinction of creator and creature, and the personal action of the triune God in and towards the world. At the heart of Gunton's theology of mediation is his methodological commitment, which holds that "Christian theology is devoted to the articulation of a gospel involving divine action in and towards the world."[8] Gunton's progression to a trinitarian theology of mediation involves a movement towards a sustained focus on divine action in and towards the world as it is attested in scripture. Schwöbel helpfully summarizes Gunton's emphasis upon mediation in his later writings as the hinge on which Christian doctrine turns.

> In his later writings, Gunton uses predominantly the concept of mediation to account for the way in which the triune being of God shapes the trinitarian action of God so as to create the world which is destined to find its fulfilment in communion with the triune God. Mediation becomes the category that explains how the immanent being of the Triune God and the trinitarian economy are related.[9]

Big doors swing on small hinges, and Schwöbel argues that mediation is the hinge on which the doors of Gunton's theology swing. Mediation is the hinge for Gunton's delineation of the act and being of the triune God, as well as the being and act of creation.[10] A trinitarian theology of mediation enables Christian

---

6. Gunton, *Father, Son and Holy Spirit*, 164.
7. Gunton, *The Christian Faith*, 5.
8. Gunton, *Father, Son and Holy Spirit*, 93.
9. Schwöbel, "Gunton on Creation," 63.
10. Schwöbel, "Gunton on Creation," 63.

theology to affirm God as the sole creator and Lord of what occurs in creation, as well as creation's relative independence from God; a freedom to be itself through relationship with God.[11] The otherness and relatedness of God and creation are at the crux of Gunton's theology, while his theology of mediation enables them to be understood as correlatives rather than rivals.[12] John Webster agrees with Schwöbel, and maintains that the major preoccupation of Gunton's mature work is finding "a more satisfactory way of relating God and creation;" his constructive trinitarian resolution to this relation is his theology of mediation.[13] Likewise, Paul Cumin concludes that a trinitarian theology of mediation stands at the heart of Gunton's theology, and William Whitney goes so far as to suggest that a summary label of Gunton's theological programme is, "A Trinitarian Mediation of Creation."[14] While many note the importance of mediation in Gunton's theology, the reach of his theology of mediation has not been fully exhausted.

Whilst Gunton uses the term "mediation" with great suggestiveness, Webster argues there is a need for greater precision and analytical accuracy.[15] Webster does not clarify in detail where there is a need for greater precision in relation to mediation, but his concerns raise definitional questions regarding Gunton's use of mediation. Cumin offers a helpful exposition of Gunton's theology of mediation, but suggests we understand communion and mediation as functionally the same concept in Gunton's work.[16] This might be true as a global statement in Gunton's thought, but it risks universalizing the concept of mediation. The specific content of mediation in Gunton's thought emerges from the details of *how* God relates creatures to Godself. Whilst mediation is a hinge term for the relation of God and creation, the shape and content of mediation are determined by the differentiated unity of the action of the Son and the Spirit in the economy.

Gunton's focus on the action of the Son and the Spirit delineates the trinitarian shape of divine mediation and what is understood to be mediated: God's redemption and perfection of the creation by the Father's two hands. Whilst upholding the ontological distinctiveness and relatedness of creator and creation, mediation points forward to God's action in the incarnation and reconciliation of all things in Christ and the Spirit's action in creation and the Church to bring all things to their eschatological destiny in relationship with God.[17] Mediation therefore includes not only what is mediated but also the shape of that mediation. The shape of trinitarian mediation is best understood by an explication of Gunton's trinitarian theology

---

11. Gunton, *Father, Son and Holy Spirit*, 94–5.
12. Gunton, *The Promise of Trinitarian Theology*, 202. For an understanding of the synergy of the otherness and relatedness of creation in Gunton's theology of mediation, see Cumin, *Christ at the Crux*, 170.
13. Webster, "Systematic Theology after Barth," 259.
14. Cumin, *Christ at the Crux*, 170. See also Whitney, *Problem and Promise*, 99.
15. Webster, "Systematic Theology after Barth," 261.
16. Cumin, *Christ at the Crux*, 183.
17. Schwöbel, "Gunton on Creation," 64.

of creation, Christology, pneumatology, theological anthropology, election, and ecclesiology. Mediation is not only the hinge on which the relation of the eternal God and temporal creation swings, but, as Schwöbel observes, it is the hinge on which Gunton's account of salvation history turns.[18] The action of the Son and the Spirit in the creation, and the relationship between the immanent and economic Trinity, *is* the theological detail of Gunton's account of trinitarian mediation. Gunton's trinitarian theology of mediation clarifies his theological method and his commitment to divine action in the economy as the beginning point for theology, as he believes we know God's eternal being only from the revelation of God's action.

Gunton's later writings are marked by a progression from trinitarian analogies of being to a trinitarian theology of mediation. Holmes notes the development in Gunton's work and suggests that his progression towards a theology of mediation avoids some of the social trinitarian risks that are attendant in his trinitarian analogies.[19] This movement towards a trinitarian theology of mediation occurs at some point in the mid-1990s, after *The One, the Three and the Many*.

An indicative example of the progression towards mediation is Gunton's use of mediation in the second edition of *The Promise of Trinitarian Theology*. The first edition of *The Promise of Trinitarian Theology* was published in 1991. In this edition, Gunton employs mediation eight times, mostly to critique Augustine's perceived tendency to replace the mediatorship of Christ with angelic intermediaries or an account of the Church as an institution mediating grace.[20] The second edition of *The Promise of Trinitarian Theology* was published in 1997, and the new preface and two additional chapters have seventeen references to mediation. After noting that "suddenly we are all trinitarians, or so it would seem," and cautioning against some of the immanentist developments that threaten the necessary ontological distinctions between divine and human being, Gunton moves on to affirm an understanding of mediation developed from Irenaeus. It is the action of the Son and the Spirit, Gunton now asserts, "to mediate the will and work of the Father in perfecting what can be called the project of creation."[21] The value of a theology of the Trinity lies in it enabling a rethinking of topics like theology and culture rather than articulating a privileged view of God. Two new major chapters are added to strengthen Gunton's quest for "a concrete rather than theoretical trinitarianism."[22] These two additional chapters focus upon the relation between Church, culture,

18. Schwöbel, "Gunton on Creation," 65.

19. Holmes, "Towards the *Analogia Personae et Relationis*," 42-3.

20. See Gunton, *The Promise of Trinitarian Theology*, 6; 8; 35-6; 51; and 97. There is one reference to the love of the Father that is mediated by the Son and the Spirit on page 82.

21. Gunton, *The Promise of Trinitarian*, xxi-xxii. Likewise, in *Theology Through the Theologians* it is the chapters first published from the mid-nineties and after *The One, the Three and the Many* that feature extended reflection on mediation. See Gunton, *Theology Through the Theologians*, Chs. 7 and 8. As an indication of the rise in the importance of mediation, there are 105 occurrences of mediation (and its derivatives) in Gunton, *Intellect and Action* and 172 occurrences in Gunton, *Father, Son and Holy Spirit*.

22. Gunton, *The Promise of Trinitarian Theology*, xxix.

and the atonement. Importantly, Gunton notes that these chapters "demonstrate the impact of not so much arguing from the Trinity to the world by analogy as thinking trinitarianly through the focus provided by the action of God in the world mediated by his 'two hands.'"[23] This emphasis upon divine action in the economy is the *leitmotif* of Gunton's later writings and his theological method.

Mediation and Method

The biblical account of God is oriented to action, not contemplation, and this, for Gunton, determines the way in which we must consider God's being.[24] God's action in the economy is divine self-disclosure and self-interpretation, and this, therefore, must be our focus. "We must place ourselves theologically where the action is, because if we turn away from God's actual historical self-identification in Jesus, we simply manufacture an idol, or a series of idols."[25] Whilst Gunton always held divine self-revelation as the proper ground of theology, especially against *a priori* accounts that determine rational limits of divine-disclosure, his later writings strengthen his commitment to this method and its fruits. As a result of this renewed commitment, Gunton's later writings are marked less by the use of philosophical and non-theological sources to buttress theological insights, and more by sustained engagements with the scriptural narrative of divine revelation and theological sources.

Gunton's later writings show most clearly that his theological method is one of commitment to God's action in the world. Given his untimely death, Gunton did not complete his projected multi-volume dogmatics. However, some of Gunton's colleagues and friends hold draft versions of the first volume of this work, which Gunton presented at King's College, and quote it in their publications. Reading their quotations of the draft enables us to garner insights of Gunton's unpublished work. The provisional title of the first volume captures the emphasis on divine action in the world: *A Christian Dogmatic Theology. Volume One: The Triune God. A Doctrine of the Trinity as Though Jesus Makes a Difference.*[26] Excerpts quoted from these drafts reinforce Gunton's theological beginning point, "because it is through the economy that scripture's God makes himself known, an account of the economy is essential to any doctrine of God's being."[27] This is further detailed in his methodology in which he holds, "We shall approach the doctrine of the Trinity according to the way of knowing, beginning with the economy of the Spirit and moving from there to the economy of the Son, the economy of the Father, and thence to the doctrine of the Triunity of God."[28] This method is an

---

23. Gunton, *The Promise of Trinitarian Theology*, xxix–xxx.
24. Gunton, *Act and Being*, 40–1.
25. Gunton, *Father, Son and Holy Spirit*, 26.
26. Jenson, "A Decision Tree of Colin Gunton's Thinking," 16 n. 2.
27. Quoted in Cumin, "The Taste of Cake," 65.
28. Quoted in Cumin, "The Taste of Cake," 66.

extension of the approach Gunton develops in *The Christian Faith*, which is a precursor to his projected dogmatics.[29] As noted, the assumption that theology must methodologically begin in the economy is now debated in contemporary theology. However, this book is concerned with understanding Gunton's trinitarian theology of culture through his methodological commitments which emerged in his theological context, rather than contemporary concerns.

The New Testament does not give a doctrine of the Trinity, Gunton maintains, but it does give a trinitarian conception of mediation through divine action in the economy.[30] *The Christian Faith*, which is Gunton's forerunner to his intended multi-volume dogmatics, begins with nine chapters on divine action in the world. It starts with the Father's work in creation mediated by the two hands and then moves to an exploration of the mediation of the Son and the Spirit that traverses all God's economic actions including ecclesiology. It is only after the exploration of the differential unity of trinitarian action in the economy that Gunton moves to a final chapter on the immanent Trinity and the triune God of Christian confession, who is revealed in the economy. "The nine foregoing chapters of this book have been designed to refute this [speculative reflections on the immanent Trinity] practically in an account of divine action in the world conceived in thoroughgoing trinitarian terms."[31] An orientation to divine action affirms, for Gunton, God's personal and loving relation with the good creation in which God gives himself to be known as the creator, redeemer, and perfecter of creation. "The theology of the economic Trinity sketched in chapters 1–9 provides an account of the trinitarian way in which God creates, shapes and perfects his creation in and through time."[32] Gunton's understanding of mediation and his commitment to a method that begins with the divine economy are in large part the result of an Irenaean turn in his thought.

Mediation and the Irenaean Turn in Gunton's Theology

In Gunton's progression to a trinitarian theology of mediation, he finds a model theologian in Irenaeus whose work is foundational for his account of divine action in the economy.[33] In his earlier writings, Gunton makes sparing use of Irenaeus

---

29. Gunton, *The Christian Faith*, xi.
30. Gunton, *The Christian Faith*, 183.
31. Gunton, *The Christian Faith*, 180.
32. Gunton, *The Christian Faith*, 180.
33. Gunton deploys the two hands motif as early as 1989, and he celebrates Irenaeus' use of *creatio ex nihilo* to defend the ontological distinction of creator and creation against the Gnostics. Similarly, Irenaeus' view of the eschatological directedness of creation appears in seed form in the late 1980s before germinating into full bloom in his later theology. See Colin E. Gunton, "The Church on Earth: The Roots of Community," in *On Being the Church: Essays on the Christian Community*, ed. Colin E. Gunton and Daniel W. Hardy (Edinburgh: T&T Clark, 1989), 73.

though many Irenaean motifs were nascent in his trinitarian relational ontology. It was in the mid-1990s, after *The One, the Three and the Many*, that Irenaeus' theology provided the framework for Gunton's theological method, doctrine of creation, employment of the two hands motif, and stress upon divine action.[34]

Gunton did not always hold Irenaeus in high esteem, and he warns against idealizing Irenaeus' theology.[35] In one important essay from the early 1990s, Gunton holds Irenaeus to be the root cause of the rationalistic view of the *imago Dei* that asserts reason as the chief ontological characteristic and criterion of humanity's likeness to God.[36] Likewise, whilst Gunton celebrates Irenaeus' theory that Adam and Eve were created childlike and developed through time, he notes that it is "not in every way satisfactory."[37]

He does not expand on what aspects are not satisfactory, but as Gunton's thought progresses any reservations regarding the orientation of humanity and creation towards perfection are resolved. Irenaeus' account of recapitulation and the eschatological orientation of the created order become vital to Gunton's understanding of creation as a project. In Gunton's early work, Irenaeus provides important suggestions for Gunton's attempts to reshape the tradition against varieties of Gnosticism, but his theology of mediation is not the *leitmotif* it becomes in his later work.[38] By the late 1990s and early 2000s, the redemption and perfection of humanity and the created order through time is unreservedly celebrated as a vital Irenaean insight. "This is an Irenaean theme: Adam and Eve's childlike nature implies a growth to maturity; but our fallenness, our turning backwards, requires the incarnation, death and resurrection of the eternal Son of God if a way forward is to be found."[39] The progression in Gunton's theology to a theology of mediation is marked by the rise of Irenaeus' theology as the framework for Gunton's emphasis on divine action in the economy. In this progression, Irenaeus moves from being an interesting contributor to Gunton's quest for trinitarian relational ontology to the greatest theologian of creation that the Church has ever had, and a model for all systematic theologians.[40]

34. Gunton is no doubt influenced by Douglas Farrow's doctoral study on Irenaeus, which he completed in 1994 under Gunton's supervision. Douglas Farrow, "Ascension and Ecclesia: On the Significance of the Doctrine of Ascension for Ecclesiology and Christian Cosmology" (PhD diss., King's College, London, 1994). In stating and exploring the Irenaean turn in Gunton's though, I am indebted to Stephen Holmes' landmark analysis of the developments in Gunton's thought. See Holmes, "Towards the *Analogia Personae et Relationis*," 32–48.

35. Gunton, *The One, the Three and the Many*, 53.
36. Gunton, *The Promise of Trinitarian Theology*, 101–2.
37. Gunton, *The Promise of Trinitarian Theology*, 115–16.
38. Gunton, *The One, the Three and the Many*, 2.
39. Gunton, *Intellect and Action*, 109.
40. Gunton, *The Christian Faith*, 10. On Irenaeus as a model for all systematic theologians, see Colin E. Gunton, "Historical and Systematic Theology," in *The Cambridge Companion to Christian Doctrine*, ed. Colin E. Gunton (Cambridge: Cambridge University Press, 1997), 15.

In Irenaeus, Gunton finds an ally against all forms of dualism, real or perceived, and a counterpart in the battle against Gnostic forces whose abstract and immaterial trajectories undermine the doctrine of creation.[41] What is necessary is an account of mediation, but this requires a careful delineation, as different means of mediation bring with them very different concepts of how God is known.[42]

Gnosticism is an archetypical heresy, in Gunton's evaluation, that reappears in various forms, especially in Western culture, philosophy, and theology. The dispute between Irenaeus and the Gnostics is a dispute about mediation and what is mediated.[43] The Gnostics hold a mediation of ascent out of the physical and material world, which they view as marred by corruption and decay, into the higher spiritual world.[44] The apportionment of good and evil in the created order is unfair, and the spiritual God of Christ has nothing to do with the marred and corrupt material world which is the result of the bungling efforts of the Hebrew Bible's creator. Redemption is by way of ascent out of the material world and into the higher spiritual realm and is achieved by a variety of angelic intermediaries.[45] Within the Gnostic hierarchy of being, the angels are divine, but not as divine as the spiritual God of Christ, and they are therefore able to mediate between the higher spiritual realm and the lower material realm.[46] The result is a twin ethics of disembodiment: the ethic of renunciation of embodied life, and the ethic of self-indulgence, both of which suffer from an inability to be at home within the world. These trends, Gunton believes, are replicated in the resurgent Gnosticism of modern sensate Western culture, which also exhibits an inability to be at home within the world.[47]

In contrast to the Gnostic theology of ascent out of the physical and material world, Irenaeus' emphasis is upon the incarnation of the eternal Word as the basis of a theology of descent into the world.[48] God comes into personal relation with the creation through the eternal Word of God incarnate, and reveals that whatever the effects of sin, the created order, and human life within it, are of supreme importance to God.[49] Irenaeus is, in Gunton's assessment, the Church's greatest theologian of creation. His account of the Son and the Spirit who mediate the Father's work of creation enables an understanding of God's free immanent involvement within the world as well as God's transcendent action towards the world.[50] By examining the action of the Son and the Spirit, Irenaeus upholds

---

41. Gunton, *The Christian Faith*, x. See also Gunton, *The Triune Creator*, 2.
42. Gunton, *Father, Son and Holy Spirit*, 164.
43. Gunton, *Father, Son and Holy Spirit*, 164.
44. Gunton, *Father, Son and Holy Spirit*, 165.
45. Gunton, *The Christian Faith*, 23.
46. Gunton, *Father, Son and Holy Spirit*, 164–5.
47. Gunton, *The Triune Creator*, 227. See also Gunton, *Father, Son and Holy Spirit*, 9–10; and Douglas Farrow, "Gunton and Irenaeus," 240–1.
48. Gunton, *Father, Son and Holy Spirit*, 165.
49. Gunton, *Father, Son and Holy Spirit*, 30.
50. Gunton, *The Christian Faith*, 10.

the unity of creation, redemption, and perfection. This unity also enables him to uphold creation's goodness and meaningfulness which are eschatologically ordered towards perfection. Irenaeus' greatness stems not only from his account of mediation, but also from his account of the distinct ontologies of creator and creation that enable their free relatedness.

The Gnostic hierarchy of being confuses the distinct ontologies of creator and creation. In contrast, Gunton celebrates Irenaeus' account of *creatio ex nihilo* as a triumph of Christian ontology. Irenaeus holds that nothing is co-eternal with God and God relies on nothing outside of his eternal being to create the world. God is sovereign and replete in the perfection of God's being as Father, Son, and Spirit. God is *a se*, and does not need the world because God is alive with self-moved life. Creation, therefore, is a sovereign and free act of God's love, who wills that there be something rather than nothing.[51] The creation is not co-eternal with God and has a temporal beginning and a spatial limitation. In Irenaeus' classic Christian ontology there are only two ontological realities: eternal creator and contingent creation; God, and all else that God has made in the created order.[52] The creation exists because God wills it to be so, and God remains sovereign over it as Lord. This, Cumin notes, is a basic tenet of the gospel according to Gunton. "That God remains distinctly himself at the same time as sustaining everything else as itself was for him [Gunton] the most basic and therefore least appealing item of a gospel against the grain of a sin-bent creation."[53] In this duality without dualism, there is no hierarchy of being and no need for intermediaries between God and the created order because the Son and the Spirit mediate the Father's loving presence and action through personal relation. Irenaeus' account of the freedom of God from creation establishes the sovereignty of God and the relative freedom of creation in its createdness, a freedom established and upheld by God's personal and loving relation with what God has made.

Irenaeus' account of *creatio ex nihilo* establishes the free relatedness of creator and creation, and asserts the relative freedom (*Selbständigkeit*) of creation in its createdness as a subsistence it receives from God.[54] God alone has being *a se* and is alive with self-moved life, whereas the creation is contingent and utterly dependent on God's gracious action *ad extra* for its life. But this distinction is not the Gnostic opposition of a higher spiritual being and a lower material being. God deems the creation to be very good in its createdness and, apart from sin, God and the world are not opposed realities.[55] God gives creation its own proper being and Irenaeus' Christian ontology derives from the goodness and integrity that God gives creation and its createdness. The distinction is between uncreated and created

---

51. Gunton, *The Triune Creator*, 9.
52. Gunton, *The Triune Creator*, 54.
53. Cumin, *Christ at the Crux*, 169–70.
54. Gunton, *Father, Son and Holy Spirit*, 95.
55. Gunton, *Act and Being*, 47.

reality, a duality without dualism.⁵⁶ From the freedom of the triune God's perfect life and love, God wills the existence of creation for its own sake. Whilst creation is entirely contingent on God for its ongoing existence, it is given its own form of freedom to be and become itself in relation to God.⁵⁷ The Christian account of ontology upholds the necessary space between the aseity and sovereignty of God and the goodness of creation, including its freedom to become what God intends it to be in relation to God.

> For the world to be truly the world, it needs a God who is both other than it and who is able to love it for itself, because it is the world to which God has given being. That is the heart of the matter. Because God as Father, Son and Spirit is already, from eternity, a structure of love – of persons in communion – the world may be brought into relation with that God without having its own reality threatened or diminished.⁵⁸

Creation's temporality and spatiality are its glory; it is a universe ordered in space and through time by God's love which enables the world to be itself in its contingent created being.⁵⁹ It is God's otherness to creation that ensures the possibility of God's free relation to the creation. "Only that which is other than something else can be related to it. Otherness and relation can therefore be seen as correlatives rather than rivals."⁶⁰ Discussion of God's otherness from and relatedness to creation raises again the question of mediation. For Gunton, as for Irenaeus, the content of this mediation is determined by the action of the Son and the Spirit who are the Father's two hands.

The sovereign and free God comes into relation with that which is not God by the mediating work of the Father's two hands, the Son and the Spirit, who are themselves substantially God. Gunton utilizes Irenaeus' two hands motif to describe the trinitarian shape of divine action in the economy. The Father's work in creation is mediated by his two hands, the Son and the Spirit, who uphold the creation in loving and personal relation with its creator. Scripture has "a disarmingly personal" way of representing the Father's action in the Son and the Spirit.⁶¹ The two hands motif establishes that mediation is a personal divine action, not the action of Gnostic intermediaries or the causal action of a distant clock-maker deity. God's

---

56. Colin E. Gunton, "Flesh and Spirit after Darwin," in *Beyond Determinism and Reductionism: Genetic Science and the Person*, ed. Mark L. Y. Chan and Roland Chia (Adelaide: ATF, 2003), 49–50.
57. Gunton, *The Triune Creator*, 9–10.
58. Gunton, *Father, Son and Holy Spirit*, 31.
59. Gunton, *Father, Son and Holy Spirit*, 140.
60. Gunton, *The Promise of Trinitarian Theology*, 202.
61. Gunton, *The Triune Creator*, 44.

action is personal action that holds the world in relation through the Son and the Spirit and directs it to its eschatological end in communion with God.[62]

> I do not think that we can do better than hold to Irenaeus' straightforward characterization of God's action in the world: the Father works, as we have already heard, by means of his two hands, the Son and the Spirit .... When you use your hands, to greet someone or to write a letter, it is you who are doing it. "God's right arm has gained the victory ... " That is not mere metaphor, but a metaphor that conveys a great and important truth. Our God's action is not immediate but mediated action.[63]

The action of the Son and the Spirit is a differentiated unity, but Gunton seeks greater differentiation than Irenaeus who tends to "place the two hands side by side."[64] Certainly, the two hands do not act separately, "like someone holding a baby in one hand and trying to bang in a nail with the other."[65] All divine action is the unified action of the one God, which is mediated in the economy in a twofold way by the Son and the Spirit.[66] But the unified action of the Son and the Spirit is distinguishable action and not merely the action of God *simpliciter*. "It remains the case, however, that if we fail to identify three distinct agents, we are not being true to the biblical witness."[67] An exploration of the biblical witness to the economic actions of the Son and the Spirit reveals they are united in their action, but they are given distinct offices and distinct forms of action in the mediation of the Father's will. Irenaeus' emphasis upon the economic action of the Son and the Spirit reinforces the approach Gunton indwells most fully in his later writings.

In Gunton's reading, which is based on received scholarship at the time, Irenaeus is an economic theologian who gives little attention to the immanent Trinity.[68] Whilst this reading of Irenaeus may now be contested, Gunton finds in Irenaeus an affirmation of his own focus upon divine action in the economy.[69]

---

62. Gunton, *Theology Through the Theologians*, 145–6.
63. Gunton, *Father, Son and Holy Spirit*, 79–80.
64. Gunton, *Father, Son and Holy Spirit*, 81. Gunton's usage of the two hands motif may have lacked some of the historical detail and nuance of Irenaeus' original conception. For a fuller historical account of Irenaeus' two hands motif, see Anthony Briggman, *Irenaeus of Lyons and the Holy Spirit* (Oxford: OUP, 2012), 104–25. Douglas Farrow argues that Gunton's use of Irenaeus is somewhat formulaic and his account of Irenaeus is idealized as an anti-type to Augustine. Farrow, "Gunton and Irenaeus," 245–8.
65. Gunton, *Father, Son and Holy Spirit*, 80.
66. Gunton, *Father, Son and Holy Spirit*, 80.
67. Gunton, *Act and Being*, 143.
68. Gunton, *The Promise of Trinitarian Theology*, xxii.
69. Jackson Lashier questions the scholarly assumption that Irenaeus was a theologian of the economy. Lashier instead argues that Irenaeus not only held to a doctrine of the immanent Trinity, his views of the economic activity of the Trinity are founded on the immanent relations of Father, Son, and Spirit. See Jackson Lashier, *Irenaeus on the Trinity*, Supplements to Vigiliae Christianae 127 (Leiden: Brill, 2014), 189–221.

Irenaeus' orientation to the economy is a strength rather than a weakness as it provides a careful self-limitation to scripture, whose limits later abstract doctrines of the immanent Trinity tend to transgress.[70] Christian dogma, Gunton argues, is only Christian when it is truly a summary of the gospel; "that is to say, proper specifications of the being of the God of Israel and Jesus and his action towards and in the world."[71] Because of this orientation to divine action in and towards the world, Irenaeus' theology does not adhere to the conceptual relationships expected of systematic theology. Irenaeus' theological method, Gunton argues, defies later scholastic logic and metaphysics, because theology is gospel before it is a system. The stress upon the economic action of God calls into question excessive systematizations determined in advance of divine self-disclosure. Faith has its own logic and strict adherence to systematic conventions risks veiling the gospel that God unveils through divine action in the economy.[72] Irenaeus' theology is systematic only in a weak sense, as the drive to articulate intra-systematic conceptual relations is secondary to his concern to articulate the extent and coherence of God's economic action.

Irenaeus' unsystematic approach to theology accords well with Gunton's dissenting tendencies that often question the tradition through an engagement with divine action in the world. Gunton certainly holds to the need for the internal unity, connectedness, and balance of theological claims, but these may not be best expressed in theological systematizations that can be determined in advance of revelation. Truth is always eschatological for Gunton, and the usefulness of systematic theology is measured by how far it can anticipate God's eschatological perfection of all things. Whilst Gunton is certainly a theologian of the tradition, he is not beholden to it and he gives precedence to God's self-disclosure that is mediated to us through God's action in creation.[73] "Systematic theology takes shape in the world as the discipline concerned to engage with the reality and implications of the economy of divine action in creation, reconciliation, and redemption as it is recorded in Scripture."[74] Before examining Gunton's theological exegesis of Genesis 1 and 2, there is a need to set his criticisms of the doctrine of creation in the context of his day and the dualistic and abstractive tendencies he attempts to overcome. It is against these tendencies that Gunton develops his quest for a more concrete trinitarianism and his theological account of culture as the right human habitation of creation.

Culture within the Bounds of Creation

Gunton's later writings on creation and culture are a constructive alternative to the dualistic and abstractive tendencies he perceives in the tradition and Western culture. The progression from trinitarian analogies of being to a trinitarian

---

70. Gunton, *The Promise of Trinitarian Theology*, xxii.
71. Gunton, *Intellect and Action*, 25–6.
72. Gunton, *Intellect and Action*, 13.
73. Gunton, *Intellect and Action*, 39.
74. Gunton, *Intellect and Action*, 43.

theology of mediation results also in an extension of earlier analyses of theology *and* culture to include a trinitarian theology *of* culture.

Theology and culture projects have taken various forms throughout theological history, but they share a common misconception of God's relation to creation. Human culture is oftentimes analysed in independence from God's providential action within it, and then, as a second step, contrasted with an account of the gospel to assess which aspects of culture conform to the gospel or not. However, as Gunton notes, human action in independence from God's prevenient action is almost a definition of sin.[75] There is a need for a theological account of human culture that is set within the wider context of the doctrine of creation, and especially God's providential action in and towards creation.

The doctrine of creation makes universal claims about reality and a theological account of human culture is best understood in relation to God's establishing and providential action in and with the creation. In his later writings, Gunton constructs a trinitarian theology of culture in which human culture is something that God creates, redeems, and perfects through the action of the Son and the Spirit. Moreover, God creates the world in such a way that it is oriented towards an eschatological perfection in the new creation that is greater than the original creation. Through God's action, human culture is enabled to contribute to the divine perfection of creation. Such human action is not independent from God, but is a sub-agency that God grants in God's redemption and perfection of the creation. In the context of humanity's cultural calling in Genesis 1, Gunton suggests "culture ... is that set of activities in which those made in the image of God share in the divine perfecting of that which was made in the beginning."[76] He substantiates this claim through a thoroughgoing trinitarian account of culture that emerges from his exposition of the mediating action of the Son and the Spirit in creation.

Creation and createdness form the basis of Gunton's trinitarian theology of culture, as culture involves God's intended meaning and purpose for creation and humanity. The universal scope of the Christian gospel means that an examination of the doctrine of creation involves all reality and its constitution in relation to God. The doctrine of creation provides a common foundation for human cultural endeavour—science, ethics, politics, and art.[77] An understanding of creation arises from engagement with biblical sources and takes shape in relation to, and conversation with, the culture of the day.[78]

There is in our day, however, a crisis in belief in the reality of creation. Developments in modernity and postmodernity, examined in Chapter 1, precipitate a loss of confidence in the belief that God has set the world on its foundations and that it is the proper place for cultural endeavour and the pursuit of truth. The right response, Gunton holds, is the reaffirmation of the rational

---

75. Gunton, "Reformation Accounts," 80.
76. Gunton, "Reformation Accounts," 80.
77. Gunton, *A Brief Theology of Revelation*, 55. See also Rae, "Colin E. Gunton," 207.
78. Gunton, *The Triune Creator*, 41–3.

viability of the doctrine of creation and an exploration of creation's meaning that is given by God's establishing and providential action.[79]

It is Gunton's exploration of God's establishing and providential action that forms the basis of his trinitarian theology of culture. The following section examines Gunton's account of Genesis 1 and 2 and his understanding of God's establishing action in creation. Chapters 4 and 5 explore his understanding of human culture in the context of God's providential action in the mediation of the Son and the Spirit. Providence claims that God not only upholds the world in being, but directs the world, which remains essentially fragile given the fall, towards its eschatological end by involvement in the daily life of his creatures.[80] Providence is God's conservation of creation understood in eschatological light through the mediating action of the Son and the Spirit.[81]

Gunton's account of the triune God's establishing and providential action is best understood in the light of the dualistic and discarnate trajectories it seeks to overcome. The doctrine of creation, Gunton argues, suffers from a long Babylonian captivity; an exile from trinitarian reflection in which it is submerged by foreign elements.[82] The long story of creation's Babylonian captivity is unified by non-trinitarian accounts of creation as an ontologically inferior material realm in contrast to an ontologically superior immaterial realm. The result is that God and material creation are negatively related, and redemption is by way of ascent from the material world into immateriality. "The effective quiescence of Christology and pneumatology in the structuring of Western theologies of creation leaves a vacuum which non-biblical ontologies rush to fill."[83] Without the necessary accounts of divine action in creation, the doctrine develops under the influence of arbitrary and impersonal forces. The action of the Son and the Spirit is crowded out by hierarchical pagan ontologies, and there is a breach between creation and salvation.[84] These forces take particular shape at different times in history, but share a common undermining of the reality and goodness of creation.

In his own setting, Gunton views the scientists of the modern era as effectively the theologians of creation.[85] Science is both liberator from Christendom's obsession with eternal heaven, and, as argued in Chapter 1, enslaver to new forms of heteronomies. Gunton celebrates the rise of science and its valuable insights into the rationality of the material world, but distinguishes this from the rise of scientism. Scientism is the backdrop of Gunton's day, and is marked by "the modernist heresy" that assumes human reason can provide objective knowledge

---

79. Gunton, *The Christian Faith*, x.
80. Gunton, *The Christian Faith*, 20-1.
81. Gunton, *The Christian Faith*, 36.
82. Gunton, *The Triune Creator*, 97.
83. Gunton, *The Triune Creator*, 102.
84. Gunton, *The Triune Creator*, 115-16. See also Gunton, *Father, Son and Holy Spirit*, 135-6.
85. Gunton, *The Triune Creator*, 125.

of all reality.[86] This mode of enquiry separates the rational human subject from the rest of creation, which is viewed as an inanimate object.

Whilst the form of alienation from reality is different from Gnosticism, as eternal heaven is no longer the focus, the detached and dispassionate human knower remains dualistically divided from the created reality it seeks to know. The world operates by the laws of nature, and is knowable quite apart from God. If there is a God, then God is the *Deus ex machina* who, like a master clock-maker, designs an intricate mechanistic world and leaves it to its own devices. God's ongoing providential government of the world is undermined, and the world is wholly explicable by material causation and the impersonal forces of the laws of nature.[87] Creation's *telos* is determined by impersonal causal forces and human progress, and divine action is restricted to the religious or historical realms. Providential action is reduced to little more than "finding gaps for divine action in an otherwise seamless web of causality."[88] Whilst much of post-Enlightenment thought held a utopian belief in human causal action, the brutality of the two world wars in the twentieth century put paid to the myth of human progress. In light of this Gunton argues for a return to the biblical doctrine of providence.[89] It is in the context of God's originating and providential action that Gunton's theology of human culture develops.

Central to Gunton's doctrine of culture is an affirmation of embodied life within the creator's good world. In place of the perceived deistic thought forms which prevailed in the English theological scene, Gunton seeks to develop an account of creation which stresses God's personal relation and action in and towards the good creation that humanity indwells. A distinctive Christian theology, according to Gunton, holds together three important themes: creation as an article of the creed; creation out of nothing; and creation "as the work of the whole Trinity, Father, Son and Holy Spirit – [which] are in some way bound up with each other, both historically and systematically."[90] These three themes, Schwobel argues, comprise the Wittgensteinian depth grammar of Gunton's systematic expression of creation which provides a wider domain of language for all surface grammar.[91]

The doctrine of creation is an article of the creed, a matter of belief that develops as the Christian response to divine revelation. The doctrine of creation is therefore not the result of self-evident natural theology nor the outcome of

---

86. Rae, "Colin E. Gunton," 206.

87. Gunton, *The Christian Faith*, 20–3. See also Gunton, *The Triune Creator*, 132–4, and Rae, "Colin E. Gunton," 209.

88. Gunton, *The Christian Faith*, 29–30.

89. Gunton, *The Christian Faith*, 33–7.

90. Gunton, *The Triune Creator*, 9. See also Colin E. Gunton, "The Doctrine of Creation," in *The Cambridge Companion to Christian Doctrine*, ed. Colin E. Gunton (Cambridge: Cambridge University Press, 1997), 141–3.

91. Schwöbel, "Gunton on Creation," 62. See Ludwig Wittgenstein, *Philosophical Investigations*, trans. G. E. M. Anscombe, 2nd ed. (Oxford: Basil Books, 1958), 168.

scientific endeavour and discovery; it is a faith claim that is "part of the fabric of the Christian response to revelation."[92] There are no *a priori* accounts of creation in advance of scripture's witness. Furthermore scripture's witness to God and God's creating action "has a disarmingly personal way of representing that action."[93] The gospel is not a system, and rather than beginning with an abstract and *a priori* account of God, Gunton begins his account of creation and culture with a theological exegesis of Genesis 1 and 2 and God's establishing action. The complex pattern of mediation in Genesis 1 and 2 reveals the sovereign God's loving creation of all things which God deems to be "very good" in their createdness. God's love is displayed in the creation of all created reality, but especially of those made in God's image. It is humanity which is "granted the capacity to respond to his love and share in his work," and this is concentrated in humanity's cultural mandate. Humanity's cultural mandate is a command to make something of the world and extend God's royal governance of creation as God's priestly representatives in creation.

Creation is out of nothing, a claim that reveals not only the distinct nature of the eternal God and contingent creation, but also their relation. Whilst not an explicit biblical claim, *creatio ex nihilo* is a summary of scriptural affirmations of God's sovereignty as a whole.[94] The sovereign and free God is unconstrained by any forces, beings, or conditions external to God's eternal being, and from this utter freedom God creates and upholds creation through love. Creation is not an extension of God's being, but the result of God's loving will that there be a reality that is distinctly other than Godself. God creates through an externalization of the love that God is as Father, Son, and Spirit in an eternal communion as the one God, and wills that creation be free to be itself.[95] Creation derives from the love of God, not from impersonal and arbitrary causal forces. It is because creation is an act of love that creatures are good and valuable for their own sake. Createdness is not a defect of being, it is an intrinsic aspect of the goodness of created being. God is not negatively related to creation, but remains in personal and loving relation with the created order through the action of the Son and the Spirit, who enable creation to be itself in relation to God and all else.[96]

God the Father is the creator of all, and his loving work is mediated through his "two hands"—the Son and the Spirit.[97] Creation is therefore a work of the whole Trinity, whose united, yet distinct, action not only establishes the creation, but also upholds and directs the creation to an end that is greater than its beginning.

---

92. Gunton, "The Doctrine of Creation," 141. See also Rae, "Colin E. Gunton," 211.

93. Gunton, *The Triune God*, 44.

94. Gunton, *The Triune Creator*, 19–20. See also Gunton, *The Christian Faith*, 17–18; and Rae, "Colin E. Gunton," 213–18.

95. Gunton, *The Christian Faith*, 17–18.

96. Gunton, *The Christian Faith*, 18, 55–6. See also Gunton, "The Doctrine of Creation," 142–3.

97. Gunton, *The Christian Faith*, 55.

God's love for creation is expressed not through deterministic and impersonal forces, but through the personal and relational action of the Son and the Spirit.[98] According to the New Testament, creation's theo-logic is determined by the *Logos*, the one in whom all things in heaven and on earth came into being and are held in being (John 1:1-3; 14; Col 1:15-20; Heb 1:3).[99] Creation is therefore "structured by the very one who became incarnate and as such part of the created order of which we are speaking."[100] Christ's incarnation reveals God's purposes for humanity and creation, and it is through his recapitulation of Adam, enabled by the Spirit, that we can discern creation's eschatological direction. This emphasis on Christ's faithful humanity, which Chapter 4 examines in detail, opens vistas on humanity's cultural calling and human contributions to the restoration of the project of creation and its reorientation towards perfection.

Creation is a project ordered through time and in space towards eschatological perfection by the mediation of the Spirit whose life-giving action recreates and transforms the created world. Whilst the Son acts immanently within creation's structures, the Spirit's transcendental action is "a mark of God's freedom toward or *over against* it – from outside, so to speak."[101] The Holy Spirit is the perfecting cause of creation whose eschatological action sets creation free to be itself and move towards its perfection by bringing it into relation with God the Father through the Son.[102] Gunton argues throughout his career for a stronger pneumatology in theology and establishes this especially in his later writings.[103] As the eschatological particularizer, the Spirit, from time to time, enables created reality to anticipate its eschatological destiny—to be that which it was particularly created to be. "God the Father perfects his creation in and through time, through his Son and Spirit enabling particular acts, events, and things, from bits of pottery to noble and self-giving actions, to be themselves, and thus to be particular anticipations of the final perfecting of all things."[104] The Spirit's perfecting work is universal and enables all forms of human culture to anticipate the end. This universal work is concentrated

---

98. Gunton, *The Christian Faith*.
99. Gunton, *The Triune Creator*, 20–2. See also Rae, "Colin E. Gunton," 225–6.
100. Gunton, "The Doctrine of Creation," 142.
101. Gunton, *The Christian Faith*, 9–10.
102. Gunton, "The Doctrine of Creation," 142.
103. Gunton holds that "No trinitarian theology is adequate without attention first to the particular shape taken by the life, death and resurrection of the second person of the Trinity incarnate, Jesus of Nazareth, and second to the characteristic form taken by the work of the Spirit who, by relating people and things to Jesus, brings about their proper perfection." Colin E. Gunton, "The Indispensable God? The Sovereignty of God and the Problem of Modern Social Order," in *Beyond Mere Health: Theology and Health Care in a Secular Society*, ed. Hilary D. Regan, Rod Horsfield, and Gabrielle L. McMullan (Kew, VIC: Australian Theological Forum, 1996), 15. For a very helpful account, see Habets, "Gunton on Pneumatology," 121–3; and Stringer, "The Lord and Giver of Life."
104. Gunton, *The Christian Faith*, 119.

in the Church and Israel—God's particular communities of redemption who mediate God's mediating action.¹⁰⁵

Beginning with Abraham and extending through Israel and to the Church, God elects concrete communities to body forth God's universal purposes for creation in their particular communal life.¹⁰⁶ A pneumatologically conditioned account of election rebalances the doctrine towards its temporal significance and emphasizes God's calling of concrete communities of redemption who display God's purposes in their common life in community—their culture. "According to scripture, God's providing takes the form of his calling particular people and groups in order to bring about his promised salvation."¹⁰⁷ The Church's common life and culture are its worship, the offering to God, through Christ and in the Spirit, of the right human habitation of creation in community. In Chapter 5, I examine Gunton's account of election and ecclesiology in relation to the Church's common life and culture as an anticipation of God's eschatological purposes that are offered to God as a living sacrifice of praise through Christ. Chapter 6 then shows the fruitfulness of Gunton's insights on the Church's worship as culture and extends them through a biblical exploration of the Lord's Supper in 1 Corinthians 11 and the politics of the Church's belonging in community.

Gunton's later writings develop his theology of creation and culture through a more consistent examination of divine action in the economy as it is witnessed in scripture. In *The One, the Three and the Many*, Gunton claims that the modern cultural crisis can be summarized as an inadequate exegesis of the opening chapters of Genesis. He states that his book can be understood as an extended exegesis of the Genesis creation narratives.¹⁰⁸ However, Gunton's exegesis of the texts is minimal, and more generally scholars are critical of the lack of biblical exegesis in his work. Randal Lyle assesses Gunton's work against the criteria of inerrancy and finds it lacking. However, Gunton does not hold the same view as Lyle regarding inerrancy and, therefore, does not adhere to the criteria.¹⁰⁹ Nonetheless, others who do not hold to inerrancy still maintain that there is a paucity of exegetical

---

105. Gunton, *Father, Son and Holy Spirit*, 178–9.
106. Gunton, *The Christian Faith*, 30.
107. Gunton, *The Christian Faith*, 30.
108. Gunton, *The One, the Three and the Many*, 2; 215–16.
109. Lyle, "Social Trinitarianism as an Option for 21st Century Theology," 55–7. See Colin E. Gunton, *Christ and Creation: The 1990 Didsbury Lectures* (Carlisle: Paternoster Press, 1992), 11–16; Gunton, *A Brief Theology of Revelation*, 64–82; Colin E. Gunton, "'All Scripture is Inspired … '?," *The Princeton Seminary Bulletin*, 14 (1993): 240–53.

description in Gunton's work.[110] Perhaps the most telling critique comes from John Webster who suggests that Gunton's theology is least persuasive when it does not pause sufficiently long over exegetical or historical description.[111] Webster's criticism is important because of his close relationship with Gunton, and because others have reinforced Webster's concerns. Nathaniel Suda, a former student of Webster, is especially critical of Gunton's Midrashic reading of the Genesis creation texts in *The Triune Creator*.[112] However, Suda's criticisms focus only on *The Triune Creator* and do not adequately capture the details of Gunton's theological exegesis of Genesis, which he develops in a variety of his later writings.

Gunton's reading of Genesis is especially important for his doctrine of creation and his theology of culture as it details the nature of God's creation project, its openness to human contributions, and its orientation towards perfection. It is within this understanding of the project of creation that humanity's cultural mandate in Genesis 1:26-28 can be understood as humanity's priestly calling, and humanity itself as those created in the image of God, to participate in the divine perfecting of that which was created in the beginning. The following section outlines the shortcomings Gunton perceives in the doctrine of creation as it has developed in the tradition. It then examines Gunton's exegesis of Genesis 1 and 2 in his later writings and shows that his exegesis not only accords with contemporary biblical scholarship, but can also be extended to enrich further his theology of human culture.

The Doctrine of Creation and God's Creative Action

Theology's Greek dualistic inheritance results in a long Babylonian captivity for the doctrine of creation.[113] The tendency in Western theology, which, according to Gunton, Augustine, and Origen exemplify, is to combine creedal and Greek influences in the construction of the doctrine of creation.[114] Origen's two-stage

---

110. David A. Höhne, *Spirit and Sonship: Colin Gunton's Theology of Particularity and the Holy Spirit* (Farnham: Ashgate, 2010), 13-15; 34-7. It is worthy of note that Höhne's criticisms and exegetical extensions of Gunton's account of Luke draw almost entirely from Gunton's early work, apart from a short section on Gunton's use of univocity in *Act and Being*. Höhne's work is very helpful, and more exegetically developed than Gunton's. However, he does not adequately engage Gunton's later corpus and overlooks the importance that Gunton gives to Luke's framing of Jesus' fulfilment and concentration of Israel in his later work. As I will argue in chapter four, this is very important to Gunton's Christology.

111. Webster, "Systematic Theology after Barth," 262.

112. Nathaniel Suda, "Aspects of Colin Gunton's Reading of Genesis 1 and 2," *Colin Gunton Research Blog*, March 14, 2006, http://guntonresearch.blogspot.co.nz/2006/03/gunton-on-genesis-1-and-2.html.

113. Gunton, *The Triune Creator*, 96.

114. Gunton, "The Doctrine of Creation," 149.

view of creation owes much, Gunton believes, to Gnostic influences, and asserts a hierarchy of being in which God creates the ideal Platonic forms and then the lower material creation. Human beings are conceived as some form of disembodied rational spirits whose embodiment in creation is the result of a pre-temporal fall in which spiritual beings lapsed in their contemplation of God. The fallen spirits fall into material reality to be trained in human bodies so that they may return to unity with the One.[115] Origen's dualistic drive to disembodiment views the world as an instrumental means to a spiritual salvation *from* the material world rather than *in* and *with* the world.[116]

Augustine avoids many of Origen's simplifications and makes a major contribution to the doctrine of *creatio ex nihilo*, but Gunton believes his flirtation with Manicheanism endows him with an ongoing Neoplatonic revulsion of the material world.[117] Augustine's two-stage hierarchical view of creation, in which God creates the Platonic forms before the lower material world, establishes an impulse to immateriality.[118] Materiality is deemed to be ontologically inferior to immateriality and this, in Gunton's assessment, undermines the goodness of the creation and establishes a divorce between God and the economy of salvation.[119] Augustine's attempts to protect God's omnipotence by establishing *creatio ex nihilo* as the result of God's abstract will ultimately deprive temporality of its true reality and significance.[120] Moreover, Gunton is especially critical of Augustine's allegorical reading of Genesis because it involves an instantaneous view of creation that opposes God and time in such a way that creation's temporality, and divine action within it, is undermined.[121] Creation's redemption is understood as a retrieval of and return to the original perfection, instead of an orientation to an end that is greater than the beginning.[122] In the final analysis, Gunton holds that Augustine's doctrine of creation fails to uphold the goodness of creation's temporality and God's relation to time and space.

Dualistic accounts of creation entered the theological bloodstream of the West in its early developments, and Gunton believes they remain a persistent nemesis in

---

115. Gunton, *The Triune Creator*, 57-9. See also Gunton, "The Doctrine of Creation," 149.

116. Gunton, *The Christian Faith*, 24. See also Gunton, *The Triune Creator*, 59-60; Gunton, *Theology Through the Theologians*, 149.

117. Gunton, *The Triune Creator*, 73-4.

118. Gunton, *The Triune Creator*, 75. See also Gunton, "The Doctrine of Creation," 149.

119. Gunton, *The Triune Creator*, 16.

120. Gunton, *The Triune Creator*, 74-6.

121. Gunton, *The Triune Creator*, 77-8. See also Gunton, "The Doctrine of Creation," 149; Colin E. Gunton, "Between Allegory and Myth: The Legacy of the Spiritualising of Genesis," in *The Doctrine of Creation: Essays in Dogmatics, History and Philosophy*, ed. Colin E. Gunton (London: T&T Clark, 1997), 56; Gunton, *The Promise of Trinitarian Theology*, 180.

122. Gunton, *The Triune Creator*, 11.

the development of theology. Whatever we make of Gunton's historiography, these dualisms serve as a foil for Gunton's theology of divine action in the economy.[123] If we are to avoid these dualistic traps, says Gunton, "we must do what Augustine failed to do and consider more closely what might be the shape of divine action in time."[124] The shape of divine establishing action requires an account of God's creation project and the complex pattern of mediation in Genesis 1 and 2.

Genesis and God's Pluriform Creative Action

Colin Gunton's theology of culture develops within his doctrine of creation and the conviction that God redeems and perfects creation through the mediating action of the Son and the Spirit. Whilst the New Testament texts are primary in Gunton's doctrine of creation, the Genesis accounts of creation reveal God's pluriform creating action and the eschatological nature of God's creation project.

At this point, Gunton is dependent on Francis Watson's exegesis of Genesis 1–2 and utilizes Watson's illuminating insights as the basis of his understanding of the texts.[125] Watson's account of God's pluriform creating action in Genesis serves as the basis for Gunton's understanding of God's creation of, and purpose for, human culture. For Gunton, Genesis 1 offers a threefold model of God's creating action that reveals a complex pattern of mediation—creation by command; creation by fabrication; and creation by mediation.[126] These three models of God's creating action enable wider theological reflection upon the sovereignty of God and the relative freedom (*Selbständigkeit*) of creation; upon creation as a project that God perfects through time and in space; and upon humanity's ministerial calling as sub-agents in God's perfecting action in creation. Watson's final model, and its stress upon humanity's ministerial calling as God's representatives in creation, is especially important for understanding Gunton's theology of culture. However, this model cannot be understood in separation from the other two models of God's creating action as they are organically united.

Gunton's Use of Francis Watson's Exegesis of Genesis

Gunton's reading of Genesis 1 occupies an important place in his doctrine of creation. Whilst he consistently holds that the interpretation of the first chapter of Genesis is crucial for the doctrine of creation, his exegetical impulse is overshadowed in his

---

123. See McNall, *A Free Corrector*, 129–30; Joshua McNall, "Gunton and Augustine," 282–3; and Neil Ormerod, "Augustine and the Trinity: Whose Crisis?," *Pacifica*, 16 (2003): 17–32.

124. Gunton, *The Triune Creator*, 84.

125. Gunton, *Revelation and Reason*, 80. Francis Watson, *Text, Church and Word: Biblical Interpretation in Theological Perspective* (Edinburgh: T&T Clark, 1994), 137–53.

126. Gunton, *Revelation and Reason*, 80. See also Gunton, *A Brief Theology of Revelation*, 69–72.

early writings by his concern about the influence of Hellenistic epistemology and the impact of its dualisms on the tradition.[127] In his later writings, Gunton engages more thoroughly with exegetical readings of the creation accounts in Genesis and employs them in service of his expanded theology of creation, mediation, and culture.[128]

Gunton's reliance on Watson's work for his exegesis of Genesis is often overlooked by his critics.[129] Watson's book *Text, Church and World: Biblical Interpretation in Theological Perspective* is a very important source for Gunton's trinitarian doctrine of creation, and his account of God's pluriform creating action.[130] Watson's analysis of the narrative dimensions of the Genesis creation accounts enables Gunton to outline the variegated forms God's establishing action takes through the mediation of the Son and the Spirit.[131] Gunton writes, "I found [Watson's work] very illuminating, he shows how Genesis 1 has a very complex pattern of mediation."[132] But Gunton's use of Watson's work, especially Watson's mediation model, is nuanced. Whilst Watson terms his third model of divine creating action the mediation model, Gunton terms it the ministerial model because mediation, in Gunton's work, is the term for all the economic actions of the Son and the Spirit. Mediation is not regarded by Gunton as a model of God's creating action, it is the theological framework within which we comprehend all the parts.[133] Instead, Gunton interprets all three models as modes of the mediation action of the Son and the Spirit, and calls the third model the ministerial model of creation. There are three models of creation in Genesis 1 according to Watson: creation by speech-act; creation by formation; and creation by mediation. While adjusting the terminology Gunton employs the insights from each to inform his trinitarian accounts of the doctrine of creation and theology of culture.

---

127. Gunton, *The One, the Three and the Many*, 53–5; 215.

128. In his later work, Gunton draws from a variety of biblical scholars as he explores the Genesis texts. Among the most prominent are Claus Westermann, Gordon Wenham, Hans Walter Wolff, Robert Grosseteste, Gabriel Josipovici, H. H. Schmidt, Gerhard von Rad, as well as a wide array of systematic theologians such as Basil, Irenaeus, Augustine, Origen, Martin Luther, John Calvin, Dietrich Bonhoeffer, Karl Barth, Jürgen Moltmann, Robert Jenson, and Gerhard May.

129. See Gunton, *The Triune Creator*, 61–2; Gunton, *The Christian Faith*, 5–8; Gunton, *Father, Son and Holy Spirit*, 138–9; Gunton, *Theology Through the Theologians*, 134, 138; Gunton, *The Barth Lectures*, 248; and Gunton, *Revelation and Reason*, 80–1.

130. See Gunton, *The Triune Creator*, 61–2; Gunton, *The Christian Faith*, 5–8; Gunton, *Father, Son and Holy* Spirit, 138–9; Gunton, *Theology Through the Theologians*, 134, 138; Gunton, *The Barth Lectures*, 248; and Gunton, *Revelation and Reason*, 80–1. Watson, *Text, Church and Word*, 137–53.

131. Gunton, *The Christian Faith*, 5.

132. Gunton, *Revelation and Reason*, 80. See also Gunton, *The Triune Creator*, 61.

133. Gunton, *The Christian Faith*, 7.

The Divine Speech-act Model

Watson wrote *Text, Church and World* against the backdrop of the deconstructionist critique of metaphysical claims to reality beyond textuality.[134] "In effect," Gunton explains to his students, "he [Watson] is going after the postmodernists who say words are all there are."[135] Watson's theological reading of Genesis 1 is motivated by two fundamental concerns. The first is to delineate the universal horizons between which the story of Jesus can be understood. Whilst the Genesis 1 account is textually mediated, its universality is integral to the narrative. The second concern is to underline the priority of the world as divine creation which is, within limits, subjected to a secondary shaping that is not confined to speech and is open to human contributions.[136] Both concerns appeal to Gunton, and the second concern is especially important to his theology of culture.

The first model of trinitarian creating action is the divine speech-act model, which Gunton terms the command model of creation.[137] Creation is accomplished by speech, but it is speech that causes an act. "If the act of creation is accomplished through speech, then speech and act are identified."[138] God creates directly through command, and entities such as light (Gen 1:3) and vegetation (Gen 1:11) come into immediate existence *ex nihilo*.[139] God commands entities that do not yet exist into being, and their coming into being is their act of obedience to God's command—as the Psalmists proclaims, "For he commanded and they were created" (Ps 148:5).[140] The speech-act model, Watson argues, is definitive in the cosmic Christology at the beginning of John's gospel, which is itself an intertextual echo of Genesis 1. "All things came into being through him [the divine Word], and without him not one thing came into being" (John 1:3). Whilst John's use of *logos* might be more closely associated with "reason" than "speech," the intertextual echoes with Genesis 1, and the connections of *logos* with speech in later parts of the gospel, suggest that the speech-act model is plausible.[141] Genesis 1 may lack the Johannine hypostatization of *logos*, but the text is clear that creation is by God's word.

"God speaks," Gunton notes, "and things happen."[142] God's Word is powerful and commands reality into being. "Again and again we find Jewish and Christian writers likening God to one who executes his intention by a mere word of command: he spoke, and it came to be."[143] Creation by command affirms God's

---

134. Francis Watson, *Text, Church and Word: Biblical Interpretation in Theological Perspective* (Edinburgh: T&T Clark, 1994), 137.

135. Gunton, *Revelation and Reason*, 80.

136. Watson, *Text, Church and Word*, 140.

137. Gunton, *The Christian Faith*, 5.

138. Watson, *Text, Church and Word*, 140.

139. Watson, *Text, Church and Word*, 140–1.

140. Watson, *Text, Church and Word*, 141.

141. Watson, *Text, Church and Word*, 140.

142. Gunton, *Revelation and Reason*, 80.

143. Gunton, *The Christian Faith*, 5. See also Bruce K. Waltke, *Genesis: A Commentary* (Grand Rapids: Zondervan, 2001), 60.

sovereignty over creation and everything in creation comes into being *ex nihilo* from his personal will and agency.[144] Creation is a divine speech-act, Gunton avers, and, unlike other Ancient Near Eastern deities, God is not dependent on or constrained by pre-existing material or other deities to create.[145] Whilst there is not a highly developed doctrine of *creatio ex nihilo* in the Genesis texts, Gunton holds that the confession of *creatio ex nihilo* is nonetheless an appropriate implication from the Genesis texts and the wider witness of scripture.[146] The confession of *creatio ex nihilo* and the witness of scripture perform a similar theological function in establishing the world once and for all by God's powerful Word.[147] "Creation is therefore by speech, by God's word. This means that there is no pre-existent material as in the creation myths. In Genesis there is no pre-existing material from which God works."[148] The command model testifies to the reality that the world was established out of nothing by the speech-act of God.

Creation by command also affirms the sovereignty, freedom, and aseity of God's eternal being as Father, Son, and Spirit, and creation as a free act of God's personal and loving will. There are only two ontological realities: the infinite, uncreated, and eternal creator and the finite, contingent, and temporal creation; a duality without dualism. There are no intermediaries or scales of being, unlike Hellenistic influences, because all created being shares an ontological homogeneity. This does not suggest that there are not variety and particularity, but that there are only two realms of being—creator and created. "This is the message of Genesis 1. Everything, from the light to the human creature, is *creation*: other than the one who made it, and so of essentially the same ontological status."[149] This is the triumph of Irenaeus' classic Christian ontology. Creation is a personal act of the sovereign God, who creates and upholds the creation in its own contingent *created* reality; its own createdness.[150]

Creation should not be comprehended as an act internal to God's own being. This is a major point of divergence between Gunton and Robert Jenson. Jenson

---

144. Gunton, *The Triune Creator*, 3.

145. Gunton, *The Christian Faith*, 4. See also Gunton, *The Triune Creator*, 17–18; and Rae, "Colin E. Gunton," 213. However, others observe that the account of creation in Proverbs 8 and the presence of the personified female figure of divine wisdom complexifies this claim.

146. Gunton cautions against reading later theological concerns into the concerns of the Genesis authors to establish a distinctive account of the trustworthy God against the capricious deities of the Ancient Near East. Gunton, *The Christian Faith*, 17–19. See also Gunton, *The Barth Lectures*, 248.

147. Gunton, *The Barth Lectures*, 248.

148. Gunton, *The Barth Lectures*, 248.

149. Gunton, "Flesh and Spirit after Darwin," 41.

150. Gunton employs this term from Christoph Schwöbel. See Christoph Schwöbel, "God, Creation and the Christian Community: The Dogmatic Basis of a Christian Ethic of Createdness," in *The Doctrine of Creation: Essays in Dogmatics, History and Philosophy*, ed. Colin E. Gunton (London: T&T Clark, 1997), 149–76.

argues that God creates by making room within his being.[151] Such proposals, Gunton argues, suggest a contraction in God's being and assert creation to be something internal to God, rather than external. The result is that creation is out of God's being, rather than out of nothing, and there develops a form of panentheism that assumes an ontological continuity between God and creation.[152] Any ontological continuity between creator and creation, Gunton believes, is a threat to God's aseity *and* the integrity of creation and its createdness.

Instead of creation as a form of internality, Gunton holds that creation is a form of externality; God's loving gift of being to creation as something that is genuinely other than God.[153] Understanding creation as a form of externality from God's being preserves the ontological freedom of God and creation, and the integrity of their distinct identities. Whilst the creation is dependent upon God for its being, God gives the creation its own reality and relative independence (*Selbständigkeit*).[154] God gives worldly reality its own significance and interacts with it in ways that respect its spatial and temporal structures. God's free relation with the creation in its createdness affirms the significance of the world as "having its own proper reality … which is to be what God makes it to be."[155] The free relation of God and creation upholds the importance of the mediation of the Son and the Spirit who show that otherness and relatedness are correlatives.

The Fabrication Model and the Project of Creation

Creation is certainly by divine Word *ex nihilo*, but the subtle nuances of Genesis 1 reveal that the divine speech-act model is not the only form of divine creating action. Gunton's concern is that an excessive emphasis upon creation by divine fiat results in imbalanced understandings of God's creating action that risk undermining the significance of materiality. If God creates only by divine fiat there develops a wholly timeless conception of God's creating action which robs creation of its spatiality and temporality.[156] Instead, Gunton, drawing from Watson, observes the distinctive verbs used in Genesis 1 to describe God's creating action, "create" (*bārāʾ*) and "make" (*ʿāśâ*), and their distinction between instantaneous creating action and creating action that takes time.

God takes time with creation and interacts with it according to its spatial and temporal structures, which God deems to be very good. In Genesis 1, God not

---

151. Gunton, *The Triune Creator*, 141–2. On Jenson, see Gunton, *Father, Son and Holy Spirit*, 103. On Fiddes, see Colin E. Gunton, "Review of *Past Event and Present Salvation: The Christian Idea of Atonement*," New Blackfriars, 71 (1990): 210.

152. Gunton, *The Triune Creator*, 141–2.

153. Gunton, *Father, Son and Holy Spirit*, 103.

154. Gunton employed the German word *Selbständigkeit* which he understood to mean "standing on its own reality." Gunton, *The Barth Lectures*, 242.

155. Gunton, *The Triune Creator*, 145, 178.

156. Gunton, *Father, Son and Holy Spirit*, 138.

only creates by speech-act, God also creates by an act of fabrication that takes time to form and shape the creation. Watson's fabrication model invites reflection on divine action that accommodates itself to the nature of the reality it brings about, like a great playwright who allows a play to conform itself to the intrinsic development of the plot.[157] Creation is created very good and is ordered towards its perfection in time and space. The fabrication model reveals that creation is a project that is eschatologically oriented towards an end that is greater than its beginning through God's timely action.[158]

In Genesis 1, entities such as light come into immediate existence, at God's command, but other entities, such as the firmament (Gen 1:6-8), come into existence through God's formation and construction *in time*.[159] The creation of the firmament involves a different model of God's creating action. Unlike light, the firmament does not immediately spring into being at God's command but is constructed by divine action conformed to temporal reality. Whilst the formula appears to follow the speech-act model of command ("Let there be"), the immediate fulfilment ("it was so") is missing. The entity does not spring immediately into being, but has to be *made*, rather than created, by God ("And God said, "Let there be a dome in the midst of the waters …. So God made the dome … ", Gen 1:6-7). The preceding refrain is not to be understood as a command which immediately brings into being the desired state of affairs, "but as the decision that constitutes its necessary but not its sufficient condition."[160] The distinct verbs used in the creation narrative, "create" (*bārāʾ*) and "make" or "do" (*ʿāśâ*), suggest that whilst God creates by command, God also decides and makes in time.[161] It is only after God constructs the firmament and separates the waters that the fulfilment narration, "it was so," is given (1:6). There is a gap between the decision ("Let there be") and its fulfilment ("And it was so") that is bridged by an act of fabrication.

Gunton's theological extension of Watson's exegesis finds support in contemporary biblical scholarship.[162] Biblical scholars note the significance of the sparing use of "create," which is only used with God as the subject in the Hebrew Bible, and the more common use of "make," which is used of God and human beings.[163] Bill Arnold reinforces Gunton and Watson's insights and notes, "it is also interesting that this [the creation of light] is the only time in Gen 1 that creation occurs by *fiat* alone. Elsewhere in the chapter God speaks and then takes action to 'make' or otherwise bring about the feature of creation."[164] Whilst debate continues

---

157. Gunton, *The Christian Faith*, 5.
158. Gunton, *The Barth Lectures*, 248.
159. Watson, *Text, Church and Word*, 141.
160. Watson, *Text, Church and Word*, 141.
161. Watson, *Text, Church and Word*, 141.
162. See Gunton, *The Christian Faith*, 5–7.
163. Leslie C. Allen, *A Theological Approach to the Old Testament: Major Themes and New Testament Connections* (Eugene: Wipf and Stock, 2014), 15.
164. Bill T. Arnold, *Genesis* (Cambridge: Cambridge University Press, 2009), 39.

regarding the significance of the distinction between "create" and "make" in the Priestly narrative, it at least highlights that creation is not atemporal. The ontological significance of creation's temporality and spatiality is Gunton's central affirmation from the text which he explores theologically. God not only creates by command, but also creates by deciding and making.[165]

The fabrication model reveals that God loves creation's createdness and accommodates God's action to the temporal and spatial structures of the created order.[166] The account of the creation of humankind is also achieved by an act of fabrication. The creation of humanity appears not as a command, but as a decision made within time: "Let us make humanity in our image … " (Gen 1:26).[167] The fabrication model offers a more intimate understanding of God's involvement with the world, in the mode of indwelling, which assumes the contact of the creator's hands with the matter being moulded. "The exalted potentate who commands (commissions?) and the artisan who labours are, in this case, one and the same, the latter perhaps a kenotic version of the former."[168] God is, in Watson's imagery, the artisan who labours, and this image echoes with an important development in Gunton's later writings. Gunton's favoured image of creation is of a project that is projected through time to an end that was greater than its beginning. In the hands of its sculptor, creation is being shaped to its intended end and destiny—perfected in Christ by the Spirit to the Father's glory.[169]

Creation, according to Gunton, is best understood in light of its eschatological direction; it is a project that is going somewhere.[170] "Gunton's repeated reference to the project of creation is," Michael Stringer rightly notes, "a way of speaking about the whole complex movement from creation through redemption to consummation."[171] The original creation was created relatively perfect: perfect and to be perfected through time.[172] Creation is not a static timeless lump of matter as some timeless accounts assert; it is like a newborn baby that is born perfect but is to be made perfect through time.[173]

> Creation is very good: perfect. But perfect is not here a static concept. There are two senses in which we can use the word. We might say that a newborn baby is 'perfect', but it is there to become something else; not something else that is no longer itself – it is not to be turned into a pig – but a mature human being

---

165. Watson, *Text, Church and Word*, 141.
166. Gunton, *The Christian Faith*, 5.
167. Watson, *Text, Church and Word*, 141.
168. Watson, *Text, Church and Word*, 143.
169. Gunton, *Intellect and Action*, 105.
170. Gunton, *The Promise of Trinitarian Theology*, 181.
171. Stringer, "The Lord and Giver of Life," 248.
172. Gunton, "Reformation Accounts," 79. See also Gunton, *Father, Son and Holy Spirit*, 110.
173. Gunton, *The Christian Faith*, 19.

who is to be made perfect through time .... There is therefore no creation 'in the beginning' without an eschatological orientation. From the beginning, it has a destiny, a purpose.[174]

Creation is best understood by dynamic, rather than static, images. Creation is imaged as a block of marble being shaped,[175] a developing play,[176] a piece of music,[177] or an unfolding artwork,[178] which, in the hands of a sculptor, playwright, musician, or artist, is perfectible through time.[179] "Thus it is that the created world is project – something projected into and through time – and so something which is real and good precisely because it, too, takes time to become what it is created to be."[180] Creation is projected in space and through time and, as Rae suggests, it cannot be thought of as a series of random events, but as a project that God is directing towards God's purposes.[181] In accordance with Gunton's interpretation, J. Richard Middleton suggests that God is imaged in Genesis as the wise artisan who attentively constructs an artful world in which he is pleased with "both the stages or process of fabrication ... and the overall outcome."[182] The fabrication model reveals that God takes time to shape and form the project of creation through divine action that accommodates itself to the spatial and temporal structures of creation.

Gunton credits his account of creation as a project to Irenaeus and Barth because of their conceptions of the relation of the eternal God to temporal creation. Whilst neither Irenaeus nor Barth employs the concept of creation as a project, they offer an integrated account of creation, redemption, and eschatological perfection through the mediation of the Son and the Spirit.[183] Life within creation is meaningful because God makes it so, and patiently loves and relates to creation in ways that enable all created reality to become what God particularly intends it to be in relation with God and all else. "The biblical notion of time as that which God gives to things for their right development is further elaborated in Genesis' depiction of God's resting on the seventh day."[184]

God takes time to achieve God's wisdom in the creation, as the temporality of human life and the created order are given to be perfected through time. "It is an

---

174. Gunton, *The Christian Faith*, 19.
175. Gunton, *Intellect and Action*, 105.
176. Gunton, *The Christian Faith*, 7.
177. Colin E. Gunton, "Three Pitfalls in Preaching Creation," *Living Pulpit*, 9 (2000): 14.
178. Gunton, "The Doctrine of Creation," 142.
179. Gunton, *Intellect and Action*, 105.
180. Gunton, *The Triune Creator*, 93.
181. Murray Rae, *Christian Theology: The Basics* (London and New York: Routledge, 2015), 27.
182. J. Richard Middleton, *The Liberating Image: The* Imago Dei *in Genesis 1* (Grand Rapids: Brazos, 2005), 77.
183. Gunton, *The Triune Creator*, 91, 164–5.
184. Gunton, *The Christian Faith*, 7.

implication of the patient wisdom of God that not only does he will a world that is very good in its temporality, but that he also continues to act in and toward it in a way appropriate to its structure."[185] Creation is certainly the act of the timeless God, but it is not a timeless act of God. Creation is an act of the eternal God in time. God patiently takes time with the creation, conforming his action to that which he makes.[186] Time is not the problem, but what takes place within it, and it is serious enough that it requires the divine wisdom of God displayed in the incarnate Son's death upon the cross.[187] God is not the enemy of time, but its creator, redeemer, and perfecter.

The movement of creation towards perfection is not primarily the result of creation's own impetus, but of divine action mediated in the economy. The doctrine of creation as it has commonly been developed suffers, in Gunton's analysis, from an orientation to protology at the expense of the necessary eschatological determinants.[188] In Irenaeus, Gunton finds a greater emphasis upon the eschatological determination of creation that necessitates an orientation to the perfection of creation rather than an emphasis on protology and the retrieval of the original creation. At the centre of Irenaeus' claim is Christology, and Jesus Christ's faithful recapitulation of humanity that is not the redemption of spiritual beings but the completion through redemption of all created reality. "Irenaeus' eschatology is not therefore one of return, *back* to spiritual conditions which prevailed before the world was created, but is a movement *forward* to the perfection of all things intended by the creator."[189]

Creation is therefore best understood as a project that is eschatologically structured towards its perfection through redemption. Theologies of retrieval and return fail to consider the accommodating shape of divine action in time or creation's eschatological direction towards perfection. Redemption is not the retrieval or return to a pre-fallen state, which leaves little room for the recreating action of the Spirit, but a reorientation towards perfection by redemption. The project of creation is restored through Jesus Christ who is the mediator of creation and redemption. Through his life, death, and resurrection Jesus Christ restores the creation, but only as a project now oriented again to its true end.[190]

God's creating action accommodates itself to that which is created, and God gives space to creation to be itself in relation to God. The eschatological destiny of the creation, which gives meaning to all else, is to glorify God by being and becoming itself in accordance with God's will. This freedom comes primarily through the divine action of the Son and the Spirit. Yet the project of creation is open to human participation and contributions. God calls humanity to act

---

185. Gunton, *Father, Son and Holy Spirit*, 141.
186. Gunton, *The Christian Faith*, 5–6.
187. Gunton, *Father, Son and Holy Spirit*, 140.
188. Gunton, *The Promise of Trinitarian Theology*, 180.
189. Gunton, *The Christian Faith*, 24. See also Gunton, *The Triune Creator*, 12, 55.
190. Gunton, *The Promise of Trinitarian Theology*, 184–5.

as priest within the creation to extend God's kingly rule throughout the world. "Creation in the beginning cannot finally be understood without its directedness to an end, because it has to be understood as God's project, a project in which he freely and graciously involves us, his personal creation."[191] God's creating action takes time, and God gives humanity a ministerial role as sub-creators in God's project of creation.[192] This leads to Watson's third model of God's creating action, the mediation model, which Gunton utilizes to develop his most important insights for his theological account of human culture.

The Mediation Model and Creation's Ministerial Calling

God creates by command, fabrication, and, finally, God also creates by mediation, which is vital to Gunton's trinitarian theology of culture. Watson's mediation model of divine creative action in Genesis 1 extends God's accommodating action in and towards temporal creation by observing God's use of existent creation as a collaborator in God's creative work. God's invitation for creation to participate in the divine creation opens horizons for an understanding of non-competitive human contributions to divine action in creation. This finds particular expression in God's priestly call for humanity to image God by stewarding the creation and extending God's royal administration of creation through faithful human action and culture. In order to understand Gunton's theology of culture, we need to carefully examine Watson's biblical account of creation's mediatorial action and humanity's calling to image God in the creation. Watson's insights from the mediation model form the basis of Gunton's understanding of God's openness to creaturely contributions to the project of creation, which enable a theological account of the meaning and significance of human culture.

Whilst God creates by command and fabrication, Watson notes, God simultaneously creates by mediation. God employs existent creation as the womb from which the rich diversity of creation is propagated.[193] God says, "Let the earth bring forth living creatures of every kind" (1:24), which is followed by, "and it was

---

191. Gunton, *The Triune Creator*, 86.

192. The stewardship model is not without its critics, especially in the context of climate crisis. Eco-theologians note that ideas of stewardship are often based upon a socio-economic hierarchy that "positions God as an absentee landlord and (some) humans as managers of the divine estate." Encoded in this model is "a political message of power and oppression, signifying a relationship of benign dictatorship, where the Earth and Earth's other-than-human communities are entities who depend for survival on the decisions made and implements by human managers." Emily Colgan, "*Kaitiaki*: The Human Vocation to Till and to Keep," in *Earth Our Parish*, ed. George Zechariah and Te Aroha Rountree (Auckland: Trinity Methodist Theological College, 2023), 28–32. See also Clare Palmer, "Stewardship: A Case Study in Environmental Ethics," in *Environmental Stewardship: Critical Perspectives—Past and Present*, ed. R. J. Berry (London: T&T Clark International, 2006), 63–75.

193. Watson, *Text, Church and Word*, 142.

so" (1:24). This is then described as a form of creation, something which God made (1:25) and the language bears close analogy with the previous creation of the heavenly lights (1:14). Whilst the heavenly lights come into existence *ex nihilo*, "in the midst of a prior vacancy," the creation of the living creatures emerges "out of the matrix of prior plenitude"; a mediated form of creation.[194] "God creates immediately by command and by fabrication, but," Watson argues, "he also and simultaneously creates mediately in employing one of his creatures as the womb out of which others proceed."[195]

The earlier creation of vegetation provides an even more striking example of the mediatorial role of creation in divine creating action. God says, "Let the earth put forth vegetation" (1:11), and it is followed by, "And it was so" (1:11). Yet in this case we are not told that "God made" as we would expect in the fabrication model, instead we are told that "The earth brought forth vegetation" (1:12), through the model of mediation. The models are not independent, and, as in the case of the propagation of the waters (1:20), God creates simultaneously by mediation and fabrication. Mediation, in this case, is a form of God's fabrication. But, Watson notes, creation's mediate action is also a form of future divine creative action. "Plants and trees are created as containers in which is preserved the precious seed which will propagate the species (v. 11), and the divine blessings that command or promise the fruitfulness of sea creatures and humans alike suggest a similar situation of mediation (vv. 22, 28)."[196]

Genesis 1 uses the three interconnected, yet distinct, models of creation: the speech-act model (which Gunton terms the command model); the fabrication model; and the mediation model (which Gunton terms the ministerial model). While the speech-act model stresses God's sovereignty over creation, and the fabrication model indicates a closer and more intimate mode of creating, the mediation model offers a collaborative account of creation's participation in God's creating action. Yet, this is never beyond God's superintending. "The creation that brings forth life does so because of the prior presence of God in the mode of indwelling."[197]

Mediation is a wide-ranging theological concept that extends beyond creation in Gunton's thought, so as noted earlier he terms Watson's mediation model the ministerial model. Amidst the manifold forms of mediation in creation, the ministerial model asserts God's enablement of the created world to serve as mediators of other parts of God's creation.[198] God enables the creation to participate as sub-agents in God's creating and perfecting action. The juxtaposition of "Let the earth bring forth … " with "God made the wild animals" shows us that creation's ministerial calling remains within the confines of God's creative action, but God

---

194. Watson, *Text, Church and Word*, 142.
195. Watson, *Text, Church and Word*, 142.
196. Watson, *Text, Church and Word*, 142–3.
197. Watson, *Text, Church and Word*, 143.
198. Gunton, *The Christian Faith*, 8.

enables creation to be itself. "Worldly agencies are enabled by divine action to achieve their own 'subcreating', not in the absolute way that God creates, but relatively, as creation from what already is."[199] This, for Gunton, is the theological basis for art, ethics, and science and the best features of human culture for the right human habitation of creation that contributes to its redemption and perfection.[200]

Creation's ministerial calling finds its most concentrated expression in the calling of humanity to be its chief ministers of creation and represent God's rule in the world. All creation is capable of generating goodness, beauty, and truth, but it is humanity in particular which is called to be God's representative and superintend creation's sub-agency in God's perfecting action.[201] Before turning to humanity's cultural mandate, it is helpful to observe, in the face of criticisms of Gunton's lack of biblical exegesis, that Gunton's account of God's pluriform creating action finds support in biblical scholarship. Moreover, Gunton's insights from Watson can be further enriched by more recent biblical scholarship.

Contemporary biblical scholars reinforce Watson and Gunton's interpretation of the highly complex and variegated account of divine creating action in Genesis, and further their insights on creation's sub-agency in God's creating action. In his extended study of the *imago Dei* in Genesis 1, Middleton notes that the creation account in Genesis 1 is highly structured and, at one level, offers a symmetrical explanation of creation by divine fiat. However, the highly complex literary variations from creation by divine fiat suggest the formulaic patterning is not simple.[202] There are nonpredictable variations in the literary patterning of Genesis 1 that confound a tightly defined formulaic and symmetrical account of creation. There are patterns of distinct divine actions in separating, dividing, and filling, but these patterns have anomalies that do not adhere to tight categorization. As examples, the execution report "and it was so" is missing or displaced in some instances, and the evaluation report "God saw that it was good" is missing in others.[203] The text is marked as much by variation as consistency, and Middleton concludes that whilst there is a pattern, "this pattern is by no means simple, obvious, or predictable. It is, on the contrary, highly complex."[204]

The complexity of the text's literary variations is, Middleton suggests, analogous to fractal geometry in contemporary chaos theory in which the subject forms its own structures. God is imaged not as the Newtonian lawgiver, but as the strange attractor who is the stabilizing force in a complex and dynamic world.[205] In accordance with Gunton's emphases, Middleton notes that God grants creation

---

199. Gunton, *The Christian Faith*, 8.
200. Gunton, *The Christian Faith*, 8.
201. Gunton, "Reformation Accounts," 80.
202. Middleton, *The Liberating Image*, 275–8. See also Arnold, *Genesis*, 30–45; Waltke, *Genesis*, 56–67; and James McKewon, *Genesis* (Grand Rapids: Eerdmans, 2008), 19–29.
203. Middleton, *The Liberating Image*, 281.
204. Middleton, *The Liberating Image*, 283.
205. Middleton, *The Liberating Image*, 284–7.

noncoercive freedom that hints at a distinct form of power that is inscribed with love and generosity and welcomes non-competitive creaturely contributions to creation.[206] God shares power with non-human creation, grants subjectivity and freedom to the cosmos, and enables the cosmos to find its own pattern in response to the creator's call.[207] God grants the firmament a godlike function of separating, as well as granting the earth (twice) and the waters (twice) participation in God's creating activity. Interestingly, Middleton highlights the risk God takes in calling the earth to produce vegetation, as at this stage in the narrative God has not engaged in the act of filling. The earth has no God-given model of filling to follow, and it is God, on the following day, who imitates the earth's creative action. "God is, rhetorically speaking, pre-empted by the earth and does not seem threatened by this."[208] Middleton's exegesis affirms the insights of Watson and Gunton and enriches their analysis of the radical collaboration and power-sharing of God in the Genesis accounts.

For all the insights of source theories about Genesis, Middleton suggests there is "a structural relationship between Genesis 1:1-2:3 and what follows."[209] God grants human agency on the sixth day, but it is not exercised until the paradise/fall story in Genesis 2-3. The literary clue that unites the narratives is the use of the conclusion formula for each day. Each of the first six days concludes with the refrain, "And there was evening and there was morning," to signal the finish of that creating action. However, this formula is missing from the seventh day, when we would expect it to appear at the conclusion of God's creation. This, Middleton argues, "leaves the attentive reader hanging and suggests that the seventh day is open-ended and unfinished," and God continues to rest having entrusted creation to humanity.[210] Such rest does not imply the "cessation of all divine action, only that the initial conditions of a meaningful world are completed."[211] God continues to act in collaboration with humanity in a world open to the exercise of creative human cultural agency. Indeed, the final word of Genesis 2:3 in Hebrew is an infinitive that reinforces the sense of open-endedness and unfinished action.[212] Gunton suggests that the openness of creation to creaturely collaborations with God is an aspect of God's providential action in which we can comprehend human culture. "The world of Genesis 1 and 2 is a place of labour, though not yet laborious labour. It is not 'paradise'. We are presented rather with an empty earth, whose

---

206. Middleton, *The Liberating Image*, 287-8. See Terence E. Fretheim, "The Book of Genesis: Introduction, Commentary, and Reflections," in *The New Interpreter's Bible Commentary*, vol. 1, ed. Leander E. Keck et al. (Nashville: Abingdon, 1994), 343-7; and Walter Brueggemann, *Genesis*, Interpretation (Atlanta: John Knox, 1982), 27-8.

207. Middleton, *The Liberating Image*, 285.

208. Middleton, *The Liberating Image*, 288-9.

209. Middleton, *The Liberating Image*, 290.

210. Middleton, *The Liberating Image*, 291.

211. Middleton, *The Liberating Image*, 291.

212. Middleton, *The Liberating Image*, 292-3.

order is in need of completion … while similarly Adam and Eve are called to till the ground."[213] God's calling of humanity to sub-agency in divine action in and towards the project of creation is established at God's creation of humanity in God's image.

The imago Dei and Humanity's Cultural Mandate

Gunton's account of the *imago Dei* develops with the progressions in his theology and provides the basis for his understanding of God's purposes for human culture. In his early accounts of the *imago Dei*, Gunton stresses the importance of its relational conception. Relational ontology is at the heart of Gunton's early writings on the *imago Dei*, and it offers a counter to Enlightenment thinkers who assume the divine image and likeness of God are found in rational human capacities.[214] Western views of the *imago Dei* suffer from the recourse to immateriality and individualism, and so Gunton proffers two alternative conceptions: humanity's ministerial calling and Barth's relational view of the image. At this stage of his development, Gunton finds the ministerial calling too literalistic and too restrictive with respect to the biblical texts, "especially in the light of the New Testament reorienting of the doctrine to Christ."[215] He is drawn to Barth's relational conception, but seeks a greater emphasis upon humanity's relation with creation. In an attempt to obviate between the weaknesses of the two alternatives, Gunton seeks a stronger theological ontology that arises from his trinitarian understanding of personhood. "Where the tradition tended to see our imagedness to consist in the possession of certain faculties, here the stress is on the ontology of personhood."[216] This accords with Gunton's ontological concerns at this stage of his career. In his later writings, Gunton overcomes his concerns with the *imago Dei* being humanity's ministerial calling by detailing the way this calling is concentrated in Jesus Christ and his faithful human habitation of creation and culture.

In the face of other Ancient Near Eastern societies, who proclaim the king as the image of God, Israel determines that all human beings are made in the image of God and bear God's likeness.[217] To be in the image and likeness of the tripersonal God whose eternal being is established in love is to be made to love— love for God, love for others, and love for God's creation.[218] The image is structural because human beings are related to God differently than the rest of the created order, and it is also relational because God places humanity in relation to other humans and the created order. Whilst there are no hierarchies in the relations of

---

213. Gunton, *The Christian Faith*, 28–9; 47–51.
214. Gunton, *The Promise of Trinitarian Theology*, 101.
215. Gunton, *The Promise of Trinitarian Theology*, 112.
216. Gunton, *The Promise of Trinitarian Theology*, 116.
217. Gunton, *The Christian Faith*, 40.
218. Gunton, *The Christian Faith*, 44.

male and female, Gunton believes there is a hierarchy in the relation of humanity with creation. Creation, he argues, cannot be fully itself without humanity.[219]

Human care for creation is important, and the call for humanity to have dominion over creation should not be understood as domination. However, Gunton argues that there is a distinction between humanity and the rest of creation, whilst recognizing that this view is unpopular in the contemporary ecological context. "To be in the image of God is to be related to God in the way that other creatures are not, and so related to the other creatures differently from the way in which they are related to one another."[220] Humanity is the crown of creation, but it is all creation that God deems very good.

In Genesis 1:28, humanity is commanded to make something of the world, and to engage with the created order in such a way that creation is enabled to become what it is created to be in worship of God.[221] The calling of stewardship is not a calling to the human domination of the world, as the difference between human and non-human creation is only relative, not absolute. Indeed, the wordplay in the Yahwist account of creation, between 'ādām and 'ădāmâ, (Gen 2:7), constrains the absolute difference between humanity and creation and stresses their shared destinies.[222] Gunton hints at the ontological unity of the Hebrew wordplay and notes that "Adam is of the earth; indeed, that is part of what the name means."[223]

The Genesis account of human dominion over the creation is expressed narratively in the context of covenant and eschatology, and the call of humanity to name the animals and tend the garden draws humanity into a covenantal relation with the creation. This covenantal relationship shares similarities with the way in which God names Jacob as Israel and is thus drawn into a covenant of promise. "To garden is to tend, while to name is a way of entering into a relation, containing elements of reciprocity, though not necessarily symmetrical reciprocity, with the other."[224] The mandate for humanity to have dominion over creation is a command

---

219. Gunton, *The Christian Faith*, 41.

220. Gunton, *The Christian Faith*, 42. See also Gunton, *Father, Son and Holy Spirit*, 112; and Gunton, "Reformation Accounts," 79. Gunton's observation that such claims about the distinction of humanity from the rest of creation are controversial has only intensified with developments in eco-theology. There are ranging critiques of the anthropocentrism that lies at the heart of claims that posit humanity in a hierarchical relationship with creation. Contemporary eco-theologies lay much greater emphasis upon the independence and autonomous agency of other than human creation, and the creation itself. Earth-centred readings of Genesis 1 and 2, as well as Job 38–40, provide important correctives to some of Gunton's claims, and open possibilities for a more ecologically conscious account of human culture. See Emily Colgan, "Reading the Bible as Waters Rise: Ecological Interpretation of Scripture," in *Science, Faith and the Climate Crisis*, ed. Sally Myers, Sarah Hemstock, and Edward Hanna (Bingley: Emerald Publishing, 2020), 115–34.

221. Gunton, *Father, Son and Holy Spirit*, 123.

222. McKewon, *Genesis*, 31–2.

223. Gunton, *Father, Son and Holy Spirit*, 177.

224. Gunton, *The Triune Creator*, 196–7.

for humanity to engage with the created order in such a way that it is enabled to join the human species in worshiping its creator.[225] It is only the human that God addresses personally and directly in the Genesis 1 narrative (1:28-30), and it is only the human who, unlike the rest of creation, receives a blessing. The address, Middleton suggests, is a calling to "extend God's royal administration of the world as authorized representatives on earth."[226] Relationality with the world is not the same kind of community as that with persons, but, God sets humanity in covenantal relationship with the created order in such a way that the destiny of the creation is organically linked with its most problematic inhabitants.

Creation's ministerial calling, for Gunton, finds its most unique and clearest expression in the calling of humanity, as those created in the image of God, to be the chief ministers of creation. Creation in the beginning had a relative perfection, but things were not yet as they were created to be. Creation is created perfect and to be perfected through time and in space, and the task of that perfecting is given to humanity to steward the creation as God's representatives. The created order cannot be fully itself without humanity's priestly action. God gives humanity the task of shaping the world not merely as a permission, but a command. Whilst it is a command, the cultural mandate should be understood dynamically and relationally, rather than as a static principle. "There is a case for claiming that culture is one of the activities implicit in the doctrine of the image of God; that is to say Genesis 1:28, 'fill the earth and subdue it', can be called a cultural mandate."[227] This is not a call to the domination of the earth, as developed from the Enlightenment's mechanistic view of the world as an inanimate object. Instead, it is a form of obedient human action that participates in the divine redemption and perfection of the project of creation.

Culture is faithful human action that participates in God's providential action in and towards that which was created very good; a participation in God's work of art. It is through the human cultural mandate and the project of creation that Gunton offers his mature definition of culture:

> Eschatologically speaking, even 'in the beginning', before the fall, things are not yet as they were created to be, because there is a task laid upon those created in the image of God and it involves both the moral and cultural, insofar as they can be separated. The agent of this perfecting is to be man, male and female together, who are placed there as God's representatives – I think we should say, sacramental representatives – in order, as part of the created order, to superintend that perfecting. In this context, culture, we might say is that set of activities in which those made in the image of God share in the divine perfecting of that which was made in the beginning.[228]

---

225. Gunton, *Father, Son and Holy Spirit*, 123.
226. Middleton, *The Liberating Image*, 289.
227. Gunton, "Reformation Accounts," 79.
228. Gunton, "Reformation Accounts," 79–80.

Humanity's calling to sub-agency in the divine redemption and perfection of creation provides theological meaning to human culture. The calling to participate in the divine perfecting of creation should not be understood as an independent human activity. Indeed, human attempts at perfecting "the world apart from God's prevenient agency is almost a definition of sin" and idolatry.[229] Rae highlights that "because the form and character of creation is determined by divine love, our participation is not coerced but enabled, not unlike the way a child may grasp a parent's extended hand as they embark upon some project together. The child's act is freely undertaken but made possible in virtue of the parent's love."[230] Humans are not co-agents but sub-agents in God's creation project.[231]

The calling of humanity to tend and work in the creation is not the result of God's punishment of humanity for sin. Nor is it a calling for humanity to attempt to build the temporary earthly-city to stave off the worst effects of sin until Christ comes to remove it all and establish the city of God.[232] Adam and Eve are given the task of ordering creation *before* the fall. Thus, culture is not a result of the fall. "Human beings shape their world, and Genesis appears not only to approve this, but encourage it: indeed, Genesis 2 makes horti*culture* the primary task that Adam and Eve perform in the place in which they are set."[233] Culture, Gunton holds, is distinct from nature in that it orders or changes the creation, like a wilderness into gardens or empty land into housing.[234] Commenting on Genesis 2, Gunton maintains that the "existence of the garden would appear to presuppose that outside it things are not so ordered, for a garden is a piece of earth which is subdued to human purposes in a way that land beyond it is not."[235] The creation and humanity are created as very good and are to be perfected through time by the right human habitation of the world.[236]

Eden is a garden, not a paradise, and it is destined to perfection. The hope of scripture is not creation's return to an Edenic beginning but the redemption and perfection of creation in a new heaven and new earth.[237] The eschatological directedness of creation overcomes the timeless conception of instantaneous creation and theologies of retrieval. As Holmes notes, such timeless views of creation offer no room for human culture, as human beings only bring to fruition the "seeds" that contain within them what will be. Everything that will exist already exists, invisibly and potentially, and there is no room for human culture or openness to creaturely contributions to the world.[238] Extrapolating on Gunton's

---

229. Gunton, "Reformation Accounts," 80.
230. Rae, "Colin E. Gunton," 217.
231. Gunton, "Reformation Accounts," 80.
232. Holmes, "Can Theology Engage with Culture?" 8.
233. Gunton, *The Christian Faith*, 50.
234. Gunton, *The Christian Faith*, 50.
235. Gunton, *Father, Son and Holy Spirit*, 109.
236. Gunton, *The Christian Faith*, 19.
237. Gunton, *The Triune Creator*, 197.
238. Holmes, "Can Theology Engage with Culture?" 9–10. See also Holmes, "Triune Creativity," 73–85.

work, Holmes maintains the biblical story offers images of the promised end that celebrate and affirm cultural advances that occur throughout time and history which have contributed to the perfecting of creation (e.g., cities, buildings, families, relationships, infrastructure, political systems, diverse peoples and languages, gardens, and the arts).[239] Whilst the creation is created very good, it is not created fully ordered or perfect; there is work to do, soil to till, gardens to tend, animals to name, cities to build, and families and communities to develop. These things happen through time, and they highlight the importance of viewing creation as a project which God is perfecting.

Perfection is not a static concept, and there is something that humans have to do with the relative freedom that they are given by God. God is like the playwright who allows the actors freedom to develop the play intrinsically, within the constraints of the plot.[240] Faithful human action, empowered as it is by the action of the Son and the Spirit, genuinely contributes to the divine perfecting of creation, and it offers a living sacrifice of praise to God for God's wise purposes in the beginning. Through the faithful humanity of the Son, and the enabling of the Spirit, human culture is able to give particular finite anticipations of the true, the good and the beautiful in advance of the eschatological redemption and perfection of all things.[241] However, this perfecting does not occur merely through human progress, but through the redemption of creation by the faithful humanity of Jesus Christ that the Spirit perfects.

Gunton is quite clear that in a fallen world, there is no perfection without redemption. Despite criticisms, Gunton takes seriously the effects of the fall on creation and its destiny. Humanity may be offered a priestly calling, but the fall shows us that aside from redemption, humanity fails in its cultural calling and, consequently, the creation fails to reach its destiny to share in the liberty of the children of God.[242] The intimate connection between humanity and creation is echoed in Paul's description of creation's teleology in Romans 8. Creation, Gunton maintains, cannot be understood in abstraction from the way it is ordered to the human race. Humanity's failure to exercise its calling is somehow responsible for creation's bondage to decay and its failure to share in the liberty of the children of God. "The exchange of liberty for slavery in one realm, the human, involves a bondage for the created world also."[243] This means that any account of the ministerial calling of humanity must also take account of the reality and extent of human fallenness and the need for a Christological definition of the *imago Dei*. The project of creation can only be achieved through the redemption that is offered in the birth, life, death, resurrection, and ascension of the faithful Son of God as a divine mediation. Similarly, there can be no thought of perfecting creation aside from the work of the Spirit, the perfecting cause, who alone makes things holy by

---

239. Holmes, "Can Theology Engage with Culture?" 14–15.
240. Gunton, *The Christian Faith*, 5.
241. Gunton, *The Christian Faith*, 50.
242. Gunton, "Reformation Accounts," 81–2.
243. Gunton, *Father, Son and Holy Spirit*, 111–12.

bringing them into relation with God through Christ.[244] Faithful human culture is set within the context of the divine action of the Son and the Spirit who mediate the Father's presence in the world, which will be examined in detail in Chapters 4 and 5.

Conclusion

This chapter has set the examination of Gunton's theology of culture in the context of his doctrine of creation, and the Father's mediation of creation through the economic action of the Son and the Spirit. Gunton's progression to a trinitarian theology of mediation results in a more consistent exploration of his theological method that prioritizes divine action as the site of divine self-revelation and self-interpretation. In Irenaeus, Gunton finds inspiration for his theological method and for his assertion of creation's material goodness and eschatological directedness. God creates the world as a distinct reality and accommodates his love and care to creation's temporal and spatial structures. More than that, God's relation with the creation is dynamic and open, and enables the created reality to participate with God in perfecting God's creation project.

The openness of creation to creaturely contributions provides a context for God's cultural calling to humanity to image God as God's priestly representatives who extend God's royal administration of the world. Humanity's cultural mandate is a call from God for humanity to participate in the divine redemption and perfection of creation. Faithful human cultural action enables the creation to be itself in relation to God and all else, and, therefore, anticipate the eschatological redemption and perfection of all things. Faithful human action is not independent from God, but is enabled by the action of the Son and the Spirit to collaborate with God in bringing about God's purposes for the world. Aside from the action of the Son and the Spirit, fallen humanity fails in its cultural mandate. A theological account of human culture, therefore, must be developed in relation with an account of the mediation of the Son and the Spirit in the economy. It is in Jesus Christ that the image of God subsists, and it is through his faithful life, death, and resurrection, enabled by the Spirit, that humanity's cultural mandate is redeemed and restored.

244. Gunton, "Reformation Accounts," 81–3.

Chapter 4

THE MEDIATION OF THE SON: HUMANITY AND HUMAN CULTURE

In one of his last works, published posthumously, Colin Gunton suggests the need for "a biblical and Trinitarian approach to culture" to replace the otherworldy drive of Platonized Christianity.[1] Instead of Platonized Christianity Gunton develops a biblical and trinitarian alternative that grounds the theology of culture in a robust Christological pneumatology.[2] Christology and pneumatology are the ground of Gunton's theology of culture because human culture is determined by the Son's mediation of faithful humanity that is enabled by the Spirit. The purpose of this chapter, and the following chapter, is to provide a detailed examination of Gunton's Christology and pneumatology as they relate to culture. This approach recognizes that Gunton develops his later *theological* account of culture through biblical and trinitarian reflection that supplements and extends his earlier analysis of Western culture.

The Mediation of the Son: Jesus Christ as Lord of Creation and Redemption

The relationship of the eternal God to temporal creation is for Gunton a central theological question.[3] Western theology commonly posits a breach between the orders of creation and redemption because it opposes God's timelessness to creation's temporality in order to preserve God's omnipotence. This stress upon God's transcendence from material creation often divorces God's timeless and instantaneous creating action from temporal saving action that takes time.[4] Creation is attributed to a monadic God who creates instantaneously by timeless divine fiat, whilst God's saving and redeeming action is conceived as redemption from temporality. Salvation is such a radically different action that there is a divorce between God's timeless creating action and God's saving and redemptive

---

1. Gunton, "Reformation Accounts," 91.
2. Gunton, "Reformation Accounts," 92.
3. Gunton, *Father, Son and Holy Spirit*, 135.
4. Gunton, *Father, Son and Holy Spirit*, 135.

action which takes time.⁵ The inability to relate the eternal God to temporal creation sets divine and created being in an oppositional framework that obstructs a proper theology of mediation. Christology, Gunton argues, needs to be much more determinative in the doctrine of creation in order to overcome the divorce between a timeless view of creation and temporal redemption. At stake is the question of mediation and how the timeless God is related to temporal creation, and the defining issue is Christology.⁶ God comes into relationship with that which is not himself through the incarnation of the eternal Son into the fullness of the fallen human estate.

Irenaeus is, in Gunton's estimation, the greatest theologian of creation, and his account of mediation provides the basis of Gunton's trinitarian theology of mediation. In contrast to the Gnostic theology of ascent out of the physical and material world, Irenaeus establishes a theology of God's descent into the world through the incarnation of the eternal Son of God in Jesus of Nazareth.⁷ In the Word made flesh, creation's Lord comes in person to remake and redeem that which through sin and evil has become subject to dissolution.⁸ The incarnation reveals that whatever the effects of sin, the created order, and human life within it, are of supreme importance to God.⁹ "According to the New Testament, creation is *through* and *to* Christ, and this means that it is, so to speak, structured by the very one who became incarnate and thus part of the created order of which we are speaking. It is good because God himself, through his Son, remains in intimate and loving relations with it."¹⁰ The incarnation is an affirmation of creaturely reality and since the Son of God took on flesh, we must confess that there is nothing inherently evil with temporal and material being.¹¹

If we are to understand God's personal relation with creation, we do so through what God reveals in the divine action of incarnation. "If you want to understand how God works in our world, then you must go through the route God himself has given us—the incarnation of the eternal Son and the life-giving action of the Spirit."¹² The incarnation is the chief model of mediation for Gunton because God's actions in Christ are sovereign and achieve their ends, whilst respecting and upholding the integrity of creation's createdness. Jesus Christ is the focus of God's involvement within creation's structures because his being, as the creator of these structures, is ordered towards creation's spatiality and temporality that he takes to himself.¹³

The vital link between the timeless God and temporal creation is found in the eternal Word, through whom all things came into being, entering the temporal

---

5. Gunton, *Father, Son and Holy Spirit*, 137.
6. Gunton, *Father, Son and Holy Spirit*, 139–40.
7. Gunton, *Father, Son and Holy Spirit*, 165.
8. Gunton, "The Doctrine of Creation," 143.
9. Gunton, *Father, Son and Holy Spirit*, 30.
10. Gunton, *The Triune Creator*, 10. See also Gunton, "The Doctrine of Creation," 142.
11. Gunton, *The Christian Faith*, 24–5.
12. Gunton, *Father, Son and Holy Spirit*, 11.
13. Gunton, *Father, Son and Holy Spirit*, 140. See also Gunton, *The Christian Faith*, 99.

created order. As the eternal Word that created and structured all things in time, it is the distinct office of the Son to be incarnate. The mediation of creation by God's eternal Word indicates that God can become "worldly" and remain wholly God.[14] Jesus Christ is, therefore, the Father's immanent action within the world, and to create through him is to create "by the mediation of the one who is the way of God out into that which is not himself."[15] The affirmation of Jesus Christ as the mediator of creation *and* redemption is a central affirmation of the New Testament and a pivotal affirmation for Gunton's theology of culture.

Whilst the Genesis texts on creation are important, Gunton holds that the New Testament offers the definitive Christian account of a trinitarian theology of creation. "The definitive New Testament contribution to the development of the doctrine is to be found in its Christological form."[16] The primary source for the doctrine of creation is the New Testament account of Christ as mediator of creation; the one by whom, through whom, for whom, and to whom all things are created and directed.[17] Creation is Christologically conditioned and the New Testament affirms Jesus Christ as the mediator, sustainer, and redeemer of creation (John 1:1-18; Col 1:15-29; Heb 1:1-4; Rev 22:1-5). The New Testament writers often utilize the Genesis accounts of creation as an invisible intertextual matrix for their assertions of a trinitarian theology of creation. The prologue to John's gospel, and the wider structure of the gospel, echoes the Genesis creation narrative in its account of creation by the Word, and John employs the days of creation as a template to interpret Jesus' ministry. There are similar intertextual echoes of Genesis in the wider New Testament, which serve as frameworks to understand the significance of Jesus Christ (e.g., Hebrews 11:3 and Revelation 4:11).[18] Along with the intertextual echoes are the direct textual claims that creation is Christologically conceived, maintained, and directed (John 1; 1 Cor 8:6; 2 Cor 4:6; Heb 1; Col 1).[19] The Colossian Hymn (Col 1:15-23) is one especially insightful example.

The Colossian Hymn affirms that creation is not only in and through Jesus Christ, but that Christ also upholds all things and directs them to their promised *telos* (end) in himself. Through the eschatological action of the Spirit, all things are directed to Jesus Christ and find their proper end in the one through whom they were created and made.[20] Reflecting on Colossians 1:16 ("for in him all things in heaven and on earth were created ... all things have been created through him and for him."), Gunton concludes that Jesus Christ is the person in whom the relation between the eternal God and temporal creation takes place. Jesus Christ is "the externalization in the world of the one who mediates all the Father's creating

---

14. Gunton, *The Christian Faith*, 10.
15. Gunton, *The Triune Creator*, 143.
16. Gunton, *The Triune Creator*, 20–1.
17. Gunton, "The Doctrine of Creation," 145.
18. Gunton, *The Triune Creator*, 21–2.
19. Gunton, *The Triune Creator*, 20.
20. Gunton, *The Triune Creator*. See also Gunton, *The Promise of Trinitarian Theology*, 185–6; and Gunton, *Father, Son and Holy Spirit*, 105.

and redeeming action."[21] Instead of creation by a monadically conceived account of God, creation is Christologically conditioned, and takes place in *Christ* rather than in God. "There is a great deal of difference between saying that all things were created in God, *simpliciter*, and that it happened and happens in Christ."[22] Gunton's trinitarian account of creation and culture is centred in the person of Jesus Christ who is the mediator of creation and redemption.

Jesus Christ is divine wisdom in action, and this has much to teach us about the form of God's providential action in creation and redemption, as well as true human culture. The New Testament authors draw from pre-existing wisdom traditions in the Hebrew Bible, in place of the esoteric Hellenistic accounts of wisdom, to characterize the distinct form of providential action found in Jesus Christ. Creation is mediated by divine wisdom (Prov 8:27), and it is this tradition that influences New Testament accounts of creation in John 1, Colossians 1, Hebrews 1, and 1 Cor 8:6. Wisdom in the New Testament is not an abstract Hellenistic virtue; it is personified in Jesus Christ who *is* wisdom.[23]

Divine wisdom, according to 1 Corinthians, is displayed most centrally at the cross.[24] God's wisdom is best understood as a form of God's gracious action in response to the disaster of the fall. God's patient wisdom is enacted through time by the re-establishment of the creation covenant with Noah and the call of Abraham to be the vehicle by whom the covenant of redemption was made with all humanity.[25] In God's redemptive action, God respects humanity and creation's need for time to become themselves. Even the cross, Gunton argues, is a form of God's wisdom that is appropriate to humanity's fallenness and the need for redirection through time. The cross is the culmination of Jesus Christ's faithful human life and career that is outworked in the midst of a fallen world. The temporality of createdness is vital for Gunton, as "our being in time is not a defect of being, but part of its goodness."[26] The divine work of redemption is established amidst the temporal structures of creation, and it is part of the wisdom of God that enables things to take their course through time as well as over-against it.[27] God respects creation's temporality and in Jesus Christ interacts with it according to its being. Creation's temporality is its glory; time is not the problem but what happens within it. In Jesus Christ, God's being is oriented to creation's spatiality and temporality that he takes to himself in the incarnation.[28]

The incarnation is not a rescue project to restore creation to an idyllic pre-lapsarian life. Creation is a project that is going somewhere; it was created perfect and to be perfected through time. The eschatological directedness of the project of creation is ordered to an end that is greater than its beginning, while the divine

---

21. Gunton, *Father, Son and Holy Spirit*, 105.
22. Gunton, *The Triune Creator*, 142–3.
23. Gunton, *Father, Son and Holy Spirit*, 132–3.
24. Gunton, *Father, Son and Holy Spirit*, 133–4.
25. Gunton, *Father, Son and Holy Spirit*, 135–6.
26. Gunton, *Father, Son and Holy Spirit*, 136.
27. Gunton, *Father, Son and Holy Spirit*, 139.
28. Gunton, *Father, Son and Holy Spirit*, 140.

purpose of the perfection of the project of creation precedes the fall. Gunton opposes what he calls dishwater Protestantism that posits the incarnation as the divine solution to a creaturely problem. "Is it really the case," Gunton asks, "that God has one shot at his world called 'creation', and because that fails then has to send his Son to pick up the pieces?"[29] Given that the relationship between creation and redemption is unified in the Lordship of Jesus Christ, Gunton contends, through Irving and Scotus, that there would be an incarnation even if there was no fall because the creation is oriented to an end that is greater than the beginning.

The incarnation is not a mere repair job, but the extension and concentration of the love of God for creation and its eschatological perfection in Jesus Christ by the power of the Spirit. Sin and the fall do not condition grace; grace redeems sin and transforms the effects of the fall. "The ways of God for his creation involve Christ, the one through whom he created and continues to uphold the universe *in any case*, and therefore he would have come – even had sin not dictated the *form* of his coming."[30] Whilst the fall may have been the formal cause of the incarnation, it is the love of God for the creation that is the efficient cause; a love that is rooted in God's being and concentrated in Jesus Christ, the Lord of creation. The efficient cause of the incarnation is the love of God for God's creature and creation, "a love rooted in his being, and begun, continued and ended in Christ."[31] Whatever else may be said of salvation, it is rooted in the love of God and God's merciful refusal to allow the creation to destroy itself. Through the incarnation, ministry, and passion of Jesus Christ, we see creation's Lord returning to his realm in human actuality in such a way that the project of creation is redirected to its proper eschatological end—the reconciliation of all things with God.[32]

The Full Humanity of the Son and Human Culture

Jesus Christ's humanity needs to be regarded as continuous with our humanity in a way that is much more radical than is usually allowed.[33] Gunton detects a persistent docetic tendency in Western theology that stresses the divinity of Jesus Christ to such an extent that his humanity is subsidiary.[34] Given Gunton's opposition to perceived dualisms and his emphasis upon embodiment, it is no surprise that he fights to oppose this trajectory. In seeking to underscore the uniqueness of Jesus Christ, Gunton senses the tradition's attempts to preserve the divinity of Jesus Christ by stressing his extraordinary birth, life, ministry, death, resurrection, and sinlessness. But Gunton queries this conflation of the uniqueness of Jesus with his sinlessness as it posits his humanity as a different kind from that which we inhabit—a form of hybrid being that screens him from the real perils

---

29. Gunton, *The Christian Faith*, 65.
30. Gunton, *The Christian Faith*, 67.
31. Gunton, *The Christian Faith*, 68.
32. Gunton, *The Promise of Trinitarian Theology*, 185.
33. Gunton, *The Christian Faith*, 99.
34. Gunton, *The Christian Faith*, 78.

of our humanity.[35] Salvation depends upon the Lord's total identification with our humanity and its fallen condition, and Gunton argues that the tradition has not given adequate weight to the humanity of the Son. If it is our humanity that is redeemed, the incarnation of the eternal Son entails total assumption of our fallen estate. The significance of Christ's assumption of our common humanity is important to Gunton because Christ mediates not only God to humanity but also humanity to God. The salvation of humanity, and the wider creation, requires the total identification of Jesus Christ with our fallen humanity, as the unassumed is the unredeemed.[36]

If the docetic tendencies of the tradition are to be overcome, then Gunton argues that we must develop an account of the incarnation that stresses the Son's full humanity and his assumption of our fallen humanity. The book of Hebrews highlights for Gunton the importance of Christ's assumption of our humanity as it confesses that Jesus Christ is "tempted in every way, just as we are – yet was without sin" (Heb 4:15). Much of the emphasis of the tradition falls upon the latter part of the verse to show the uniqueness of Jesus Christ should be determined by his sinlessness. However, this comes at the expense of the emphasis of the earlier half of the verse that Christ is tempted in his humanity "just as we are."[37] As Jerome Van Kuiken observes, Gunton understands Christ's share in our common fallen humanity as hereditary and social. His humanity is drawn from his mother, who is thoroughly fallen, and he is born and lives amidst a fallen social setting. "Thus through both heredity and social setting, Christ was conditioned by fallenness."[38] It is through the medium of his fallen flesh that Christ "works his healing into the fabric of the universe."[39] Gunton's emphasis upon Christ's full assumption of our fallen humanity, sin apart, develops through the work of Edward Irving. This emphasis upon the genuineness of Christ's humanity and human action is an important aspect of Gunton's quest for a more concrete trinitarianism, and is vital to his theology of culture.

In the work of Irving, Gunton finds an alternative theological trajectory to the docetism he detects in the tradition. Irving provides an important emphasis upon the Son's assumption of our full humanity, whilst remaining without sin, that offers greater importance to the genuineness of his human action.[40] In the incarnation, Jesus Christ assumes the common stock of our fallen humanity, but Gunton stops short of employing Irving's language of Christ's fallen flesh, because

---

35. Gunton, *Father, Son and Holy Spirit*, 152.

36. Gunton, *Father, Son and Holy Spirit*, 152. Gunton is here referring to Gregory of Nazianzen's famous dictum, "that which He has not assumed He has not healed." Gregory of Nazianzen, *To Cledonius the Priest Against Apollinaris* 101 (*NPNF* 7:440).

37. Gunton, *Father, Son and Holy Spirit*, 152-3.

38. E. Jerome Van Kuiken, *Christ's Humanity in Current and Ancient Controversy: Fallen or Not?* (London and New York: T&T Clark, 2017), 46.

39. Van Kuiken, *Christ's Humanity in Current and Ancient Controversy*, 46.

40. Gunton, *Theology Through the Theologians*, 151. See also Gunton, *The Christian Faith*, 102; and Gunton, *Father, Son and Holy Spirit*, 153-7.

it is prone to misunderstanding. "Because it is people, not flesh, who sin and are fallen perhaps it would make the point more adequately if we were to say that the matter from which the Spirit builds a body for the Son is that same corrupt matter as that which constitutes the persons of other human beings."[41] The person of Jesus Christ is certainly free of sin's taint, but the humanity he assumes is, like ours, post-lapsarian. Jesus Christ must share in the full conditions of our taint, Gunton maintains, if his freedom from sin is to be mediated to us. Christ is constituted of the same humanity which we share, part of the created order, that is subject to decay and in need of redemption.[42]

Christ's life is one of real struggle and temptation that is overcome by the Spirit's enabling, as it is the Spirit who perfects this representative sample of humanity. His sinlessness is not a result of his immanent possession of the Spirit, but his obedience to the Father's will by the power of the Spirit enabling him. It is the eschatological Spirit who enables Jesus Christ to resist temptation and sin, and equip and empower him in his particular humanity and calling.[43] The second section expands the significance of this accent in Gunton's thought, as some scholars raise concerns about the passivity of the Word and the potential separation of the Word and the Spirit.

Alongside his emphasis upon the uniqueness of Jesus Christ as the eternal Son incarnate, Gunton believes there also needs to be a stress upon his ordinariness.[44] The birth of Jesus Christ is certainly a miraculous new divine initiative of salvation, but equally significant is the fact that this is realized through one who is fully human. "A real human being is shaped from the flesh of the Virgin by the Father's creator Spirit."[45] Likewise, the resurrection is certainly a miracle, but its importance also lies in the Spirit raising Jesus Christ from the dead as the first fruits of our redeemed humanity. It is our common humanity that is redeemed and raised to a new form of eschatological life.[46] This is very important in Gunton's work, because salvation is not limited to Christ's death on the cross making atonement for sin. Christ's human life is redemptive, as it is a triumphant recapitulation of Adam's fallen humanity.

Christ's faithful recapitulation of Adam's fallen humanity is a redemptive mediation of God through which Christ goes over the sorry story of human sin but, unlike Adam, emerges triumphant.[47] The incarnation of Jesus Christ into our common stock of humanity is not only related to the redemption of our

41. Gunton, *The Christian Faith*, 102. See also Van Kuiken, *Christ's Humanity in Current and Ancient Controversy*, 46–7.
42. Gunton, *Intellect and Action*, 15.
43. Gunton, *Intellect and Action*, 15.
44. The uniqueness and the ordinariness of Jesus Christ are another mediatorial tension in which Gunton asked, "Can we have our cake and eat it? A saviour whose exceptionableness is that of a man who is in some ways not exceptional." See Gunton, *Father, Son and Holy Spirit*, 153.
45. Gunton, *Father, Son and Holy Spirit*, 153.
46. Gunton, *Father, Son and Holy Spirit*, 154.
47. Gunton, *Father, Son and Holy Spirit*, 162.

humanity, though it is certainly not less. Of equal importance is Christ's fulfilment of the human calling to mediate God's rule on earth and bring about creation's redemption from its bondage to decay. Gunton draws from Irenaeus to develop a theology of Christ's recapitulation of Adam and Israel which informs his account of the *imago Dei* and humanity's cultural mandate. Like the doctrine of creation, Christology is at the centre of the *imago Dei* and humanity's cultural mandate.

Jesus Christ, the imago Dei, and Humanity's Cultural Mandate

In his early writings on the *imago Dei*, Gunton explores the relational structuring of the image for humanity's relationship with God, humanity, and the created order. The emphasis upon the relational conception of the image offers a relational ontology in contradistinction to rationalistic Enlightenment understandings that centre the image in human reason.[48] In his later writings, Gunton draws from Irenaeus' account of recapitulation to extend his relational ontology through a more sustained examination of the Christological conditioning of the *imago Dei* and humanity's cultural mandate.

Jesus Christ's faithful recapitulation of Adam's story reveals him to be the true human who mediates God's redemption and restoration of the *imago Dei* in humanity after the fall.[49] Jesus Christ not only mediates God's redemption to humanity, his recapitulation of Adam also mediates humanity to God as the representative human. The career of Jesus Christ is a recapitulation of the career of Adam whose life is marred by sin. But, unlike Adam, Jesus Christ emerges triumphant over sin and evil through his human faithfulness as the second, and eschatological, Adam.[50] Jesus Christ is the eschatological Adam in whom God recapitulates the human story, "achieving the redemption of the lost creation by doing in triumph what Adam failed to do in defeat. As Adam failed to be the human being made in the image of God, so Christ, by becoming human, not only corrects what is wrong, but brings to perfection what was begun in creation."[51] A biblical and trinitarian account of mediation and the *imago Dei* is concentrated in Jesus Christ's triumphant recapitulation of humanity.

The New Testament account of the *imago Dei* reinterprets its meaning in and through Jesus Christ. The doctrine of the *imago Dei* is not an overtly prominent theme in scripture, and when it is used in the New Testament it is assimilated almost exclusively to Christ. The New Testament, for the most part, restricts the attribution of the image of God to Jesus Christ, who represents true humanity.[52] Following the fall, the image of God is distorted in humanity and creation fails to be set free to become itself in worship of God. The Christological redefinition of the *imago Dei* means that in Jesus Christ we are concerned with the redemption of

---

48. Gunton, *The Promise of Trinitarian Theology*, 109–6.
49. Gunton, *Father, Son and Holy Spirit*, 165–7.
50. Gunton, *Father, Son and Holy Spirit*, 162.
51. Gunton, *Father, Son and Holy Spirit*, 29.
52. Gunton, *The Christian Faith*, 122. See also Gunton, *The Triune Creator*, 196.

the distorted image and the inbreaking of the new creation in him. "The doctrine of Christ as the Second Adam has therefore this function, to show that the destiny of the created human being – the first Adam – is in some sense bound up with him."[53] Not only is there no perfection apart from Jesus Christ, the end is not attained without the redemption that is found in him. Jesus Christ, the Lord of creation and redemption, upholds humanity in the image of God because it is in him that the image subsists.[54] In his later work, Gunton developed his Christologically conditioned theology of the *imago Dei* in specific relation to humanity's cultural calling in Genesis 1:26-28.

Humanity's cultural mandate comes to occupy a vital place in Gunton's later works, particularly those after *The Triune Creator*. In his earlier writings, Gunton explores the ministerial and relational accounts of the *imago Dei* and observes weaknesses in both. The ministerial account is too literalistic and restrictive with the biblical texts, and Barth's relational account underplays the importance of the non-human creation. Gunton's remedy to these weaknesses is, at this point, a stronger theological ontology, based upon his trinitarian understanding of personhood.[55] In his later writings, it is Christology and the concrete mediation of the Son in the economy, rather than relational trinitarian personhood, that unite the ministerial and relational conception of the image in Gunton's thought.

The material creation cannot be understood apart from its ordering to the human race as humanity is called to represent and mediate God's rule within the world. This is humanity's calling to rightly inhabit creation in such a way "as to enable the created order to be itself as a response of praise to its maker."[56] Because of the fall, humanity fails to exercise the ministry of stewardship in creation and both are subjected to the bondage to decay in which they do not attain the freedom and destiny that God intends. "As things are, the human race fails in its cultural mandate, and, *consequently*, the remainder of creation fails to be offered in praise of its Maker."[57] This bondage to decay is expressed in Genesis through the cursing of the earth (*'ădāmâ*) as a result of humanity's (*'ādām*) fall, such that work is no longer pleasant but laborious, toilsome, and unpleasant.[58] The life and ministry of Jesus Christ can be understood as the faithful expression of humanity's ministerial calling to stewardship of the creation.

The gospel writers interpret Jesus' life, ministry, and teaching through the context of the creation narrative in Genesis and God's re-establishment of his rule over the creation. "If we are to be true to the theology of creation which forms the foundation for everything else, we must hold that as the minister of God's kingdom this man re-establishes God's writ over the whole of the fallen creation."[59] This is explicit in Romans 8 and its echo of Genesis 1–3 and the relationship of

---

53. Gunton, *The Triune Creator*, 202.
54. Gunton, *The Triune Creator*, 207.
55. Gunton, *The Promise of Trinitarian Theology*, 116.
56. Gunton, *The Triune Creator*, 12.
57. Gunton, "Reformation Accounts," 81–2.
58. Gunton, "Reformation Accounts," 82.
59. Gunton, *The Christian Faith*, 106–7.

'ādām and 'ădāmâ. Romans 8:20 sets the creation's subjection to futility in the context of humanity's fall. Gunton detects here an echo of the cursing of the earth in Genesis 3:17.[60] The eschatological destiny of 'ādām and 'ădāmâ is intrinsically linked such that humanity's exchange of its ministerial calling for idolatry results in the creation's bondage too.[61] The ministry of Jesus Christ is the fulfilment of humanity's calling and through the eschatological 'ādām, the Spirit renews 'ădāmâ from its bondage to decay to enjoy the glorious freedom of the children of God.[62] The theological importance of Christ's recapitulation of humanity necessitates an examination of the human career of Jesus Christ as a redemptive mediation by God.

Much of the tradition, in Gunton's analysis, stresses the cross as the centre of God's atoning work to such a degree that Christ's particular life and ministry are of little significance.[63] Atonement is certainly centred in the cross, but Gunton maintains that the human career of Jesus Christ must also be understood as a constitutive part of the gospel of grace and God's redemptive mediation. In his recapitulation of Adam, Jesus Christ takes up humanity's failed calling and exercises the human calling to stewardship in the creation through his human career. Only in Jesus Christ "does there live and act one truly exercising the promised human authority over creatures."[64] It is only in Jesus Christ that we know what is right human habitation of the world and true human culture, for his life is empowered and perfected by the eschatological Spirit.[65]

Christ's life is a microcosm through which the Spirit enables this representative sample of the created world to become that which it was created to be.[66] The project of creation and humanity's ministerial calling is concentrated in Jesus Christ, and he exercises the ministry of human stewardship and culture as the eschatological Adam. In Christ, the eschatological Adam, creation is offered back to God, perfected as a result of the faithful exercise of humanity's cultural mandate. God's universal purposes are inaugurated and achieved through the particular life, ministry, and career of Jesus Christ, who restores the project of creation to its proper *telos* (end) in and through his own person. "The reconciliation of all things to God can be achieved only by him who is at once Christ the creator *and* a human being who restores the project of creation to its proper destiny by what he does."[67]

In the incarnation and human career of Jesus Christ we encounter creation's Lord returned to claim his own in human actuality.[68] But this divine mediation is not the work of a wonder worker; it is the work of a truly human agent who

---

60. Gunton, *Father, Son and Holy Spirit*, 111.
61. Gunton, *Father, Son and Holy Spirit*, 112.
62. Gunton, *Father, Son and Holy Spirit*, 111–12.
63. Gunton, *Father, Son and Holy Spirit*, 169–73. See also Gunton, *Intellect and Action*, 123–5.
64. Gunton, *The Christian Faith*, 46.
65. Gunton, "Reformation Accounts," 93.
66. Gunton, *Father, Son and Holy Spirit*, 117.
67. Gunton, *The Promise of Trinitarian Theology*, 186.
68. Gunton, *The Promise of Trinitarian Theology*, 185.

exercises the human calling to stewardship in the creation by the right human habitation of the world. Jesus' ministry is that of a truly human agent exercising the human call to stewardship in the creation.

Whilst some of Jesus' healings adhere to the speech-act model of divine (re)creating, others follow the mediation model of divine (re)creating. Referring to the instances of God's variegated creating action in Genesis, Gunton argues that "Jesus' healings according to Mark are sometimes by word alone and sometimes through physical interaction with the material world (compare here the different forms of God's creating action in Genesis 1)."[69] In the stilling of the storm, creation responds to the Word of its Lord ("Peace! Be still!" Mark 4:39) and is set free from its bondage.[70] But divine fiat is not the only form of recreating action Jesus displays, and later in Mark we find Jesus is unable to perform miracles (Mark 6:5) by divine command.

Whilst Jesus acts by divine command, he also acts by mediation that accommodates itself to temporal creation. In a different recreating mode, we find that the healing of a blind man takes time. After Jesus' initial interaction with the blind man, where he puts saliva on his eyes and touches him, the blind man sees people as trees. It is only after another interaction, where Jesus touches his eyes again, that the man's sight is restored (Mark 8:22-26).[71] "Jesus' healings are accommodated to the condition of those in need of healing."[72] The Lord of creation, Gunton concludes, respects creation's temporality and accommodates his action in partnership with the ministerial calling of the creation and its creatures.[73] The healings and exorcisms are eschatological anticipations that the Spirit enables, in collaboration with faithful human action; the beginnings of the eschatological kingdom that has no end.[74] Christ's ministry and human career is empowered by the Spirit as an eschatological anticipation of the renewal of all things in time, through which the creation is set free to be what it was created to be in praise of its maker.

Jesus Christ's victorious recapitulation of Adam's fallen humanity is won through his faithful obedience to the Father's will. Jesus Christ's obedience was not the result of an automated saintliness; it is learned as he responds to the Spirit leading and maintaining him, as a weak and needy human, in faithfulness to the Father.[75] Gunton turns especially to the book of Hebrews for his Christology, in particular its stress upon Christ's human obedience and victory over temptation

---

69. Gunton, *Father, Son and Holy Spirit*, 154.
70. Gunton, *Father, Son and Holy Spirit*, 155.
71. For an account of this text that utilizes insights from sensory disability to overcome stereotyped ableist readings of the text, see Louise J. Lawrence, *Sense and Stigma in the Gospels: Depictions of Sensory-Disabled Characters* (Oxford: Oxford University Press, 2013), 31–56.
72. Gunton, *Father, Son and Holy Spirit*, 155.
73. Gunton, *Father, Son and Holy Spirit*, 155.
74. Gunton, *Father, Son and Holy Spirit*, 117.
75. Gunton, *The Christian Faith*, 103.

through what he suffered.⁷⁶ The reference to "what he suffered" should not be limited to the cross; it should include the cross that Jesus Christ bore throughout his entire ministry. What Jesus Christ suffers in his human ministry is primarily the temptation to be God's Son in a way that is different than God intends. "This temptation of Jesus, so important for the author to the Hebrews, is clearly central to his learning of obedience, because it concerns, at two of its many levels, both what it means to be a true Israelite and what it means to obey God rather than the devil."⁷⁷

Christ's triumphant recapitulation of Adam's fallen humanity is a triumph of obedience and not Adamic self-assertion. "As Adam fell, so Jesus stands and walks with God."⁷⁸ If Christ is to fulfil humanity's cultural mandate, Gunton maintains that it must be a truly human obedience to the Father by the Spirit. Christ's obedience and sinlessness are not due to his divine nature constituting him unable to sin (*non potuit peccare*) or accept the temptations of the devil. Nor is it that Christ is able not to sin through human effort (*potuit non peccare*) because this suggests that human beings are able to do the will of God in their own strength. This results in an undermining of his full humanity. Instead, Gunton proposes a pneumatologically developed alternative: Jesus Christ is *enabled* not to sin by the Spirit's perfecting action. It is the Spirit who upholds Jesus Christ in his human obedience to be the particular Israelite that the Father calls him to be.⁷⁹ The recapitulation and concentration of Adam *and* Israel in Jesus Christ is an important progression in Gunton's theology of culture. The gospel is concerned with particularities, and Christ's faithful obedience as a Jewish man is displayed in the concrete social, political, and moral context of first-century Israel and Israel's story.⁸⁰

Jesus Christ the True Israelite and the Right Human Habitation of the World

Jesus Christ cannot be known and understood aside from his particular Jewish humanity. What makes Jesus who he is particularly is his relationship to Israel and Israel's God.⁸¹ The importance of Israel in Gunton's thought develops especially in his later writings, and this has particular impacts on his Christology and his account of human culture. However, the significance of Israel to Gunton's Christology, pneumatology, and ecclesiology has not received adequate recognition in Gunton scholarship.

An important exception is the work of David Höhne, who notes the prominence of Israel in Gunton's theology. Gunton refers especially to Luke-Acts to establish the Jewish particularity of Jesus. However, Höhne observes that Gunton's lack

---

76. See Stephen R. Holmes, "Foreword," in Gunton, *Father, Son and Holy Spirit*, x.
77. Gunton, *The Christian Faith*, 105.
78. Gunton, *The Christian Faith*, 105.
79. Gunton, *The Christian Faith*, 105–6.
80. Gunton, *Father, Son and Holy Spirit*, 64–5.
81. Gunton, *Intellect and Action*, 106.

of exegetical detail limits the depth of his insights regarding the particularity of the Son as the climax of Israel's drama. Höhne rightly argues that Gunton's work could be furthered by a more thorough exegesis of Luke-Acts that recognizes Luke's intertextual account of Jesus as Israel's Davidic king.[82] In a different vein, Terry Wright, in his chapters on Gunton and divine providence, and Gunton and eschatology, notes the importance of Israel in Gunton's theology. Given the themes of Wright's chapters, he pays particular attention to Gunton's pneumatological account of the election of Israel and the Church as elect communities. Aside from these two important exceptions, not enough attention is given to the significance of Israel in Gunton's later Christology, ecclesiology, and culture.[83]

Gunton detects a persistent supersessionism in the tradition that undermines Christ's Jewishness and interprets his significance in abstraction from his historical context and formation in Israel.[84] Instead, Gunton stresses that the incarnation of Jesus Christ is his incarnation into the particular context and story of Israel. "Israel, we might say, provides the logic of christology, so that the Old Testament lays down the framework within which both Jesus himself, so it would appear,

---

82. David A. Höhne, *Spirit and Sonship: Colin Gunton's Theology of Particularity and the Holy Spirit* (Farnham: Ashgate, 2010), 17, 44–5. Höhne's critique and subsequent development of Gunton's work in conversation with Dietrich Bonhoeffer and an exegesis of Luke-Acts produce some important enrichments of Gunton's work. Höhne notes an important potential line of enquiry that could be furthered by placing greater emphasis on Gunton's later writings, as well as more recent intertextual readings of Luke-Acts and the Isaianic New Exodus. For example, see Holly Beers, *The Followers of Jesus as the "Servant": Luke's Model from Isaiah for the Disciples in Luke-Acts* (London: Bloomsbury/T&T Clark, 2015); Issac W. Oliver, *Luke's Jewish Eschatology: The National Restoration of Israel in Luke-Acts* (New York: OUP, 2021); Michael E. Fuller, *The Restoration of Israel: Israel's Re-gathering and the Fate of the Nations in Early Jewish Literature and Luke-Acts* (Berlin: De Gruyter, 2006); Richard Bauckham, *The Jewish World around the New Testament* (Grand Rapids: Baker, 2008), 325–70; and David W. Pao, *Acts and the Isaianic New Exodus* (Grand Rapids: Baker, 2000).

83. Wright notes that whilst Gunton's views on providence emerged initially in *The Triune Creator*, they were fully matured in his later work, especially in *The Christian Faith*, through his theology of the election of Israel and, in Christ, the church. Wright argues that the addition of election to the doctrine of providence results in Gunton defining providence as *the* action, not just *an* action, of God according to the scriptural narrative. Wright's work on Gunton's theology of providence shares many of the arguments of this book regarding the shape of Gunton's later theology and the importance of divine action and mediation as it is revealed in the scriptural narrative. See Terry J. Wright, "Colin Gunton on Providence: Critical Commentaries," in *The Theology of Colin Gunton*, ed. Lincoln Harvey (London: T&T Clark, 2010), 153–60; and Terry J. Wright, "Gunton on Eschatology," in *T&T Clark Handbook of Colin Gunton*, ed. Andrew Picard, Myk Habets, and Murray Rae (London: T&T Clark, 2021), 147–8.

84. Gunton, *The Christian Faith*, 81. See also Gunton, *Intellect and Action*, 84–6.

and his first interpreters understood his significance."[85] Jesus Christ's calling as the second Adam needs to be understood in relation to God's particular historical actions in the covenants of promise with Israel. Jesus Christ, Gunton holds, is both the second Adam and the true Israelite in fulfilment of God's purposes, and he recapitulates Adam's humanity *and* Israel's story. Without this necessary link to the Hebrew Bible and Christ's triumphant recapitulation of Israel's story through obedience, Gunton argues that we cannot understand the nature of his sonship and faithful humanity.[86]

Jesus Christ is born into Jewish genetics and the lineage of the people who carry the promise and burden of fallen human life. Gunton notes that the gospel narratives, especially Luke's gospel, situate Jesus Christ in full solidarity with the people of Israel, and his ministry is that of the true Israelite.[87] His early life and formation are in the Jewish community, through the Jewish scriptures, and at the Jewish temple. Jesus' baptism is set in the context of John the Baptist's proclamation of judgement upon disobedient Israel, and this setting signifies his identification with their plight.[88]

It is in his identification with Israel's disobedience that the Spirit descends upon him, and we learn of his calling to true sonship. As God's eschatological other, the Spirit drives Jesus into the wilderness where he faces the same temptations as Israel. "The Spirit is the mediator of particularity in being the one who forms a body for the Son – *this* Jewish child of *this* Jewish mother – comes upon him in baptism, drives him into the wilderness to be tempted and there supports him so that he may become the particular Israelite that he was called to be and become."[89] Through these temptations, Jesus learns obedience and where Israel failed, Jesus does not. It is through obedience that Jesus is the true Israelite and the faithful Son of the Father. "Jesus is not only obedient Israel, but the eternal son of God become, in Luther's words, proper man."[90] In his recapitulation of Israel's calling, Jesus reveals that whilst Israel may be called God's son (Jer 31:9; Hos 11:1-2), he is the eternal Son of God and faithful sonship is determined in him.[91]

Israel's election and calling are a particular calling for the sake of anticipating God's universal purposes in creation in time. The promise to Abraham is that he and his descendants will be the source of salvation for all people. God's callings, promises, and covenants with Israel are the means through which God advances God's merciful and saving action in the creation.[92] God's universal purposes for the right human habitation of the world are displayed through the particular means of Israel's social, moral, and political order. Like the Church, which we will examine in the next chapter, Israel is a community of redemption whose life is a form of

85. Gunton, *The Christian Faith*, 80.
86. Gunton, *Father, Son and Holy Spirit*, 65.
87. Gunton, *The Christian Faith*, 103.
88. Gunton, *The Christian Faith*, 103–4.
89. Gunton, *Intellect and Action*, 80.
90. Gunton, *Father, Son and Holy Spirit*, 66.
91. Gunton, *Father, Son and Holy Spirit*, 64–5.
92. Gunton, *The Christian Faith*, 68–9.

culture instituted by God.[93] The shape of Israel is determined by the covenants, the law, the offices, and institutions that were given by God through which human life is reoriented to the end for which it was created. As such, Israel's life is ordered to a form of life and worship, a living sacrifice of praise to God, which is structured to God's purposes in creation and redemption.

Israel's law (Torah), Gunton avers, is given as a framework for Israel's habitation of creation and human life under God in gracious response to God's unmerited goodness. "Torah thus embraces those things expected both generally of any human being and more specifically and in detail of the group which was saved out of Egypt and made a people for God's glory."[94] The Torah concerns Israel's vertical relation with God and its horizontal communal relations. It requires forms of action that give glory to God through personal integrity, just social order, and respect for the land and its creatures.[95] Just as God is different from the world, so Israel, through the law, is called to a distinct form of life. This distinct life is an ethic of creation that is lived out among the nations—a form of human culture within the created order. As Chapter 5 will show, Gunton examines Paul's employment of the Torah (especially in 1 Corinthians) and notes its ongoing importance in relation to the Church's culture and ethic. Along with the Torah, Israel is given the offices of prophets, priests, and kings, to order its social, moral, and political life towards covenant faithfulness and God's eschatological purposes in the creation.[96]

Israel's offices are given so that Israel's social life is ordered to display God's purposes, the right human habitation of the world. Gunton maintains that they reveal to us a form of redeemed human culture.[97] It is through these offices that God holds Israel in its elected vocation as minister of God's providential purposes in the world and maintains its faithfulness to the covenant.[98] The office of Israel's kings is to dispense justice within Israel, defend it from external threats, and maintain Israel in obedience to its calling among the nations. The office of the prophets is to speak and embody God's truth, and recall recalcitrant Israel to covenant loyalty through politically charged and symbolic marginal messages. The office of priests, which becomes particularly important in Gunton's Christology and theology of sacrifice, is to reorder Israel's relationship with God and one another through priestly sacrifice.[99] This reordering takes place through the exchange of something (an animal or an offering) for something else (cleansing or forgiveness).

The concept of a priestly sacrifice is vital to Gunton's theology, especially his Christology and theology of culture. The relationship of the human and non-human creation reminds us of the human calling to offer creation back to God in

---

93. Gunton, *Father, Son and Holy Spirit*, 121.
94. Gunton, *The Christian Faith*, 48–9. See also Gunton, *Intellect and Action*, 89–90.
95. Gunton, *The Christian Faith*, 49. See also Gunton, *Intellect and Action*, 83–90.
96. Gunton, *The Christian Faith*, 69.
97. Gunton, *The Christian Faith*, 70.
98. Gunton, *The Christian Faith*, 69.
99. Gunton, *The Christian Faith*, 70.

thanksgiving. Sacrifice also reminds us that apart from God's redemptive action, we are unable to offer ourselves (*'ādām*) and creation (*'ădāmâ*) back to God as a living sacrifice that is holy and acceptable.[100] Gunton draws from Calvin to show that these offices are not abolished in Christ, but find their fulfilment and concentration in him.[101]

Humanity and Israel's calling are concentrated in Jesus Christ as the fulfilment of humanity's cultural mandate in Genesis 1:26-28, as well as Israel's offices of prophet, priest, and king. "In his person, and through the various acts and phases of his historic career, Jesus fills the offices and institutions of Israel with distinctive and definitive meaning. ... Israel's offices are so concentrated in him that the old wineskins are burst open by the new and heady brew: in his person he *is* prophet, priest and king."[102]

As the eschatological prophet, Jesus Christ speaks as one with authority and power, and his symbolic acts of cleansing and renewal call Israel back to God. Jesus Christ is Israel's eschatological king, against all other contenders, who re-establishes God's reign and rule in his ministry of the kingdom. Christ's kingdom is not of this world and he is not elevated to glory, but to a cross. His death upon the cross fulfils all righteousness as he accepts the judgement and consequences of the human failure to live by the law.[103] Yet the cross is the means of his elevation to glory as even in the crucifixion Christ's obedience to the Father reveals him to be the true and faithful human being.[104] In his subsequent resurrection and ascension, Jesus Christ is enthroned as humanity's true and eternal king over all creation.[105]

The final office of priest is the most important for Gunton's theology of culture and his understanding of humanity's priestly calling. In his priestly ministry, Jesus Christ offers himself sacrificially in such a way that priest and sacrifice come together in his person as the perfect sacrifice. "In the Old Testament the priest is one who makes sacrifices to God on behalf of the people by bringing the gifts of the people to God. In this new order of things, the priest *is* the sacrifice and his gift to God the Father is that of himself, of his *life*."[106] The priesthood is realized eternally in Christ's self-offering of his perfect humanity as a sacrifice of praise in obedience to the Father by the power of the Spirit (Heb 9:14). "Jesus' life as a whole is an expression of that priesthood over creation that is the human calling outlined in Genesis 1.26-8 as the calling of those created in God's image .... In

---

100. Gunton, *The Christian Faith*, 71.
101. Gunton, *Father, Son and Holy Spirit*, 174–5. See also Gunton, *Intellect and Action*, 125–6.
102. Gunton, *The Christian Faith*, 72.
103. Gunton, *The Christian Faith*, 74–5. See also Gunton, *Intellect and Action*, 85–100 and Gunton, *Father, Son and Holy Spirit*, 228.
104. Gunton, *The Christian Faith*, 107.
105. Gunton, *The Christian Faith*, 70.
106. Gunton, *The Christian Faith*, 77. Italics original.

priestly fashion, as God made man, he brings together loving creator and hostile creature."[107]

Gunton's theology of Christ's priesthood and sacrifice is important to his account of the atonement, as well as his understanding of the ascension and human culture. These concentrations in Christ coalesce in Gunton's account of human culture that observes Christ's concentration of Israel's and humanity's cultural calling, which enables an understanding of Christ *as* eschatological human culture.[108]

Jesus Christ as Eschatological Human Culture

As the eschatological Adam and the true Israelite, Jesus Christ fulfils humanity's ministerial calling and offers us a view of true human culture and the right human habitation of the world.[109] Utilizing Robert Jenson's work, Gunton proposes that we can understand Christ as culture.[110] Christ is the eschatological Adam, the true Israelite, whose life is the obedient participation of creation in God's economic acts, in fulfilment of humanity's cultural mandate. It is only in Christ, the eternal Word and the true human being, that we observe the fulfilment and concentration of Israel's promises and humanity's ministerial calling mediated to God and the creation.

In Jesus' ministry of the Kingdom of God we see the Spirit enabling faithful human action to interact with creation in such a way that storms are stilled, diseases healed, and demons are exorcised as creation is set free to be itself in praise of its maker. Similarly, we see true human culture in his friendship with sinners,

---

107. Gunton, *The Christian Faith*, 112.

108. Gunton, "Reformation Accounts," 82.

109. Naomi Reese examines Gunton's pneumatology for the development of a public theology, which, in her usage, is more broadly a theology of culture. In comparison to other theologians of culture, Reese finds a much greater stress upon pneumatology and eschatology in Gunton's work. Reese makes good use of Gunton's pneumatology and his stress upon the eschatological action of the Spirit in the project of creation. However, her account of Gunton's theology of culture separates his pneumatology too far from his christology and, as such, Gunton's christological determination of culture and humanity's cultural mandate is overlooked. A sustained engagement with Gunton's christological definition of human culture would further strengthen Reese's engagement and critique of Niebuhr's Christ and culture typologies, as well as Carson's critical development of them. See Naomi Noguchi Reese, "Colin E. Gunton and Public Theologians: Toward a Trinitarian Public Theology," *Evangelical Review of Theology*, 41 (2017): 150–65. See also Reese, "Seeking the Welfare of the City," 208–54.

110. Gunton, "Reformation Accounts," 82. See Robert W. Jenson, "Christ as Culture 1: Christ as Polity," *International Journal of Systematic Theology*, 5 (2003): 323–9; Robert W. Jenson, "Christ as Culture 2: Christ as Art," *International Journal of Systematic Theology*, 6 (2004): 69–76; and Robert W. Jenson, "Christ as Culture 3: Christ as Drama," *International Journal of Systematic Theology*, 6 (2004): 194–201.

welcome of outcasts, love of enemies, and creation of a renewed community.[111] In him we see the first fruits of creation being set free from its bondage to decay by faithful human action, and the finite perfection of creation in anticipation of the promised end. "It is a material human body which is offered perfect to God the Father through the eternal Spirit in the context of a particular ministry (that of Israel's prophet, priest and king) in a particular religo-political context."[112]

These finite anticipations of the perfection of the project of creation are the result of the ministry of the eschatological Spirit who empowers Jesus Christ to be the true human being who expresses redeemed human culture. "It is the perfecting Spirit's action which becomes the means of the re-constitution of the cultural mandate in its God-given form in this particular instance."[113] Christ is true human culture because he is, by the Spirit, the eschatological Adam and the true Israelite, who pioneers and perfects our faith as the one fully alive human being.[114]

If we understand Jesus Christ as culture, the criteria for assessing true human culture must be Christological and human culture can only offer a sacrifice of praise to God when it conforms to Christ.[115] "[The] criteria by which we assess whether – or in which respects – a work of culture is the praise of God or some form of sin must be Christological, because only in Jesus do we know what right culture is."[116] This is not a simple straight-line process, for the cross, which is regarded as the supreme blasphemy, becomes by the Spirit the source of true wisdom and the means through which humanity can praise God. Yet if created being is to praise God, it must praise God in the way God is praised by the incarnate Son.[117] In him, Adam's priestly calling to stewardship over the creation is concentrated and fulfilled. It is in him, who is at once the true human and the Lord of creation, that we see the perfection of the project of creation in anticipation of the renewal of all things. Yet, there is no true human culture or perfection of the project of creation aside from the death and resurrection of Jesus Christ.[118]

The Crucified and Risen Son and Human Culture

If humans can contribute to the eschatological perfection of the project of creation, does this lead to a progressive eschatology that is too optimistic about humanity and fails to adequately regard human fallenness? For all its suggestiveness, Gunton's account of the eschatological perfection of the project of creation is criticized

---

111. Gunton, *Father, Son and Holy Spirit*, 117.
112. Gunton, "Reformation Accounts," 82.
113. Gunton, "Reformation Accounts," 82.
114. Gunton, *The Christian Faith*, 77.
115. Gunton, "Reformation Accounts," 92.
116. Gunton, "Reformation Accounts," 93.
117. Gunton, "Reformation Accounts," 93.
118. Gunton, *The Promise of Trinitarian Theology*, 183.

for an under-developed hamartiology that lacks the necessary staurocentrism. William Whitney claims that Gunton's theology of creation *is* his doctrine of salvation to such a degree that he holds a creational soteriology in which "the saga of redemption *is* the creation story."[119] Whitney's criticism captures the concerns others, such as Brad Green, hold about Gunton's hamartiology. Given the criticisms of Gunton's soteriology, this section examines the importance of his account of Christ's death, resurrection, and ascension and its implications for his theological account of human culture, as well as defending his work against its critics. Gunton certainly holds to the perfection of creation, and human contributions to that perfection, but these are established only through "the narrow gate of the historic cross and resurrection of Jesus of Nazareth."[120] Humanity's participation in the perfecting of the project of creation is Christologically determined and defined by Christ's sacrifice of obedient humanity in praise and worship to God.

Brad Green maintains that Gunton's assessment of Modernity reduces sin to be a noetic problem that is simply incorrect thinking about God and the world which needs correcting. What is missing, Green argues, is an account of hamartiology that asserts human sin as that which needs cleansing and reordering by the gospel. Green contrasts Gunton's noetic account of hamartiology with his understanding of Paul's stress in Romans 1 on humanity's sinful suppression of the knowledge of God.[121] Sin is not merely the wrong cultural ideas about God that require the right ideas about God, but "culture must also glorify God and give thanks to Him, and this latter emphasis is missing in Gunton."[122] Green establishes his charge of a noetic hamartiology through his reading of *The One, the Three and the Many* and *Enlightenment and Alienation*, which are primarily analyses of Modernity's epistemology and cosmology. As a result, Green reads Gunton's cosmological and philosophical accounts of Modernity as though they represent his definitive theological account of sin and soteriology, and fails to adequately engage Gunton's wider corpus.

A careful engagement with Gunton's full corpus, especially his later work, shows that Gunton gives multiple chapters to the themes of sin, the false exchange, self-glorification, slavery, unfreedom, and Christ's redemption. In *The Christian Faith*, Gunton begins his three chapters on the mediation of the Son with a section on "The Concept of Sin," as Christ's significance is directly related to

---

119. Whitney, *Problem and Promise*, 103.
120. Gunton, *The Promise of Trinitarian Theology*, 183.
121. Brad Green, "Colin Gunton and the Theological Origin of Modernity," in *The Theology of Colin Gunton*, ed. Lincoln Harvey (London: T&T Clark, 2010), 171. See also Green, *Colin Gunton and the Failure of Augustine*, 170–3.
122. Green, *Colin Gunton and the Failure of Augustine*, 173. This criticism of Gunton is repeated in Anizor, *Trinity and Humanity*, 99.

God's overcoming of sin and the effects of the fall.[123] Gunton's earlier writings on the contours of Modernity and the drive to autonomy are best understood as a detailed explication of the contours of sin in our context.[124] Modernity's drive to autonomy represents a contemporary expression of human sinfulness in which the creature chooses a form of unfreedom masquerading as freedom.[125] Gunton's wider writings on sin are much richer and more nuanced than his critics recognize, and more penetrating than their proposals.

All scripture, Gunton unequivocally holds, assumes a disrupted relation between God and humanity. Gunton maintains that the universal fallenness of humanity is the result of humanity's refusal to glorify God and its idolatrous self-glorification.[126] "There is a case for saying that for Scripture all depends on the disrupted relation to God, which is best understood in terms of idolatry. … In our context, that must be construed to mean that sin is that human attitude and action which gives glory to anything other than the God of Scripture."[127]

In his theological account of human freedom, Gunton sets the human quest for autonomy from God in the context of human sinfulness and idolatry and, against Green's criticisms, utilizes Romans 1 as his primary text.[128] The explicit definition of sin in Romans 1 implicitly informs a wide hamartiological semantic range that Gunton uses to describe human sin: slavery, unfreedom, autonomy, self-glorification, false exchange, and bondage.[129] The primary sin of human beings, according to Gunton, is a false exchange in which human beings exchange the truth of God for a lie and worship the creature instead of the creator. Sin, as Paul describes it in Romans 1, takes the form of a false exchange in which humanity exchanges the glory of God for self-glorification in many guises. The litany of false

---

123. Gunton, *The Christian Faith*, 59–63. Anizor and Whitney highlight that there are only five pages directly devoted to sin in *The Christian Faith*. However, they fail to see the explicit and implicit role that sin plays in Gunton's ongoing arguments in the book, especially through Gunton's use of the family of theological synonyms for sin such as idolatry, false exchange, slavery, unfreedom, and self-glorification. Likewise, they do not mention the multiple chapters dedicated to sin in *Intellect and Action* or Gunton's later detailed account of sin in his chapter on reconciliation. See Gunton, *Intellect and Action*, 83–100, 121–38, 156–73, and 174–92; and Colin E. Gunton, "Towards a Theology of Reconciliation," in *The Theology of Reconciliation*, ed. Colin E. Gunton (London: T&T Clark, 2003), 167–74.

124. See Gunton, *Intellect and Action*, 91, 172; and Gunton, "Towards a Theology of Reconciliation," 167.

125. Gunton, *Intellect and Action*, 166.

126. Gunton, *Intellect and Action*, 157.

127. Gunton, *Intellect and Action*, 157.

128. Gunton, "Towards a Theology of Reconciliation," 167. For an extended discussion on the concept of exchange in the Old Testament concept of holiness and sacrifice, and its eschatological concentration in Jesus Christ, see Gunton, *Intellect and Action*, 83–100.

129. For a detailed account of his theological analysis of the contours of Modernity's sin, see Gunton, *Intellect and Action*, 156–73. See also Gunton, *The Christian Faith*, 59–63.

exchanges in Romans 1 offers examples of sinful forms of human idolatry that arise from the original false exchange at the fall, the root of human sin.[130]

The modern myth of self-realization is a further expression of the sin of Babel in which humanity denies its God-given creatureliness in exchange for self-glorification. Genesis 11 repeats the language of divine creating action in Genesis 1, "Let us make," and employs it mockingly to depict human self-assertion and humanity's attempt to make itself like God: "Let *us* make bricks ... Come, let *us* build ourselves a city, with a tower that reaches to the heavens" (Gen 11:3-4).[131] Human beings have disrupted the order of creation by exchanging their creatureliness for a lie and denying their true identity as creatures of God who worship the creator and image God in the creation. "The essence of sin," Gunton concludes, "is to attempt to be like God in ways other than that laid down for those who, because they are finite in time and space, are also limited in their capacity for knowledge and achievement. Sin is for the creature to think and act as if it were the creator."[132] Importantly, Gunton states that it is sin that prevents people from being holy, and culture "from being truly the praise of God and things from being wholesome and good."[133]

For all the devastating effects of sin, the false exchange is usurped by the sweetest exchange in which the incarnate Son of God endures the wrath of God on the cross of Gethsemane for our sake.[134] Modernity's sinful false exchange of God-given creaturely freedom for slavery and unfreedom is only overcome by reconciliation. "Reconciliation is at the heart, because there the false exchange (Romans 1) is displaced by the 'blessed exchange' of the cross."[135] At the heart of Gunton's account of sin and reconciliation is Paul's theology of the cross and

---

130. Gunton, "Towards a Theology of Reconciliation," 167.
131. Gunton, *The Christian Faith*, 60-1.
132. Gunton, *The Christian Faith*, 60.
133. Gunton, *The Christian Faith*, 71.
134. Gunton, "Towards a Theology of Reconciliation," 167. Hans Schaeffer incorrectly argues that Gunton's theology of God's actions towards sin is never qualified as wrath or anger. Gunton explicitly argues this point in *The Christian Faith*. In relation to God's justice and judgement, Gunton states that "the wrath of God is integral to his relations with the world. Wrath is the form that holy love takes when it is rejected, and it involves the rejection of the actions of those who put themselves outside the love of God." Whilst Gunton does not want to separate God's wrath from God's love, because punitive punishment is not an end in itself, it is clear that, in Christ, God's love accepts that breaches of the law entail consequences. In Jesus Christ, God endures the divine wrath on our behalf as an act of divine self-giving and mercy, and the due punishment for human sin is transformed by the gift of Christ's sacrifice in which evil and death are overcome. See Gunton, *The Christian Faith*, 75-6. For Schaeffer's comments, see Hans Schaeffer, *Createdness and Ethics: The Doctrine of Creation and Theological Ethics in the Theology of Colin E. Gunton and Oswald Bayer* (Berlin: Walter de Gruyter, 2006), 99.
135. Gunton, *Intellect and Action*, 172.

"the sweetest exchange" in which "μεταλασσω becomes καταλασσω."[136] Before we examine Gunton's theology of atonement in relation to culture, we need to clarify, against critics, the centrality of the cross to Gunton's transformative eschatology and the perfecting of the project of creation.

Sin, Salvation, and the Perfecting of the Project of Creation

Gunton is an avowed Reformed theologian and minister, yet some believe his account of the perfecting of the project of creation moves his soteriology in non-Reformed directions towards a "creational soteriology."[137] Yet Gunton contends that he is working in Calvin's tradition and he explicitly develops his view of sin and atonement from Calvin.[138]

The Church, Gunton holds, with Calvin, stands or falls by the doctrine of justification by faith, and sin must be understood as infidelity and idolatry.[139] Furthermore, nothing escapes the corrupting effects of sin, which has injected itself like a poison throughout the entire universe.[140] As a result of the universal extent of human fallenness, there is a radical incapacitation and corruption of all created reality, human and non-human, which results in the universal bondage of humanity.[141] Even the most altruistic acts are tinged with elements of self-seeking and self-serving.[142] Whilst Gunton is working within the Reformed tradition, he distinguishes between Calvin's biblical approach to theology and the later federal approach that utilizes scripture in service of *a priori* theological systems.[143] Many of the traditional sin and salvation schemas, and the accompanying accounts of total depravity, Gunton deems to be unsatisfactory. Total depravity is often misconstrued to mean that there is nothing good in human beings, which Gunton

---

136. Gunton, *Intellect and Action*, 91.

137. Whitney, *Problem and Promise*, 105. Whitney draws from John Webster's contention that Gunton's view of soteriology can be "curiously flat." See Webster, "Systematic Theology after Barth," 262.

138. Gunton defends Calvin's theology of atonement and Calvin's legacy because he believes it to be "manifestly worthy of defence," see Gunton, *Intellect and Action*, 130.

139. Gunton, *Intellect and Action*, 124.

140. Gunton, *The Christian Faith*, 62.

141. Gunton, *Intellect and Action*, 160.

142. Gunton, *The Christian Faith*, 62.

143. Gunton, *Intellect and Action*, 136. Whitney suggests that Gunton could be understood as a Neo-Calvinist, given his shared commonalities with Neo-Calvinism. However, Gunton believes there is a critical distinction to make between Calvin and Calvinism. See William Baltmanis Whitney, "The Correlation Between Creation and Culture in the Theology of Abraham Kuyper and Colin E. Gunton," in *The Kuyper Center Review. Volume 3: Calvinism and Culture*, ed. Gordon Graham (Grand Rapids: Eerdmans, 2013), 82–3. On Gunton's distinction between Calvin and Calvinism, see Gunton, *Intellect and Action*, vii–viii; 121–4, 136–7.

holds to be theologically and empirically false. We see many instances of the good, the true and the beautiful (a phrase Gunton commonly uses for culture), because God's providential action overrules the full consequences of the fall and we do not reap everything we sow.[144] The stress upon total depravity risks undermining the goodness of the created order, which Gunton seeks to uphold within his account of redemption.

Any account of redemption must maintain the nature of creation's temporality and spatiality. God's redemptive action is the redemption *of* created reality not redemption *from* created reality. Creation is a project that is ordered to eschatological perfection through time and in space. Accordingly, God's redemption in Christ is not an escape plan but the crown of creation. Yet some scholars allege that Gunton's claims about the perfecting of creation are developed aside from the cross of Christ. Gunton is charged with a progressive eschatology that lacks the necessary focus on the cross. Whitney and Uche Anizor argue that Gunton holds a creational soteriology that often sounds like an improvement process, which finds completion at the eschaton.[145] They detect an ambivalence in Gunton when it comes to sin's impact on creation, and note, with Hans Schaffer, that Gunton is inclined to speak of creation "as an ordered whole without the elements of sinful disorder."[146] These criticisms in general, and Whitney's taxonomy of creational soteriology in particular, do not adequately observe the centrality of redemption in Gunton's account of the perfecting of creation. The sources that are employed to establish this critique are based on Gunton's early writings and fail to engage patiently with Gunton's later writings on the topic. As a result, these critiques succumb to the *Hauptbriefe* in Gunton's writings and fail to engage adequately with his later works.[147]

Gunton is committed to an account of the perfection of creation and concrete reality, but he is overtly clear that there can be no perfection of creation without redemption, because "there is no manifest and unambiguous *progress*."[148] Against optimistic suggestions of progressive eschatology, Gunton holds that the painful realities of human history remind us that there are no resolutions apart from transformative eschatology. "Apart, that is to say, from a conception of God's action in the world which takes far more seriously sin, death and evil as forces which threaten the project, and threaten it radically, there is either no project, or it is destined for failure."[149]

Any account of creation's perfecting which does not go through the narrow gate of Christ's death as the sole basis of the reconstitution of creation fails to take

---

144. Gunton, *The Christian Faith*, 62.
145. Whitney, *Problem and Promise*, 104 and Anizor, *Trinity and Humanity*, 81.
146. Schaffer, *Createdness and Ethics*, 237.
147. For a definition of *Hauptbriefe* ("main letters"), see p. 3, fn 5.
148. Gunton, *The Promise of Trinitarian Theology*, 183. See also Gunton, *Father, Son and Holy Spirit*, 25.
149. Gunton, *The Promise of Trinitarian Theology*, 183.

adequate account of the extent of the fall.[150] "The project of creation is achieved only through its redemption, not simply through its perfecting; or rather by its perfecting through redemption – by its release from its bondage to decay."[151] The fall represents a crisis, an elemental crisis in the cosmos, in which powers and principalities (τὰ στοιχεῖα τοῦ κόσμου Col 2:8) enslave the creation to forces beyond its control. Jesus' ministry is a titanic struggle against these, actively evil, powers and principalities that prevent the perfecting of creation. The ministry of Jesus of Nazareth is at once truly human, and that of the cosmic Lord returned to claim his own. It is his obedient recapitulation of humanity, even to death on a cross, that is the means through which the crisis is averted, the project of creation is restored to its proper end, the at-one-ment of all things with God.[152]

Reconciliation is solely centred in the mediation of Jesus Christ and the Spirit, and Gunton guards this against any theological imbalance that minimizes this claim. Some overly moralistic accounts of the Church's action displace the theology of redemption into the Church's moral action and virtue. The cross is reduced to a form of exemplarism that lays upon human agents a burden too heavy to bear and reduces Christ to a historical model to replicate.[153] A stronger hamartiology is needed, Gunton argues, because our settled disposition, in the wake of the fall, is in need of radical renewal. The slavery to which we are in bondage can only be broken by redemption that comes from God the creator and redeemer of our humanity in the form of Jesus Christ the mediator by the Spirit.[154]

A careful engagement with Gunton's full body of work leaves no doubt that the fallenness of humanity, and, consequently, creation, is a vital assumption in his theological project. Suggestions that Gunton upholds a progressive eschatology, a diminished eschatology, or a creational soteriology are misrepresentations of his work that need to be abandoned. A more nuanced engagement with Gunton's theology of the project of creation sees it as centred in the death and resurrection of Jesus Christ as an obedient sacrifice offered in praise of God. Creation's release from the bondage to decay does not come through human efforts at progress but through the redemption of all things in the cross of Jesus Christ.

The Cross, Sin, and the Sacrifice of Jesus Christ

It is at the cross that God deals with the human condition as it really is, whilst also respecting its spatial and temporal structures.[155] A detailed account of Gunton's theology of the atonement is beyond the scope of this book, but we will focus

---

150. Gunton, *The Promise of Trinitarian Theology*, 183.
151. Gunton, "Reformation Accounts," 82.
152. Gunton, *The Promise of Trinitarian Theology*, 184–6.
153. Gunton, *The Christian Faith*, 109–13.
154. Gunton, *Intellect and Action*, 110.
155. Gunton, *Father, Son and Holy Spirit*, 136.

in this section on the implications of his understanding of the atonement for a theology of culture.[156]

Gunton is very clear that the reconciliation of humanity with God through the atoning death and resurrection of Jesus Christ is the heart of the Christian faith. "If the preaching of the cross and its outcome is not at the centre of worship and life, we are no longer about the Father's work. Reconciliation with God through the work of Christ is that without which nothing else will work."[157] The cross is the centre of God's justifying action in relation to human sin, but as we have seen, it is also the centre of a much wider act of justification by God.[158] The redemption of humanity and creation is centred in the mediating action of Jesus Christ who is the concentration of faithful Israel and true humanity by the Spirit's power. The sacrifice of Jesus Christ is the priestly self-offering of obedient humanity as a living sacrifice of praise to God the Father by the Spirit.

Much of Gunton's early writings on the atonement are set against the backdrop of foundationalism and seek to give an account of the atonement metaphors against the encroachment of rationalism. Metaphors are indirect, yet truthful, speech about God, in which language is seconded by the gospel and the meaning of words is reshaped by the new reality they attempt to describe.[159] Gunton develops three metaphors: victory, judgement, and sacrifice. The cross is a victory over sin, evil, the enemy, and death, but it also renews our understanding of the meaning of victory. Victory is "the kind of thing that happens when Jesus goes to the cross."[160] Yet Christ's victory is not established merely through the cross, as his whole human career is a victory of human obedience to the Father. "Jesus' [victory] is a divine victory won through the human faithfulness and sheer intransigence that only the empowering Spirit can effect. It begins in his life and climaxes in his death."[161] Jesus' victory at the cross is that of the faithful human, the second Adam. Whilst he

---

156. For a sustained account of Gunton's doctrine of atonement, see Murray Rae, "Gunton on Atonement," in *T&T Clark Handbook of Colin Gunton*, ed. Andrew Picard, Myk Habets, and Murray Rae (London: T&T Clark, 2021), 91-104. See also Justyn Terry, "Colin Gunton's Doctrine of the Atonement: Transcending Rationalism by Metaphor," in *The Theology of Colin Gunton*, ed. Lincoln Harvey (London: T&T Clark, 2010), 130-45; Murray Rae, "The Travail of God," *International Journal of Systematic Theology*, 5 (2003): 47-61; and Andrew Picard, "Colin Gunton," in *T&T Clark Companion to the Atonement*, ed. Adam J. Johnson (London: Bloomsbury T&T Clark, 2017), 527-32.

157. Gunton, *Father, Son and Holy Spirit*, 175.

158. Gunton, *The Promise of Trinitarian Theology*, 178.

159. Colin E. Gunton, "Universal and Particular in Atonement Theology," *Religious Studies*, 28 (1992): 459-62. See also Rae, "Gunton on Atonement," 95-6, 103; Rae, "The Travail of God," 47-51; and Picard, "Colin Gunton," 527-8.

160. Gunton, *The Actuality of Atonement*, 79.

161. Gunton, *The Christian Faith*, 74.

himself is not in need of redemption, he brings redemption through his victorious life in the realm of death, which he conquers by obedience to the Spirit.[162]

Judgement and justice have to do with God's rule over the creation and its perfecting, and injustice is whatever inhibits this eschatological *telos*. Under the conditions of the gospel, judgement is personalized as the action of God's holy love in which the one who has the right to judge does not behave in the way we expect of judges. Following Barth, Gunton argues that Jesus Christ is the judge, the judgement, and the judged; he is the judged judge on our behalf who concentrates and fulfils the Torah.[163] "If the presence of God was once in some way realised – concentrated – in tabernacle, temple, land, law, and people, it is now concentrated in this one Jew, who becomes them all, and, in our context, specifically becomes Torah that is to say, the mediator – as the ascended Lord – of the presence of God on earth."[164] Jesus Christ is the concentration and fulfilment of the law. Accordingly, there is more continuity than discontinuity in the New Testament's account of the Jewish law.[165] Christ is born under the law, brought up as a son of the law, keeps it, teaches it, sometimes reinterprets it in himself, and is sentenced under it. Just as Christ's baptism constitutes his solidarity with Israel in judgement, in his death, Christ accepts on behalf of others the consequences of God's just judgement of humanity's sin and failure to live by the law.[166]

Christ's cry of dereliction from the cross is the cry of the incarnate Son's total identification with the lost human condition. "Most simply, it is the cry of an Israelite expressing the self-distancing of that people from God as a result of their sin, the completion of Jesus' identification with Israel in his baptism."[167] However, this does not mean that God is punishing Jesus instead of sinners, but that in Christ God achieves an exchange—the one who knew no sin became sin for us. Jesus' cry of dereliction is the horror of one who "dies in the space from which God has taken away his loving presence, to the effect that he bore the just judgement of God upon sin in order that others might be freed not from all judgement, but from the judgement that brings death."[168] He accepts the judgement of the law on behalf and in place of human beings who fail to live by the law and endures it for our sake.

On the cross, Jesus Christ bears God's judgement on sin, not so that sinners will not be judged, but that God's judgement would be received as discipline. "Christ, we might say, bears anticipatorily the eschatological judgement of death – he goes

---

162. Gunton, *The Christian Faith*, 108.

163. Gunton, *The Actuality of Atonement*, 110. See Karl Barth, *Church Dogmatics* IV/1: *The Doctrine of Reconciliation*, ed. G. W. Bromiley and T. F. Torrance, trans. G. W. Bromiley (Edinburgh: T&T Clark, 1956), 231–83.

164. Gunton, *Intellect and Action*, 98.

165. Gunton, *Intellect and Action*, 89–91.

166. Gunton, *The Christian Faith*, 74–5. On the continuity of the Torah in the New Testament see also Gunton, *Intellect and Action*, 85–91.

167. Gunton, *Act and Being*, 130.

168. Gunton, *The Christian Faith*, 75.

to *hell* – in order that those who trust in God through him should be able to bear the judgement that cleanses rather than annihilates."¹⁶⁹ The metaphor of judgement should not be understood as an indication of God's abstract and retributive justice. This notion of justice risks separating the work of the Son from the Father, as though they have different ends in view, and pits God against God.¹⁷⁰

Drawing upon Calvin, Gunton stresses instead that the cross is concerned with life and "the indulgent Father who gives us himself in his Son."¹⁷¹ Jesus Christ certainly bears the penalty for sin, but the cross is not limited to the question of penalty. Christ's suffering under the judgement of God serves reconciliation and life in such a way that God's love is the priority.¹⁷² We must, Gunton holds, understand Christ's faithful obedience and sacrifice as an act of love, not as the passive acquiescence of the Son to the alien will of the Father. Christ's work of obedience "*derives from* God's love; it does not *establish* it."¹⁷³ Instead of penal substitution, Gunton prefers Christoph Schwöbel's suggestion of a mediatorial substitution in which Christ takes our place "in such a way that we are truly brought to God."¹⁷⁴ Jesus Christ certainly takes the place of sinners at the cross, but it is as an unsubstitutionary sacrifice because only he is able to achieve reconciliation by the sacrificial offering of his faithful human life.¹⁷⁵

Sacrifice is the third of the metaphors Gunton examines and it holds expansive implications for our understanding of the nature of creaturely reality and redeemed human culture.¹⁷⁶ The sacrifice of Jesus Christ carries two important meanings for Gunton: firstly, the sacrifice of Christ as the mediator between God and humanity, and, secondly, the offering of living sacrifices to God—a certain form of human living that exercises the priestly calling to offer creation back to God as a sacrifice of praise.¹⁷⁷ In his earlier writings, Gunton develops a theology of sacrifice in the shadow of his search for transcendentals and concludes that sacrifice is an essential mark of divine and human being.¹⁷⁸ The reciprocal giving and receiving

---

169. Gunton, *The Christian Faith*, 162.
170. Gunton, *Intellect and Action*, 126.
171. Gunton, *Father, Son and Holy Spirit*, 170.
172. Gunton, *Father, Son and Holy Spirit*, 172. See also Gunton, *Intellect and Action*, 127–8.
173. Gunton, *Intellect and Action*, 127. Italics original.
174. Gunton, *Father, Son and Holy Spirit*, 171.
175. Gunton, "Towards a Theology of Reconciliation," 171.
176. Gunton, *Father, Son and Holy Spirit*, xvii. Gunton also states that the "third of the metaphors is in many ways the crucial one, because of the central significance of sacrifice for our theme." Gunton, *The Promise of Trinitarian Theology*, 187.
177. Gunton, *The Promise of Trinitarian Theology*, 187.
178. Gunton, *Father, Son and Holy Spirit*, 200. This essay was first published as Colin E. Gunton, "Atonement: The Sacrifice and the Sacrifices. From Metaphor to Transcendental?," in *Trinity, Incarnation, and Atonement: Philosophical and Theological Essays*, ed. Ronald J. Feenstra and Cornelius Plantinga (Notre Dame: Notre Dame University Press, 1989), 210–19.

that constitutes the sacrificial triune God can be echoed in the created order by the Spirit enabling, through the sacrifice of Christ, true human giving and receiving.[179] This takes the form of human culture that liberates the creation through the sacrificial dynamic of mutual giving and receiving, and is a finite echo of God's eternal being and purposes for the world.[180]

Sacrifice in Gunton's later writings is situated in the context of the theology of mediation and takes us to the heart of the Trinity and the heart of humanity and creation's calling which is worship; the offering of a living sacrifice of praise to God through right habitation of the world. Israel's institutions are given for the sake of the right human habitation of the world. This is a form of culture in which God's purposes are ministered in the world in fulfilment of the calling of humanity as the priest of creation.[181] This priestly calling is concentrated in the person of Jesus Christ who, as our great high priest, offers his faithful life as the perfect sacrifice of praise to the Father from within the created order.[182] The life and death that is so central to the priestly writings is now concentrated in the death and resurrection of Jesus Christ who is put to death for our sins and raised for our justification.[183] The sacrificial sphere draws us towards a theology of exchange; the one in whom the priesthood is concentrated substitutes himself in the place of sinners and offers his life as a sacrifice.[184]

Jesus Christ is the mediator between God and humanity, and his spotless sacrifice from within the human sphere is the saving action of God. While humanity is utterly culpable for its grave predicament, humanity is incapable of resolving its predicament because it cannot offer an untainted sacrifice. Only God can save the creation that has gone astray, yet, the offering must be a truly human offering. Salvation is achieved by the one who is both divine and human: Jesus Christ the mediator who offers a truly obedient humanity to God from within the heart of the human condition.[185]

Jesus Christ, the great high priest, brings us to God in a particular way—through his perfect sacrifice and his eternal humanity. We have no need to look for a distant mediator since Jesus Christ is our brother who holds his hand out to us. Nor is there any reason to fear that he is unaware of our ills and human limitations

---

179. As we will see in Gunton's ecclesiology, Gunton's early work is marked by the suggestion that divine being can be echoed in the created world through relationality. In his later work, the use of echo as an analogical bridge between divine and created being recedes almost entirely.

180. Gunton, *The Promise of Trinitarian Theology*, 204–6. This essay was first published in the first edition of *The Promise of Trinitarian Theology* (Edinburgh: T&T Clark, 1991), 162–76.

181. Gunton, *The Christian Faith*, 71.

182. Gunton, *Father, Son and Holy Spirit*, 157.

183. Gunton, *Intellect and Action*, 97.

184. Gunton, *The Christian Faith*, 70–1.

185. Gunton, *Father, Son and Holy Spirit*, 170.

as he has taken our infirmities to himself so that he may be the mediator of our salvation who reconciles humanity to God in himself.[186] In this way he becomes the means for the sacrifice of praise of the whole of creation. "Jesus' life as a whole is an expression of that priesthood over creation that is the human calling outlined in Genesis 1.26-8 as the calling of those created in God's image."[187] Through his faithful obedience, Jesus Christ offers a living sacrifice of Adam's recapitulated humanity in triumph; humanity fully and truly alive, as God intended it to be.

The project of creation is created to be perfected as a result of the exercise of humanity's priestly calling. "The human project is to be completed in the presentation before God of a form of life made possible by Christ's atoning death."[188] It is the mediation of the Spirit to perfect the created world by bringing it into relation with God through Christ, and the Spirit enables "projectings" in time of the promised end.[189] Romans 12 calls humanity, in Christ and by the Spirit, to present our embodied life as a living sacrifice of praise that so indwells the creation that the creation is enabled to be offered as a sacrifice of praise to God.[190] The sacrifice of praise to God is worship, the faithful human response to God and humanity's primary calling. Yet it is embodied worship to which human beings are called in relation to one another, the creation and God. Finite perfections therefore take the form of human culture in the world; a way of living in relationship to God, one another and the creation that is a living sacrifice of praise to God.

The Spirit is at work in all human culture, not just religious culture, enabling anticipations of the perfection of God's project in the present as they conform to the life, career, and death of Jesus Christ. We can determine if a form of human culture is a sacrifice by the measure of its right or wrong use of creation that brings worship and glory to God.[191] "All human 'ethics', all right use of creation, all offering of creation to God the Father, perfected through Christ and in the Spirit; in sum, all right habitation of the world God has made and redeemed on the cross of Christ, takes form under that promise, whether it knows it or not."[192]

While the Spirit's work in the present is not limited to the Church, the Church is the community that is instituted by the Spirit as a particular form of culture centred around the one truly perfected life.[193] The Church's social and political life and institutions are forms of holy culture instituted by God through which human life is ordered to creation's end. The Church's life is enabled by the Spirit, from time

---

186. Gunton, *Father, Son and Holy Spirit*, 172. Quoting John Calvin, *The Epistle of Paul the Apostle to the Hebrews and the First and Second Epistles of Peter*, trans. W. B. Johnson (Grand Rapids: Eerdmans, 1963), 55.

187. Gunton, *The Christian Faith*, 112.

188. Gunton, *The Promise of Trinitarian Theology*, 189.

189. Gunton, *The Promise of Trinitarian Theology*, 189.

190. Gunton, *The Triune Creator*, 235.

191. Gunton, *The Triune Creator*, 235.

192. Gunton, *The Triune Creator*, 236.

193. Gunton, "Reformation Accounts," 82.

to time, to offer a sacrifice of praise because the body of Christ participates in the ascended Christ's self-offering to the Father. As we will examine more fully in the next chapter, the cultic actions of the Church are instances of embodied worship offered in relation with the created order.[194]

The Lord's Supper is especially important to Gunton, as the Church's common life in relation with God, one another, and creation is offered through the fruits of the earth (the grain and grape) as a sacrifice of praise for God's wise purposes in creation. Chapters 5 and 6 detail the way the Lord's Supper, in Gunton's thought, encompasses embodied human social, moral, ethical, and political life in community and offers it through Christ and in the Spirit as an eschatological sacrifice of praise. In order to understand the extent of Gunton's account of sacrifice, we need to trace his understanding of Christ's resurrection and ascension, and the import of his eternal priesthood for a theology of human culture.

The Resurrection and Ascension of the Great High Priest and Human Culture

In Gunton's thought, the promise of Jesus' baptism, that he would be the one who fulfils all righteousness in his identification with sinful humanity, is fulfilled in his resurrection. The resurrection is an eschatological act in which God raises Jesus Christ from the dead by the power of the Spirit as a vindication and validation of this particular human being.[195] The Spirit's eschatological action is the means of the reconstituting of the cultural mandate in its God-given form in and through the person of the incarnate Son.[196] The resurrection attests that true human life is found only here in the one human who images God as the one just, truthful, and free human being. "For others to realise the image and likeness of God now involves being brought into reconciled relation with God the Father through him; indeed, in Paul's expression, being conformed to him."[197] In his incarnation, Jesus Christ is made priest, and humanity the sphere of his priesthood. In his resurrection, Jesus Christ is raised up as the great high priest—the confirmation of his eternal priestly ministry in which he offers himself to the Father as the true human being and the focus of our worship.[198]

The liberation of the created order from its bondage to decay comes through an act of redemption and transformation by the eschatological Adam. Resurrection, for Gunton, is not firstly about immortality, but about God's purposes in creation that are realized through the faithful humanity of God's Son and the transformation of all things in him.[199] His victory over death through human faithfulness brings creation's bondage to decay to a *telos* in which death no longer has dominion over

---

194. Gunton, *Father, Son and Holy Spirit*, 122.
195. Gunton, *The Christian Faith*, 111–12.
196. Gunton, "Reformation Accounts," 82.
197. Gunton, *The Christian Faith*, 123.
198. Gunton, *Father, Son and Holy Spirit*, 54.
199. Gunton, *The Christian Faith*, 153.

the creature or creation. The life of the new age is not a rescue from materiality to immateriality, but the transformation of materiality in new ways.

The post-resurrection appearances of Jesus Christ reveal that the resurrection is a resurrection to a new form of bodily life in relation to the created order. "The one who breathed into Adam the breath of life now raises the second Adam to new life by the transformation of his body not to bodiliness but to a new form of bodily life."[200] The new creation is continuous with the old, but, by the perfecting action of the Spirit, brings about creation's transformation in anticipation of the eschatological perfection of the created order through the redemption of Jesus Christ.[201] As the imagery in the book of Revelation shows, the resurrection is not immortal life after death, but the completion of earth's transformation by the power of the Lamb and his cross.[202] In the New Jerusalem, human cultural advances that have contributed to the perfecting of creation are celebrated and affirmed.[203] The resurrection is God's transformation of the creation through the faithful human action of creation's Lord, and the fulfilment of humanity's cultural calling. "The resurrection of the flesh, of the whole person, is the completion of the promise inherent in Genesis 1.26-28, because those created in the image of God are to be perfected in the context in which they were created."[204] The resurrection is the fulfilment of the promise of the reconciliation of all things through Jesus Christ, through which the creation is liberated from its bondage to decay and brought to share in the glorious freedom of the children of God.

In the ascension, the high priesthood and eternal kingship of Jesus Christ are realized and our humanity, and its priestly calling in creation, is brought before God through his eternal sacrifice. Jesus Christ is ascended to the right hand of the Father and is permanently and universally the means of human access to God.[205] His priesthood is an eternal priesthood that, in priestly fashion, brings together the loving creator and hostile humanity. "That priesthood is now permanent and eternal, a living way for others to go confidently before their maker."[206] Importantly for Gunton, Jesus Christ is raised in his human particularity and humanity is drawn to participate in his eternal filial relationship with the Father by the Spirit. This participation in Christ's eternal humanity is not a form of *theosis* or divinization of humanity because Christ's high priesthood is exercised in his continuing humanity. It is through his perfected eternal humanity that humanity's calling to image God

---

200. Gunton, *Father, Son and Holy Spirit*, 118.
201. Gunton, *Father, Son and Holy Spirit*, 118.
202. Gunton, *The Christian Faith*, 154.
203. Holmes, "Can Theology Engage with Culture?" 14–15.
204. Gunton, *The Christian Faith*, 154.
205. Gunton, *The Christian Faith*, 112.
206. Gunton, *The Christian Faith*, 112.

is restored and realized.²⁰⁷ In this way, the history of the truly human person of Jesus Christ is not over, but continues as the second Adam reigns until the end of the age when he delivers the kingdom of God to the Father who will then be all in all.²⁰⁸ Worship is therefore the context in which we can understand the ongoing ministry of Jesus Christ who presents our humanity, and the created order, to the Father as a sacrifice of praise through his eternal sacrifice.²⁰⁹

Some have argued that Gunton's account of Christ's ascended ministry is somewhat blunted by the stress he places upon the mediation of the Spirit in the economy after the resurrection. Michael Stringer and H. Paul Santmire argue that apart from his formal claims of the resurrection and ascension of Christ, Gunton remains noticeably silent on the concreteness of Christ's ascended ministry.²¹⁰ Stringer and Santmire sense that Gunton's delineation of mediation creates dispensations in which the ongoing ministry of the ascended Christ becomes subsumed under the ministry of the Spirit in the Church. Following the resurrection, Santmire maintains, Gunton's theology of mediation becomes one-handed and the Spirit "basically runs the show."²¹¹ Likewise, Stringer suggests that Gunton's pneumatological focus is so strong that the ascended ministry of the Risen One does not feature prominently in his trinitarian theology.²¹² However, Gunton's distinction between the post-resurrection ministry of the Son and the Spirit must be read in light of his Reformed emphasis upon the bodily absence of the Risen Lord whose presence is mediated by the Spirit.

Gunton's divergence from his mentor, Robert Jenson, provides a helpful clarification of the importance of Christ's bodily absence in Gunton's thought.²¹³ Despite an enduring friendship and the rich theological interactions between Gunton and Jenson, they disagreed over the nature of Christ's presence in the Church. For Gunton, the importance of embodied particularity means that the risen Christ is particularly located at the right hand of the Father as the ascended Lord.²¹⁴ Christ's ascended body is particular, and is therefore not a ubiquitous presence in the world through the Church, nor is his presence raised up into the body of the Church. At the Lord's Supper, Christ is absent, and his presence is

---

207. Gunton, *The Promise of Trinitarian Theology*, 205. Whitney's suggestion that Gunton's understanding of election shares similarities with Eastern Orthodox views of divinization and theosis misrepresents Gunton's stress upon the importance of human particularity and the ontological distinction between divine and created being. Whitney, *Problem and Promise*, 108.

208. Gunton, *Father, Son and Holy Spirit*, 29.

209. Gunton, *Father, Son and Holy Spirit*, 54.

210. H. Paul Santmire, "So That He Might Fill All Things: Comprehending the Cosmic Love of Christ," *Dialog*, 42 (2003): 262.

211. Santmire, "So That He Might Fill All Things," 262.

212. Stringer, "The Lord and Giver of Life," 250.

213. Gunton, *Father, Son and Holy Spirit*, 219–21, and 96–103.

214. Gunton, *Father, Son and Holy Spirit*, 219.

mediated by the Spirit. Jenson's Lutheran tradition holds to a greater sense of Christ's immanence in the Church, and Christ can be understood to be immanently present in, under, or around the elements.[215]

The intricacies of these debates are beyond this book, but it is important to note that Gunton's theology of the ascension is informed by his Reformed tradition and the particularity of Christ's ascension to the Father's right hand. "The new dispensation depends on Jesus' absence, which is to be succeeded eventually by his return in glory."[216] Christ presents his continuing humanity before the Father on our behalf, and his bodily absence is the occasion for the sending of the Spirit to mediate Christ's ongoing significance and ministry.[217] The particular presence of Jesus Christ at the right hand of the Father is the basis upon which Gunton develops his account of pneumatology and ecclesiology in such a way as to uphold the *Selbständigkeit* between the creator and creation. This, in Gunton's theology, gives the necessary space and freedom for the Spirit's activity in and beyond the Church in the redemption and perfection of the project of creation. "The ascended Jesus is the Jesus made present by the Spirit in the sacraments, the communion of the people of God and wherever the Kingdom is realised in the world."[218]

In Gunton's theology, the one whose incarnate life and ministry of faithfulness and obedience was empowered by the Spirit now sends the Spirit to empower eschatological action for the perfection of creation.[219] The Spirit's perfecting work is universal, but it is concentrated in the Church which the Spirit gifts with eschatological life to realize in human particularity the reality of what God has achieved in Jesus Christ. The Spirit enables the Church in its worship and life to mediate the work of the mediator from time to time. The Church is not the gospel, nor the *telos* of the gospel, but the Church is the community of the gospel whose life in flesh and blood community is a gift of the Spirit.[220] "The Church is the place – the living space – where the kingship, priesthood and prophetic work of Jesus is appropriated – taken on board, we might say. It is therefore a particular form of social existence ordered by the Spirit of God the Father by virtue of its relation to this one and only life lived truly as the image of God."[221] Before examining the Spirit's action in the world and in the Church, there is a need to comprehend the Spirit's perfecting action in the incarnation and human career of Jesus Christ.

---

215. Gunton, *Father, Son and Holy Spirit*, 219–20.
216. Gunton, *The Christian Faith*, 112.
217. Gunton, *Father, Son and Holy Spirit*, 119.
218. Gunton, *Father, Son and Holy Spirit*, 156.
219. Gunton, *Father, Son and Holy Spirit*, 179.
220. Gunton, *Father, Son and Holy Spirit*, 179.
221. Gunton, *The Christian Faith*, 123.

Pneumatological Christology: The Action of the Son in the Spirit

Any account of the Son's mediation requires an account of the Spirit's action as the two hands do not act separately. All divine action is the unified action of the one God, yet we are able to consider the distinct action of the Spirit within the united action of the Godhead.[222] In order to understand the action of both hands of God, we need to examine the Spirit's action in relation to Jesus Christ and the Spirit's empowerment of Christ's faithful humanity. Much of this has been covered in the preceding material, so the focus is now upon the mediation of the Spirit in Jesus Christ's incarnation, career, resurrection, and ascension. The distinct *persona* and action of the Spirit within the unity of the Godhead are vital to Gunton's theology. Unsurprisingly, therefore, it is his pneumatology that has received the most attention in the scholarly reception of his work.[223]

For Gunton, the Spirit's action is not limited to internality or the application of Christ's benefits, because the Spirit is not an immanent causal force but the divine person whose office is transcendent action. Gunton is drawn to sources in the tradition that give much greater weighting to the distinct action of the Spirit, and he makes particular use of Basil of Caesarea's depiction of the Spirit as the perfecting cause.[224] The Spirit is the perfecting cause, and scripture very often depicts the action of the Spirit as God acting eschatologically. "For the New Testament especially, wherever the Spirit is, there the conditions of the last times are anticipated."[225] It is the Spirit who directs creatures to where God wants them to go, which is their perfected destiny as creatures. It is the Spirit who empowers Jesus Christ to be the eschatological Adam, and it is the Spirit who leads and equips the Church to be the community of Jesus Christ in anticipation of the communion of the last days.[226]

The Spirit, Jesus Christ, and Human Culture

An early critique of Gunton's Christology raised questions about the importance of pneumatology to Christology. Whilst the first edition of *Yesterday and Today* enjoyed a warm reception, Geoffrey Nuttall raised an important concern through

---

222. Gunton, *Father, Son and Holy Spirit*, 80.

223. Gunton's pneumatology has been the direct subject of four doctoral theses. See David A. Höhne, "Spirit and Sonship: Colin Gunton's Theology of Particularity" (PhD diss., University of Cambridge, 2007) published as Höhne, *Spirit and Sonship*; Reese, "Seeking the Welfare of the City"; Stringer, "The Lord and Giver of Life"; and Harris, "Holy Spirit as Communion," published as I. Leon Harris, *The Holy Spirit as Communion: Colin Gunton's Pneumatology of Communion and Frank Macchia's Pneumatology of Koinonia* (Eugene: Wipf and Stock, 2017). See also Habets, "Gunton on Pneumatology," 121–36.

224. Basil of Caesarea, *On the Holy Spirit*, 16.38.6 (*NPNF* 8:23).

225. Gunton, *Father, Son and Holy Spirit*, 76.

226. Gunton, *Father, Son and Holy Spirit*, 76–7; 81.

private correspondence. He noted that it is odd for a book on Jesus Christ to contain so few references to the Spirit.[227] In the epilogue to the second edition, Gunton acknowledges that Nuttall's critique spurred his interest in Edward Irving and alternative voices in the tradition who gave greater weighting to the distinct action of the Spirit than has traditionally been the case.[228] As a result of his engagement with Irving and these alternative voices, Gunton places strong emphasis upon the humanity of the Son, his self-emptying into the fallen human condition, and his empowerment by the Spirit.

These Christological developments are dependent on Gunton's search for a greater *persona* for the Spirit in the incarnation and the enabling of Christ's human vocation.[229] In addition to Irving, Gunton also turns to the work of John Owen who holds to the transcendence, rather than immanence, of the Spirit.[230] These two British theologians offer dissenting voices to the tradition and its immanent accounts of pneumatology.[231] Undoubtedly, Gunton is influenced by Alan Spence and Graham McFarlane and their doctoral studies on Irving and Owen, and, in turn, Gunton undoubtedly influences their work.[232] Whatever the influences, the shared voice of dissent against the pneumatological accounts of the tradition and their constructive counter-proposals are important to Gunton's work.

Like much of Gunton's work in other areas, his criticisms of the dominant pneumatological perspectives of the tradition serve as foils for his constructive work. In Gunton's analysis, the tradition suffers especially from forms of modalism that reduce the personal agency of the Spirit to little more than the application of Christ's work to the Church and the individual believer. The roots of the

---

227. Colin E. Gunton, *Yesterday and Today: A Study of Continuities in Christology*, 2nd ed. (London: SPCK, 1997), 221.
228. Gunton, *Yesterday and Today*, 221.
229. Gunton, *Yesterday and Today*, 222.
230. Gunton, *Theology Through the Theologians*, 191.
231. Gunton, *Yesterday and Today*, 223. See also Gunton, *Theology Through the Theologians*, 151–68.
232. See Graham W. P. McFarlane, *Christ and the Spirit: The Doctrine of the Incarnation According to Edward Irving* (Carlisle: Paternoster, 1997) and Alan Spence, *Incarnation and Inspiration: John Owen and the Coherence of Christology* (London: T&T Clark, 2007). Gunton wrote a foreword to McFarlane's book, and McFarlane acknowledged that it was Gunton who introduced him to Irving. McFarlane, *Christ and the Spirit*, vii. See also Graham W. P. McFarlane, "Gunton and Irving," in *T&T Clark Handbook of Colin Gunton*, ed. Andrew Picard, Myk Habets, and Murray Rae (London: T&T Clark, 2021), 327–38. In his PhD acknowledgements, Spence noted his indebtedness to Gunton's supervision and encouragement to engage deeply with the work of Owen. Interestingly, Spence also acknowledges his gratitude to Graham McFarlane and he notes that their debates between Owen and Irving sharpened his thinking. Alan Spence, "Incarnation and Inspiration: John Owen and the Coherence of Christology" (PhD diss., King's College, London, 1989), 9. Later published as Spence, *Incarnation and Inspiration*.

Western depersonalization of the Spirit, Gunton believes, are found in Augustine. Augustine fails to identify a particular *persona* for the Spirit, because he develops his pneumatology from general concepts of being, such as love and gift, rather than from the Spirit's particular action in the economy.[233] Whilst deeply indebted to Barth for so much of his work, Gunton is critical of his pneumatology and holds that Barth's theology verges, at times, on a form of modalism.[234] Barth's pneumatology limits the work of the Spirit to the application of the benefits of Christ to the believer, which has the effect of making the Spirit functionally subordinate to the Son.[235] This is a deeply problematic position according to Gunton, and it leads him to accuse Barth of Augustinianism.[236] In place of general concepts of being, Gunton seeks to develop his pneumatology from the Spirit's eschatological action in the economy.

In place of the under-developed pneumatology of the tradition, Gunton develops a pneumatology that shows much greater appreciation of the distinct personal action of the Spirit within the undivided unity of the Godhead.[237] He argues that the Spirit is often depersonalized in Western accounts, and reduced to the cause of subjective religious experiences or other internalized actions.[238] Catholics tend to internalize the Spirit within the institution of the Church, while Protestants are inclined to internalize the Spirit's action to the individual, which develops into forms of rationalism and experientialism.[239] On the one hand, Hegel's account of the movement of *Geist* within history conceives of the Spirit's action within rationalistic human progress, while, on the other hand, Schleiermacher and Pentecostalism consider the Spirit's action to be located primarily within the ecstatic experiences of the individual. In both cases, the Spirit's agency is reduced to internal causality, and the transcendent and eschatological action of the Spirit is lost.[240]

The Spirit is not God's immanent action, and nor is the Spirit the immanent possession of Jesus Christ. The Spirit is God's perfecting cause of creation—the Lord and giver of natural and eschatological life.[241] The Spirit's action in the economy draws creation forwards towards its perfection in Christ. Gunton is

---

233. Gunton, *The Promise of Trinitarian Theology*, 48–50. See also Gunton, *Theology Through the Theologians*, 109–111.

234. Gunton, *Becoming and Being*, 235.

235. Gunton, *Theology Through the Theologians*, 105–6.

236. Gunton, *Father, Son and Holy Spirit*, 95.

237. Gunton, *Becoming and Being*, 235. See especially, Gunton, *Theology Through the Theologians*, 105–28.

238. Colin E. Gunton, "Holy Spirit," in *The Oxford Companion to Christian Thought*, ed. Adrian Hastings et al. (Oxford: OUP, 2000), 305.

239. Gunton, "Holy Spirit," 305. See also Gunton, *The One, the Three and the Many*, 147–9; and Gunton, *The Triune Creator*, 170.

240. Gunton, "Holy Spirit," 306.

241. Gunton, *Theology Through the Theologians*, 118.

wary of the Western conception of the Spirit, which he traces to Augustine, as the bond of love. This has the effect of turning the Spirit's action into another form of internality in which the Spirit closes the circle of divine being. Rather, Gunton proffers the suggestion that the Spirit perfects the love of the Father and the Son by focusing it outwards. God's eternal being-in-communion is marked by ecstatic love that is focused outward towards the other, and this is the basis for God's creating action.[242]

The human life and career of Jesus Christ are enabled by the Spirit's eschatological action. The Spirit works alongside Jesus as God's free and life-giving action in and towards the world.[243] Such an emphasis upon the Spirit's distinct action preserves Christology from docetic tendencies that suggest "Jesus was in some way pushed around by the Word, by his 'divine nature.'"[244] Jesus Christ certainly is the Word, but he is the Word self-emptied fully and truly into the condition of human flesh whilst remaining at one with himself. "We therefore conclude that it is by the power of the Spirit that the incarnate Word is maintained in faithfulness to the Father while being 'weak and needy man.'"[245] The corollary of Gunton's emphasis upon the humanity of Jesus Christ is his emphasis on the Spirit. This is important to his theological account of human culture. Jesus Christ is Luther's "proper man," the second and eschatological Adam. Humanity's ministerial calling in Genesis 1:26-28 is concentrated in Christ, and it is the action of the Spirit that maintains him in right relation to the Father.[246]

In place of an over-emphasis upon Christ's extraordinariness as the eternal Word, Gunton suggests we also consider the ordinariness of Jesus Christ's humanity. In the gospels, particularly Luke's birth narrative, Christ's significance derives not only from the miraculous new divine initiative of salvation, but also from the salvation that is realized through his authentic human flesh and blood.[247] The authenticity of his humanity is vital, and it is the work of the Spirit in and with Jesus Christ that enables him to be the particular person he is. It is the life-giving action of the Spirit which forms a fully human body for the Son in the womb of Mary. Likewise, it is the Spirit who guides the incarnate Son as he grows in wisdom and stature, comes upon him at his baptism, drives him into the wilderness, and sustains him to resist the temptations of the devil in the wilderness that he might be the particular Israelite that he is called to be and become. "The Spirit is the one by whom the Father enables him to speak the truth, heal the sick and endure Gethsemane .... In sum, the Spirit is the mediator of the Son's relation to the Father in both time and eternity."[248] Through the human career of Jesus Christ, God is at

---

242. Gunton, "Holy Spirit," 306.
243. Gunton, *Theology Through the Theologians*, 115–16.
244. Gunton, *The Christian Faith*, 103.
245. Gunton, *The Christian Faith*, 103.
246. Gunton, *The Christian Faith*, 103.
247. Gunton, *Father, Son and Holy Spirit*, 153.
248. Gunton, *Intellect and Action*, 80.

work by the power of the Spirit, reversing the accumulated history of sin and re-establishing, in anticipation, the creation's orientation towards its perfection.[249]

Jesus Christ is the bearer of authority and constitutional power from God because he is endowed with the Spirit and obediently exercises the offices of Israel by the power of the Spirit.[250] With reference to Irving, Gunton notes that the Spirit gives Jesus the charisms of the offices as he grows through various stages of his human ministry and development. At his baptism, he is anointed a prophet, but his eternal priesthood is gifted after his resurrection and ascension. The Spirit is therefore a personal agent who is active in various ways at different stages in Jesus' ministry and growth. "He [Irving] can thus speak of different 'measures' of the Spirit's being given."[251] At the resurrection, we see that the Spirit is the giver of eschatological life who breathes eschatological life into the new Adam and transforms Jesus' body into the age that is to come; the first-born of the new creation.[252] In his post-resurrection appearances, Jesus remains bodily, but his embodied life is transformed and perfected, such that he transcends some of the limits of temporal and spatial existence without forsaking them.[253] The resurrected body of Jesus Christ is miraculously transformed by the Spirit into another kind of body that relates to the created order in such ways that we see the first fruits of the perfecting of creation.

The Relationship of the Spirit and the Word

Gunton's pneumatological Christology focuses attention on the humanity of Jesus Christ and his faithful human life, but some believe this comes at the cost of an account of the eternal Word. John Webster reviews Gunton's reading of Barth, especially his criticisms of Barth's pneumatology, and holds that Gunton's reading of Barth is a presentation of the *grandes linges* that critiques by generalization. Gunton needs to heed his own advice on Barth and, "read the man himself!"[254] Webster takes issue with Gunton's claim that Barth has little if any real interest in Jesus' human action and that this is coupled with an under-developed pneumatology. For Webster, this is an extraordinary and ill-informed judgement. Moreover, Gunton's criticism that Barth's pre-temporal view of election lacks the pneumatological conditioning necessary to avoid the briars of Neoplatonism, is "a sour and uninformed judgement."[255] Rather, Gunton's criticisms are in fact the result of a deficiency in his own theology—namely the lack of a sustained and systematic account of Christology. For all its suggestiveness, the prominence Gunton gives to the Spirit risks separating the Word from the Spirit in such a way that it "gives

---

249. Gunton, *The Christian Faith*, 79.
250. Gunton, *Theology Through the Theologians*, 117.
251. Gunton, *Theology Through the Theologians*, 117.
252. Gunton, *Father, Son and Holy Spirit*, 118.
253. Gunton, *The Christian Faith*, 153.
254. John Webster, "Gunton and Barth," in *The Theology of Colin Gunton*, ed. Lincoln Harvey (London: T&T Clark, 2010), 27–9. On Gunton's advice to students, see Gunton, *The Barth Lectures*, 9.
255. Webster, "Gunton and Barth," 25–7.

little room to the Word's ongoing activity in the history of the incarnate one."[256] The lack of treatment of the eternal Word weakens Gunton's ability to resist forms of adoptionism and exemplarism, even though he never falls into them.

Webster is not alone in his criticisms of Gunton's pneumatological Christology. Paul Molnar also raises concerns about Gunton's theology of the Spirit and the Word. Gunton's stress upon Jesus' humanity can sometimes eliminate the significance of "his being the Word incarnate and at times actually tends to separate the actions of the Word and the Spirit."[257] In his desire to emphasize the full humanity of the Son, Gunton has a tendency to oppose the Word against the Spirit rather than upholding the action of the Word which takes place in and through the action of the Spirit.[258] A more active account of the Word incarnate would uphold the mystery of the Son of God incarnate in the unity of his divine and human natures. "Barth insists that Jesus's human actions are never merely the actions of a human being who was not also the eternal Son of God."[259]

Oliver Crisp agrees and holds that those who seek a greater *persona* for the Spirit face the dilemma of God the Son having a reduced role in the incarnation and the action of the Spirit overdetermining Christ's actions. Whilst the doctrine of inseparable operations holds that all the external works of God are trinitarian, many external works are "the particular preserve of one divine person, upon whom they terminate. In the case of the incarnation, this is God the Son."[260] It is the particular work of God the Son to be incarnate and attributing the Son's obedience to the Spirit risks dividing God's external works. Furthermore, it is unclear how the human Christ has more of the Spirit than any other creature. A simpler and more satisfactory theological claim, Crisp suggests, is "that God the Son is incarnate by the fiat of the Father, and with the Spirit's help, though it is God the Son who is the divine person particularly at work, as it were, in and through his human nature." Whilst the incarnation is the united action of the triune God, "it terminates upon the person of the Son."[261]

In like manner, Molnar raises objections about Gunton's account of the Spirit's perfecting of the Son's relationship with the Father. Why does the divine being need perfecting in Gunton's thought, and "is it not perfect by virtue of the fact that God exists as the one who loves in freedom?"[262] The divine being is not like the created order, and the Trinity is not a project that is to be perfected through time. Anizor asks, "Is [the divine communion] not already perfect by virtue of what it is: the communion that is God who loves in freedom?"[263] Gunton would, of course,

---

256. Webster, "Gunton and Barth," 28.
257. Paul Molnar, *Divine Freedom and the Doctrine of the Immanent Trinity*, 2nd ed. (London: T&T Clark, 2017), 494.
258. Molnar, *Divine Freedom and the Doctrine of the Immanent Trinity*, 495.
259. Molnar, *Divine Freedom and the Doctrine of the Immanent Trinity*, 508.
260. Crisp, "Gunton on Christology," 84.
261. Crisp, "Gunton on Christology," 85.
262. Paul D. Molnar, review of *Father, Son and Holy Spirit: Toward a Fully Trinitarian Theology*, by Colin E. Gunton, *Pro Ecclesia* 14 (2005): 496.
263. Anizor, *Trinity and Humanity*, 52.

offer an affirmative reply to these questions. However, Gunton's suggestion that the Spirit completes the divine life by orienting it outwards militates against his stress upon the *Selbständigkeit* of the creator and creation, and threatens his account of God's aseity. Any account of divine becoming, which Gunton opposes, risks undermining the eternal divine perfection. Rather than celebrating, with Cumin, Gunton's unique account of divine aseity as an "open dynamic of personal love,"[264] there is a need for caution. Webster, Molnar, Crisp, and Anizor are right to suggest the need for a stronger account of the Word in Gunton's Christology to ensure that the Word is not separated from the Spirit.[265]

Gunton's concerns about the encroachment of docetism and dualisms lead him to attempt to reformulate orthodox Christological doctrine in unconventional ways. Positively, this results in many suggestive biblical and theological insights for human culture, not least Christ's recapitulation of Adam and Israel through his faithful humanity. Negatively, it results in him pushing at some doctrinal boundaries that need to be more vigorously maintained.[266] Gunton's caution about the Chalcedonian language of two natures, and its impersonal drive towards abstraction and dualism, leads him to proffer some awkward constructions that threaten to undermine the activity of the Word incarnate. Gunton is uncomfortable with the language of natures because he believes it risks a form of abstraction in which two externally related qualities are cobbled together. However, his suggestion that in Jesus Christ we see the coming together of two movements in a single personal action undermines some of Gunton's own stress upon theological ontology.[267] Crisp rightly observes that "this is a case of Gunton being less careful than he ought to have been."[268] Likewise, Gunton's concern that the Word pushes Jesus Christ around risks the belief that "Jesus' humanity needs somehow to be protected from the determination of the Word if it is to have integrity."[269] Here, as with his nervousness about the *logos asarkos*, Gunton's penchant for detecting and overcoming dualisms may have weakened his work.[270]

---

264. Cumin, *Christ at the Crux*, 189.

265. Anizor, *Trinity and Humanity*, 120-3. See also Molnar, *Divine Freedom and the Doctrine of the Immanent Trinity*, 494-526; and Webster, "Gunton and Barth," 22-8.

266. Crisp is especially critical of Gunton's attempts to reformulate an account of Christ's two wills and his revision of the Chalcedonian two natures doctrine. See Crisp, "Gunton on Christology," 86-9.

267. Gunton, *The Christian Faith*, 94-6. For trenchant critiques, see Crisp, "Gunton on Christology," 88-9; and Alan Spence "The Person as Willing Agent: Classifying Gunton's Christology," in *The Theology of Colin Gunton*, ed. Lincoln Harvey (London: T&T Clark, 2010), 59-63.

268. Crisp, "Gunton on Christology," 88.

269. Webster, "Gunton and Barth," 28.

270. On Gunton's caution with the *logos asarkos*, see Gunton, *Father, Son and Holy Spirit*, 96. In this work, Gunton notes again his dissent with Robert Jenson on christology, even if he agrees with Jenson's concern that the *logos asarkos* can posit a God behind God that undermines divine revelation in the economy. Gunton's dissent is an affirmation of the *extra Calvinisticum*, even if it features rarely in his work.

The positive contributions of Gunton's turn to divine action in the economy need not be lost, but there is scope to strengthen Gunton's insights by a fuller account of the activity of the eternal Word in the ministry of Jesus Christ. Webster summarizes the criticisms of Gunton's Christology by noting that the lack of a sustained and systematic account of the Son of God is one of the oddest lacunae in Gunton's work.[271] There is scope for future research on Gunton to engage, strengthen, and extend his treatment of Christology, especially in relation to a theology of the eternal Word, in ways that enrich his orientations rather than supplant them.

Conclusion

This chapter has examined Gunton's theological account of culture through the mediation of the Son in the Spirit. The important criticisms of Gunton's Christology do not undermine the significance of Gunton's emphasis upon the humanity of Jesus Christ or his Christological definition of humanity's cultural mandate, but they rightly require greater strengthening of his theology of the eternal Word. Gunton's constructive theological account of human culture remains fruitful and generative, not least because his stress upon the concentration of creation, the *imago Dei*, and Israel's calling in the person of Jesus Christ provides a theological basis for human culture. Jesus Christ is the eschatological Adam and faithful Israelite by the empowerment of the eschatological Spirit; a representative sample of true humanity and human culture that is offered as a sacrifice of praise to the Father. Through Jesus Christ, the Spirit enables anticipations of the redemption of all things by setting the creation free to be itself in relation to God through Christ. Such anticipations can occur in the most unlikely places and in the most unlikely ways, as Christ is creation's Lord and present in all the world.[272]

Christ's universal lordship over all things in heaven and on earth is concentrated in his lordship over the Church, the body of Christ. The Church is not elected primarily for a unique future destiny out of the world, but is chosen from the world as a community with whom the destiny of the world is in some way bound up.[273] The Church, therefore, is the historical realization of God's eternal purposes to bring all things into unity under Jesus Christ by the Spirit's power. Chapter 5 examines Gunton's theology of the Church as a community of redemption that God elects to display God's purposes in creation. The Church is a form of redeemed culture that the Spirit, from time to time, enables to anticipate God's redemptive purposes for all creation in its common life and culture.

271. Webster, "Gunton and Barth," 28.
272. Gunton, "Reformation Accounts," 90.
273. Gunton, *Intellect and Action*, 148.

Chapter 5

THE MEDIATION OF THE SPIRIT: THE CHURCH AND HUMAN CULTURE

Colin Gunton is a theologian of the Spirit, and his account of the mediation of the Spirit funds a more concrete trinitarianism that is expressed in human culture in the world and in the Church's common life. This chapter explores Gunton's pneumatology in relation to his trinitarian theology of culture, which culminates in the Church's offering of worship at the Lord's Supper. The first section examines the Spirit's eschatological action that, from time to time, enables those who are created in God's image to achieve finite anticipations of the promised end. The second section turns to Gunton's writings in ecclesiology and explores them in relation to his theology of culture. It is Gunton's later writings in ecclesiology that offer some of his most important claims regarding a theology of human culture. Gunton's ecclesiology examines the concrete shape of the Church's life in community as an expression of its elect identity. God elects the Church as a representative community of redemption whose concrete life is enabled, from time to time, to be a distinctive form of eschatological culture. The Church offers its life and culture as a sacrifice of praise and worship to God through Christ by the Spirit's enabling, which culminates at the Lord's Supper.

The Spirit, Human Culture, and the Perfecting of Creation

The Spirit is the perfecting cause who enables human culture to contribute to finite perfections of creation in anticipation of the perfection of all things.[1] Finite perfections are the Spirit's eschatological enabling of creation to give approximations of God's perfect purposes for the project of creation.[2] Creation, humanity, and human culture are called to worship God by being what God created them to be in relation to God, one another, and the created order. Worship is not something limited to the Church's liturgical life, but a way of being human in the world. In

---

1. Gunton, *The Christian Faith*, 50. Gunton continues to use the classic refrain of the good, the true, and the beautiful to encompass all forms of right human habitation of the world.
2. Gunton, "Reformation Accounts," 93.

connection to human contributions to God's perfecting of creation, we examine Gunton's criterion for assessing human culture and the central calling of humanity to worship. In a fallen world, it is not obvious what makes for a human cultural contribution to the redemption and perfection of creation. Gunton develops a Christological criterion for assessing human cultural contributions as a sacrifice of praise in and through Christ's perfect sacrifice. Human cultural contributions praise God only when they conform to the way God is praised by the incarnate Son.

Gunton's Theological Definition of Human Culture

Human culture, broadly defined, is that set of activities through which human beings engage with one another and the world.[3] In culture, humans order and change the world around them, turning wilderness into gardens, barren land into housing, or, alternatively, forests into deserts.[4] In line with this, the cultural mandate in Genesis commands human beings to shape and change the world as part of their priestly calling. An eschatological account of creation, however, goes further. It sets human culture in the context of the perfecting of that which was created very good.[5] Accordingly, Gunton defines culture as the Spirit's enabling of humanity to collaborate with divine action in completing and perfecting God's work of art—the project of creation.[6]

Gunton's theology of culture develops within the Reformation tradition and seeks to extend the Reformers' insights biblically and theologically. The Reformers' theology of culture is a revised biblical conception of the relation between God and the world that replaces what Gunton views as the fusion of Christian and pagan culture that emerged in Christendom.[7] In place of the division of culture into two realities—spiritual and material—the Reformers offer a two-era view: the old and the new. This in turn provides a seedbed for science and politics, and many of our modern institutions developed under its impulses.[8] However, the Reformation's revisions of Christendom's theology of culture did not solve all problems.

The Reformers tend, in Gunton's assessment, towards a dialectical theology of culture rather than a trinitarian one. Luther's dialectic between the lost world of the fall and the new world of the gospel threatens to constrain the Spirit's action to that which is consciously Christian.[9] Luther's rather bleak view of human culture lacks the robust pneumatology that is found in Calvin. As a Reformed scholar,

---

3. Gunton, *The Christian Faith*, 50.
4. Gunton, *The Christian Faith*, 50.
5. Gunton, *The Christian Faith*, 50.
6. Gunton, *The Christian Faith*, 50.
7. Gunton, "Reformation Accounts," 84.
8. Gunton, "Reformation Accounts," 89.
9. Gunton, "Reformation Accounts," 90.

Gunton is heavily indebted to Calvin's theology of culture and actively stands in continuity with it.

In Gunton's estimation, Calvin's theology of culture offers a more optimistic view of human culture than Luther's because it is more pneumatological. The Spirit, according to Gunton's reading of Calvin, is the universal perfecting cause whose rays of divine light shine through the whole human race.[10] Despite the fall, there remain traces of natural endowments in humanity. These natural endowments enable Calvin to celebrate human political, scientific, mathematical, and artistic skills as gifts of the Spirit. However, Gunton is cautious about suggestions of residual natural endowments as they assume human capacity aside from the gift of the Spirit, and risk separating the Spirit from the Word as a force for divine good.[11] In Gunton's assessment, where Luther tends to see culture as a function of the fall, Calvin tends towards an utilitarian view of culture, "pagan culture is good when it is useful to us."[12]

Gunton seeks to strengthen the Reformers' account of human culture through his Christology and pneumatology that brings eschatology to bear on the present. The Spirit is not an immanent ecclesial force, but the perfecting cause of creation who sets creation free by bringing it into relation with the Father through the Son. Because Christ's lordship is over all creation, not just the Church, the Spirit's perfecting action is universal, not merely ecclesial. There is no limit to the Spirit's sphere of action. Rather, the Spirit enables finite human cultural perfections in the Church and in all the world.[13]

The Spirit is the Spirit of freedom who brings all things into unity under the universal lordship of Jesus Christ. Jesus Christ can be found where the gospel is not consciously lived, and all right human culture is a gift of the Spirit's perfecting action.[14] Indeed, pagan culture is part of the universal lordship of Jesus Christ and the free work of the Spirit who enables it to worship God in its own particular way.[15] The Spirit enables all forms of human reconciliation and a variety of cultural action beyond the Church. "Wherever there is between human beings the kind of love instantiated in Jesus and wherever there is good use of the created world for science and art; wherever, that is to say, the world in all its aspects is enabled to praise its maker, there is the work of the perfecting Spirit."[16] Scripture celebrates craftsmanship, music, and architecture as given by the Spirit, good in themselves and meaningful ways of praising God. "All right culture, by whomever it is formed, is the gift of God the Spirit through Christ, and so the gift of God's perfecting action."[17]

---

10. Gunton, "Reformation Accounts," 86–7.
11. Gunton, "Reformation Accounts," 90–1.
12. Gunton, "Reformation Accounts," 92.
13. Gunton, *The Christian Faith*, 178.
14. Gunton, *The Christian Faith*, 51. See also Gunton, "Reformation Accounts," 90.
15. Gunton, "Reformation Accounts," 92–3.
16. Gunton, *The Promise of Trinitarian Theology*, 191.
17. Gunton, *The Christian Faith*, 51.

The language of inspiration offers Gunton the opportunity to explore the work of humanity as sometimes attributable to the work of the Spirit.[18] The common language of a "mysterious inner light" that shines forth from human culture can, Gunton suggests, be set in a theological account of the Spirit's action in creation.[19] True human culture is the gift of the Spirit, and the language of inspiration (breathed by the Spirit), used in secular and religious contexts, captures the Spirit's inspiration of right human habitation in the world. A cricket stroke may be inspired, Gunton suggests, and so too may be a piece of art, as it is through particular human actions within the created order that the Spirit enables finite anticipations of creation's perfection.[20] Inspiration in art, and culture more broadly, is a gift that is given to artists from beyond themselves and orders their work.[21]

At this point, Gunton goes on to examine art as an example of human cultural agency and a contribution to the perfection of creation. In art, human agents interact with the material world to produce beautiful and useful things. Because the creation is coherent and meaningful, the artistic use of the world is also meaningful and can anticipate the redemption and perfection of all things in Christ when the Spirit enables it. Whether religious or not, true art is a creative gift of the Spirit who enables anticipations of the good, the true, and the beautiful in the present. "Art is thus one of the human ways of participating in God's project of creation."[22]

Inspired art is "action for the glory of God," but it need not result in a quest for the Spirit's otherworldly or miraculous cultural action. The Spirit's action is not only in the extraordinary but in ordering the ordinary material world and its capacities to anticipate God's eschatological purposes.[23] The Spirit's realization of truth, goodness, and beauty occurs within the capacities intrinsic to the creation, yet there remains the difficult question of how to assess what equates to an enhancement or degradation of the good, the true, and the beautiful. For instance, the development of Twenty 20 cricket has resulted in new innovations in stroke play which many initially regarded as ugly aberrations. Gunton notes the difficulty and reminds us that "[what] constitutes the proper perfecting of any particular created being is not clear, and subject to much argument."[24] This is especially the case when we consider the nature of human sin and the fall. Human cultural contributions are not neutral, and some forms of human culture are a participation in the culture of death.

---

18. Gunton, *Father, Son and Holy Spirit*, 123.
19. Gunton, *Father, Son and Holy Spirit*, 124.
20. Gunton, *The Christian Faith*, 51.
21. Gunton, *The Triune Creator*, 234.
22. Gunton, *The Triune Creator*, 234.
23. Gunton, *The Triune Creator*, 234.
24. Gunton, *The Triune Creator*, 229.

The Spirit, Sin, and Human Culture

Any theology of culture must give adequate account of the disruptive effects of the fall and sin. "In a fallen world, there is no perfection without redemption, without labour to overcome the backwards direction taken by the whole created order, and restored only in Christ."[25] All human culture, whether it knows it or not, is either an enhancement or degradation of the good, the true, and the beautiful; it is either a participation in God's perfecting of creation or a participation in the culture of death.[26] As the history of politics and the pollution of the ecosystem show, the Spirit's perfecting work is only achieved against opposition.[27]

Human cultural contributions are not value free and may be as much an expression of the culture of death as a contribution to the divine perfecting of creation. Humans are certainly called to horticulture and husbandry, yet Gunton notes that some forms of animal rearing are exploitative and fail to show due respect for the life they share with humanity.[28] It is not clear when such alteration of the ecosystem is a proper human action that frees the creation to be itself, and when it is a misuse that exploits, and therefore frustrates, creation. Too often, the human dominion of creation is interpreted as the human domination of creation to devastating effect.[29] As Gunton reminds us, humanity fails in its cultural mandate and the project of creation can only be achieved through the redemption that God achieves through Jesus Christ.[30]

The nature of sin not only impacts our assessment of human culture, but also impacts our ability to make theological sense of sin's unreality. How can the fallen human mind assess whether culture contributes to the perfecting of creation or to the culture of death? How can we judge between the appropriate killing of an animal and its improper exploitation?[31] Theological assessments of cultural contributions must take account of the limitations that arise from human sin, as well as the limitations of theology's ability to describe sinful human cultural contributions. Sin is, as Barth argues, irrational and absurd—humanity's rebellious choice to reject and deny the reality of its God-given creatureliness in favour of the unreality of sin.[32] As Holmes notes, in an essay heavily indebted to

---

25. Gunton, "Reformation Accounts," 82.

26. Gunton, *The Christian Faith*, 50–1. Gunton draws from Pope John Paul's encyclical on the gospel of life and his description of some modern ethical life as a culture of death. Pope John Paul II, *Evangelium Vitae*, 12. w2.vatican.va/content/john-paul-ii/en/encyclicals/documents/hf_jp-ii_enc_25031995_evangelium-vitae.html. See Gunton, *Father, Son and Holy Spirit*, 125–6.

27. Gunton, *Father, Son and Holy Spirit*, 121.

28. Gunton, *Father, Son and Holy Spirit*, 125.

29. Gunton, *Father, Son and Holy Spirit*, 89. See also Gunton, *The Promise of Trinitarian Theology*, 115.

30. Gunton, "Reformation Accounts," 82.

31. Gunton, *Father, Son and Holy Spirit*, 125.

32. Barth, CD IV/1, 406.

Gunton's work, theology cannot provide meaningful explanation for sin as sin is theologically meaningless.[33] "[Those] things that God does not will are unlikely to be illuminated by investigation into God …. [No] rational discourse can identify anything more than the bare fact of the existence of such realities, because they are, in essence, irrational."[34] A theology of culture, therefore, needs to respect the inherent tensions and limitations of making theological sense of human culture when it is sinful.

Given the universal extent of sin, Gunton distinguishes between what God wills and what God permits. Utilizing the imagery in Revelation 6, he shows that while the dark forces of sin are allowed to have their day, their action is not beyond God's sovereign authority and restraint. The use of divine passives for the riders in Revelation 6:1-8 (ἐδόθη αὐτῷ στέφανος (6:2); ἐδόθη αὐτῷ λαβεῖν τὴν εἰρήνην ἐκ τῆς γῆς (6:4); ἐδόθη αὐτοῖς ἐξουσία ἐπὶ τὸ τέταρτον τῆς γῆς (6:8)) shows that even though God does not will these evil forces, God permits them to take their destructive course for a time to reveal the outcome of the way humanity is determined to go. The resulting chaos does not have its own independent authority and remains subject to divine restraint and limitation—one-fourth and no more (Rev 6:8).[35] Gunton concludes that God permits, but does not will, activities that "disrupt the purposes of creation and impede its perfecting."[36] There remains, however, the question of how we are to evaluate human habitation of the world. For this reason, Gunton develops and refines a theological criterion for assessing right human habitation of the world.

Culture, Finite Perfections, and the Criterion of a Sacrifice of Praise

Worship is humanity's *telos*—the creature's offering of the right human habitation of the world as praise and thanks to God for God's wise purposes in creation. This worship is a form of human culture and life in community, and so Gunton develops his criterion for judging the Spirit's perfecting action in relation to this end.[37] He turns to Romans 12, an influential chapter for his theology of culture, and Paul's account of humanity's offering of embodied worship. The right human

---

33. Holmes, "Can Theology Engage with Culture?" 5–6.

34. Holmes, "Can Theology Engage with Culture?" 5–6.

35. Gunton, *Father, Son and Holy Spirit*, 161. Craig Koester's interpretation of Revelation reinforces Gunton's point and Koester notes that divine restraint and limitation are literary features the author employs throughout Revelation. "Authority over a fourth of the earth shows the magnitude of the threat as well as its limit: one-fourth, not more." Craig Koester, *Revelation: A New Translation with Introduction and Commentary*, The Anchor Yale Bible (New Haven and London: Yale University Press, 2014), 398.

36. Gunton, *Father, Son and Holy Spirit*, 161.

37. Gunton, *The Promise of Trinitarian Theology*, 190.

habitation of God's world effects the offering of humanity and creation as a sacrifice of praise for God's purposes in the world and anticipates the Spirit's perfection of all things.

Gunton proposes that the criterion by which we may assess right human habitation of the world is the sacrifice of praise. This is an extension of his account of Christ's priestly self-sacrifice. "There is one criterion which is universal, and it is that right behaviour to the material world is that which offers those particular events and being with which we have to do as a sacrifice of praise to God."[38] A sacrifice of praise to God is not a human effort at bringing in the kingdom, but the perfected offering of created particulars in their own proper way and time. The evaluative question for cultural contributions is, "Does this offer to God the creator the sacrifice of praise of the perfected creation?"[39] Gunton's criterion does not answer each and every question, or provide universal answers, but it provides a theological framework for an analysis of particular forms of created being in relation to creation's eschatological end.

In his later writings on the theology of culture, Gunton refines his criterion for assessing human culture further through Christological reflection. In a fallen world, it is only in Jesus Christ that we know what is right human culture. As the eschatological Adam, it is Jesus Christ's particular human life, death, and resurrection that offer faithful human praise to God. From his account of Christ *as* eschatological human culture, Gunton maintains that culture, Christian or not, offers a sacrifice of praise to God when it conforms to Christ and his faithful human life, death, and resurrection. "[The] criteria by which we assess whether – or in which respects – a work of culture is the praise of God or some form of sin must be Christological, because only in Jesus do we know what right culture is."[40] Even so, the realities of human sin mean that moving from Christ's humanity as true human culture to judgements on human culture more broadly is highly complex and requires wisdom from God. It is all too easy to mistake the work of the Spirit, who, for instance, turns the cross of Christ from the supreme blasphemy into the means of praising God.[41]

Gunton pursues the development of a criterion for assessing human culture, and extends his thought on the sacrifice of praise through the concept of finite perfections. As we have seen, finite perfections featured in *The One, the Three and the Many*, but there they were explored in relation to the open transcendentals and Gunton's theology of analogy. With the progression in his thought, Gunton refines the concept of finite perfections further through his theology of divine

---

38. Gunton, *The Triune Creator*, 230.
39. Gunton, *The Triune Creator*, 231.
40. Gunton, "Reformation Accounts," 93.
41. Gunton, "Reformation Accounts," 92–3.

action in the economy. Wisely, Gunton does not give a highly developed framework for assessing human cultural contributions. He does, however, conclude that any assessment of finite human perfections must be controlled by Christology.

> The central criterion will be whether an action, event or thing praises the One who made it, and praises it in the way he was praised by his incarnate Son; but the nature of the perfection will be different according to the nature of that which is judged. This means the humblest artefact can there succeed, the most beautiful act of worship fail.[42]

All human action is human in the weak sense, but not all human action is human in the strong sense that it conforms to the pattern of truly human action as it is revealed in Jesus Christ by the Spirit.[43] Our assessment of the true, the good, and the beautiful, inside and outside the Church, is defined by the true Adam who is the fulfilment of the *imago Dei* and humanity's cultural mandate.

Gunton's Christological criterion offers a framework for interpreting human culture, as it is in Christ that humanity and creation find their proper end in worship of the Father. It is in worship that creation's end is anticipated in humanity's presentation of embodied life in communion with God, one another and the creation to the Father through the Son and in the Spirit. Romans 12, with its reference to offering embodied life as worship, is the central text of Gunton's understanding of worship which concerns all of embodied life—culture.[44] The whole creation is called to worship God by becoming what God particularly created it to be. Yet, the world has systematically organized itself in such a way that it is prone to worship the creature rather than the creator.[45] Over against this, Gunton proposes that an account of the Spirit's enabling of true human culture finds its particular expression in the Church as a concrete community of worship whose life is reordered to God through Christ.[46]

Gunton's Early Ecclesiology: The Being of God and the Being of the Church

As a dissenting theologian and congregationalist minister, Gunton seeks to renew ecclesiology from a static and institutional view of the Church to an understanding

---

42. Gunton, "Reformation Accounts," 93.
43. Gunton, *Father, Son and Holy Spirit*, 161.
44. Gunton, *Father, Son and Holy Spirit*, 229.
45. Gunton, *The Promise of Trinitarian Theology*, 175.
46. Gunton, "Reformation Accounts," 82–3.

of the Church as a dynamic visible community in a post-Christendom context.[47] Gunton's ecclesiology is critical and constructive. His criticisms of the Church's institutional, political, and theological failings serve as foil to his insistence on the Church as a visible community. Too often ecclesiology assumes an over-realized eschatology of the institution that imbues it with divine historical authority. What is needed is to balance Christ's historic *institution* of the Church with the Spirit's *constitution* of the Church in the present as God's eschatological community.

Gunton establishes his trinitarian theology of the Church as an eschatological community against his cultural and theological criticisms of the Church. To this end he brings together insights from Cappadocian trinitarian ontology and John Owen's account of the Church's life as a pneumatological community. In his early writings on the Church, Gunton suggests that the Church's life in community is a form of concrete culture that God the Spirit enables to be a "finite echo" of the Trinity.[48] Such claims face criticism for forms of social trinitarianism that risk drawing analogical connections between divine and human being too easily. However, these critiques of Gunton's concept of the Church as a finite echo of God's being do not adequately observe the strict apophatic qualifications and limitations that Gunton insists upon. Furthermore, many of the criticisms project Gunton's open transcendentals on to his early ecclesiology, despite the fact that aside from *The One, the Three and the Many* Gunton does not utilize the concept of open transcendentals in his ecclesiology. The *Hauptbriefe* in Gunton's writings is especially strong in regard to his ecclesiology, and results in a misrepresentation

---

47. Gunton observes that being Christian in this era became synonymous with being born European. A detailed account of Gunton's analysis of Christendom would recognize that whilst his critique of the church in Christendom is strong, not all was loss. Gunton is clear that the history of the church's Constantinian settlement is overwhelmingly problematic, and the church regularly abused its power. Yet, he is careful not to fall prey to the fashionable reductionism of Christendom. He cautions that too much can be made of the church's transformation of faith into oppression. Whilst the church did grasp at the reins of political power to achieve its end, it was not in every way a bad thing. Not all within Christendom was loss, and it resulted in the development of many incomparable forms of culture in Western science, art, music, education, medicine, and aesthetics. On the reach of Christendom, see Gunton, *Father, Son and Holy Spirit*, 204. On the need for a nuanced account of Christendom, see Colin E. Gunton, "The Spirit as Lord: Christianity, Modernity and Freedom," in *Different Gospels: Christian Orthodoxy and Modern Theologies*, ed. Andrew Walker (London: SPCK, 1993), 75, and a later account in Gunton, *The Christian Faith*, 120. Martin Sutherland and Michael Jinkins note the popularity of reductionist accounts of Christendom that fail to take account of the nuances of church history. See Martin Sutherland, "Pine Trees and Paradigms: Rethinking Mission in the West," in *Mission without Christendom: Exploring the Site. Essays for Brian Smith*, ed. Martin Sutherland (Auckland: Carey Baptist College, 2000), 131–48; and Michael Jinkins, *The Church Faces Death: Ecclesiology in a Post-Modern Context* (Oxford: OUP, 1999), 58–63.

48. Gunton, *The Promise of Trinitarian Theology*, 73.

Gunton's Critical Ecclesiology: Christendom's Institutional Church

In the Christendom era, the Church grasped at the reins of political power to achieve its ends, often with disastrous effects in the East and the West. Gunton utilizes Harnack's historical account to argue that the Eastern Church is influenced by Neo-Platonism's hierarchically structured reality that grades existence into degrees of being.[50] The ontological achievements in Christology and trinitarian theology are not extended into ecclesiology, and the Church assumes itself to be an earthly shadow of a heavenly hierarchy.[51]

Developments in Western ecclesiology are, in Gunton's view, even more dismal. The West derives the Church's being by analogy to an earthly empire or an imperial army, which results in authoritarian and institutional conceptions of the Church.[52] When it becomes the official religion of the Roman Empire, the Church imitates earthly political empires and places increasing stress on hierarchy, clericalism, and authoritarianism.[53] As the official religion of the Empire, the Church in the West has been viewed as a mixed company of the saved and the lost. Gunton observes two resulting developments: firstly, a stress upon the institutional nature of the Church and the tendency to see the bishops as the real Church who impose unity by employing hierarchical power.[54] The being of the Church, therefore, does not come from the congregation of the faithful, because not all the Church are faithful, but from relation to its hierarchical leaders.[55] Secondly, there is a platonizing distinction between the mixed company of the visible Church and the pure invisible Church. The true Church is invisible and known only to God, and the visible Church is but a Platonic shadow.[56] The institutional accounts of the Church and its abuse of authority and power are not, in Gunton's view, primarily the result of political shortcomings, but of theological failures—especially the failure to conceive the Church in the light of the Trinity.

The Christendom Church's ecclesiology fails, in Gunton's assessment, because it does not root the Church in the triune being of God. "The conclusion must be that the conception of God as a triune communion made no substantive contribution

---

49. For a definition of *Hauptbriefe* ("main letters"), see p. 3, fn 5.
50. Gunton, *The Promise of Trinitarian Theology*, 58.
51. Gunton, *The Promise of Trinitarian Theology*, 58.
52. Gunton, *The Promise of Trinitarian Theology*, 58.
53. Gunton, *The Promise of Trinitarian Theology*, 58–60. For a helpful summary of Gunton's views, see Anizor, "A Spirited Humanity," 27; and Anizor, *Trinity and Humanity*, 151–5.
54. Gunton, *The Promise of Trinitarian Theology*, 59.
55. Gunton, *The Promise of Trinitarian Theology*, 59.
56. Gunton, *The Promise of Trinitarian Theology*, 59.

to the doctrine of the Church."⁵⁷ Because the insights of a distinctively Christian trinitarian ontology that defines the being and nature of Christ and the Trinity are not consistently realized in ecclesiology, foreign ontologies rush to fill the theological vacuum. As a result, Gunton argues that distortions of dogma enter the Church's bloodstream early and develop into atheological political settlements that have a deleterious impact on the way the Church understands and organizes itself.⁵⁸

These theological criticisms of the institutional Church provide a starting point to establish more robust theological alternatives. As we have seen, Gunton opposes all forms of dualism and abstraction, real or perceived, and seeks concrete and embodied alternatives. The following section examines his criticisms of Christendom's monism and the dominance of an ontology of the invisible.⁵⁹ These dogmatic distortions, along with the misappropriation of the Spirit and a docetic ecclesiology, assert a logical link between the institutional Church and God. The effect is the undermining of the being and nature of the Church as a community.

Gunton's Critical Ecclesiology: Monism and Its Dogmatic Distortions

In his early writings, Gunton seeks to show that different theologies of the Trinity generate different ecclesiologies. Monadic accounts of God, he avers, produce ecclesiologies that abstract the real being of the Church from the concrete community of persons in relation. Here Gunton repeats his familiar critique of Augustine's doctrine of the Trinity and its modalistic tendencies, and argues that this influences Augustine's institutional ecclesiology. Augustine, in Gunton's view, posits the institutional being of the Church as ontologically prior to the historical relationships of the visible community.⁶⁰ These modalistic tendencies undermine the significance of the Church as a visible community and fail to realize the Cappadocian trinitarian revolution in ontology. "An institution is not, as such, a community, because its existence is independent and logically prior to the persons who become part of it."⁶¹ The Church as an institution is a historically given reality to which relationships are appended, and its unity is constrained to a uniformity at the expense of its rich diversity. The Church is an institution, but it is how we conceive Christ's historic institution of the Church that matters.

That Jesus Christ institutes the Church as a historically given reality is unproblematic; however, the way we conceive of Christ's instituting authority is of critical importance. The roots of the Church's institution are found in God's call to Abraham and his offspring to be a blessing to the nations. It is Jesus Christ however

---

57. Gunton, *The Promise of Trinitarian Theology*, 60.
58. Gunton, *Theology Through the Theologians*, 190. See also Gunton, *The Promise of Trinitarian Theology*, 60–1.
59. Gunton, *The Promise of Trinitarian Theology*, 82.
60. Gunton, *The Promise of Trinitarian Theology*, 74.
61. Gunton, *Theology Through the Theologians*, 198.

who faithfully takes up this call and realizes God's purposes and his "ministry, death and resurrection achieved the instituting of the body—his body—which is the historic Church."[62] How we understand this instituting action of Christ and its effects on the present are crucial dogmatic, rather than historical, questions.[63]

The docetic christologies of the tradition spawn docetic ecclesiologies that assume the Church is endowed with Christ's authority. Docetic ecclesiologies assert an over-realized eschatology of the Church as an institution that asserts logical links between Christ's instituting authority and its possession of divine authority.[64] If, as Gunton argues, Christendom's ecclesiology is docetic, because its Christology is docetic, then this accounts for why and how the clergy understand themselves to be an extension of Christ's authority over the institution of the Church. Christology's tendency to universalize is transmogrified into a premature universality of the Church's significance at the expense of its creaturely nature.[65] The Church's authority is historically ontologized quite aside from its temporal and spatial obedience.

What kind of ecclesiology, Gunton asks, might derive from equal stress upon the significance of Jesus Christ's incarnation and contingent humanity that is conditioned by the Spirit?[66] Jesus Christ's victory of human faithfulness over temptation was won by his free acceptance of the Spirit's guidance, not some form of inbuilt divine programming.[67] The Church cannot, therefore, claim more for itself than for Christ. There is a need to give adequate account of the Church's fallible humanity and the Spirit's enabling action. However, the tendency in the church's tradition is to combine a docetic Christology with an unbalanced pneumatology that domesticates the Spirit within the Church.

Gunton believes that, on a cynical reading, the history of the Church can be stated as "the story of the misappropriation of the Spirit."[68] A crude summary would be that the promise of the Spirit's presence with the Church is turned into a claimed ecclesial possession. The over-realized eschatology of the Church as an institution reduces the Spirit to an immanent causal force whose gifts and promises are internal to the Church. The Church's tendency then is to identify the Spirit's action with the Church's action.[69] The docetic Christology that over-determines the Church's being coincides with an immanent pneumatology that under-determines the reality of the Church's humanity. At issue is the failure, especially in the West, to give the Spirit the kind of personal particularity that is needed to identify the Spirit's work and action in the world. As with a docetic Christology, what is needed

---

62. Gunton, *Theology Through the Theologians*, 198.
63. Gunton, *The Promise of Trinitarian Theology*, 64–5.
64. Gunton, *The Promise of Trinitarian Theology*, 66–7.
65. Gunton, *The Promise of Trinitarian Theology*, 67.
66. Gunton, *The Promise of Trinitarian Theology*, 66–7.
67. Gunton, *The Promise of Trinitarian Theology*, 67.
68. Gunton, *Theology Through the Theologians*, 187.
69. Gunton, *Theology Through the Theologians*, 188.

is a greater emphasis upon the humanity of the Church and the transcendence of the Spirit. The Spirit is not an immanent causal force within the institution, but God's eschatological transcendence who acts externally upon the Church.[70] In scripture, the Spirit is God's freedom and otherness who acts over and within the creation to anticipate in the present, through finite and contingent means, the things of the age to come.[71]

Whilst Jesus Christ institutes the Church as a historical institution, it is the action of the Spirit that constitutes the Church as a community in time and space. Here, Gunton draws from John Zizioulas who argues that if the Church is merely a historically given institutional reality, it is inimical to human freedom.[72] As the Spirit liberates Jesus Christ from relegation to past history by raising him from the dead with eschatological life, so the Spirit liberates the Church from institutionalism.[73] The Spirit is God's transcendent otherness from the world, who brings eschatological life into the present. The Church is not primarily a historical institution to which community is added; "the movement of an already-given reality."[74] Instead, the Spirit constitutes the Church in the present through the visible gathering of believers as a community in anticipation of the renewal of all things.

In place of the static institutionalism of the tradition, Gunton proffers a dynamic account of the Church as a visible community that the Spirit enables, from time to time, to anticipate eschatological reality. To achieve this, Gunton draws together insights on pneumatology and community from Zizioulas and Owen to construct a pneumatological ecclesiology of the Church as a dynamic eschatological community. Gunton's congregationalist and dissenting commitments are clearest at this point, and his ecclesiology stresses the Spirit's enabling of the visible communal life of the Church.

In his constructive ecclesiology, Gunton seeks to replace logical links between God and the institutional Church with theological and personal links for a trinitarian theology of the Church as a community. As we have seen, Gunton diagnoses two major distortions of dogma that militate against a trinitarian theology of the Church as a concrete community: a monadic doctrine of God that results in an abstract definition of the Church and a misappropriation of the Spirit as a causal force within the Church.[75] In the light of this he offers a twofold remedy: firstly, a Cappadocian corrective that would develop a full trinitarian account of the Church, and secondly, Owen's insight that the Church is the visible community of persons-in-relation.

70. Gunton, *Theology Through the Theologians*, 189–90.
71. Gunton, *The Promise of Trinitarian Theology*, 67.
72. Gunton, *Theology Through the Theologians*, 197–8. See Zizioulas, *Being as Communion*, 126–32. It is important to note that although Gunton (a Reformed congregationalist minister) and Zizioulas (a Greek Orthodox bishop) share very similar views on the Trinity, they have very different views on ecclesiology and ecclesial structures.
73. Gunton, *Theology Through the Theologians*, 198–9.
74. Gunton, *Theology Through the Theologians*, 199.
75. Gunton, *The Promise of Trinitarian Theology*, 56.

Gunton's Constructive Ecclesiology: Trinitarian Ontology and the Being of the Church

The question of the being of the Church, Gunton argues in his early writings, is "one of the most neglected topics of theology."[76] The historical lack of sustained trinitarian reflection that roots the being of the Church in the triune being of God allows foreign ontologies to fill the void. With the waning of Constantinianism and the loss of the Church's privileged position in the social order there is a need to develop an account of the Church as a community. To achieve this, Gunton searches alternative historical sources that resist the over-realized claims of institutionalism and offers an account of the Church as a community.[77] In doing so, he turns to Zizioulas and the Cappadocians to develop his claim that "the sole proper ontological basis for the Church is the being of God, who is what he is as the communion of Father, Son, and Spirit."[78]

God's being is a dynamic communion of distinguishable but inseparable persons—three persons in *perichoretic* interrelation. Whilst the Greek Fathers did not develop an explicit trinitarian ecclesiology, they did lay the groundwork for its development.[79] Most importantly, their ontological revolution offers a new concept of being that has important ecclesiological implications.[80] The doctrine of the Trinity replaces all logical conceptions of God's relation to the world, or to the Church in particular, with personal and theological relations.[81]

The Cappadocians developed a theology of communion or community that Gunton believes focuses ecclesiological questions. Because God is not a static hierarchy of being, but a dynamic community of persons in *perichoretic* relation, the Church, as a creature of God, cannot be conceived as a static hierarchical institution. In this way, Cappadocian ontology opens the way for a trinitarian theology of Church where the relations of the particular persons constitute the being of the Church. "May not the actual relations of concrete historical persons constitute the sole—or primary—being of the Church, just as the hypostases in relation constitute the being of God?"[82] The Church is called to be a community of *koinōnia* because it has its being from the triune God who exists in eternal *perichoretic koinōnia*. In Gunton's *perichoretic* ecclesiology, the Church is to reflect or "echo" at its own level the kind of being that God is eternally. There is an indirect analogy between God and the Church, Gunton avers, in which the Church is called

---

76. Gunton, *The Promise of Trinitarian Theology*, 56.

77. Gunton explores the work of Tertullian and Novatian and notes that their opposition to institutionalism led them to be suspected of heresy. However, there is in their work the beginnings of an account of the church as community where the conditions of the life to come can be realized in the present. Gunton, *The Promise of Trinitarian Theology*, 61–4.

78. Gunton, *The Promise of Trinitarian Theology*, 71.

79. Gunton, *Theology Through the Theologians*, 196.

80. Gunton, *Theology Through the Theologians*, 196.

81. Gunton, *The Promise of Trinitarian Theology*, 72.

82. Gunton, *The Promise of Trinitarian Theology*, 74.

to be a finite echo of God's eternal being-in-relation.[83] "The Church is called to be the kind of reality at a finite level that God is in eternity."[84]

Gunton's suggestion that the relational dynamics of the divine persons can be echoed in the Christian community faces much criticism, especially that of projectionism. Webster cites Gunton's work when he cautions that the analogical use of trinitarian formulae as bridge terms can give the impression of effecting the passage between creator and creation too comfortably.[85] Anizor amplifies Webster's caution, and senses that Gunton is in danger of reading too much creaturely reality into the Trinity.[86] More directly, Justin Stratis insists that Gunton's analogical echo requires a very strict qualification because, "the type of *caritas* enjoyed by the Trinity is as different from the life of the creature as the creature is from the Creator."[87] These cautions are important, especially given Gunton's stress upon the ontological distinction of creator and creation. However, they do not observe the apophatic limitations Gunton places upon the analogy of echo. The ontological distinction between divine and human being is central to Gunton's work and he is conscious of the need to be careful to avoid confusing their distinct ontologies.

Any attempt to draw finite links between divine and human being must, Gunton argues, attend to the necessary limits of divine and human being. The necessary theological control for any analogical link between divine and human community is the doctrine of creation.[88] Ecclesiology must be rooted in the triune God *and* make allowance for the fact that the Church is a created reality. As a created reality the Church is finite and contingent, entirely dependent on divine action for its being. There are no logical links, Gunton maintains, that allow us to base the unity of the Church on the unity of God, or, conversely, the diversity of the Church on the diversity of God's being.[89] God's relation to the Church is not logical or symmetrical, but asymmetrical and personal. It is God's free and personal action, through the frail humanity of the Son and the perfecting action of the Spirit, that makes the Church a community of the triune God.[90] Conceiving the Church in the image of the humanity of Christ upholds the necessary space between divine and created being that is so vital for the integrity of their distinct ontologies.

---

83. Gunton, *The Promise of Trinitarian Theology*, 73.

84. Gunton, *The Promise of Trinitarian Theology*, 80.

85. Webster, "'In the Society of God,'" 206.

86. Anizor, *Trinity and Humanity*, 164–5.

87. Justin Stratis, "A Person's a Person, No Matter How Divine? The Question of Univocity and Personhood in Richard of St Victor's *De Trinitate*," *Scottish Journal of Theology*, 70 (2017): 388.

88. Gunton, *The Promise of Trinitarian Theology*, 71–2.

89. "That would be to move too quickly, playing with abstract and mathematically determined concepts and exercising no theological control over their employment." Gunton, *The Promise of Trinitarian Theology*, 71.

90. Gunton, *The Promise of Trinitarian Theology*, 71–2.

It may surprise some to note that Gunton cautions against any direct attempts to construct ecclesiology from the immanent Trinity and the supposed patterns of relationship between the persons of the Godhead.[91] In language reminiscent of Karen Kilby, Gunton observes that there must be "a duly apophatic treatment of the trinitarian relations," that does not "claim such detailed knowledge of the inner constitution of the godhead that we can attempt direct and logical readings-off of that kind."[92] Any analogy between God and the Church, Trinity and community, must be an indirect analogy or a finite echo that bodies forth the divine personal dynamics.[93] Gunton goes to lengths, rarely recognized by his critics, to develop a qualified account of the indirect analogy of the Church as a finite echo of the Triune communion.[94] The finite echo is, in accordance with Khaled Anatolios' arguments outlined in Chapter 2, an analogy of likeness within radical unlikeness.[95] The finite echo is Gunton's attempt to conceive the Church's being in its concrete relationships and not an ontologically prior institutional reality to which relationships are appended.[96]

The Cappadocians did more to lay the ontological framework for ecclesiology, Gunton suggests, than they did to develop it.[97] Gunton is discontent with simply a trinitarian ecclesiology in ontological mode, and turns to Owen's pneumological Christology to co-opt his work for constructing a theology of the Church as a concrete visible community. It is at this point that Gunton's Reformed, congregationalist, and dissenting commitments to the visible gathered community, in place of the Church as an institution, are clearest. The combination of a Cappadocian theology of being and Owen's theology of pneumatological community, both of which Gunton co-opts for his own purposes, informs Gunton's early writings on the Church as a visible eschatological community in the present.

---

91. Gunton, *The Promise of Trinitarian Theology*, 73.

92. Gunton, *The Promise of Trinitarian Theology*, 73. See Kilby, "Perichoresis and Projection," 432–45.

93. Gunton, *The Promise of Trinitarian Theology*, 73–4.

94. A more even-handed reading would acknowledge, with Stephen Holmes, that Gunton does not bluntly collapse trinitarian relationality into an account of society. Stephen R. Holmes, "Gunton, Colin Ewart (1941–2003)," in *New Dictionary of Theology: Historical and Systematic*, 2nd ed., ed. Martin Davie et al. (Downers Grove: IVP, 2016), 385. Julie Green rightly notes Gunton's apophatic analogy of echo grounds the being of the church in the being of God and the personal relational dynamics. The trinitarian dynamics of personal being need not be reduced to a simplistic social trinitarianism. See Julie Kaye Green, "The Worldly Church: The Relationship between Church and Culture as Perichoretic Necessity with Particular Reference to Colin Gunton" (PhD diss., University of Aberdeen, Scotland, 2014), 189–90.

95. Anatolios, *Retrieving Nicaea*, 233.

96. Gunton, *The Promise of Trinitarian Theology*, 74.

97. Gunton, *Theology Through the Theologians*, 196.

John Owen, the Spirit, and the Church as a Concrete Visible Community

John Owen is an important source for Gunton as he is a British voice who shares Gunton's dissenting perspective and stress upon the visible community of disciples in the present. Owen argues that whilst the Reformers certainly brought about a reformation of doctrine, they did not develop a theology of community.[98] The Reformation sought to establish the Church as a communion of saints, but its sociality and polity remain wed to the external and legal pressures of the state at the expense of community.[99] Gunton develops his account of pneumatological ecclesiology from Owen who contributes two important *foci*: the transcendence of the Spirit and the concrete community of the Church. Owen's theology of the Church as community can be extended by integrating it with the insights of trinitarian ontology. By bringing Owen into dialogue with the Greek theologians, Gunton hopes to "say something important about how we may conceive the action of the Spirit in one central area of his work; that is in relation to the Church."[100]

Owen's theology of the Spirit's transcendence runs against the grain of the tendency to conceive of the Spirit as an immanent causal force.[101] Owen's Christology, like Edward Irving's, seeks to overcome the docetism implicit in the tradition by placing greater emphasis upon the humanity of the Son whose faithfulness is enabled by the Spirit rather being than over-determined by the Word.[102] The Spirit is not identified with human action because the Spirit is a distinct person of the Godhead whose particular actions are over-against the creation. The Spirit, in Owen's thought, is a distinct *hypostasis* who performs a wide range of eschatological actions in relation to the incarnate Son, liberating him to be the Messiah of God.[103] The Spirit's being and action are characterized by freedom and authority that bring about God's eschatological purposes. What kind of ecclesiology, Gunton asks, might derive from a greater stress upon the ecclesiological significance of Jesus Christ's humanity that is conditioned by the Spirit?[104]

The Spirit's presence is not fixed within the institution of the Church, but is a dynamic, and unpredictable, transcendent presence, that blows where the Spirit wills.[105] Like the rebalancing of Christology, there needs to be a greater emphasis upon the Church's createdness and contingency. The Church does not possess the Spirit, but, like the incarnate Son, is enabled and empowered by the Spirit to anticipate God's new community. Having explored Owen's theology of the Spirit's

---

98. Gunton, *The Promise of Trinitarian Theology*, 74.
99. Gunton, *Theology Through the Theologians*, 191.
100. Gunton, *Theology Through the Theologians*, 190.
101. Gunton, *Theology Through the Theologians*, 191.
102. Gunton, *The Promise of Trinitarian Theology*, 69.
103. Gunton, *Theology Through the Theologians*, 192.
104. Gunton, *The Promise of Trinitarian Theology*, 66–7.
105. Gunton, *Theology Through the Theologians*, 192.

transcendence, Gunton turns to examine his contribution to a theology of Church as community.

Owen's congregationalist ecclesiology employs Aristotelian categories to establish the nature of the Church as a visible community. The visible believers are the material cause of the Church. Their voluntary coalescence into congregations is the formal cause of the Church and visible local Church communities are the final cause or *telos*. The being of the Church, therefore, consists in its nature as a community, which Owen terms a visible Church-state.[106] "According to this conception," Gunton argues, "it is the actual believers as they are constituted a community who make a Church, not some supposed invisible underlying structure."[107]

Gunton detects in Owen's ecclesiology an echo of Cappadocian ontology. This is especially the case as Owen's language shifts from Aristotelian terminology towards Cappadocian trinitarian theological conceptions of person, cause, and relation.[108] The Church has its being from the persons gathered in community, not an *a priori* ontological institution to which persons are appended. "The result is that Owen's doctrine of the Church is an echo of the Greek theology of the Trinity according to which God *is* what the three persons are in relation to one another. The outcome is an ecclesiology in which the Church is understood by analogy with the Trinity."[109] Again, Gunton is clear that this is not a direct reading-down of divine being on to the nature of community, but an attempt to understand the nature of the Church through theological concepts developed from the doctrine of God as Trinity. This, in Gunton's perspective, avoids tendencies to draw analogies from the army or the state and sets the analogy between creator and creation.[110]

For all Owen's insights, Gunton senses in him a failure to bring together his two great contributions: the distinct action of the Spirit and a theology of the Church as community. Owen offers little on the Spirit as the creator of community on earth, and especially regarding the saints' communion. His emphasis upon the voluntary coalescence of the gathered Church risks importing Enlightenment ideals of the

---

106. Gunton, *Theology Through the Theologians*, 193.

107. Gunton, *Theology Through the Theologians*, 193.

108. Gunton, *Theology Through the Theologians*, 192–3. See also Gunton, *The Promise of Trinitarian Theology*, 74–5.

109. Gunton, *Theology Through the Theologians*, 193.

110. Gunton, *Theology Through the Theologians*, 194. Gunton draws heavily from Adolph Harnack's analysis in Adolf Harnack, *History of Dogma*, trans. Neil Buchanan, 7 vols. (New York: Dover Publications, 1961). Gunton uses Cyprian as an example of the early impulse to develop the church by imperial analogies. Whilst there is not a direct analogy between the church and an earthly empire, Cyprian's letters "breathe a spirit of authoritarian commitment to the unity of the church with an empire." Gunton, *The Promise of Trinitarian Theology*, 58–9. For Cyprian's analogy of the church as an Army, see Cyprian, *The Epistles of Cyprian*, 46.2; 54.1 (*ANF* 5:324). A more common analogy of the church as an army is Clement, *The First Epistle of Clement to the Corinthians*, 37 (*ANF* 1:15).

freedom of the individual *from* community that undermines the gospel's freedom in and for community.[111] Without a pneumatological determination of freedom, there is a risk that Owen's voluntarism could be read as a theological legitimation of secular individualistic autonomy and its assertion of freedom *from* relationship. The gospel does not offer freedom *from* relationship but freedom *in* relationship; the Spirit frees us in and for relationship with God and one another through the community of the Church.

The Spirit is not only the creator of faith, as Owen proclaims, the Spirit is also the creator of community—the one through whom the Father realizes the communion of the saints on earth.[112] Life in the community of the Church is not the result of human togetherness, but the action of the Spirit who is the creator of community. Gunton's early writings in ecclesiology bring together Owen's two ideas, along with Cappadocian ontology, to develop a pneumatological account of the Church as a visible eschatological community.

The Visible Church as an Eschatological Community of the Spirit

Ecclesiology, for Gunton, is not an abstract topic, but takes shape within the world in the visible community of disciples and their common life together in the Spirit. In place of the abstract ecclesiology of the tradition, Gunton stresses the visibility of the Church as God's eschatological community that displays the first fruits of the kingdom in its common life. The recourse to an ecclesial ontology of the invisible needs correction by an ontology of the visible community that upholds the pneumatological aspects of the Church in balance with the Christological aspects. The Spirit's eschatological action in the present enables the Church to be God's community of the end that embodies God's purposes for all things.[113] A pneumatologically balanced ecclesiology allows an exploration of the shape the Church takes in the present, which invites consideration of the Church's common life and culture as the experience of the freedom of the Spirit in community. "The link that must be made is between the Spirit as the source of freedom and the being of the Church as community."[114]

The tradition is strong in affirming that we are not free unless we are set free by the sacrifice of Christ, yet this freedom must be realized in the present if it is to be more than ideological. It is the Spirit's action to realize the Church's freedom in the present by constituting the Church as God's eschatological community in anticipation of the renewal of all things.[115] At this point Gunton turns to the doctrine of election and suggests a pneumatological revision that considers the temporal significance of election and the Church's elect vocation as God's eschatological community in the present.

---

111. Gunton, *Theology Through the Theologians*, 194.
112. Gunton, *Theology Through the Theologians*, 195–6.
113. Gunton, *Theology Through the Theologians*, 200.
114. Gunton, *Theology Through the Theologians*, 200.
115. Gunton, *Theology Through the Theologians*, 200.

The doctrine of election holds that before the foundation of the world, God elects humanity to fellowship through Jesus Christ, but as Gunton notes it is often ordered to a pre-temporal past that over-determines the present. Whether in the traditional theology of double predestination or in Barth's reworking of election in a universal direction, the orientation is to a decision in the past that over-determines humanity's future apart from us.[116] Gunton suggests that without undermining the Christological dimensions of election, we consider the temporal implications of the Spirit's action in the present.

The Spirit liberates humanity by bringing humanity into relation with the Father through the Son in the community of Christ's body—freedom in relationship with God and one another. "He liberates us, that is to say, by bringing us into community; by enabling us to be *with* and *for* the brothers and sisters whom we did not choose."[117] The Spirit is God's transcendent otherness who sets us free in relationship and community, because to be free in the biblical tradition is to be in community.[118] In Gunton's later ecclesiological writings, the pneumatological rebalancing of the doctrine of election is central to his ecclesiology and theology of culture. He develops his thoughts on election in relation to the Church's calling as a representative community, whose distinctive common life and culture anticipate God's redemptive purposes for creation.

In his early writings, Gunton develops his concern for the ontology/being of the Church through the cosmic ecclesiologies of the deutero-Pauline letters. This allows him to set the Church's common life in eschatological perspective. The vision of the Church in Ephesians and Colossians grounds the Church's being and life in the Father's purpose to reconcile all things to himself through the Son and in the Spirit.[119] The eschatological vision of ecclesiology in Ephesians is, on Gunton's reading, "the climax of New Testament ecclesiological thinking."[120] The mystery of God's purposes to bring all creation to its eschatological destiny and unity in Christ (Eph 1) is prefigured in the Church as God's new community in the Spirit

---

116. Gunton, *Theology Through the Theologians*, 201.

117. Gunton, *Theology Through the Theologians*, 201.

118. Gunton, *Theology Through the Theologians*, 201.

119. Gunton, *The Promise of Trinitarian Theology*, 81. See also Gunton, *Theology Through the Theologians*, 203.

120. Gunton, *Theology Through the Theologians*, 203. Gunton's assessment finds strong support in the work of N. T. Wright who argues that the vision of the scandalous unity of the church is as central to Paul's theology as justification by faith. The unity of God's people is central to Paul's thought, and Wright argues that if this gives way, everything comes crashing down. Having reviewed the importance of unity across the undisputed Pauline letters, Wright concludes that what is found to be central in the undisputed letters of Paul turns out to be summarized in Eph 2:11–3:21. N. T. Wright, *Paul and the Faithfulness of God* (Minneapolis: Fortress Press, 2013), 385–402. See also Andrew Picard, "No Longer Strangers: Disabled Ontology and the Church as Meaningful Community in Liquid Modernity," in *Theology and the Experience of Disability: Interdisciplinary Perspectives from Voices Down Under*, ed. Andrew Picard and Myk Habets (London: Routledge, 2016), 68–9.

(Eph 2–3). "The Church is called to be the community that plays a central part in the perfecting through Christ of the created order. But the perfecting is the work of the Spirit."[121] The Spirit gives gifts of grace to build the community so that its communal life and worship anticipate the reconciliation of all things in Christ.[122]

Likewise, in the Colossian hymn (Col 1:15-19), Gunton notes the role of the Church as the body of the cosmic Christ, the head of the Church. "[The] Church is the body called to be the community of the last times, that is to say, to realise in its life the promised and inaugurated reconciliation of all things."[123] The cosmic ecclesiologies of Colossians and Ephesians capture the note of sheer being that underlies the Church; an eschatological identity to which she is called to be and become as the Spirit enables. As we will see in the following section, Gunton's later ecclesiological writings assume the Church's ontological identity and explore in more detail the concrete shape of the Church's life in community. In this later work, Gunton draws most especially from 1 Corinthians as it is here that Paul works out the Church's common life in community as a concrete expression of eschatological culture.

The heart of the Spirit's constituting action is found in worship, through which the Spirit constitutes the Church as God's eschatological community in the present. Gunton affirms the Reformed pattern of worship and interprets it through his account of the Son's institution and the Spirit's constitution of the Church. At the call to worship, the opening words of scripture proclaim the gospel and call the Church to worship. Interpreted pneumatologically, Gunton suggests that through the word of the gospel, the Spirit constitutes the institution of the Church as a community of worship in the present that stands, in its particular time and space, before God. "The Spirit lifts the community to the Father through the Son: and therefore we must say that the Church is constituted as the Spirit, through the word of the gospel – the risen Christ becoming concrete in the present – calls the community into being."[124]

In a similar way, the sacraments can also be understood pneumatologically. At baptism, the Spirit reconstitutes the Church anew by incorporating new persons into relationship in the community. Paul's claim that at baptism there is a new creation (2 Cor 5:17) is best understood corporately, rather than individualistically. The Church is constituted anew as the Spirit reconstitutes the relationships of the community and makes it ever and again the people of God and the body of Christ. Likewise, at the Lord's Supper, the Spirit constitutes the community of the Church in its *koinōnia* with God and one another around the table of the Lord.[125] Gunton's account of the sacraments stresses the life of the community in the particularities of the present rather than the historical past. "Thus there is no timeless Church: only a Church then and now and to be, as the Spirit ever and again incorporates

---

121. Gunton, *Theology Through the Theologians*, 203.
122. Gunton, *Theology Through the Theologians*, 203.
123. Gunton, *The Promise of Trinitarian Theology*, 81.
124. Gunton, *Theology Through the Theologians*, 202.
125. Gunton, *Theology Through the Theologians*, 203.

people into Christ and in the same action brings them into and maintains them in community with one another."¹²⁶ The Church's common life in *koinōnia* is a gift of the Spirit's constituting action and an echo of the personal dynamics of the triune God. As such the Church's life in community is a form of eschatological culture that is instituted by the Son and constituted and reconstituted by the eschatological Spirit as an anticipation of God's purposes for all creation.

In summary, Gunton's early ecclesiological writings capture some of his most important themes in ecclesiology and culture in an embryonic form, which he develops and extends in his later writings. His conception of the Church as a community is also best understood as a claim about the culture of the Church as an eschatological community. In his early writings, Gunton's interest is in establishing the being and nature of the Church as a community. In pursuit of this goal, he draws from trinitarian ontology, pneumatology, and the cosmic ecclesiologies of Ephesians and Colossians. This results in a significant emphasis upon the relational nature of the Church as a community that echoes the triune God, as opposed to the Church as an institution. Gunton's early writings utilize the insights of trinitarian ontology to establish the nature of the Church, while his later writings explore the shape, detail, and texture of the Church's concrete life in community—the Church's eschatological culture.

With the progression in his thought, Gunton's later writings on ecclesiology and culture are marked by a consistent methodological exploration of divine action in the economy, biblical exegesis, and the perfecting of the project of creation. Gunton develops many of his earlier themes and extends their theological meaning and import by a detailed exploration of the Church's common life as God's elect community that embodies and performs God's eschatological purposes for creation. As such, Gunton's later ecclesiological writings offer important extensions of his thought, especially in relation to his trinitarian theology of culture. These developments, however, have not been adequately examined by Gunton scholars, as his later ecclesiology is often interpreted through the lens of his earlier writings. The *Hauptbriefe* in the reception of Gunton's ecclesiological writings results in interpreters melding later insights with earlier formulations without recognizing the developments in his thought.

The *Hauptbriefe* in Gunton's Ecclesiological Writings

Gunton's ecclesiology is the subject of much critical scholarly attention, even though he does not offer a fully developed doctrine of the Church. The common focus of this attention is Gunton's attempt to ground the Church's being in the being of the triune God. Scholars contend that Gunton's open transcendentals are central to his trinitarian project, especially his ecclesiology, and critique the perceived social trinitarian analogies and projections. Yet, as we have seen, the open transcendentals play no part in his early ecclesiological writings, aside from

---

126. Gunton, *The Promise of Trinitarian Theology*, 82.

The One, the Three and the Many, even if his apophatic analogy of a finite echo bears some conceptual resemblances. Furthermore, while the open transcendentals certainly feature in *The One, the Three and the Many*, Gunton ceases to develop the concept in his later writings. There is a *Hauptbriefe* in the critical reception of Gunton's ecclesiology that gives excessive prominence to his earlier writings and veils many of the developments in his later writings.

Bernard Nausner and Leon Harris incorrectly assume that "Gunton's ecclesiology is built upon the idea of *open transcendentals*."[127] Harris establishes this conclusion by citing Gunton's chapter on "The Community," yet this chapter makes no mention of the open transcendentals at all. Harris' analysis projects the open transcendentals into Gunton's later thought and veils the particular claims of Gunton's distinct works.[128] In his earlier writings on Gunton's ecclesiology, Uche Anizor focuses his analysis of Gunton's eccleisology on Gunton's ecclesial ontology and asserts the centrality of the open transcendentals.[129] Likewise, Roland Chia bases his study of Gunton's ecclesiology on the assumption that "Gunton develops a communio-ecclesiology based on his understanding of relationality as a transcendental."[130] Similarly, while Julie Green engages Gunton's full corpus, she utilizes it in service of her own proposals for the *perichoretic* relationship between Church and culture.[131] Naomi Reese is also struck by Gunton's suggestive ontological accounts of the Church as a community, but limits her exploration to his early writings.[132] All these works provide some helpful analysis of Gunton's ecclesiology, especially his earlier work on the being of the Church. However, the scholarly reception and critiques of the open transcendentals overwhelm their analyses, and veil many of the particular claims Gunton develops in his distinct contributions to ecclesiology.

Given the emphasis upon the open transcendentals, it is surprising to note that, aside from *The One, the Three and the Many*, Gunton does not utilize the concept of

---

127. Harris, "Holy Spirit as Communion," 153. Italics original. For Nausner's analysis, see Nausner, "The Failure of a Laudable Project," 411–13.

128. Harris, "Holy Spirit as Communion," 153. Harris cities Gunton, *The Promise of Trinitarian Theology*, 2nd ed., 56.

129. Anizor, "Spirited Humanity," 29. Anizor repeats this conclusion in Anizor, *Trinity and Humanity*, 150. Anizor assumes the legitimacy of Nausner's critique of Gunton and the centrality of the open transcendentals to Gunton's project, and references Nausner's work in his critiques of Gunton's ecclesiology.

130. Chia, "Trinity and Ontology," 452.

131. Green argues that the analogy of echo and the concept of *perichoresis* between the church and the life of God extend to the relationship of church and culture. However, she fails to take adequate account of Gunton's apophatic control of the finite echo that carefully limits its univocal usage. Green, "The Worldly Church," 9–10.

132. This is striking given that Reese does highlight Gunton's later writings on the church and Israel as forms of redeemed culture, but overlooks their significance for Gunton's ecclesiology. Reese, "Seeking the Welfare of the City," 159–68. In this extended section on Gunton's ecclesiology, Reese gives no sustained engagement with Gunton's later writings on ecclesiology.

open transcendentals in any specific ecclesiological writings—early or late.[133] This is not to dispute Gunton's link between the open transcendentals and ecclesiology in *The One, the Three and the Many*, but it is to contest the assumption of their centrality to his ecclesiology.[134] We have already seen that the open transcendentals represent a particular trajectory in Gunton's work, which he discontinues in his later writings. Elevating the open transcendentals to a central place in Gunton's ecclesiology imposes an *a priori* assumption of their foundational worth on to texts that do not employ them. Furthermore, it focuses upon the criticisms of Gunton's open transcendentals and subsumes his other important constructive contributions in ecclesiology.

The preoccupation with the open transcendentals may account for the lack of sustained engagement with many of Gunton's most important insights into ecclesiology. It is only in more recent writings by Anizor, Wright, and Kelly Kapic, that the importance of Gunton's pneumatological account of the doctrine of election is beginning to be recognized. Likewise, until recently, little has been made of Gunton's accounts of Israel and the Church as redemptive communities whose sociality, polity, and ethics are a form of eschatological culture shaped by the Torah for the right human habitation of creation.[135] The centrality of the Lord's Supper as the culmination of human worship culture in community is often overlooked, and the importance of the Lord's Supper to Gunton's work is often misrepresented. In his book on Gunton's theology, Anizor begins his section on the Lord's Supper with the assertion that Gunton does not devote much space to it.[136] This assertion is odd given that elsewhere in the book Anizor notes the importance of the Lord's Supper for Gunton's ecclesiology and theology of culture.[137] He rightly observes that the

---

133. See Gunton, *The Promise of Trinitarian Theology*, 56–82; Gunton, *Theology Through the Theologians*, 187–205; Gunton, *Intellect and Action*, 101–20, 139–54; Gunton, *Father, Son and Holy Spirit*, 201–15, 216–34; and Gunton, *The Christian Faith*, 119–38.

134. On the link between the church and the open transcendentals, see Gunton, *The One, the Three and the Many*, 217–19.

135. Anizor, "Gunton on Ecclesiology," 157–8; Wright, "Colin Gunton on Providence," 154–60; and Wright, "Gunton on Eschatology," 147–8; and Kelly M. Kapic, "Gunton and Owen," in *T&T Clark Handbook on Colin Gunton*, ed. Andrew Picard, Myk Habets, and Murray Rae (London: T&T Clark, 2021), 350–4. Kapic critiques Gunton's selective use of aspects of Owen's work, such as embracing Owen's Spirit Christology, whilst trying to avoid elements, such as double predestination, which he finds distasteful.

136. Anizor, *Trinity and Humanity*, 161.

137. Anizor, *Trinity and Humanity*, 162. Uche Anizor's first two engagements with Gunton's ecclesiology focus on Gunton's early writings and their trinitarian account of the ontology of the church; the place of pneumatology; and the proper role of christology. See Anizor, "Spirited Humanity," 26–34. Anizor revises his article in his later book *Trinity and Humanity*, 156–62, and begins to engage with Gunton's later ecclesiology. However, his revision is limited to an overview of some of Gunton's later ecclesiology that is subsumed into the analysis he derives from Gunton's earlier ecclesiological writings. Anizor's most recent account of Gunton's ecclesiology observes the developments in Gunton's writings on ecclesiology and dedicates a section to Gunton's later writings. The result is a more detailed and nuanced outline of Gunton's ecclesiology. See Anizor, "Gunton on Ecclesiology," 156–65.

Supper, in Gunton's thought, is an anticipation of the renewal of all things and the Church's offering of a sacrifice of praise. Yet he does not set this in the context of Gunton's argumentation that it is the culmination of human life in community that is redeemed and perfected by the Spirit.

In his book that introduces Gunton's theology, Anizor provides a helpful analysis of Gunton's early writings in ecclesiology; however, he elevates Gunton's use of the finite echo analogy beyond its original scope. This imbalance in Anizor's analysis results in him projecting the language of "echo" into texts where Gunton does not utilize it. According to Anizor, the meal, in Gunton's thought, "is to represent reconciled and whole relationships that are a finite echo of the eternal *koinōnia* of the Trinity."[138] To substantiate this claim, Anizor cites Gunton's article on the Lord's Supper in 1 Corinthians, but Gunton does not employ the concept of the church as an echo in this article or in its republication as a chapter in *Father, Son and Holy Spirit*.[139] In these first forays into Gunton's ecclesiology, Anizor provides an important analysis of Gunton's thought on the Lord's Supper, but he does not uphold the Supper's centrality in Gunton's thought as the culmination of the Church's worship.[140] For Gunton, it is at the supper that the Church offers its life and culture as a sacrifice of praise in and through Christ's self-sacrifice by the Spirit. Whilst Gunton is critical of the traditional debates on sacramentality, he holds the Lord's Supper to be the culmination of the Church's social, political, and ethical calling in the context of worship.

In his most recent publication on Gunton's ecclesiology, Anizor provides a much richer and more detailed reading that also recognizes the progression in Gunton's ecclesiology. He rightly distinguishes Gunton's early emphasis upon a trinitarian ontology of the Church from his later exploration of the eschatological dimensions of the Church.[141] This distinction should not be pressed too far, Anizor rightly notes, as the strands remain interwoven. However, the acknowledgement of progression in Gunton's ecclesiology strengthens Anizor's analysis and he captures the importance of election, ethics, and eschatology in Gunton's ecclesiology in greater detail. In this work, Anizor no longer upholds his earlier assertion that Gunton devotes little space to the Lord's Supper. Instead, Anizor highlights the centrality of a theology of Church's sociality in Gunton's interpretation of Paul's

---

138. Anizor, *Trinity and Humanity*, 162.

139. Colin E. Gunton, "'Until He Comes': Towards an Eschatology of Church Membership," *International Journal of Systematic Theology*, 3 (2001): 187–200. Gunton, *Father, Son and Holy Spirit*, 216–34.

140. Anizor explores the Lord's Supper in a discreet section on the topic, and later adds some further important ideas on the church and worship. However, he does not engage deeply with Gunton's claim that the church offers its life in the Spirit as a sacrifice of praise through Christ's great sacrifice. Anizor, *Trinity and Humanity*, 161–2; 175–6.

141. Uche Anizor, "Gunton on Ecclesiology," in *T&T Clark Handbook on Colin Gunton*, ed. Andrew Picard, Myk Habets, and Murray Rae (London: T&T Clark, 2021), 163.

account of the Lord's Supper in 1 Corinthians.[142] Anizor's more recent analysis captures the centrality of the Church's primary calling in Gunton's thought—to worship God. But the Church's worship cannot be abstracted from its concrete life in the social and political matrix of life in the contemporary world. The sociality, polity, and ethics of the Church's common life together *are*, for Gunton, the Church's offering of worship.

In Gunton's later writings, he assumes the Church's ontological identity and goes on to explicate the shape of the Church's concrete being as an eschatological community. He provides more sustained exegesis of biblical texts to establish his claims about the Church's concrete life that is the outcome of divine action in the economy. The following section explores Gunton's later forays in ecclesiology with a particular eye to the Church as a form of redeemed human culture, whose sociality, polity, and ethics (culture) are enabled by the Spirit to anticipate, through Christ, the redemption of all things. Through his theology of mediation, Gunton gives greater attention to the divine action of the Son and the Spirit in the economy, and this results in extended exegesis of the New Testament in general, and 1 Corinthians in particular. It is in 1 Corinthians, Gunton maintains, that Paul works out an account of the Church as a distinctive form of culture that God shapes through the action of the Son and the Spirit.[143] Gunton's ecclesiology and theology of culture culminate at the Lord's Supper, and it is here that the Spirit enables the Church to offer its distinctive and representative way of living in the world as a sacrifice of praise to God through the sacrifice of Jesus Christ.

Gunton's Later Ecclesiology: The Church and Eschatological Culture

Gunton's later writings detail the shape of the Church's concrete social, political, and ethical life as an embodiment of its God-given identity and the offering of a living sacrifice of praise.[144] Ecclesiology is increasingly important in Gunton's later writings, yet Holmes notes how unfamiliar Gunton scholarship appears to be with this move. Holmes traces Gunton's rising interests in ecclesiology to a lecture series he delivered at Fuller Seminary, and mid-week Bible study he gave on 1 Corinthians at Brentwood United Reformed Church.[145] Given the lack of sustained engagement with Gunton's later ecclesiological writings, the following section notes the progression in Gunton's thinking on the Church and delineates his developed account of the Church as a form of redeemed human culture. Gunton's trinitarian theology of culture is best understood through his account

---

142. Anizor, "Gunton on Ecclesiology," 164–5. However, Anizor continues to insert Gunton's earlier account of echo into his reading of Gunton's theology of the Lord's Supper at Corinth despite the fact that Gunton does not use language of echo in this essay.
143. Gunton, *Father, Son and Holy Spirit*, 119.
144. Gunton, *The Christian Faith*, 135.
145. Holmes, "Foreword," in *Father, Son and Holy Spirit*, x.

of the redeeming and perfecting action of the Son and the Spirit in creation. It is the Son and the Spirit who elect and form the Church as an anticipation of God's promised end.

In his later writings on the Church, Gunton affirms his earlier stance on the nature of the Church's being and extends it to give a detailed account of the Church's concrete life that is enabled by divine action. This section gives prominence to Gunton's exegetical use of 1 Corinthians because, among other things, Gunton believes that this letter is especially concerned with the Church as a distinctive kind of eschatological culture.[146] "It is not an exaggeration to say that in a number of Paul's letters, especially perhaps the First Letter to the Corinthians, we see being hammered out before our eyes the distinctive form of culture that the Church was and is."[147] The diverse forms of relationship to God, one another and the created order constitute the Church's particular form of human culture and community.[148] Like Israel, the Church is a community of redemption whose life is shaped by the historic actions of God as a form of culture instituted by God.[149]

Gunton's trinitarian theology of culture focuses upon the Church as a representative community that God elects to represent God's purposes in the world, whose life in community is an offering of embodied worship. Gunton's ecclesiology brings together the interrelated themes of Israel, election, the Torah, the Church's sociality, polity, and ethics, and the Church's distinctive way of being in community as a sacrifice of praise. It is at the Supper where the Church's life in community, the Church's culture, is offered by the Spirit, through Christ's self-offering of true humanity, as a sacrifice of praise.

The Spirit and Election: The Temporal Calling of Israel and the Church

The doctrine of election is vital to Gunton's ecclesiology, as God elects the Church with Israel to serve God's purposes in the world. But Gunton believes the doctrine of election suffers from non-worldly abstractions in which pre-temporal concerns over-determine eschatology to such an extent that the end is determined by the beginning.[150] The biblical doctrine of election, Gunton argues, is much more this-worldly and communal than traditional abstract and non-temporal accounts allow. What is required is a rebalancing of the Christological over-determination of election and the pneumatological under-determination. The Spirit is the perfecting cause who enables anticipations of the promised future to be realized in the present.

A pneumatological rebalancing of election observes the temporal calling of Israel and the Church as God's representative communities who anticipate God's ultimate

---

146. Gunton, *Father, Son and Holy Spirit*, 119.
147. Gunton, *Father, Son and Holy Spirit*, 119.
148. Gunton, *Father, Son and Holy Spirit*, 119.
149. Gunton, *Father, Son and Holy Spirit*, 121.
150. Gunton, *Intellect and Action*, 141.

purposes for creation through the Spirit's enabling. God's universal purposes are realized through particular means. God elects Israel and the Church as communities of redemption through whom the Spirit realizes eschatological life in community. A pneumatological rebalancing of election and its temporal significance stresses the qualitative dimension of God's elect communities, rather than quantitative speculations of the post-temporal destinies of individuals.[151] Israel and the Church are communities of redemption; they are types of culture instituted by God and ordered to the end of worship through their distinctive form of life in community.[152]

Aside from Anizor's helpful analysis, Gunton's reworking of the doctrine of election has received little scholarly attention.[153] Anizor extends his earlier account of temporal election in Gunton, and observes that God elects Israel and the Church as particular communities that serve God's universal purpose of the reconciliation of all things.[154] As Anizor notes, "The Church's election is inescapably bound to God's cosmic purposes and their temporal outworking …. Election is about the Church living out its purpose both as a harbinger of the communion that will ultimately exist and as those called to participate in God's recreative work."[155] Election is certainly vocation for Gunton, but he holds that election is eschatological divine action before it is human vocation.[156] The Church, like Israel, is called to be different from the nations. The Church's elected life as a community of redemption is instituted and shaped by God's historic actions to be a form of eschatological culture.[157] As communities of the covenants, Israel and the Church are determined by divine action. Their temporal life is reoriented to the end for which they were created: worship as concrete life in community.[158]

Gunton's Pneumatological Rebalancing of the Doctrine of Election

The doctrine of election, according to Gunton, suffers from an imbalance towards protology that over-determines the doctrine at the expense of the eschatological determinants of election.[159] The danger Gunton senses is that the tendency towards individualistic and other-worldly abstractions risks narrowing the purposes of God

---

151. Gunton, *Intellect and Action*, 145.
152. Gunton, *Father, Son and Holy Spirit*, 178.
153. Green, Harris, Chia, and Stringer make little or no mention of Israel or election in their accounts of Gunton's ecclesiology or pneumatology.
154. Anizor, *Trinity and Humanity*, 4. For his later interpretation of Gunton, see Anizor, "Gunton on Ecclesiology," 157–8. Anizor also highlights Gunton's critique of Barth's orientation to pre-temporality and the past that over-determines the end. Anizor, *Trinity and Humanity*, 32–3.
155. Anizor, "Gunton on Ecclesiology," 158.
156. Gunton, *Intellect and Action*, 152.
157. Gunton, *Father, Son and Holy Spirit*, 121.
158. Gunton, *Father, Son and Holy Spirit*, 121.
159. Gunton, *Intellect and Action*, 141.

and undermines concrete life within temporal creation.[160] Traditional accounts of election are in danger of turning the good news of God's prevenient grace in the election of humanity to fellowship into God's predetermination in such a way that history is closed to the recreating action of the Spirit.[161] In the doctrine of double predestination, election is reduced to God preordaining a limited number of individual souls to an otherworldly salvation, whilst consigning the vast multitude to an eternal rubbish heap.[162] As a result of these otherworldly speculations, the doctrine of election becomes an impersonal abstraction which divorces the gospel from the Church and reduces the Church to little more than a heavenly waiting room.[163]

The universality of Barth's Christological reworking of election is a welcome reprieve from the double decree. God's purposes are for universal salvation and Barth rightly holds that all humanity is elect *de jure* in God's eternal election of humanity in Christ.[164] However, Gunton argues that the pretemporal determination advances an impersonal definition of election abstracted from the created order and the actual reconciled relations of embodied persons.[165] Election is irrevocable and is certainly an expression of the definiteness of God's love that creates and sustains faith, but it is not determinism.[166] New Testament eschatology has a greater orientation to the destiny of the material creation as the context in which humanity is inexorably bound.[167] Reconciliation is certainly universal in intent, as Barth proposes, but it is not yet fully realized or perfected. The Spirit perfects Christ's complete work by realizing God's eschatological purposes in time, especially through the community of the Church.[168] Without denying any of Barth's Christological advances, Gunton seeks to extend his work through a stronger pneumatological determination of election that emphasizes the temporal significance of election and God's calling of communities of redemption.

In place of the tendency to see the whole of humanity elected immediately in Christ, Gunton proposes that humanity is elected mediately through God's calling and formation of Israel and the Church by the Spirit's particular eschatological action.[169] God elects communities, rather than individuals from within the communities. Election, therefore, is not primarily concerned with quantities

---

160. Gunton, *The Christian Faith*, 127.
161. Gunton, *Intellect and Action*, 141.
162. Gunton, *Intellect and Action*, 154.
163. Gunton, *Intellect and Action*, 151–2.
164. Gunton, *The Christian Faith*, 162–3.
165. Gunton, *The Christian Faith*, 163. It is important to note that Gunton holds a warm view of Barth's doctrine of election "as once an eternal and temporal act, and the greatness of his treatment is its interlocking, interweaving, of eternal and historical divine act." Gunton, *Intellect and Action*, 143–4.
166. Gunton, *Intellect and Action*, 146.
167. Gunton, *Intellect and Action*, 144.
168. Gunton, *The Christian Faith*, 164.
169. Gunton, *Intellect and Action*, 150–1.

but qualities—not the number of individuals, but the purpose of the election of such quantities.[170] What is muted in traditional accounts, Gunton believes, is the eschatological action of the Spirit enabling right human action in the community of the Church in anticipation of the reconciliation of all things.[171] God's universal purposes are achieved through particular communities and people, as is appropriate to a world structured through space and in time.[172] A pneumatological account of the doctrine of election turns attention from other-worldly speculation of the complement of heaven to a this-worldly account of God's election of Israel and the Church as intermediate communities who mediate God's mediation.[173]

Gunton's later writings on Israel and the Church draw from Jenson and his stress upon the Church's continuity with Israel. Israel's election is eternal and their hardening and rejection is temporary in order that God's purposes would extend to the Gentiles.[174] The Church is engrafted into an existing root and shares in Israel's election through Jesus Christ.[175] The Church is grafted into an expanded Israel through Jesus Christ, which embraces the Gentiles in fulfilment of God's promises to Abraham. God's calling of the Church, in part, is for the sake of Israel as the reconstituted Israel is "called as a living challenge to Israel to be truly the people of God."[176] Together, Israel and the Church are called out from the rest of humanity as priestly representatives of all humanity, but unlike Israel the Church includes within it people from all nations and tribes. Divine election is not God's selection of one preferred group over another, but the election of one group "for the sake of and on behalf of others."[177]

As priestly representatives for all the nations of the earth, Israel and the Church are called on behalf of the world to a distinctive way of being that anticipates the redemption of all things.[178] The election of the people of God is not, therefore, oriented to a unique destiny outside of the world, but a unique calling within the world—to display God's purposes in their concrete common life.[179] Christ's universal mediation of creation is displayed through the Spirit's election of particular communities on behalf of the whole of creation.[180] This pneumatological rebalancing of the doctrine of election orients us not only to the concrete communities of Israel and the Church, but also to their culture as a form of eschatological community life that the Spirit enables to anticipate the end. This

---

170. Gunton, *Intellect and Action*, 145.
171. Gunton, *Intellect and Action*, 146.
172. Colin E. Gunton, *The Christian Faith*, 127.
173. Gunton, *The Promise of Trinitarian Theology*, 176.
174. Gunton, *Intellect and Action*, 145.
175. Gunton, *Intellect and Action*, 152.
176. Gunton, *The Christian Faith*, 126.
177. Gunton, *The Christian Faith*, 164.
178. Gunton, *The Christian Faith*, 166.
179. Gunton, *Intellect and Action*, 147–8.
180. Gunton, *Intellect and Action*, 148.

distinctive way of life together in the world is a form of worship that offers praise and thanksgiving to the creator for God's gracious purposes in the beginning.

Torah, Holiness, and the Church's Distinctive Life in Community

In Gunton's work, the importance of embodied life in community cannot be overstated, as it is a form of worship. Gunton holds that the single leading idea of scripture is life, and for this reason he makes life the defining emphasis of *The Christian Faith*.[181] Gunton's wider work on the role of the Torah and holiness is best understood in the context of this emphasis upon life and the right human habitation of creation. The right human habitation of creation is a form of redeemed human culture that the Son and the Spirit enable as an offering of worship and praise to God.

Holiness means to be set apart, and God's difference from the world is God's holiness. God elects Israel and the Church from among the peoples of the nations to be communities that are different.[182] Such difference does not imply a sectarian relocation from the world, but a different way of being within the social and political structures of the world.[183] This difference is realized, above all, in Israel's and the Church's distinctive ways of being human in community.[184] Whilst holiness remains Israel and the Church's calling, they repeatedly fail in this calling and remain entirely dependent on God's ongoing grace to restore and renew them to be who God intends them to be. Gunton believes the Torah is best understood as a framework for liberated life, grace embodied in community, rather than laws by which to abide.[185] The two tables of the Decalogue shape relationship with God and relationship with the world as an expression of the freedom that God's grace and forgiveness creates in community. "The new vertical relationship is bodied out in a new horizontal set of relations and their consequent responsibilities."[186] The law details the shape of these new relationships and responsibilities for the right human habitation of creation in relation to sexual relations, bodily fluids, clothing fabric, and the cultivation of land; in short, all embodied life.[187]

Gunton draws from Jacob Milgrom's work on Leviticus to argue that priestly theology is in part an attack on pagan cosmology that seeks to establish a redeemed

---

181. Gunton, *The Christian Faith*, x–xi.
182. Gunton, *The Christian Faith*, 148.
183. Gunton, *The Christian Faith*, 131.
184. Gunton, *Intellect and Action*, 89.
185. Gunton, *The Christian Faith*, 140.
186. Gunton, *The Christian Faith*, 149.
187. Gunton, *Intellect and Action*, 89–90. See also Gunton, *Father, Son and Holy Spirit*, 229. Gunton relies upon Jacob Milgrom's commentary on Leviticus for his understanding of the Levitical law and its theological account of morality, sociality, and ethics. See Jacob Milgrom, *Leviticus 1–16*, Anchor (London: Doubleday, 1991).

human ethic within creation.[188] Israel's holiness code and sacrificial system shifts impurity and defilement from the superstitious realm of the pagan mythological canopy and resettles it in the framework of the rejection of death and the choosing of life.[189] Sacrifice is, therefore, not concerned with manipulating or appeasing benevolent and malevolent forces, but with the whole ecology of Israel's social and political realities that restore order to a disordered creation.[190]

The Levitical holiness code is important to Gunton because of its continuing influence in the New Testament and the shape of the Church's culture. When it comes to the Church, Gunton is careful to argue that Israel's law and way of being in the world are in no way abrogated. Israel's law is not set aside, but fulfilled, concentrated, and often intensified, in the person and work of Christ and encompassed in the Church's calling.[191] Jesus Christ is the *telos* of the law (Rom 10:4) while the disordered creation is addressed through the sacrificial death and resurrection of creation's incarnate Lord. Christ's sacrifice provides a new basis for the law through Christ's cleansing, justifying, and sanctifying death which is appropriated to the Church.[192] Paul sees no contradiction between proposing a theology of justification by faith as well as life in community within the framework of the law. The law has ongoing significance and is given new meaning in and through the death and resurrection of Jesus Christ and new life in the Spirit.[193]

The Christological concentration of the law sets holiness and virtue in the context of grace conferred. The distinctions between clean and unclean human actions, created objects, and interpersonal relations assume that creation's wholesome order has been disordered. The sacrificial system, which is very important in Gunton's thought, can be understood as God's gracious dispensation for dealing with forms of disorder. Paul's repetition of the Levitical holiness code is concerned with the fruit of reconciliation in the new community rather than conformity to an abstract account of the law.[194] Human virtue and holiness should be understood from a theology of redemption and perfection to which all human effort and striving are a graced response.[195] As things are, the creation is deformed and there is need for reforming before there can be the forming of the Church

---

188. Gunton, *Intellect and Action*, 90. Leviticus demythologizes the Ancient Near Eastern belief in a metadivine realm that influences deities and spawns benevolent and, mostly, malevolent entities that lead followers to try and tap into the realm to acquire magical powers to coerce the deities and their will. See Milgrom, *Leviticus 1–16*, 42.

189. Milgrom, *Leviticus 1–16*, 47.

190. Milgrom, *Leviticus 1–16*, 49–51. See also Gunton, *Father, Son and Holy Spirit*, 228–9.

191. Gunton, *Intellect and Action*, 91–2. See also Gunton, *The Christian Faith*, 126–7; Gunton, *Father, Son and Holy Spirit*, 220.

192. Gunton, *The Christian Faith*, 150.

193. Gunton, *The Christian Faith*, 150.

194. Gunton, *Intellect and Action*, 95–6.

195. Gunton, *Intellect and Action*, 109.

in right human habits and habitation. "Accordingly, the Church cannot become a school of virtue unless she is first a community that lives and proclaims the forgiveness of sins achieved by the life and particularly the death of Jesus Christ her Lord as the sole basis of the reconstitution of the disabled human will."[196] The kingdom of God is not brought in by the Church's virtuous activity but Christ's sacrifice, and justification by faith is the basis of the Church's redeemed human culture. "In traditional terms, justification is the precondition of sanctification."[197]

The Church's holiness, like righteousness, is conferred by the Spirit sanctifying the community of the justified in anticipation of the redemption and perfection of all things. Sanctification is the calling given to and demanded of the Church to be different, and the Spirit sanctifies the Church by conforming its life to Christ and training it in Christ's ways of love.[198] As Christ's love is oriented outwards, rather than inwards, so the Church is schooled in exocentric righteousness by the Spirit in an eschatological way of being in relationship.[199] The Church's holiness and human virtue in community is one of the ways the Spirit anticipates the end as settled dispositions are shaped in good works. Gunton notes the importance of the Torah to Paul's gospel. Paul's reinterpretation of the law and holiness for the Church at Corinth shows that the law remains a framework for eschatological life that is anticipated in the present.[200] Paul's social, political, and ethical injunctions to the Church at Corinth restate the Torah as the framework for the Church's embodiment of an eschatological form of life in community. For Gunton, 1 Corinthians provides important insights into the Church as a form of culture.[201]

The Church as an Embodiment of Eschatological Culture

Ecclesiology is eschatological at heart. Accordingly, Gunton develops his views on the Church's polity, sociality, and ethic as anticipated eschatology. In the wake of Christendom, the Church's most common error is an over-realized eschatology. There is a balance needed that maintains an eschatological reserve and acknowledges the limits of what we can expect of the Church in the light of the fall and sin.[202] The fading of the Church's political and social settlements in Christendom provides a pressing need for greater balance with respect to the Church's relation to the social order in which it is set. This requires reflection on

---

196. Gunton, *Intellect and Action*, 113.

197. Gunton, *Intellect and Action*, 113.

198. Gunton, *The Christian Faith*, 150–1. See also Gunton, *Father, Son and Holy Spirit*, 218. Gunton gives an extended account of the Spirit's sanctifying action in Gunton, *The Christian Faith*, 147–52.

199. Gunton, *Intellect and Action*, 116.

200. Gunton, *The Christian Faith*, 149–50. See also Gunton, *Intellect and Action*, 92–6 and Gunton, "Reformation Accounts," 83.

201. Gunton, "Reformation Accounts," 83.

202. Gunton, *Father, Son and Holy Spirit*, 217–18.

the kind of social, political, and ethical entity the Church is. Gunton thus develops his eschatological account of the Church through a conscious engagement with the Church's cultural context in the West.[203]

Gunton's views on the Church as an eschatological community are worked out in dialogue with Jenson. Whilst there are many convergences in their thought, Gunton notes a divergence between himself and Jenson regarding the Church as the body of Christ and their respective Reformed and Lutheran traditions. Jenson's understanding of the body of Christ carries immanentist overtones that posits the Church *as* the kingdom of God on earth, rather than its representative.[204] For all the near identification of the Church with Christ, Paul's theology of the body of Christ (1 Cor 12:12-31) has an equally strong movement to distinguish Christ from the Church.[205] Christ's presence is not immanent within the Church, but transcendent as the absent and ascended Lord whose presence is mediated by the Spirit.[206] Christ is present in the Church by the Spirit's eschatological action that enables the Church, from time to time, to be what it is elected to be: a community enabled by the Spirit to be a social embodiment of the gospel of Jesus Christ.

Whilst appreciative of Gunton's work, John Colwell is troubled by Gunton's use of the pneumatological disclaimer that the Spirit is present in the Church "from time to time." Colwell believes this is a "disturbing qualification," and charges Gunton with ecclesiological occasionalism that risks making the Spirit's presence in the Church capricious.[207] I suggest however that Colwell's critique overplays the occasionalism of the Spirit's presence in Gunton's ecclesiology, which attempts to maintain a careful balance. Gunton does not hold, as Colwell argues, that the Spirit's presence in the Church is capricious. But Colwell's proposal of Christ's promised, and sacramental, presence in the church by the Spirit risks the over-realized eschatology that Gunton attempts to avoid. The suggestion that the Church is "the means of the presence of Christ within the world" offers an immediacy of God's presence in the Church that Gunton avoids because it risks confusing divine and human ontologies.[208] Gunton opposes all monophysite overtones that make over-realized claims for the Church, and this is the basis of his major divergence from Jenson.[209] Instead, he argues that the one true sacrament is Jesus Christ whose person cannot be confused with the Church. All other sacraments derive from Jesus Christ and his sacrifice, and this derivation cannot be forgotten. The sacraments are appendices to the Word, and secondary to Christ's atoning sacrifice.[210] Gunton

203. Gunton, *Father, Son and Holy Spirit*, 219.
204. Gunton, *Father, Son and Holy Spirit*, 219-21.
205. Gunton, *The Christian Faith*, 132.
206. Gunton, *Father, Son and Holy Spirit*, 230.
207. John E. Colwell, "Provisionality and Promise: Avoiding Ecclesiastical Nestorianism?," in *The Theology of Colin Gunton*, ed. Lincoln Harvey (London: T&T Clark, 2010), 103.
208. Colwell, "Provisionality and Promise," 112.
209. On Gunton's debates with Jenson, see Gunton *Father, Son and Holy Spirit*, 91-106; 219-25; and Gunton, *The Christian Faith*, 121-2, 129-30.
210. Gunton, *Father, Son and Holy Spirit*, 226.

maintains that the "risen [and absent] Lord is made present only by the Father's Spirit, and any institution claiming in some sense automatically to mediate – let alone to be – the presence of Christ or automatically be in possession of the Spirit is in danger of subverting its own constitution."[211]

The incarnation, along with pneumatology and eschatology, is the key to ecclesiology.[212] The Church is the living space where Jesus' offices as the eschatological prophet, priest, and king are appropriated. Furthermore, the Church derives its community and culture from Christ's bodily incarnation, death, resurrection, and ascended reign. This means the Church is a particular form of social existence that the Spirit orders to God and God's purposes by relating the Church to the one and only human life lived truly as the *imago Dei*.[213] As a community, the Church is being conformed into the image and likeness of God by being brought into reconciled relation with God the Father through Jesus Christ.[214]

The Church is a creature of the Word, incarnate and proclaimed. As a creature of the Word, Gunton holds that the Church's being is maintained by two important practices: words and actions. God's actions in Jesus Christ's life, death, and resurrection are such that the proclamation of these events is the means God uses to make Christ's divine and saving action concrete.[215] Gunton extends his earlier accounts of Christ's institution of the Church by showing *how* Christ institutes the Church as a creature of the gospel. The Church's first proclamation of the gospel made the Church an instituted form of being together in Jesus Christ that took concrete shape in time and space.[216] The proclamation of the gospel, through preaching and the Church's scripture, orders the Church's social life around Jesus.[217] Because Jesus Christ is the Word who spoke and acted in particular ways within the created order, the Spirit shapes the Church by words and actions that conform its life to Christ's career, and brings the Church's social life in worship to the Father through Jesus Christ.[218] Yet, Word alone does not adequately capture the significance of the Son's involvement within the structures of createdness.

The incarnation demands a broader conception than solely the spoken word, and it is the gospel sacraments that enable the Church to give "corresponding expression to this aspect also in her worship."[219] Gunton believes that traditional views of the sacraments, as the outward and visible signs of an inward and invisible grace, risk an implicit dualism of inner and outer that turns attention away from materiality. The sacraments should not be reduced to individual internality but extended to

---

211. Gunton, *The Christian Faith*, 122.
212. Gunton, *Father, Son and Holy Spirit*, 230, 233.
213. Gunton, *The Christian Faith*, 123.
214. Gunton, *The Christian Faith*, 123.
215. Gunton, *The Christian Faith*, 123–4.
216. Gunton, *The Christian Faith*, 124.
217. Gunton, *The Christian Faith*, 125.
218. Gunton, *The Christian Faith*, 128.
219. Gunton, *The Christian Faith*, 129.

include "concrete material and historical realities."[220] Christ's incarnation and atonement are God in action not only inwardly, but outwardly in such a way that the invisible becomes visible.[221] The sacraments celebrate Christ's life in word and action. It is Christ who presents a perfect offering of worship to the Father in the Spirit and so realizes humanity's cultural mandate of Genesis 1: "to exercise dominion of creation as God's representative on earth."[222] The Church's worship is therefore related to the offering of its words and actions that the Spirit conforms and unites with Christ and his self-offering of faithful humanity as worship.

The Church's Concrete Life as Worship: Sociality, Polity, and Ethics as Embodied Culture

The Church's primary calling is to worship God in and for God's self; the creaturely offering of praise and thanksgiving to the One who has created and redeemed us. Yet the nature of the One who is worshipped requires us to qualify the shape of the Church's primary calling to worship.[223] "The triune God is one whose triune *koinōnia* has overflowed into the creation and redemption of a world he loves, and particularly those creatures he has made and remade in the image of his Son Jesus." The Church's worship, therefore, cannot be abstracted from the created order and its social and political matrix.[224] Worship and life, according to Gunton, are interrelated realms; it is from this premise that he develops his trinitarian account of the Church's concrete life in community as, from time to time, a form of eschatological culture.[225]

The Church's distinctive way of being in the Spirit is a form of culture—a way of living together in response to God's mercies. "The Church is the society whose distinctive way of being in the world – distinctive polity, we might say – is oriented to God primarily in terms of thanksgiving and worship."[226] This worship should not be understood narrowly but as the offering of all life to God through the Church's concrete life, such that questions regarding the nature of the Church are best addressed by exploring "the kind of social order that it represents."[227]

If the Church is continuous with Israel, then it follows that, like Israel, the Church is an organized way of being in the world.[228] Gunton appropriates Jenson's view of the Church as a distinctive social and political reality. "It has, or more accurately is, a polity, a way of being politically and socially in the world."[229] Unlike

---

220. Gunton, *The Christian Faith*, 129.
221. Gunton, *The Christian Faith*, 130.
222. Gunton, *The Christian Faith*, 130.
223. Gunton, *Father, Son and Holy Spirit*, 228.
224. Gunton, *Father, Son and Holy Spirit*, 228.
225. Gunton, *The Christian Faith*, 129.
226. Gunton, *The Christian Faith*, 127.
227. Gunton, *The Christian Faith*, 127–8.
228. Gunton, *Father, Son and Holy Spirit*, 221.
229. Gunton, *Father, Son and Holy Spirit*, 221.

Israel, it is through the rite of baptism that the Spirit forms the community as Christ's body and unites it as a community. As a united community of the Spirit, the Church's polity is an anticipated eschatology—an embodiment that anticipates the promised eschatological kingdom of peace and God's reconciliation of all things in Christ. Gunton follows Jenson's suggestion that the Church's distinctive sociality and polity necessitate a distinctive ethic, which Paul develops especially in 1 Corinthians through his use of the Decalogue.[230]

Gunton's account of the Church's eschatological difference and holiness expressed through its sociality, polity, and ethics is best understood in the context of his constructive theology of culture. To develop his theology of the Church as a form of eschatological culture, which culminates in the Church's embodied worship at the Lord's Supper, Gunton turns to 1 Corinthians. It is at the Lord's Supper that we are given insight into the nature of the Church whose right social embodiment of the gospel anticipates the end.[231]

Paul's Corinthian Correspondence and the Church as God's Eschatological Community

As a social and political institution, the Church is called to live differently in the world. "The Church is a social and political reality that does things differently from other institutions, because it is eschatologically different, which means that the basis of its being and authority are also radically different."[232] Gunton examines this form of difference through the ongoing significance of the Torah for the Church, and gives particular emphasis to Paul's use of the Torah in 1 Corinthians that forms the Church's life together in the world.[233] Gunton's exploration of the Torah has received little attention in scholarship to date, and I maintain that Gunton's exploration of the Torah in relation to the Church forms a vital part of his theology of culture.

Paul's first letter to the Church at Corinth is concerned with Torah, and the roots of his thought stem from his Jewish background. "In chapter after chapter of this letter, Paul is concerned with what can only be called Torah, which means not merely law but the whole gracious divine dispensation for human living on earth and in the body."[234] Paul is concerned with the right social, political, and ethical embodiment of the gospel as an expression of the Church's eschatological nature. The Corinthians are called to give allegiance to the Torah, and Paul recapitulates the Decalogue as the charter for the holy people of God.[235] His moral teaching

---

230. Gunton, *Father, Son and Holy Spirit*, 221.
231. Gunton, *Father, Son and Holy Spirit*, 221–2.
232. Gunton, *Father, Son and Holy Spirit*, 222.
233. Gunton, *The Christian Faith*, 130–1.
234. Gunton, *Father, Son and Holy Spirit*, 228.
235. Gunton, *The Christian Faith*, 131.

begins with a restatement of Levitical law (Lev 18:8) concerning sexual morality (1 Cor 5:1) and the following chapter unfolds as a republication of the Decalogue.[236]

In 1 Cor 6:9-10, Paul restates the Decalogue to delineate the social, political, and ethical sphere within which the Church, like Israel, exercises its calling to be a holy and different community.[237] Paul's summary of the Decalogue reminds the Church that Israel's law is still their law, and he upholds it as "the canon by which membership of the community of salvation is measured."[238] As Paul's wider argument develops, he draws a close connection between Jesus' bodily resurrection and the seriousness of what Christians do in and with their bodies (1 Cor 6:12-20).[239] Crucially for Gunton, and his concern for embodiment, it is what we do in and with our bodies that reflects our loyalties, as the fruits of redemption include the proper relational use of the body.

Gunton examines Paul's ethical injunctions through the lens of eschatology and community. In what way, he asks, can we say that the end is realized in the Church's life?[240] Gunton's answer is that the end is realized through the Church's embodiment and performance of the gospel. It is in and through our bodies that we relate to God, others, and the world, and it is in the Church's common life in community that the eschatological end is embodied and performed.[241] Sharing meals in pagan temples is not immediately problematic for Paul because their gods do not exist. Yet, flaunting one's freedom without concern for Christian neighbours is a sin against love and community (1 Cor 8:1-13).[242] Furthermore, while the idols are non-existent, Christians eating in pagan temples are misplaced because how we use our bodies reflects our ultimate allegiance and loyalty. Like Christians who take recourse to pagan law courts to settle intra-Church disputes (1 Cor 6:1-7), those that eat in temples are bodies out of place.[243] By entering these realms they allow different lords and gods to exercise their authority over them and demand their allegiance. "To eat with non-existent idols is to enter a social and political sphere in competition with that of the God of Israel …. Those who are to judge angels place themselves under the authority of the demonic."[244] Paul is not demanding Christian seclusion from society, but insisting that the Church

236. Gunton, *Intellect and Action*, 92.
237. Gunton, *Intellect and Action*, 93.
238. Gunton, *Father, Son and Holy Spirit*, 228.
239. Gunton, *Intellect and Action*, 93–4.
240. Gunton, *Father, Son and Holy Spirit*, 221–2.
241. Gunton, *Intellect and Action*, 93–5.
242. Gunton, *Father, Son and Holy Spirit*, 222.
243. Gunton, *The Christian Faith*, 131.

244. Gunton, *Father, Son and Holy Spirit*, 222. Ben Witherington captures Gunton's point when he suggests for Paul it is the venue, not the menu, that is problematic. Ben Witherington III, *Torah Old and New: Exegesis, Intertextuality, and Hermeneutics* (Minneapolis: Fortress Press, 2018), 252.

lives into its identity as an eschatologically distinct social and political reality whose allegiance and authority are different from other institutions.

In a similar vein, those who transgress sexual boundaries enter into constitutive relations that are contrary to the eschatological kingdom.[245] We are what we do in and through our bodies, and what we do in and with our bodies anticipates what we shall be eschatologically.[246] Citing Genesis, Paul argues that ungodly sexual union undermines the significance of the perpetrator's union with Christ (1 Cor 6:16-19).[247] Those who reject the gospel's renewal of their embodied relationships threaten to destroy the Church's body politic and must be excluded, even if only temporarily, for the sake of the body of Christ and its embodiment of the gospel. Breaking community life is breaking the Church's eschatological being and its witness as God's eschatological community. Paul's concern in all his ethical injunctions is the right social embodiment of the gospel.[248] Given all this, we can conclude that Gunton's exploration of the Torah and holiness is set within an eschatological framework through which God shapes the Church into a form of eschatological culture. It is this culture and life that are offered in worship to God and culminates at the Lord's Supper.

The Lord's Supper and the Church's Culture in Community

Gunton's trinitarian theology of culture culminates at the Lord's Supper, as it is here that we see the Church as a form of human culture consciously oriented to the death of Christ and living out praise in forms of community that anticipate the eschatological banquet.[249] The Lord's Supper gives important insight into the nature of the Church as an eschatological community whose common life gives a representative offering of humanity in relation to God, one another, and creation as a sacrifice of praise.[250]

Gunton's account of the Church and the Lord's Supper arises from his communitarian exegesis of 1 Corinthians, as it is here that "the theological, incarnational, ritual, social and ethical dimensions of the Supper belong so inextricably together."[251] Gunton asserts that the passage in 1 Corinthians where the Lord's Supper is discussed is devoted to the Church's sociality, polity, and ethics as much, if not more, than its sacramentality and eucharistic worship. Central to the Supper are the twin foci of right relation with God and right relation with embodied human beings.[252] Drawing from Jenson, Gunton treats the Supper

---

245. Gunton, *Father, Son and Holy Spirit*, 223.
246. Gunton, *Father, Son and Holy Spirit*, 223.
247. Gunton, *Father, Son and Holy Spirit*, 223–4.
248. Gunton, *The Christian Faith*, 131.
249. Gunton, *The Christian Faith*, 134.
250. Gunton, *Father, Son and Holy Spirit*, 222; 228–9.
251. Gunton, *The Christian Faith*, 130.
252. Gunton, *The Christian Faith*, 131.

as a subspecies of the meal in general. The social event of eating and drinking together as an act of worship is of equal importance to the Supper as its eucharistic significance.[253]

Paul's concerns about the Corinthians' celebration of the Lord's Supper focus upon their life as a gathered community rather than the sacramental elements. Despite the traditional debates, Gunton holds that the real weight of 1 Corinthians 11 is not primarily a discussion about Christ's presence in the bread and the wine, but the Church's social and political constitution.[254] "The passage," Gunton argues, "is devoted to the Church's polity, its social and political constitution, as much as eucharistic worship, indeed, more than that, at least if the latter is narrowly conceived."[255] 1 Corinthians 11 begins with matters of ecclesial polity and the particular issues associated with head coverings and worship. It then goes on to expose the scandal of carrying over into the Church social divisions that fail to give witness to God's desired political order under Christ.[256] It is in the context of the Church's eschatological polity and sociality that we are given words of the institution, which are a simple restatement of the remembrance of what Jesus once did.[257]

Gunton draws from Caird's exegesis to argue a Reformed perspective that the narrated passion and resurrection determine the Church and its worship, not the Eucharist.[258] The sacraments are appendices to the Word and secondary to Christ's atoning sacrifice.[259] Paul's warning of eating and drinking unworthily is best understood as reference to the issues of the Church's sociality and polity. References to the elements are not associated with their properties, as the bread is paralleled by the cup, not wine, and cup is a symbol of Christ's crucifixion. Paul's use of κρίνω and its cognates in 1 Cor 11:27-34 shows that to share the cup is to undergo judgement as godly discipline and communal reconciliation to avoid eschatological judgement.[260] Godly discipline is part of the Spirit's sanctifying action that shapes God's people in their eschatological identity while those who resist the Spirit's action risk condemnation.[261]

---

253. Gunton, *Father, Son and Holy Spirit*, 222. See also Gunton, *The Christian Faith*, 131–2.
254. Gunton, *Father, Son and Holy Spirit*, 225.
255. Gunton, *Father, Son and Holy Spirit*, 225.
256. Gunton, *Father, Son and Holy Spirit*, 225. For a recent influential treatment of this passage by one of Gunton's former students, see Lucy Peppiatt, *Women and Worship at Corinth* (Eugene: Wipf and Stock, 2015), 21–43. See also Lucy Peppiatt, "Gunton on Community," in *T&T Clark Handbook of Colin Gunton*, ed. Andrew Picard, Myk Habets, and Murray Rae (London: T&T Clark, 2021), 215–16.
257. Gunton, *Father, Son and Holy Spirit*, 225.
258. Gunton, *Father, Son and Holy Spirit*, 225.
259. Gunton, *Father, Son and Holy Spirit*, 226.
260. Gunton, *The Christian Faith*, 133.
261. Gunton, *The Christian Faith*, 134.

At this point, Gunton notes the disagreement amongst biblical scholars on the correct translation and meaning of "the body" in 11:29, and concludes it is at best a guess.[262] From the wider context of Paul's communitarian concerns in the passage, Gunton concludes that the body being discerned (διακρίνων, 11:29) is the community of the Church, not the eucharistic elements. "If a body is being unrecognized, that body is the community whose social structure is being torn apart by bad behaviour rather than inadequate sacramentology."[263] The problems at Corinth are not a failure to believe that the bread and the wine are theoretically Christ's body and blood, but a failure to love one another with the love of Christ.[264] The Church must give reverent discernment to the shape of its common life, as the Church's polity and sociality are an eschatological witness.

Gunton is aware that his reading of the text may be accused of reducing the passage to ethical moralizing, but in his opinion this misses the primacy of the Church's offering of worship through the realities of its common life.[265] Such worship is not a naturally occurring phenomenon, as worship is offered through those who continue to behave in ways that frustrate the rule of God.[266] It is the Spirit's action, not human action, that shapes the Church's worship by conforming its common life to Christ. The Church's worship is, therefore, a form of eschatological ethics, an eschatological interim ethic that is highly concrete and embodied, and concerns obedience and love.[267] The Spirit enables the Church to offer itself, through Christ, as a living sacrifice of praise—a representative offering of the first fruits of creation and God's promised kingdom.

The theme of sacrifice is vital to Gunton's view of eschatological ecclesiology and culture as the Spirit enables Christ's sacrifice to form the Church's worship and life as a sacrifice of praise to God for God's gracious intentions in the beginning.[268] Whilst Gunton's communitarian reading finds strong support in scholarship,[269] he is surprisingly muted on the Passover as a liturgical setting for the Lord's

262. Gunton, *Father, Son and Holy Spirit*, 226.
263. Gunton, *Father, Son and Holy Spirit*, 227.
264. Gunton, *The Christian Faith*, 133.
265. Gunton, *Father, Son and Holy Spirit*, 227–8.
266. Gunton, *Father, Son and Holy Spirit*, 231.
267. Gunton, *Father, Son and Holy Spirit*, 231.
268. Gunton, *Father, Son and Holy Spirit*, 228.
269. Along with Caird, Gunton draws from the work of Richard Hays for his communitarian interpretation. Richard B. Hays, *First Corinthians*, Interpretation (Louisville: John Knox Press, 1997), 200–3. For some examples of contemporary accounts that support Gunton's communitarian interpretation see Dennis E. Smith, *From Symposium to Eucharist: The Banquet in the Early Christian World* (Minneapolis: Fortress Press, 2003), 191–200; Kenneth E. Bailey, *Paul through Mediterranean Eyes: Cultural Studies in 1 Corinthians* (London: SPCK, 2011), 322–4; Pheme Perkins, *First Corinthians*, Paideia Commentaries on the New Testament (Grand Rapids: Baker, 2012), 145; and Edward Adams, "The Shape of the Pauline Churches," in *The Oxford Handbook of Ecclesiology* (Oxford: OUP, 2018), 135–6.

Supper.[270] Other scholars note the importance of the Passover background, as well as Greco-Roman dining practices, to Paul's presentation of the Lord's Supper. Thus, a greater reflection on Paul's employment of the Passover would further strengthen what Gunton wants to achieve. The Supper is certainly the reconciliation of the community in Christ, but, as Murray Rae shows, it is also pedagogical formation that schools the Church in the grammar of the gospel.[271] This maintains Gunton's emphasis upon divine action and the eschatological community by giving particular shape to the Spirit's action in the formation of the Church.

Likewise, while Gunton goes to great lengths to show Paul's stress upon community, his account of the body assumes an apolitical neutrality about the Church's common life that does not adequately capture the politics of belonging in community that dominate the letter. Reconstructions of the setting of the Corinthian meals note the likely influence of banqueting and symposium traditions from Roman associations.[272] Paul's concern is that the Corinthian meals ape the social and political hierarchies that dominate Roman banqueting traditions, and for this reason he commands a contrasting body politic. A theology of belonging in the body invites reflection on the Church's body politic and engagement with the details of privilege and power in the Church's polity and sociality. Chapter six upholds the fruitfulness of Gunton's account of the Lord's Supper and theology of human culture and extends it through an engagement with contemporary questions regarding the politics of belonging.

For alternative accounts that stress the Passover background see Anthony C. Thiselton, *The First Epistle to the Corinthians: A Commentary on the Greek Text*, NIGTC (Grand Rapids: Eerdmans, 2000), 871–4; 888–94; and Joseph A. Fitzmeyer, *First Corinthians: A New Translation and Commentary*, Anchor (New Haven and London: Yale University Press, 2008), 444–8.

270. Gunton does not refer to the Passover in his extended treatments of the Lord's Supper in Gunton, *The Christian Faith*, 131–4 or Gunton, *Father, Son and Holy Spirit*, 216–34. Nonetheless, it is important to note Gunton is aware of the importance of the Passover to the Lord's Supper, which he addresses in an earlier chapter (first published in 1989) on "Atonement: The Sacrifice and the Sacrifices," in Gunton, *Father, Son and Holy Spirit*, 197.

271. Murray Rae, "The Liturgical Shape of Christian Life," *Knox Centre for Ministry and Leadership*, http://knoxcentre.ac.nz/wp-content/uploads/2012/11/The-Liturgical-Shape-of-Christian-Life.pdf, 13–14. Another helpful exploration of the metaphor of sacrifice in Paul's writings, and in relation to the Lord's Supper and its Passover background, see Jane Lancaster Patterson, *Keeping the Feast: Metaphors of Sacrifice in 1 Corinthians and Philippians* (Atlanta: SBL Press, 2015), 145–57.

272. Kloppenborg, *Christ's Associations*; Taussig, *In the Beginning was the Meal*; Lee, *The Lord's Supper in Corinth*; and Smith and Taussig, ed., *Meals in the Early Christian World*.

The Supper, the Sacrifice, and the Church's Living Sacrifice of Praise

The Church's celebration of the Lord's Supper is the culmination of Gunton's Christological and pneumatological account of human culture. It is at the Supper that the Spirit enables the Church to offer humanity in right relation to God, one another and creation as a sacrifice of praise through the sacrifice of Christ.[273] The Spirit enables the Church's interim ethic to be, from time to time, a form of "unworldly" behaviour that takes the shape of obedience and love that makes Christ's past redemption of humanity take effect in the present material world in anticipation of the perfection of all things.[274] The Church's interim ethic is an eschatological interim ethic because it is enabled by the Spirit who perfects created being by bringing it into relation with the Father through the Son.[275] The Church's worship, life, and ethic are an eschatological sacrifice of praise because they are book-ended by two other sacrifices: the remembered atoning sacrifice of Christ and the anticipated sacrifice when Christ hands over all things, perfected by the Spirit, to the Father.[276]

Among the polyvalent meanings of sacrifice, Gunton proposes worship and thanksgiving as among the most important. Worship and thanksgiving in 1 Corinthians are foundationally worship and thanksgiving for Christ's sacrifice, but right worship and right conduct belong together.[277] Paul's recapitulation of the Torah in 1 Corinthians suggests that the Church's sacrifice of praise is the sacrificial and obedient offering of its sociality, polity, and ethics that chooses the way of life and not death.[278] Gunton cross-references one of his most influential verses (Rom 12:1) to argue that the primary sacrifice or offering is embodied life; "offer your bodies as a living sacrifice." As in 1 Corinthians, Gunton argues that the Romans text is concerned with the sociality and polity that the Church bodies forth in its common life. It is the Church's right human habitation of creation through the rich plurality of offerings of the diverse members that makes a single sacrifice of praise. The Church's life and culture are, therefore, an eschatological offering of praise and thanksgiving before God; praise in the form of human culture that perfects perfection.[279]

The Church's sacrifice of praise needs to be understood in relation to Gunton's understanding of election, humanity's cultural mandate, and the perfection of creation. The Church's election serves a representative function through which God's universal purposes for creation are displayed in its particular common life together.[280] The Church's celebration of the Supper anticipates the true human

---

273. Gunton, *Father, Son and Holy Spirit*, 119.
274. Gunton, *Father, Son and Holy Spirit*, 231–2.
275. Gunton, *Father, Son and Holy Spirit*, 232.
276. Gunton, *Father, Son and Holy Spirit*, 233–4.
277. Gunton, *Father, Son and Holy Spirit*, 228–9.
278. Gunton, *Father, Son and Holy Spirit*, 229.
279. Gunton, *Father, Son and Holy Spirit*, 229.
280. Gunton, *The Christian Faith*, 134.

community of the end and the images of an eschatological banquet where all will be reconciled to God, one another, and the created order. "That is to say, universal fellowship with God is representatively anticipated in the congregation's eating together."[281] The Spirit enables the Church to offer its common life together, its sociality, polity, and ethics, to God as a representative sacrifice of praise for God's purposes in creation.[282] Humanity's cultural mandate (Gen 1:26-28) is focused in the person of Jesus Christ, the one truly perfected human life, who fulfils humanity's calling and offers his own self-offering of faithful humanity to the Father in the Spirit. Christ's perfect sacrifice is the means for the sacrifice of praise of the whole of creation, and the Church's life emerges from his faithful human sacrifice. At the Supper, the Church's life in community and in creation is united by the Spirit to Christ's great self-offering by the Spirit as a sacrifice of praise to the Father that perfects the project of creation.[283]

Importantly for Gunton, the Supper incorporates not only the Church's relationship with God and one another, but also its relationship with creation in fulfilment of the cultural mandate in Genesis. The cultural mandate involves relationship to God expressed in relationship to one another and the wider creation.[284] Despite much Protestant resistance to materiality, the sacraments representatively incorporate the wider created world through the use of water, and grain and grape, in the Church's sacrifice of praise.[285] As baptism utilizes the natural substance of water for worship, the Lord's Supper utilizes nature manufactured by human interaction. The grain and grape are natural elements that are changed, manufactured by human hands to become bread and wine. As fruits of nature manufactured by human cultural agency, the bread and the wine incorporate humanity's cultural mandate in the Church's sacrifice of praise in and through Christ's sacrifice as the true human being and the mediator of creation.[286] "Just as Jesus' body was formed from the dust of the earth, so these physical creatures become the means whereby the whole created world is taken up, by anticipation, into the praise of the creator."[287] The Supper is at once nature and culture. It weaves together the promised resurrection of Christ with the cultural mandate that what human beings do in and with the world will be somehow taken up into the reign of God so that humanity and creation can praise their creator.[288]

In the Church's celebration of the Supper, human culture is offered redeemed and restored through Christ's sacrifice. It is at the Lord's Supper that humanity's cultural mandate finds its richest expression through Christ's sacrifice, the

---

281. Gunton, *The Christian Faith*, 134.
282. Gunton, "Reformation Accounts," 92.
283. Gunton, *The Christian Faith*, 130–4. See also Gunton, "Reformation Accounts," 92.
284. Gunton, *Father, Son and Holy Spirit*, 232–3.
285. Gunton, *The Christian Faith*, 134.
286. Gunton, *Father, Son and Holy Spirit*, 233.
287. Gunton, *The Christian Faith*, 134.
288. Gunton, *Father, Son and Holy Spirit*, 233.

Spirit's eschatological perfecting, and the Church's life in community with God, one another, and the wider creation. The Church's elect calling as God's new community represents humanity to God and God's purposes to creation through the Church's right human habitation of creation, enabled by the divine action of the Son and the Spirit. The Church's distinctive form of redeemed human culture, in right relation with God, one another and creation, anticipates God's universal purposes for humanity and the creation—to be and become what God particularly intended them to be in praise of their maker.

Conclusion

This chapter, together with Chapters 3 and 4, shows that Gunton's trinitarian theology of culture is best understood through an exploration of Gunton's doctrine of creation, Christology, pneumatology, and ecclesiology. Due to the *Hauptbriefe* in Gunton reception, these leading themes in Gunton's thought have not been adequately examined. This chapter, therefore, attempts to fill a gap in Gunton research by examining his *theological* account of culture and showing how his leading theological themes unite to establish a trinitarian theology of culture. Gunton's quest for a concrete trinitarianism finds expression in his trinitarian theology of culture, which is most fully developed in his later writings. The Spirit is the perfecting cause who anticipates the conditions of the end of time in the present. Such finite anticipations occur inside and outside the Church through various forms of human culture. Yet, the Spirit is present in and towards the Church in particular ways to enable it to be God's representative community, the body of Christ. The Church's nature as a creature of the triune God is expressed through the concrete shape of the Church that is formed by the action of the Son and the Spirit. The Church is a distinctive form of eschatological culture enabled by the Son's redeeming human sacrifice and the Spirit's perfecting action. As we have seen, the Church's life in community is a gift of God that is presented back to God as a representative offering of worship for God's universal purposes for creation. Such worship culminates at the Lord's Supper as it is here that the Church's life in communion with God, one another, and creation anticipates the eschatological banquet. It is not a banquet based on the Church's best communal intentions, but a Supper centred on the Lamb's sacrifice and the Spirit's eschatological perfecting.

Chapter 6

THE CHURCH, THE LORD'S SUPPER, AND HUMAN CULTURE AS A LIVING SACRIFICE OF PRAISE

Colin Gunton's trinitarian theology offers important analyses of Western culture and provides significant insights for a *theological* account of human culture in general. His theological account of culture arises from his doctrines of the Trinity, creation, Christology, pneumatology, and ecclesiology, and culminates in the Church's worship at the Lord's Supper. As we have seen in Chapter 5, the Lord's Supper is the culmination of human worship and culture in which humanity and creation are offered to God as a sacrifice of praise in and through Christ's faithful self-offering in the Spirit. This chapter shows the ongoing fruitfulness of Gunton's theology of culture by examining the Lord's Supper as one example of how his theology of culture helps us to understand the transformative work of the Spirit in bringing human culture and sociality to its intended goal in Christ.

Gunton's account of the Lord's Supper focuses primarily on Paul's instructions to the Church at Corinth and stresses the Church's communal and eschatological identity.[1] The scandal of social and economic divisions at the Supper is the Church's failure to embody the gospel's transformation of human relationships and its elect eschatological identity.[2] Whilst noting the scandal of the divisions in the Church, Gunton does not detail the shape of these divisions, or Paul's criticisms of the Church's politics of belonging. Given his context, with its concerns about the dominance of the natural sciences in modernity and the inroads of deism's abstract theological accounts, this lack in Gunton's treatment is understandable.[3] It is the intention of this present chapter to build upon his assessment of the Supper in the context of contemporary cultural concerns. To do so, I will examine the Church's politics of belonging in the context of ableism, and thus demonstrate the

---

1. In his preface to the chapter on the Lord's Supper, Gunton states, "the Lord's Supper ought to be understood in its communal and, indeed, ethical dimensions before its 'ritual' significance can be adequately construed. Once again in this chapter an effort is made to relate what is said about the Supper to eschatology and the life of the community." Gunton, *Father, Son and Holy Spirit*, xvii.
2. Gunton, *Intellect and Action*, 117–18.
3. Rae, "Introduction," in *T&T Handbook of Colin Gunton*, 2–3.

way in which the triune God transforms the Church's culture and its representative embodiment of God's universal purposes.[4]

Theology and the Rise of the Cultural Sciences

In a work that expands upon Gunton's theology of culture, Stephen Holmes observes the increasing centrality of the cultural sciences in contemporary academic discourse. The rise of the cultural sciences shares some similarities with the rise of the natural sciences in the seventeenth century, and the way they became central to academic discourse. Any disciplines in the seventeenth century that did not engage with the discoveries and claims of the natural sciences risked marginalization and exposed themselves to the charge of obscurantism. A similar case can be made, Holmes suggests, for the role the cultural sciences have in the academic discourse of our own time. Even the natural sciences must now consider the cultural conditioning of their empirical knowledge.[5] In this changed context, a theological account of culture needs also to engage with the pressing questions the cultural sciences raise about the sociological and political powers that are sedimented within social systems, social structures, and knowledges. This includes the hegemonic powers that are embedded within Christianity's knowledge claims and ecclesial social structures. Some argue that theology's God-talk "serves no purpose other than the legitimization of improper hegemonies."[6] Holmes rightly stresses that to ignore the charges of theology's entanglement with totalizing and colonizing forces is to risk "removing oneself from the mainstream of public discourse, of speaking in such a way that only those who already agree will listen, whilst others will simply laugh or mock, not quite believing that anyone can have failed so thoroughly to keep in touch with the modern questions."[7]

Although theology is not driven by demands for relevance, it cannot be so sectarian that it is only heard within the Lord's vineyard.[8] Holmes acknowledges that theology has indeed been misused for the maintenance of improper hegemonies, and must accept, with due humility, the critique that bad theology is oppressive to so many women and non-Westerners.[9] As noted, Gunton writes in the face of the dominance of the natural sciences and their influence upon theology and culture,

---

4. Laurence L. Welborn, "How 'Democratic' Was the Pauline *Ekklēsia*? An Assessment with Special Reference to the Christ Groups of Roman Corinth," *NTS*, 65 (2019): 303–4. Whilst this chapter offers exegetical insights on 1 Corinthians 11:17-34, these are drawn from secondary sources in biblical scholarship and are intended to extend Gunton's proposals in systematic theology rather than to break new exegetical ground.

5. Holmes, "Can Theology Engage with Culture?" 1.
6. Holmes, "Can Theology Engage with Culture?" 1.
7. Holmes, "Can Theology Engage with Culture?" 2.
8. Holmes, "Can Theology Engage with Culture?" 3.
9. Holmes, "Can Theology Engage with Culture?" 3–4.

and he rarely engages with the cultural sciences and their critiques of power. When he does, his main concern is to challenge the epistemological veracity of relativism.[10] Given his historical context, many of the questions the cultural sciences raise about unjust power structures remain unrecognized or unchallenged in Gunton's work.[11] However, Gunton does observe that Paul's account of the wisdom and power of the cross in 1 Corinthians dismantles assumptions of divine power and "privileges a certain way of exercising power."[12] The remaining chapter of this book seeks to extend Gunton's insights on human culture in the context of the rise of the social sciences and their criticisms of theology's support of improper hegemonies.

Gunton's theology provides the resources necessary for a theological account of culture that can be furthered through an engagement with contemporary discussions of the Church's sociality and sociological politics.[13] This extension of Gunton's work accords with some of Gunton's colleagues and students who have gone on to develop a variety of engagements with the cultural sciences that show the ongoing fruitfulness of his theological account of culture.[14] The gospel is, as Gunton asserts, embodied in the Church's sociality, polity, and ethics, and a consideration of the Church's embedded power structures details the shape of the Church's embodiment of the gospel and enriches an understanding of its sacrifice of praise.

Theology, the Cultural Sciences, and the Politics of Belonging

In her recent work, Sarah Coakley argues for systematic theology's need to address its intersectional entanglements with issues of gender, race, and class

---

10. For example, see Gunton, *Intellect and Action*, 39–41; Gunton, *The Christian Faith*, ix–x, 12–14; Gunton, *The Promise of Trinitarian Theology*, 162–77; Gunton, *The One, the Three and the Many*, 104–5; Gunton, "Knowledge and Culture," 96; and Gunton, "Proteus and Procrustes," 65–80. Overall, Gunton's concern is that all language is apophatically purged of everyday connotations if it is to serve trinitarian theology. See Colin E. Gunton, "Editorial: Orthodoxy," *IJST*, 1 (1999): 117.

11. In a 1992 essay, Gunton opposes the exclusion of women from ministry role and maintains it is a denial of the gospel. However, his criticism of Sally McFague's relativistic deployments of metaphor in theology do not engage her important criticisms of patriarchal power. See Gunton, "Proteus and Procrustes," 65–80.

12. Gunton, *The Christian Faith*, 15–16.

13. Welborn, "How 'Democratic' Was the Pauline *Ekklēsia*?," 290.

14. See Holmes, "Can Theology Engage with Culture?"; Murray A. Rae, "The War on Terror in Ruatoki," *International Journal of Public Theology*, 2 (2008): 277–91; Murray A. Rae, *Theology and Architecture: The Art of Place* (Waco: Baylor University Press, 2017); Paul Louis Metzger, *The Word of God and the World of Culture: Sacred and Secular through the Theology of Karl Barth* (Grand Rapids: Eerdmans, 2003); and Christoph Schwöbel, "Europa ohne Gott? Ansichten eines säkularen Zeitalters," in *Christentum und Europa: XVI. Europäischer Kongress für Theologie*, ed. Michael Meyer-Blanck (Leipzig: Evangelische Verlagsanstalt GmbH, 2019), 106–19.

through engaging the contrapuntal voices of philosophy, political thought, and sociology. In place of theological approaches that politely excuse themselves from lived realities, Coakley advances the need for theology's engagement with the cultural sciences in order to comprehend its messy entanglements with the hegemonies of the modern patriarchal and racial conditions.[15] Such engagements are difficult and complex because the Church is, at times, complicit in making discriminatory power structures part of theology and the gospel. What is required, Coakley maintains, is a theological investigation that draws from a wide array of human evidences to do greater justice to the complexities of theology's fusion with issues of racism, sexism, and ableism.[16] If the Church is determined only by metaphysical proclamations, aside from its historical manifestations, how can the Church recognize and confess its own sin?[17] The way the Church not only condones but perpetuates the powers and privileges encased in the structures of society is often not obvious as the power, dominance, and violence of structural privilege are largely invisible to those who inherit and enact it.[18] The cultural sciences highlight how society has worked, as well as outlining the shape of how transformation occurs now. Enquiries from the cultural sciences into the way the Church maintains societal

---

15. Coakley, *God, Sexuality, and the Self*, 43–51.

16. Sarah Coakley, "Knowing in the Dark: Sin, Race and the Quest for Salvation. Part 1: Transforming Theological Anthropology in a Théologie Totale," *The Princeton Seminary Bulletin*, 32 (2015): 112–13. John Webster sounds an important warning about recent forays into the relation between ecclesiology and ethnography and stresses that the church cannot be reduced to its socio-historical manifestations. There is a distinction between the church's principle *res* and proximate *res*, and the church cannot be reduced to an empirical historical reality because its movements and action are not merely natural acts, but creaturely movements moved by God. Ontological primacy is therefore not given to socio-historical realities or evidences of the church, but God and all things as God orders them. There is more to the church's historic and social action than meets the eye, and the phenomenon of the church is not exhausted by its manifestation. A theological account of the Church, Webster argues, must precede and shape any observable account from cultural sciences. Webster, "'In the Society of God," 201–4, 220–1.

17. Christopher Craig Brittain, "Why Ecclesiology Cannot Live by Doctrine Alone: A Reply to John Webster's 'In the Society of God,'" *Ecclesial Practices*, 1 (2014): 8.

18. Brittain, "Why Ecclesiology Cannot Live by Doctrine Alone," 20–5. See also Coakley, "Knowing in the Dark," 111–12, and Andrew Picard, "From Whiteness towards Witness: Revelation and Repentance as Unbelonging to Empire," in *The Art of Forgiveness*, ed. Philip Halstead and Myk Habets (Lanham: Lexington Books/Fortress Academic, 2018), 246–51. For a recent account of the relationship of theology, ecclesiology, and social science in Bonhoeffer's thought, see Michael Mawson, *Christ Existing as Community: Bonhoeffer's Ecclesiology* (Oxford: OUP, 2018), 176–86.

power structures enable the Church to confront that which it hides and give particular shape to its sin. The cultural sciences also offer a more concrete and particular account of the Church's experience and expression of God's grace lived communally through its social and political life.

The rise of the cultural sciences sheds light on the historical, social, and political contexts of scripture and its meanings. Scripture is not merely a transcendent divine revelation; it is embedded within diverse social and political contexts, from and to which the biblical authors write. The cultural sciences better enable us to comprehend scripture's concrete rhetoric, resistances, and claims. Recent developments in New Testament studies stress the importance of insights from cultural studies to enrich the reading of New Testament texts in their religio-political contexts. Richard Horsley observes that much New Testament study separates first-century religion from politics in ways that distort their fundamental unity and the socio-political import of scripture.[19] The rise of postcolonial studies and socio-political readings of scripture has resulted in a greater appreciation of the intricate weavings of religion and politics in the New Testament. The insights from these approaches enable a more particular discernment of the issues Paul addresses regarding the Lord's Supper at Corinth.[20]

Paul's Corinthian correspondence provides guidance regarding the Lord's Supper. As Gunton stresses, it is in Paul's corrections and exhortations that "the theological, ritual, social and ethical dimensions of the Supper belong so inextricably together."[21] The Lord's Supper is a social event whose end is the right social embodiment of the gospel.[22] Taking Gunton's stress upon the sociality and polity of the Lord's Supper, the following section seeks to build upon that by exploring social-scientific readings of Paul's admonitions. Paul's criticisms of the Church at Corinth, and his demands for them to embrace a distinct polity, sociality, and ethics, are set in continuity with and resistance to the established

---

19. Richard A. Horsley, "The First and Second Letters to the Corinthians," in *A Postcolonial Commentary on the New Testament Writings*, ed. Fernando F. Segovia and R. S. Sugirtharajah (London: T&T Clark, 2007), 220-1. Steven Friesen makes a similar criticism of the false disjunction of "religion" and "politics" in interpretations of the book of Revelation. See Steven J. Friesen, *Imperial Cults and the Apocalypse of John: Reading Revelation in the Ruins* (Oxford: OUP, 2001), 14-15. Friesen goes on to observe the possibilities and limitations of postcolonial studies for accounts of ancient and modern imperialisms.

20. Horsley, "The First and Second Letters to the Corinthians," 220-1.

21. Gunton, *The Christian Faith*, 130.

22. Gunton, *The Christian Faith*, 131-2.

socio-political institutions of the Roman empire and its local particularities.²³ Social-scientific readings thus provide a more nuanced understanding of the abuses at Corinth, the influence of Roman culture, and Paul's Christological alternatives. If the Lord's Supper is the culmination of human culture and worship, then the Church, in the first- or twenty-first century, must give attention to its sociality and sociological politics—its culture.²⁴ A careful consideration of the politics of belonging in the text invites contemporary reflections on the politics of belonging in the Church and its right social embodiment of the gospel as an expression of transformed human culture.

The Church at Corinth in Light of the Roman Associations

Paul's use of ἐκκλησία situates the early Christ communities amongst the Greco-Roman *polis* and its political assemblies.²⁵ The term denotes the civic assemblies of male citizens in the Greek cities, including the period of the Roman Empire, who

---

23. In his study of Roman associations, John Kloppenborg critiques the habit of Christian scholarship to dramatize the uniqueness of the Christ assemblies and their difference from other associations. Kloppenborg acknowledges that many of his readers will find this emphasis irritating, but historiography is not apologetics. Whilst there are innovative practices in the Christ assemblies, there are greater similarities between Paul's rhetoric and the expectations of Roman associations and their bylaws regarding group sociality and polity. This is an important corrective that enables the differences to stand out with special prominence. However, Kloppenborg's corrective needs to also take account of Paul's challenge to the Roman political assumptions embedded in the meal rituals of the Lord's Supper, and Paul's ironic critiques of Roman ideals of power. See John S. Kloppenborg, *Christ's Associations: Connecting and Belonging in the Ancient City* (New Haven and London: Yale University Press, 2019), Kindle Location 67–72 of 13065. On the technologies of Roman meals and Paul's subversion of their rituals, see Hal Taussig, *In the Beginning Was the Meal: Social Experimentation and Early Christian Identity* (Minneapolis: Fortress Press, 2009), 115–43.

24. McRae, "Eating with Honor," 166–8.

25. Significant debate exists among scholars as to whether Paul borrows from Jewish Septuagint usage or the standard Greek usage for local assemblies. See Paul Trebilco, "Why Did the Early Christians Call Themselves ἡ ἐκκλησία?," *NTS*, 57 (2011): 440–60, and George H. Van Kooten, "'Ἐκκλησία τοῦ θεοῦ: The 'Church of God' and the Civic Assemblies (ἐκκλησίαι) of the Greek Cities in the Roman Empire: A Response to Paul Trebilco and Richard A. Horsley," *NTS*, 58 (2012): 522–48. Richard Last helpfully suggests it is best to hold that there is a surplus of meaning in Paul's use of the term, rather than limiting it to singular or binary influences. Richard Last, "*Ekklēsia* outside the Septuagint and the *Dēmos*: The Titles of Greco-Roman Associations and Christ-Followers' Groups," *Journal of Biblical Literature*, 137 (2018): 963–9. Furthermore, John Kloppenborg argues that how the term functions in Paul's discourse is more important than the origins of Paul's usage, and civic ἐκκλησία is attested at Corinth. Kloppenborg, *Christ's Associations*, Kindle Location 6121 of 13065.

exercise various forms of power to determine the affairs of the state or *polis*. "In the apostle's time, the word [ἐκκλησία] was located in a very crowded intersection of cultural, political, social, and economic forces."²⁶ Paul's use of ἐκκλησία mimics the established civil discourse, and his imagination of the Christ groups in the Roman Empire can be mapped onto the imperial organization of the Roman cities.²⁷ In the context of Roman cities, Roman private associations provide an important social and political context in which to understand the dynamics of the early Christ groups. Whilst private associations did not often employ the term ἐκκλησία, their imitation of Roman civic values formed them as "cities writ small."²⁸

Recent New Testament studies highlight Roman associations and their associational meals as an important historical, social, and political milieu for understanding the Pauline Christ communities. Because of this association studies are of particular importance to 1 Corinthians 11.17-34.²⁹ In the Roman Empire, between the two poles of family and polis there was a large variety of private associations, guilds, clubs, and *collegia* in the Roman Empire that organized themselves around patron deities, extended family, diasporic identity, a neighbourhood, or a trade and profession. These associations existed in nearly every city and town in the ancient Mediterranean, and their gatherings primarily served a cultic, social, and political function.³⁰ Given that participation in the public civic ἐκκλησία was reserved for the elite, the associations provided distinct environments where the sub-elite could participate in leadership and decision-making irrespective of legal status, ethnicity, rank, or social status.³¹ As such, the associations functioned as "free-spaces" that integrated the sub-elite into the *polis* and enabled lower-status people to "play at democracy."³² Whilst associations were distinct from the *polis*, they mimicked civic values, like democratic practices,

---

26. Young-Ho Park, *Paul's Ekklesia as a Civic Assembly: Understanding the People of God in Their Politico-Social World* (Tübingen: Mohr Siebeck, 2015), 2.

27. Kloppenborg, *Christ's Associations*, Kindle Location 6121 of 13065.

28. John S. Kloppenborg, "Associations, Christ Groups, and Their Place in the *Polis*," *Zeitschrift für die Neutestamentliche Wissenschaft*, 108 (2017): 16-17. See also Kloppenborg, *Christ's Associations*, Kindle Locations 6052-4 of 13065.

29. Lee, *The Lord's Supper in Corinth*, preface. See also Kloppenborg, *Christ's Associations*. Laurence Welborn highlights the difficulty posed by the mutilation of the Corinthian epigraphic ruins for reconstructing associational life. See L. L. Welborn, "How 'Democratic' Was the Pauline *Ekklēsia*?" 300.

30. Kloppenborg, *Christ's Associations*, Kindle Location 2219 of 13065.

31. For an account of the reigning elite in ancient Corinth, see Welborn, "How 'Democratic' Was the Pauline *Ekklēsia*?" 300-2. For an especially detailed account of Roman associations, drawn from wider inscriptional, numismatic, and epigraphic evidence in the Roman Empire, see Kloppenborg, *Christ's Associations*.

32. John S. Kloppenborg, "Associations," 14-17. See also Michael J. Rhodes, "Formative Feasting: Practices and Economic Ethics in Deuteronomy's Tithe Meal and the Corinthian Lord's Supper" (PhD diss., University of Aberdeen, Scotland, 2019), 246-8. Now published as Michael J. Rhodes, *Formative Feasting: Practices and Virtue Ethics in Deuteronomy's Tithe Meal and the Corinthian Lord's Supper* (New York: Peter Lang, 2022).

honorific decrees, rosters of members, and common banquets, in such a way that they were a mini-*polis*.³³ The associations may not have commonly adopted the term ἐκκλησία for their meetings, but they provide a likely influence upon the early Christian communities and offer insight into possible reconstructions of their demography and social dynamics.³⁴

The private associations were populated by the sub-elite, and provided networks that created a sense of belonging as well as opportunities to enhance social capital and prestige. The demographics of the associations "ranged from citizens to aliens resident in cities, from the freeborn to freedmen and freedwomen and slaves, from associations of handworkers and artists to cultic groups."³⁵ The elite served as patrons and patronesses of the private associations, but they rarely, if ever, attended. Instead, their patronage provided financial and material resources, access to wider social networks and social capital, and legitimacy in wider civic society. In return, patrons received public honours in various forms, and loyalty from the associations.³⁶ The social status and social capital provided by the network and its patrons were especially important in an environment that did not provide social support for those facing illness, death, funerals, unemployment, disease, or dislocation.³⁷

33. John S. Kloppenborg, "Associations," 16–17. See also Kloppenborg, *Christ's Associations*, Kindle Location 6052-4 of 13065.

34. John S. Kloppenborg, "Precedence at the Communal Meal in Corinth," *Novum Testamentum*, 58 (2016): 171. Laurence L. Welborn maintains that there are only three instances where the term ἐκκλησία was employed for private associations. Welborn, "How 'Democratic' Was the Pauline *Ekklēsia*?" 294. For more on the parallels between Roman associations and the early Christ groups, see McRae, "Eating with Honor," 165-81; Edward Adams, "First-Century Models for Paul's Churches: Selected Scholarly Developments Since Meeks," in *After the First Urban Christians*, ed. Todd D. Still and David G. Horrell (London and New York: T&T Clark, 2009), 69–70; Edward Adams, *The Earliest Christian Meeting Places: Almost Exclusively Houses?* (London and New York: T&T Clark, 2013), 119–24; Richard Last, *The Pauline Church and the Corinthian* Ekklēsia: *Greco-Roman Associations in Comparative Context* (Cambridge: CUP, 2016), 1–80; Last, "*Ekklēsia* Outside the Septuagint and the *Dēmos*," 959-80; Philip A. Harland, *Associations, Synagogues, and Congregations: Claiming a Place in Ancient Mediterranean Society* (Minneapolis: Fortress Press, 2003), 1–87; Taussig, *In the Beginning Was the Meal*, 88–102; Smith, *From Symposium to Eucharist*, 13–46; and Dennis E. Smith and Hal E. Taussig, ed., *Meals in the Early Christian World: Social Formation, Experimentation, and Conflict at the Table* (New York: Palgrave Macmillan, 2012).

35. Kloppenborg, *Christ's Associations*, Kindle Location 1508-9 of 13065.

36. See Kloppenborg, *Christ's Associations*, Kindle Location 1183–1517 of 13065.

37. McRae, "Eating with Honor," 165–6. See also Kloppenborg, *Christ's Associations*, Kindle Location 1705 of 13065.

6. The Church, the Lord's Supper, and Human Culture

Meals as Social and Political Performances

A regular feature of associational life was the communal meal or banquet. Meals were perhaps the most common social practices of the associations, and provided glue for the fabric of the social network as well as contexts for the performance of social status, social identity, and group belonging.[38] Embodied in these occasions was the tension between ideals of social equality and the realities of social stratification. A study of the meal dynamics thus provides a helpful context for understanding the particular issues Paul addresses at Corinth.[39] The Lord's Supper, according to Gunton, is best understood as a subspecies of the meal in general.[40] Gunton's claim finds support in recent developments in biblical studies that have given focused exploration of meals in the Greco-Roman world.[41]

Eating together was an important aspect of life in Roman antiquity, and communal meals were the most common practice among the associations and guilds of the Roman Empire.[42] Although Paul's Christ assemblies were not associations, associational banqueting practices are a likely influence on early Christian dining practices. "The emergence of early Christianity is impossible to contemplate," Taussig maintains, "without the meal and the organizational form of Hellenistic associations."[43] Research into the central role that meals played in the emergence of early Christianity, especially in the associations of the Hellenistic Mediterranean, has been an important field of growing research in the last twenty years.[44]

Structurally the Greco-Roman meal consisted of two phases: the meal proper (a δεῖπνον in Greek or *cena* in Latin), which entailed simple fare such as bread and wine, followed by a drinking party (συμπόσιον in Greek or *convivium* in Latin). The transition from the δεῖπνον to the συμπόσιον was marked by the libation, an

---

38. Kloppenborg, "Precedence at the Communal Meal in Corinth," 201.

39. Rhodes, "Formative Feasting," 250.

40. Gunton, *Father, Son and Holy Spirit*, 222. Gunton quotes approvingly of Jenson's account that all meals are intrinsically religious occasions, and were especially understood this way in Israel.

41. The Society of Biblical Literature founded a Seminar on Meals in the Greco-Roman World in response to the work of Matthias Klinghardt, *Gemeinschaftsmahl und Mahlgemeinschaft: Soziologie und Liturgie frühchristlicher Mahlfeiern*, TANZ 13 (Tübingen and Basel: Francke, 1996) and Dennis Smith, *From Symposium to Eucharist*. See Hal Taussig, "Introduction," in *Meals in the Early Christian World: Social Formation, Experimentation, and Conflict at the Table*, ed. Dennis E. Smith and Hal E. Taussig (New York: Palgrave and Macmillan, 2012), 1.

42. Kloppenborg, *Christ's Associations*, Kindle Location 4482 of 13065. As Taussig maintains, "there was a common meal tradition throughout the Greco-Roman Mediterranean that lay at the basis of all active meals of the Greco-Roman era, whether they be gentile, Jewish, or Christian." Taussig, "Introduction," 2.

43. Taussig, *In the Beginning Was the Meal*, 100. See also Harland, *Associations, Synagogues, and Congregations*, 74–7.

44. Taussig, *In the Beginning Was the Meal*, 88.

elaborate formal ritual ceremony led by a *symposiarch*. In the δεῖπνον tables were removed, the floor swept, and water was passed around to wash hands. A common cup of wine, dedicated to the deity, was often shared among those reclining, and then poured out on the floor or into a hearth. Participants uttered prayers and songs in unison to patron deities and the imperial cult, and celebrated distinguished guests and patrons.[45] Examining ancient sources on libation ceremonies, Matthias Klinghardt notes the liturgical similarities to Christian practices and concludes, "[in] light of this evidence there can be no doubt that 'the cup of blessing which we bless' (τὸ ποτήριον τῆς εὐλογίας ὃ εὐλογοῦμεν: 1 Cor 10:16) refers to the libation cup and the accompanying prayer."[46]

Such a claim must also hold in tension the undoubted influence of the Passover on Paul's understanding of the Lord's Supper. In agreement with Michael Rhodes, I maintain that Greco-Roman banquets and the Passover informed both Paul's and the Corinthians' perspective on the Lord's Supper.[47] It is beyond the scope of this book to engage this debate, but whatever the likely antecedents, "the *telos* of such meals included an embedded intention to form the politics of the community and the moral character of those who engaged in them."[48] In the Greco-Roman

---

45. Taussig, *In the Beginning Was the Meal*, 23–6, 74–9. See also Smith, *From Symposium to Eucharist*, 28–31; Lee, *The Lord's Supper in Corinth in the Context of Greco-Roman Private Associations*, Kindle Location 499 of 6673; and Klinghardt, "A Typology of the Communal Meal," 11–12.

46. Klinghardt, "A Typology of the Communal Meal," 12. Klinghardt's emphasis upon the Greco-Roman dining tradition as the background to the Lord's Supper needs to be supplemented by the clear influence of the Jewish Passover for Paul's understanding of the meal. Dennis Smith observes that the Mishnah account of the Jewish Passover conforms to the structure of the Greco-Roman banquet. Moreover, the literary form of the Haggadah "is related to the literary form of the symposium. This correlates with the point made earlier in this study that the symposium literary tradition tended to dominate virtually all reports of meals in this period." Smith's conclusion is that rather than viewing the Jewish meals in the Second Temple period as a unique phenomenon, they are best understood in the broader world of the Greco-Roman banquet. There are most certainly distinct Jewish understandings of the Passover, which influence Paul's theology of the Lord's Supper, but the *form* of Jewish meals in the Second Temple period is embedded within Greco-Roman banqueting structures. Smith, *From Symposium to Eucharist*, 147–50, 171–2. In chapter five, I have argued for the likely theological influence of the Passover in Paul's account of the Lord's Supper, and observed the need to interpret Paul's theological presentation of the Lord's Supper in the context of the Passover. For an extended discussion of the influence of the first-century Passover meal on Paul's theological understanding of the Lord's Supper, see Rhodes, "Formative Feasting," 254–7.

47. Rhodes, "Formative Feasting," 254–7.

48. Rhodes, "Formative Feasting," 257. See the earlier argument in chapter five, especially Rae, "The Liturgical Shape of Christian Life," 13–14, and Patterson, *Keeping the Feast*, 145–57.

meal structure, the συμπόσιον followed the libation and was regarded as the high point of the meal. The host then provided after-dinner entertainment in the form of conversation (table talk), speeches, songs, alcohol, music, dancing, games, and sexual pleasures.[49] The ideals and goals of Greco-Roman banquets were community, equality, friendship, grace, generosity, and beauty, yet this was set in tension with a highly stratified sociality and polity.[50]

The meals were highly stratified occasions in which seating arrangements, food quality, and portions were carefully considered to honour guests according to rank and status. Encoded within the meal were important messages about social hierarchies, social boundaries, and social status. Drawing from Mary Douglas, an anthropologist, Dennis Smith holds that "the defining of boundaries is primary to the social code of banquets."[51] In the context of Rome's hierarchical stratification, with its sharp differentiations of power, wealth, and status, associations provided fictive equality in which entrenched social hierarchies were somewhat porous. "[Because] associations tended to mimic the political and social hierarchies of the city, their meals allowed members to participate in a polity from which, outside the association, they were excluded."[52]

The internal social dynamics of the associations therefore created social stratifications that were not found outside of the *collegium*. Slaves, lower-status people, and poorer members of the community could experience an elevated social status within the non-elite associations, including serving on rotating leadership rosters, that could not be enjoyed in wider society.[53] As such, the communal meals were sites for the performance of fictive equality as well as intense competition for social status and recognition.[54] The fictive equality of the associations often conflicted with competition for social status, and this was especially prevalent in the practices of food allocation and seating arrangements. Meals and seating were much less about nourishment and comfort, and much more about the performance of social status concretized in the banquet itself.[55]

---

49. Smith, *From Symposium to Eucharist*, 34–8. See also Taussig, *In the Beginning Was the Meal*, 36–53; Klinghardt, "A Typology of the Communal Meal," 12–14; Smith, *From Symposium to Eucharist*, 34–42; Lee, *The Lord's Supper in Corinth*, Kindle Location 1028–1110 of 6673; and Bruce W. Winter, *After Paul Left Corinth: The Influence of Secular Ethics and Social Change* (Grand Rapids: Eerdmans, 2001), 154–8.

50. Taussig, *In the Beginning Was the Meal*, 26–7. See also Smith, *From Symposium to Eucharist*, 7–12; and Klinghardt, "A Typology of the Communal Meal," 14–17.

51. Smith, *From Symposium to Eucharist*, 9, 42–6. See also McRae, "Eating with Honor," 165–6; Taussig, *In the Beginning Was the Meal*, 26–32; and Lee, *The Lord's Supper in Corinth*, Kindle Location 296 of 6673.

52. Kloppenborg, *Christ's Associations*, Kindle Location 3165 of 13065.

53. Lee, *The Lord's Supper in Corinth*, Kindle Location 4290 of 6673. See also Kloppenborg, *Christ's Associations*, Kindle Location 5115 of 13065.

54. Kloppenborg, *Christ's Associations*, Kindle Location 5083 of 13065.

55. Kloppenborg, *Christ's Associations*, Kindle Location 3170 of 13065.

Meals were performative more than nutritional, and the "point of the meal was not to dine sumptuously but to *see oneself* as dining with the group and to *let others see it*."[56] Technologies of belonging at the meal brought the ideals of community (κοινωνία), equality (ἰσότης), and good order (εὐκοσμία) into conflict with social stratification. The distribution of food at the meals aimed at equality, but equality in the ancient world was often measured geometrically, where the portion of food is proportional to the position within the group, rather than arithmetically, where all members receive the same portion.[57] The practice of geometric equality was not regarded as inherently offensive, but the determination of who received greater portion could result in uncivil behaviour and strife that undermined fellowship.[58]

Likewise, seating arrangements at associational meals were designed according to honour and status. The *triclinium* was the Roman-styled dining area in which three couches were designed in a pi-shape. The three couches were attributed with social status, and, as the couches had different heights at each end, seating within each couch carried different social significance. Social status was displayed by which couch, and which end of the couch, guests reclined upon.[59] While recent scholarship problematizes the reduction of Christian meeting spaces solely to the household setting, especially the assumption of Christ groups using a *triclinium* within a Roman villa, this does not undermine the likelihood of stratified seating arrangements and meal allotments.[60] These insights into the social dynamics of the Roman associational meals provide important insights into the nature of the schisms of the Christ groups at Corinth.

The Political and Social Schisms at the Lord's Supper in Corinth

Study of the associations, especially the cultic associations and occupational guilds, provides insight into the schisms at Corinth that trouble Paul, as well as the alternative sociological politics he espouses. Gunton observes that those who uphold economic and social divisions fail to comprehend and practice the reality of the Lord's Supper, as "the proper practice of worship bears fruit in transformed human relations."[61] The gathering of the Christ communities at Corinth was fractious affairs where the "haves" behaved in ways that humiliated the "have

---

56. Kloppenborg, *Christ's Associations*, Kindle Location 3173-4 of 13065 (italics original). See also Lee, *The Lord's Supper in Corinth*, Kindle Location 339 of 6673.

57. Kloppenborg, *Christ's Associations*, Kindle Location 4754-8.

58. Lee, *The Lord's Supper in Corinth*, Kindle Location 3282-3 of 6673.

59. Lee, *The Lord's Supper in Corinth*, Kindle Location 1128-39 of 6673.

60. For an important discussion of the range of possible early Christian meeting places, see Edward Adams, *The Earliest Christian Meeting Places*; and Adams, "First-Century Models for Paul's Churches," 60-78. Kloppenborg agrees with Adams' work, but notes that stratified seating arrangements were entrenched irrespective of physical locations. See Kloppenborg, *Christ's Associations*, chapter 3.

61. Gunton, *Intellect and Action*, 117.

nots" (τοὺς μὴ ἔχοντας, 11:22).[62] Paul employs mockery and irony to condemn the actions of the "haves" towards the "have nots." Social-scientific reconstructions of associations at Corinth enable insight into his political and social rhetoric.[63]

Schisms had developed in the Corinthian community to the extent that Paul contends that their gatherings are "not for the better but for the worse" (11:17). In gathering for the worse, the "haves" enact their social privilege in ways that shame and humiliate the "have nots" by reinforcing social stratifications.[64] The schisms are related to the inequality of food and drink distributions at the meal where some go hungry and others get drunk (11:22). Given the background of Roman associational meals, these divisions accord with the likely competitive behaviours within the social dynamics of such meals. Paul criticizes the competitive behaviour of the "haves" at the banquet as it not only denigrates and shames the "have nots," but also distorts the Church's sociality and polity such that it is not really the Lord's Supper that they eat (11:20).[65] Instead of eating the Lord's Supper (κυριακὸν δεῖπνον), Paul sarcastically chides "the haves" for reducing the meal to a private banquet (ἴδιον δεῖπνον, 11:21) that, as Gunton argues, undermines the Church's eschatological identity.[66]

There is debate concerning the specific behaviours Paul addresses regarding the Lord's Supper. Some argue that the temporal reference of προλαμβάνω (to take beforehand, 11:21) taken in conjunction with Paul's command ἀλλήλους ἐκδέχεσθε (wait for one another, 11:33), suggests that the wealthier members arrived early and feasted whilst the poor arrived late as a result of long working hours.[67] However, Kloppenborg and Lee hold that this projects post-industrial

---

62. The use of "haves" and "have nots" to discuss the factions at Corinth is a common scholarly convention drawn from Paul's condemnation of those whose behaviour humiliates those who have nothing (or "have not" μὴ γὰρ οἰκίας οὐκ ἔχετε εἰς τὸ ἐσθίειν καὶ πίνειν; ἢ τῆς ἐκκλησίας τοῦ θεοῦ καταφρονεῖτε, καὶ καταισχύνετε τοὺς μὴ ἔχοντας; 1 Cor 11:22). See Welborn, "How 'Democratic' Was the Pauline *Ekklēsia*?" 309, and Rhodes, "Formative Feasting," 258.

63. Welborn, "How 'Democratic' Was the Pauline *Ekklēsia*?" 299.

64. Rhodes, "Formative Feasting," 264–6. See also Michael J. Rhodes, "Arranging the Chairs in the Beloved Community: The Politics, Problems, and Prospects of Multi-Racial Congregations in I Corinthians and Today," *Studies in Christian Ethics*, 33 (2020): 517–20.

65. In the setting of Roman associational meal practices, κυριακὸν δεῖπνον can also mean Emperor's banquet or imperial banquet. See Kloppenborg, "Precedence at the Communal Meal in Corinth," 168.

66. Kloppenborg, *Christ's Associations*, Kindle Location 5087 of 13065. See Gunton, *Father, Son and Holy Spirit*, 230–4.

67. For example, see C. K. Barrett, *The First Epistle to the Corinthians* (New York: Harper and Row, 1968), 262; Gerd Theissen, *The Social Setting of Pauline Christianity*, ed. and trans. John H. Schütz (Edinburgh: T&T Clark, 1982), 151–3; and Barry D. Smith, "The Problem with the Observance of the Lord's Supper in the Corinthian Church," *Bulletin for Biblical Research*, 20 (2010): 536–9.

revolution caricatures of the idle rich and the working poor on to the text.⁶⁸ Instead of over-employment, the seasonal demand for products created structural unemployment in ancient economies and agrarian societies. Within the domestic sphere, wealthy patrons employed large households of slaves to display the owner's status and avoid the undignified reliance on external workers.⁶⁹ Kloppenborg concludes there is no reason to think the patterns of proliferation of workers in non-elite households differed from elite households, as economic rationalization was not the goal.⁷⁰

Instead, Kloppenborg argues for a non-temporal reading of προλαμβάνω (11:21) as "devours" instead of "to take beforehand," and ἐκδέχεσθε (11:33) as "receive/welcome" or "entertain" one another rather than "wait" for one another.⁷¹ Taken as non-temporal verbs, the stress of the text is on those devouring preferential portions rather than lateness. Similarly, Kloppenborg contends that Paul commands them to receive/welcome one another, rather than to wait for one another.⁷² On this account, it is competitive behaviours and individual performances of status that are hallmarks of gathering for the worse as they threaten the collective values of the community, a common issue in Roman associations.

Paul's condemnation of the behaviour of the "haves" demands a distinct body politic for the Christ gatherings instead of their mimicking of existing forms of sociality and polity. "Thus, in insisting that there be no divisions and hierarchically differential consumption of the Lord's Supper in the *ekklēsia* but rather an expression of the solidarity of the community, he is also insisting that his assembly's celebration be dramatically different from the usual meal patterns in which differences in status were affirmed and embodied."⁷³

In his attack on the behaviours of the "haves," Paul seeks to overturn the asymmetrical reciprocity and power dynamics that are enmeshed in the honour

---

68. Kloppenborg, *Christ's Associations*, Kindle Location 5020–81 of 13065. Lee and Kloppenborg cite evidence that shows the wealthy elite were often late to meals. "*None of the association bylaws we know thought to comment on late arrival as an issue of concern … the ancient reader, attuned to the metrics of group honor, seems to have been more worried about absenteeism, since this endangered the honor of the group. Late arrival was evidently not an issue.*" Kloppenborg, *Christ's Associations*, Kindle Location 5034–9 of 13065.

69. Kloppenborg, *Christ's Associations*, Kindle Location 5043–66 of 13065.

70. Kloppenborg, *Christ's Associations*, Kindle Location 5071 of 13065.

71. Kloppenborg, "Precedence at the Communal Meal in Corinth," 198–201. See also Lee, *The Lord's Supper in Corinth*, Kindle Location 1676–94 of 6673 and Winter, *After Paul Left Corinth*, 144–52.

72. Kloppenborg, "Precedence," 202. See also Kloppenborg, *Christ's Associations*, Kindle Location 5071–5111 of 13065; Lee, *The Lord's Supper in Corinth*, Kindle Location 1675–1737 of 6673; and Rhodes, "Formative Feasting," 289–90.

73. Horsley, "The First and Second Letters to the Corinthians," 235.

and shame codes of patronage and beneficence.[74] Paul's horror, as Gunton argues, is that the continuance of economic and social divisions undermines the Church's eschatological identity that is rooted in Christ by the Spirit. The Church's distinct eschatological identity is displayed in its embodied life; a social and political reality that does things differently from other institutions.[75] "Its due ordering is disrupted by greed, insensitivity and the importing from the outside world of social divisions which," Gunton stresses, "are forbidden in the new order in Jesus Christ."[76] Paul deplores the use of honour and shame conventions at the Lord's Supper, and stresses God's inversion of the reciprocal expectations of patronage and power through Christ's self-giving action on the cross. Ambitious clamoring for prestige and power misconstrues the proclamation and embodiment of the Supper and despises the Church of God (1 Cor 11:22).[77] "Honor no longer comes from the acknowledgment of good deeds or benefaction by one's equals .... Honor comes from God, who represents abundance: 'for the earth and its fullness are the Lord's' (1 Cor 11:26)."[78]

Instead of the honour and shame code, Paul asserts strong fictive kinship groups based on communal upbuilding, mutual servanthood, and power in weakness. Furthermore, as Rachel McCrae argues, the intrinsic link between acts of beneficence and the bestowal of honours is theologically severed as "[it] is God who is now the supreme patron and source of all beneficence."[79] The host of this meal is Christ himself, not any earthly dignitary or patron, and the Church is

---

74. McRae, "Eating with Honor," 180. John K. Chow provides a helpful outline of Roman patronage in John K. Chow, *Patronage and Power: A Study of Social Networks in Corinth*, JSNTSS 75 (Sheffield: Sheffield Academic Press, 1992), 30–3. See also Gregg Gardner, "Jewish Leadership and Hellenistic Civic Benefaction in the Second Century BCE," *JBL*, 126 (2007): 327–43.

75. Gunton, *Intellect and Action*, 98–9. See also Gunton, *Father, Son and Holy Spirit*, 223.

76. Gunton, *The Christian Faith*, 132.

77. Rhodes, "Formative Feasting," 269.

78. McRae, "Eating with Honor," 180.

79. McRae, "Eating with Honor," 180. On Paul's critique and inversion of patronage in the wider Corinthian correspondence, see David J. Downs, *The Offering of the Gentiles: Paul's Collection for Jerusalem in Its Chronological, Cultural and Cultic Contexts* (Tübingen: Mohr Siebeck, 2008), 127–46; John K. Chow, *Patronage and Power*, 175; Stephen J. Friesen, "Paul and Economics: The Jerusalem Collection as an Alternative to Patronage," in *Paul Unbound: Other Perspectives on the Apostle*, ed. Mark D. Given (Peabody: Hendrickson), 49–51; Winter, *After Paul Left Corinth*, 203–5; Frank J. Matera, *II Corinthians: A Commentary*, New Testament Library (Louisville: Westminster John Knox Press, 2003), 184; Young and Ford, *Meaning and Truth in 2 Corinthians*, 179; Victor Paul Furnish, *II Corinthians: Translated with Introduction, Notes, and Commentary*, Anchor (New York: Doubleday, 1984), 506–7; and Steve Walton, "Paul, Patronage and Pay: What Do We Know about the Apostle's Financial Support?," in *Paul as Missionary: Identity, Activity, Theology, and Practice*, ed. Trevor J. Burke and Brian S. Rosner (London and New York: T&T Clark, 2011), 220–33.

invited to understand that the Lord's Supper is a sharing (κοινωνία) in Christ's body and blood (10:16).[80] It is the *Lord's* Supper, and as Gunton notes, it is Christ who is present as host by the action of the Spirit.[81] Therefore, there are to be no hierarchical divisions, and believers are to imitate Christ and his self-giving.[82]

The apostle uses the meal ritual to create a new Christian social identity based upon humility, mutual servitude, and the love that Jesus taught, and he expects the Christians in Corinth to turn away from the pivotal values of the Mediterranean world. "Paul changes the value system of the Lord's Supper to recognise God as the divine patron, attributive honor as the gift of the Holy Spirit, and distributive honor as a life devoted to servitude and love for others."[83] Through divine action in the economy, the Church's embodiment of the gospel is a form of resistance to the socio-political assumptions underlying the prevailing customs.

The inhabitants of Roman Corinth held honorific competition as a prized cultural value, and it is likely these ambitions and practices are being carried over into the Christian ἐκκλησια.[84] Such ambition is not merely individual competitiveness, but the embodiment of Roman imperial ideals as they are interpreted at Corinth. The ἐκκλησια at Corinth apes the established Roman political and social structures and fails to realize or embody the distinctive way of being the gospel calls forth. Paul's criticisms of the Corinthians' celebration of the Lord's Supper subvert not only the hierarchical social stratifications but also their basis in imperial ideologies. Taussig argues that the early Christian meals are sites of ritual formation in resistance to Roman imperialism.[85] Most obviously, the central celebration of Christ's crucifixion is set in the Roman context where crucifixion is capital punishment for insurrection. The proclamation of Christ's death until he comes reminds the Christ groups that the community's solidarity is centred in "the Roman crucifixion of Jesus as an anti-Roman rebel leader and his vindication in exaltation, from which he will come to terminate the imperial order."[86]

Embedded within the rituals of the Lord's Supper are counter-claims that resist Roman ideologies and invite an understanding of the meal gatherings as a counter-society whose resistance centres in the cross.[87] The ritual libation cup after supper

---

80. Rhodes, "Formative Feasting," 276–7.

81. Gunton, *The Christian Faith*, 133. See also Gunton, *Father, Son and Holy Spirit*, 224–5. As argued in chapter five, Gunton rejects over-realized accounts of the church's relation to Christ and holds that Christ is absent physically as transcendent Lord, but present by the action of the Spirit.

82. Horsley, "The First and Second Letters to the Corinthians," 235.

83. McRae, "Eating with Honor," 181.

84. Last, *The Pauline Church and the Corinthian Ekklēsia*, 158.

85. Taussig, *In the Beginning Was the Meal*, 115.

86. Richard A. Horsley, "The First and Second Letters to the Corinthians," 235.

87. Taussig, *In the Beginning Was the Meal*, 118. See also Rhodes, "Formative Feasting," 272–3 who also notes Paul's deliberate echo of the politically liberative Passover narrative.

celebrates the memory of the Lord Jesus as the patron deity whose death is proclaimed until he comes, and the new covenant in his blood forms social and political loyalty and solidarity.[88] The ritual blessing of the bread, the songs, teachings, and storytelling at the meal utilize the common form of Roman dining but invert their social and political ideologies in and through Christ's crucifixion. "This confrontational subject matter near the heart of most early Christian meals combined with the major interest of these meals in representing an alternative world and its attendant behavior to mark them as events of substantial resistance to Rome."[89]

The meals of the Christ groups invite a shift in imagination and allegiance from the ideologies of Roman imperial power, privilege, and hierarchies to the foolishness of Christ's cross as God's paradoxical divine action and grace. For Paul, it is the cross of Christ that renews the Church, and its understanding of power, and establishes its meal as an anti-imperial performance of an alternative sociological politics. The Church is the community that embeds the politics of the cross in its social, political, and ethical life and culture which the Spirit enables to be an expression of God's eschatological kingdom. As Gunton stresses, "Those who are conformed to Christ's image are ground and pressed along with the wine and bread into a common form: the body of Christ, a fellowship of service which nourishes the world with its love, the blessing of the supper carrying over into an ethic."[90]

Paul's Theology of Foolishness as Social and Political Counter-Testimony

Paul's understanding of the Church's sociality and polity is rooted in the defining reality of Christ's crucifixion as foolishness (μωρία 1 Cor 1:18). In the cross of Christ, God chooses foolishness, and this is a paradox and a scandal to the aspiring elite of Corinth. The foolishness of the cross stands in contrast to the wisdom of the learned elite, who found Paul's account of the inferiority and servility of himself and the Church unappealing and weak.[91] Paul sarcastically condemns the pretensions of the elite who behave as though they reign as kings—an allusion to the satrist's language for abusive patrons (1 Cor 4:8).[92] Instead, Paul images himself

---

88. Taussig, *In the Beginning Was the Meal*, 131–4.

89. Taussig, *In the Beginning Was the Meal*, 139.

90. Gunton, *Intellect and Action*, 118–19.

91. Calvin J. Roetzel, "The Language of War (2 Cor. 10:1–6) and the Language of Weakness (2 Cor. 11:21b–13:10)," *Biblical Interpretation*, 17 (2009): 92. See also C. Andrew Ballard, "Tongue-tied and Taunted: Paul, Poor Rhetoric and Paltry Leadership in 2 Corinthians 5:13," *Journal for the Study of the New Testament*, 37 (2014): 63.

92. Welborn, "How 'Democratic' Was the Pauline *Ekklēsia*?" 299. See also L. L. Welborn, "Inequality in Roman Corinth: Evidence from Diverse Sources Evaluated by a Neo-Ricardian Model," in *The First Urban Churches 2: Roman Corinth*, ed. James R. Harrison and L. L. Welborn (Atlanta: SBL Press, 2016), 73–5; and L. L. Welborn, "The Corinthian Correspondence," in *All Things to All Cultures: Paul among Jews, Greeks, and Romans*, ed. Mark Harding and Alanna Nobbs (Grand Rapids: Eerdmans, 2013), 226–9.

as a fool, a well-known figure in Roman and Greek tragic comedy, and utilizes the buffoonic mimic character whose transgressive behaviours represent a lower-class anti-type of weakness and deficiency.[93] The fool is the anti-thesis of Roman sophistication and the exaggerated behaviours of the role are deliberately repulsive. As the secondary actor in a mime, the fool was a grotesque lower-class buffoon who mimicked the performance of the main actor, "comically misinterpreting and reacting to him."[94]

In response to the elitist assumptions of the Corinthian sophisticates, Paul offers a list of repulsive anti-credentials (1 Cor 4:9-13) that utilizes theatrical foolish discourse and hyperbole to establish apostolic authority through the power of Christ's cross.[95] Laurence Welborn notes that reference to the theatre (θέατρον, 4:9) situates Paul's discourse in the context of a Roman play. God's exhibition of the apostles as last of all (4:9) likely refers to the conclusion of a patron's lavish theatrical entertainment in which the mimes followed various higher aesthetical forms as the "after-pieces."[96] Paul's striking description of his paradoxical experience as an apostle captures the social experience of mimes, most of whom were slaves that the social elite held in contempt. Welborn proposes that Paul portrays himself as the well-known character of a befuddled orator whose ramblings reveal his weakness and lack of training in the skills and arts of rhetoric and oratory (2:1-5).[97] As the wise fool, Paul self-identifies with those deemed poor, weak, deformed, grotesque, and marginalized "to rebuke the educational privilege and social authority of the Corinthian elite."[98] Instead of established Roman ideals for leadership, Paul offers the paradoxical wisdom of Christ's crucifixion as a contemptible Roman slave, which, despite Corinthian protestations, survives all ridicule through God's vindication.

Through his role-play of the fool, Paul comes to accept foolishness as the gift of following Christ's cruciform way. "Because Paul believes that, in the cross of Christ, God has affirmed nothings and nobodies, he is able to embrace the role of the fool as the authentic mode of his own existence."[99] Paul's theology of foolishness draws

---

93. L. L. Welborn, *Paul, the Fool of Christ: A Study of 1 Corinthians 1-4 in the Comic-Philosophic Tradition* (London: T&T Clark, 2005), 34-48. See also Laurence L. Welborn, "The Runaway Paul," *The Harvard Theological Review*, 92 (1999): 122-31.

94. Laurence L. Welborn, "Μωρός γένεσθω: Paul's Appropriation of the Role of the Fool in 1 Corinthians 1-4," *Biblical Interpretation*, 10 (2002): 424. "[Paul's] identification with this social type involves a conscious appropriation of the corresponding theatrical role." Welborn, *Paul, the Fool of Christ*, 50.

95. Welborn, *Paul, the Fool of Christ*, 83-6.

96. Welborn, "Μωρός γένεσθω," 428-9. "The Greek word is θέατρον, which is, first of all, a building, a place for public assemblies, and then, as here, what one sees at a theater, a play."

97. Welborn, "Μωρός γένεσθω," 430.

98. Welborn, *Paul, the Fool of Christ*, 116.

99. Welborn, *Paul, the Fool of Christ*, 250.

from this well-known repulsive comic character to reveal God's paradoxical action in the cross of Christ. The foolish paradox of the cross redefines expectations of leadership and the Church's understanding of rank and status. The Corinthian performance of the Lord's Supprt defies Paul's theology of foolishness which has its basis in the cross of Christ. As Rhodes argues, "their meals are unfitting and unworthy to be called the Lord's because they fail to embody the character of the Lord's own status-destroying other-loving Supper."[100] Through the cross, God dismantles Roman ideologies of power and social stratification, and offers a doctrine of election that is entirely distinct from Roman hierarchies.

Cruciform Foolishness and God's Electing Purposes

God's embrace of foolishness shapes the politics of belonging in the Church and extends Gunton's insights regarding the Church's elect calling to a distinct way of being, a form of culture, that anticipates the redemption of all things. Gunton's emphasis on the temporal aspects of election opens horizons on the concrete particularities of the Church's calling to display God's purposes in the world that can be filled out further from socio-cultural readings of 1 Corinthians.

In Gunton's thought, the Church's election is a representative calling to be a distinct community whose common life and culture are enabled by the Spirit to sometimes anticipate God's universal purposes.[101] Paul's theology of foolishness enriches and extends Gunton's insights through God's choice, or election, of the marginalized and disenfranchised to be the centre of the Church's life. God's paradoxical election shapes the Church's polity and sociality in and through the experience of marginality and disenfranchisement in resistance to sedimented structures of power. It is not so much that the social is founded on the salvific, but, as Rhodes suggests, the social is an aspect of the salvific.

> [In] speaking of the God whose gospel includes choosing the 'have nots' precisely to bring to naught worldly social hierarchies (11:26-29) and the powers of this age that embrace them (2:6), we would be closer to the mark to declare that the social is *one constitutive aspect of* the salvific. Indeed, following the explicitly social line of Paul's argument reveals the depth of his theology.[102]

In the conflict at Corinth, Paul intervenes on behalf of the disenfranchised and marginalized to proclaim God's electing purposes that are to be displayed in the Church's concrete life.

In paradoxical contradiction to the values of these elite Christians, Paul asserts: "But God chose (ἐξελέξατο ὁ θεός) the foolish of the world, in order to shame the

---

100. Rhodes, "Formative Feasting," 282.
101. Gunton, *Father, Son and Holy Spirit*, 178.
102. Rhodes, "Formative Feasting," 283–4.

wise, ... the weak of the world, in order to shame the strong, ... the low-born of the world and the despised, things that are nothing, to nullify the things that are."
(1 Cor 1.27-8)[103]

Set against the increasingly oligarchic context of first-century Corinth, Welborn maintains that the democratic character of the Corinthian ἐκκλησία "appears more pronounced and unmistakable."[104] God's election of those regarded as nothings and nobodies undermines entrenched assumptions of privilege, power, and social stratification.

The logic of the Church's sociological politics is, at root, theological. "The logic of the crucial paragraph in 1 Cor 1.26-31 seems to be this: the sociological fact that the majority of those who experienced the 'calling' of the gospel were uneducated, poor and low-born led Paul to the conclusion that God had chosen the multitude of the nothings and nobodies."[105] When it comes to the politics of belonging in the Church, "Paul assures this multitude of nobodies, 'all things are yours' (πάντα γὰρ ὑμῶν ἐστιν, 1 Cor 3.21)."[106] Yet, Paul's account of the Church is not that of a flat democracy. God establishes a body that gives greater honour and dignity to those who appear weaker. The cross of Christ reveals that God has no regard for preexisting social capital or social stratification. Instead, the politics of God's electing purposes privilege the marginalized and those who lack honour and dignity.[107]

Cruciform Foolishness and the Body of Christ

In stressing the need for unity in the Church, Paul utilizes and subverts the common Roman political metaphor of the hegemonic body that compares the body-politic with the human body (1 Cor 12:12-31). This was a conservative Roman metaphor that reinforced the natural order and unity of Rome's hierarchical stratification of the social body in which the strong rule the weak. The Emperor was the head of a unified body, whose natural order brought "peace and security, while subjugating all others to this rule."[108] Yet, for Paul, the Church has an entirely different

103. Welborn, "How 'Democratic' Was the Pauline *Ekklēsia*?" 303. Welborn cites Alain Badiou's observation that Paul's language is "the most radical statement" in the history of the West. Alain Badiou, *Saint Paul: The Foundation of Universalism*, trans. Ray Brassier (Stanford: Stanford University Press, 2003), 47, cited in Welborn, "How 'Democratic' Was the Pauline *Ekklēsia*?": 303–4.

104. Welborn, "How 'Democratic' Was the Pauline *Ekklēsia*?" 302.

105. Welborn, "How 'Democratic' Was the Pauline *Ekklēsia*?" 307.

106. Welborn, "How 'Democratic' Was the Pauline *Ekklēsia*?" 307.

107. Rhodes, "Arranging the Chairs in the Beloved Community," 521–3.

108. Yung Suk Kim, *Christ's Body in Corinth: The Politics of a Metaphor* (Minneapolis: Fortress Press, 2008), 49. See also Rhodes, "Arranging the Chairs in the Beloved Community," 521–3; Horsley, "The First and Second Letters to the Corinthians," 235; Welborn, "The Corinthian Correspondence," 223; and Dale B. Martin, *The Corinthian Body* (New Haven: Yale University Press, 1995), 87–136.

body politic that subverts the conservative Roman usage and problematizes elite assumptions about social stratifications. Instead of the hierarchical social stratification of society, the superior are not to claim greater honour and instead must recognize the indispensability of those society deems inferior (1 Cor 12:22-26). Again, the basis of the Church's sociality and polity is not charity, but God's electing action, which is indicated by the use of an *inclusio* as a directing tool: "But as it is, God arranged the members of the body (12:18) ... But God has so arranged the body (12:24)." Anthony Thiselton argues that translations of the second aorist middle indicative ἔθετο as "God arranged," "God appointed," or even "God set," weaken the sense in which divine election of an individual is "inextricably bound up with his purposes for an individual within (ἐν with the dative) the Church."[109]

It is God's electing action that determines how the Church is composed and crafted together, not the prevailing elitist assumptions of Corinthian society.[110] "But in Paul's community, honor is given to all, not by social status but by God's radical love and justice. All in Paul's community are equal partners of God's Church."[111] More than mere equality, though, Paul argues that God has a preferential option for the marginalized and deliberately privileges those who are conceived socially as inferior. In Paul's body language, the less presentable and respectable body parts (12:22-23) are a likely euphemism for male genitals. Paul's deployment of this language "suggests that such parts not only play an essential role within the body, but also that their 'unpresentableness' is socially constructed."[112] God actively chooses to order the Church to give greater honour to those parts that are socially constructed as inferior. Gathering for the better is not merely an apolitical democratic notion of togetherness, but the subversion of societal norms of power and privilege that are carried over into the Church. Whilst Paul's democratic impulse is important, it arises from the theological conviction that God has arranged the body in this paradoxical and foolish manner.[113]

The use of the body in 1 Corinthians alludes to the corporate nature of embodied fellowship and its witness to God's eschatological purposes.[114] "The Church is

---

109. Thiselton, *The First Epistle to the Corinthians*, 1004.

110. Thiselton notes that the verb συνεκέρασεν (first aorist indicative) is used of a painter mixing colours, or a musician composing a harmony. He concludes, "No role or way of mixing the compound lies outside the sovereign choice of God. It is only God's **giving** (δούς, aorist participle of δίδωμι) that provides objective grounds for one's place within *the body*." Thiselton, *The First Epistle to the Corinthians*, 1010.

111. Yung Suk Kim, "Reclaiming Christ's Body (*soma chrisou*): Embodiment of God's Gospel in Paul's Letters," *Interpretation*, 67 (2013): 22.

112. Rhodes, "Arranging the Chairs in the Beloved Community," 522, citing Martin, *The Corinthian Body*, 95–6.

113. Welborn, "How 'Democratic' Was the Pauline *Ekklēsia*?" 304.

114. David J. Downs, "Physical Weakness, Illness and Death in 1 Corinthians 11:30: Deprivation and Overconsumption in Pauline and Early Christianity," *NTS*, 65 (2019): 574–5.

to work out this reality *as a countercultural community*, within which believer's statuses are radically redefined, regardless of whether their location in Greco-Roman social strata is changed."[115] The paradoxical body of Christ is the social and political manifestation of God's paradoxical gospel, whose centre is found in Paul's theology of foolishness that undermines social privilege and demolishes "hierarchies from the inside out."[116]

In his polemic against the Corinthian's gathering for the worse, Paul demands they reject Roman ideas of competition for social rank and status. Instead, they are to gather for the better and embrace the foolishness of the cross. Paul's call to receive/welcome one another is (11:33), therefore, a call to display God's eternal purposes for humanity through the radical hospitality of sharing a full meal together in community that betrays Roman ideals for the sake of witness to Christ's cross. It is through receiving one another in practical acts of love and mutuality, irrespective of rank or status, that the congregation receives Christ and embodies God's electing purposes.[117]

Implications for the Church's Culture Today: Disability, Ecclesiology, and the Politics of Belonging in Community

Paul's theology of foolishness demands the overcoming and dismantling of the powers that are embedded in the structures of society and the Church through the foolish power of Christ's cross. As Rhodes rightly observes, Paul's body politics challenges the Church's entanglement with the modern racial condition and the hierarchies of power that arise from hegemonies such as race, class, gender, and ability/disability.[118] In Gunton's terms, such ecclesial gatherings for the worse fail to offer the Church's common life as a sacrifice of praise to God. Communion with one another is broken by improper hegemonies such as white privilege and ableism, and so too the Church's communion with God—the Supper is no longer the *Lord's* Supper. What is required is not a democratic demand for unity in an unchanged ecclesial power dynamic, a kind of balancing of the books, but receiving/welcoming and privileging the socially marginalized in their otherness and particularity, whatever the happy or unhappy consequences.[119]

---

115. Helen Morris, "The City as Foil (Not Friend nor Foe): Conformity and Subversion in 1 Corinthians 12:12-31," in *The Urban World of the First Christians*, ed. Steve Walton, Paul R. Trebilco, and David W. J. Gill (Grand Rapids: Eerdmans, 2017), 145.

116. Rhodes, "Arranging the Chairs in the Beloved Community," 522.

117. Rhodes, "Formative Feasting," 290.

118. Rhodes, "Arranging the Chairs in the Beloved Community," 524-6.

119. Rhodes, "Arranging the Chairs in the Beloved Community," 526-8. For my own explorations of the confluences of theology, church, and power in relation to ableism and whiteness, see Picard, "No Longer Strangers," 53-72; and Picard, "From Whiteness Towards Witness," 241-68.

Paul's demand to privilege the socially undesirable sheds particular light on the Church's welcome of people with disabilities. In her important book *The Disabled God*, Nancy Eiesland highlights the exclusive structures of the Church's body language, which she identifies as the conscious and unconscious meanings embedded in the Church's rituals, practices, structures, and traditions. "In the church, the body practices are the physical discourse of inclusion and exclusion. These practices reveal the hidden 'membership roll,' those whose bodies matter in the shaping of liturgies and services."[120] Eiesland, a wheelchair user and person with a disability, finds the sharing of the Eucharist as a dreaded and humiliating remembrance. For all the Church's attempts at inclusion, she finds the Church's "architectural barriers, ritual practices, demeaning body aesthetics, unreflective speech, and bodily reactions" leave her feeling like a trespasser in an able-bodied kingdom.[121] At the Eucharist, whilst able-bodied people fill the front of the sanctuary and kneel to receive communion, ushers signal to Eiesland that she need not go forward because she is a wheelchair user. Instead, she is offered the sacrament alone in her seat, after everyone else has been served. As a result, the sacrament is transformed from a corporate reality to a solitary one. The Eucharist shifts "from a sacrilization of Christ's broken body to a stigmatization of my disabled body."[122] The Church, for Eiesland, is a "city on a hill" which is "physically inaccessible and socially inhospitable" for people with disabilities.[123]

The Church has a long and sordid history of exclusion and violence towards people with disabilities, and, as Bill Hughes, a sociologist and disability scholar, observes, it functioned as one of the vital powers in modernity's civilizing mission.[124] Modernity's obsession with order building positioned the disabled body as abnormal in the tyranny of normalcy. Modernity's construct of the normative "clean and proper" body is the self-sufficient male subject, and disabled bodies are the messy and unruly inverse reflection. "In the kingdom of the 'clean and proper body', disability is the epitome of 'what not to be.'"[125] Disability and human difference are pathologized in modernity's somatic hierarchies that deem

---

120. Nancy L. Eiesland, *The Disabled God: Toward a Liberatory Theology of Disability* (Nashville: Abingdon, 1994), 112.

121. Nancy Eiesland, "Encountering the Disabled God," *The Other Side*, 38 (2002): 10.

122. Eiesland, "Encountering the Disabled God," 10.

123. Eiesland, "Encountering the Disabled God," 10.

124. Bill Hughes, "Civilising Modernity and the Ontological Invalidation of Disabled People," in *Disability and Social Theory: New Developments and Directions*, ed. Dan Goodley, Bill Hughes, and Lennard Davis (London: Palgrave Macmillan, 2012), 19–21. See also Bill Hughes, "Impairment on the Move: The Disabled Incomer and Other Invalidating Intersections," *Disability and Society*, 32 (2017): 470–2; Bill Hughes, *A Historical Sociology of Disability: Human Validity and Invalidity from Antiquity to Early Modernity* (London: Routledge, 2020), chapters 5 and 6; and Brian Brock and John Swinton, eds., *Disability in the Christian Tradition: A Reader* (Grand Rapids: Eerdmans, 2012).

125. Hughes, "Civilising Modernity," 22.

the strange other "as 'dirt' as 'matter out of place.'"[126] The stranger's strangeness threatens "to poison the comfort of order with suspicion of chaos."[127]

In modernity's order-building project, difference and otherness were corrected, ordered, and assimilated or else excluded, banished and hidden from view. Disability was treated through medicalization and the horrors of eugenics, sterilization, shock therapies, and psychosurgery in the war against alterity.[128] People with disabilities endured the "great confinement" of total institutions, in which their difference was exorcised behind the thickest of stone walls and they were laid to rest in "a state of suspended extinction."[129] The great confinement is an act of purification to preserve the ideals of a pure society. As Hughes writes, "[the] science of rehabilitation was the bourgeois solution to the demon of imperfection. If the demon could be exorcised then the 'cleansed' individual could be returned to the orderly world. If not, then she was confined forever in the invisible spaces behind the high walls where the 'others' lived."[130]

Hughes utilizes the work of Zygmunt Bauman, a Polish social theorist, to observe the different forms of exclusion that result for people with disabilities in the shift from solid modernity to liquid modernity. In his later writing, Gunton also draws upon Bauman's analysis of modernity and postmodernity. What follows extends Hughes' use of Bauman in relation to disability in liquid modernity by drawing from a wider array of Bauman's more recent scholarship.[131]

The shift from solid modernity, and the society of producers, to liquid modernity, and the society of consumers, has created a very different relationship to strangeness. The rise of globalization has resulted in the normalization of otherness, difference, and strangeness. The ordered society of solid modernity, with its heavy structures, has been melted into liquid modern flux, flow, and change. Globalization has ushered in the rise of the global free-market economy, mass communication, technology, global travel, and the development of the global village. Human mobility has drastically increased and cartographic boundaries are of little significance. Coupled with this is the despatialization of time, mass migration, and the spatial compression of the world. Liquid modernity has

---

126. Bill Hughes, "Bauman's Strangers: Impairment and the Invalidation of Disabled People in Modern and Postmodern Cultures," *Disability and Society*, 17 (2002): 573.

127. Zygmunt Bauman, *Modernity and Ambivalence* (Cambridge: Polity Press, 1991), 56.

128. Hughes, "Bauman's Strangers," 575–6.

129. Zygmunt Bauman, *Postmodernity and Its Discontents* (Cambridge: Polity Press, 1997), 19. See also Hughes, "Bauman's Strangers," 575.

130. Hughes, "Bauman's Strangers," 575–6.

131. The sustained use of Zygmunt Bauman's work in relation to Gunton is appropriate given that Gunton himself utilized Bauman's analysis of modernity. Indeed, Bauman's analysis of solid modernity and liquid modernity accords with Gunton's interpretation of the ailments of Western culture. On Gunton's use of Bauman, see Gunton, *The Promise of Trinitarian Theology*, 162–3.

melted solid human collectives such as society, citizenship, and nationhood, and disturbed settled categories of "us" and "them." Liquid modern life, Chris Rumford suggests, is marked not simply by the rise of strangers but the development of the universal condition of strangeness.[132] The stranger has moved from invisibility and confinement to visibility and the un-excludability of otherness.[133] "The 'other' comes out into the world and shows herself and will not go away."[134] Liquid modernity has resulted in the decarceration of people with disabilities from total institutions, which now face a social reckoning for the horrors of their systemic abuse.[135] But whilst the forms of amelioration of the stranger have changed, many of the oppressive impulses towards the stranger appear in new guises.

The rise of globalized consumer capitalism has recast everything in the image of the consumer market as commodities to be bought and sold in a market-mediated world. Consumers are defined first and foremost as *homo eligens* ("the chooser").[136] Freedom is the freedom to choose from a range of consumer products. In online shopping, consumer products are set in the role of the docile and obedient Cartesian object, whilst consumers are raised to the rank of the emancipated sovereign subject.[137] It is not only goods that are recast into the mould of the market, the consumer is also recast as a sellable commodity.[138] The burden of meaning-making and identity formation is no longer found in stable local communities, which are on the move, or large human collectives such as national identity and citizenship. Instead, it falls upon the shoulders of the individual and their life-politics.[139]

The society of consumers brings modernity's turn to the individual home to roost. Now, each emancipated individual must create desire and demand for themselves and bear the responsibility for their social acceptability, and bear it individually.[140] Identities are projects in need of constant attention as the pace of change means that remaining a desirable product is a sentence to hard labour and insecurity.[141] Those who are not fleet-footed enough to keep up with the style pack risk exclusion, stigmatization, and social estrangement. For people

132. Chris Rumford, *The Globalization of Strangeness* (New York: Palgrave Macmillan, 2013), 10–21.

133. Ulrich Beck, "For a Cosmopolitan Outlook," http://www.euroalter.com/2010/ulrich-beck-for-a-cosmopolitan-outlook/.

134. Hughes, "Bauman's Strangers," 579.

135. In Aotearoa New Zealand, the Government has established a Royal Commission of Inquiry into Abuse in Care to examine historic state-based and faith-based abuse.

136. Zygmunt Bauman, *Consuming Life* (Cambridge: Polity, 2007), 61.

137. Bauman, *Consuming Life*, 16–17.

138. Bauman, *Consuming Life*, 57. See also Zygmunt Bauman and Leonidas Donskis, *Moral Blindness: The Loss of Sensitivity in Liquid Modernity* (Cambridge: Polity, 2013), 28. Bauman suggests that the Liquid Modern version of the Cartesian *cogito* is "I am seen, therefore I am," and the more I am seen the more I am.

139. Zygmunt Bauman, *Liquid Modernity* (Cambridge: Polity, 2000), 3–8.

140. Bauman, *Consuming Life*, 56–61.

141. Bauman, *Consuming Life*, 110–11.

with disabilities, liquid modernity may have resulted in the decarceration from total institutions, but the commodification of personhood creates new forms of exclusion and estrangement.

Bauman observes that there are collateral casualties in consumerism. The collateral casualties are the uncommoditized men and women who are "flawed consumers." Through their supposed poor choices, sloth, or lack of skill, they have failed to capitalize on consumer freedom and all the life chances on offer.[142] Social acceptability is individualized in consumerism, and Bauman's "flawed consumers" are those individuals who have failed to exercise their rights as a consumer. They now must lick their individual wounds alone and in private.[143] In solid modernity, the solid structures of the state took primary responsibility for the poor and the disabled. In the highly individualized environment of consumerism the responsibility is shifted primarily on to the individual.

Consumerism offers individuals the right to sovereign self-assertion through consumer choice, however, not every individual can act equally on that right.[144] Individuals may create themselves as a desirable product for others to "friend," "follow," or "tag," yet some are freer than others. People with disabilities face widespread social, political, and environmental barriers which significantly limit this supposed freedom. Stigmatization, discrimination, lack of adequate healthcare and rehabilitation services, inaccessible information, and lack of participation in decisions which directly affect them all contribute to the barriers people with disabilities face. These barriers contribute to people with disabilities experiencing poorer health, lower educational achievements, fewer economic opportunities, and higher rates of poverty than people without disabilities.[145]

People with disabilities are often among the collateral casualties of consumerism and have to face the exclusion and stigmatization that comes in consumerism with being a source of "unfreedom." In the past, the pain of those excluded or stigmatized was treated as a collective issue that required a collective response such as total institutions. In the highly individualized society of consumerism, people with disabilities must find biographical solutions to systemic problems. The state, the Church, and unions are no longer solid structures to which people with disabilities can connect. Freedom in the liquid modern version of life is freedom *from* the other and any of the burdening demands that they might make upon other solo performers. As Bauman argues, "the collateral victim of the leap to the

---

142. Zygmunt Bauman, *Collateral Damage: Social Inequalities in a Global Age* (Cambridge: Polity, 2011), 8.

143. Bauman, *Collateral Damage*, 151–6.

144. Bauman, *Collateral Damage*, 64–7.

145. Alana Officer and Tom Shakespeare, "The World Report on Disability and People With Intellectual Disabilities," *Journal of Policy and Practice in Intellectual Disabilities*, 10 (2013): 86.

consumerist rendition of freedom prevalent in the 'liquid' phase of modernity is the Other as the prime object of ethical responsibility and moral concern."[146]

Community in Liquid Modernity

In liquid modernity, the idealized community offers freedom and security together in the right doses—the security of holding hands and the freedom to let go.[147] There is the individual freedom to move and explore, but also security from any burden-creating, space-reducing, or guilt-inducing other who limits individual freedom, flexibility, or independence. Relationships are "pure relations" that are offered on commodified terms with "no strings attached."[148] Life in liquid modernity is to be enjoyed, not suffered. The sovereign individual is given the security of knowing they can "block," "unfriend," or "hide" any space invaders who may spoil their freedom. Responsibility for the other morphs into responsibility for oneself.[149]

Relationships and community are patterned on the relationship between buyer and commodities bought. "Commodities are not expected to outstay their welcome and must leave the stage of life once they start to clutter it up."[150] At the same time, buyers do not and are not expected to swear loyalty to their purchases. "Relationships of the consumerist type are, from the start, 'until further notice.'"[151] Care for the other is measured by the level of unfreedom that such care would create. Bauman concludes that whilst a "consumerist attitude may lubricate the wheels of the economy; it sprinkles sand into the bearings of morality."[152]

Bauman examines consumer community spaces and notes that they are designed for the mis-meeting of strangers. Mis-meetings are the chance interactions in malls, cinemas, cafés, resorts, and airport lounges which have no past or future, and are "not to be continued."[153] These "empty places" are designed for mis-meetings which are marked by the culture of civility. Empty spaces are purified places that offer security from any meddlers, loiterers, beggars, or intruders who invade the consumer's precious space.[154] Attendees are secure in the knowledge that no person's particularity will be allowed to impinge upon their freedom. Encounters in empty places may be unavoidable, but they are designed to be brief and shallow

---

146. Zygmunt Bauman, *The Art of Life* (Cambridge: Polity, 2008), 108.

147. Zygmunt Bauman, *Community: Seeking Safety in an Insecure World* (Cambridge: Polity Press, 2001), 19–20. See also Zygmunt Bauman, *Culture in a Liquid Modern World* (Cambridge: Polity Press, 2011), 20–1.

148. Bauman and Donskis, *Moral Blindness*, 14.

149. Zygmunt Bauman, *Does Ethics Have a Chance in a World of Consumers?* (Cambridge, MA and London: Harvard University Press, 2008), 54.

150. Bauman, *The Art of Life*, 15.

151. Bauman, *The Art of Life*, 15.

152. Bauman and Donskis, *Moral Blindness*, 15.

153. Bauman, *Liquid Modernity*, 95–6.

154. Bauman, *Liquid Modernity*, 97–8.

as everyone is just passing through. "Shopping/consuming places offer what no 'real reality' outside may deliver: the near-perfect balance between freedom and security."[155]

Unlike solid modern institutions, empty spaces are not cleansed of strangeness, alterity, or otherness. Their appeal is found in the kaleidoscopic difference that is present, whilst simultaneously ensuring that all differences are neutered, sterilized, and tamed.[156] "Empty spaces are first and foremost empty of *meaning*. Not that they are meaningless because of being empty: it is because they carry no meaning, nor are believed to be able to carry one, that they are seen as empty."[157] In such meaning-resistant spaces, it is a condition of entry that the particularities of the individual's identity are left at the door. Unlike the high street, one is unlikely to encounter protests regarding the barriers to inclusion that people with disabilities relentlessly face.[158] Empty spaces embrace diversity and otherness whilst purifying them of their particularities so all difference is neutered.[159] Liquid modern purification is more subtle than its solid modern forebear, but no less radical.

In solid modernity, diversity was confined as part of purified community, but it is celebrated in liquid modernity for the sake of kaleidoscopic community. This celebration of difference and diversity is not, however, a sign of welcome for the stranger's strangeness. bell hooks argues that in a consumer society, minority cultures are depersonalized, instrumentalized, commodified, and consumed as an object of desire in the identity construction of majority culture. Otherness and difference are kitschified as desirable exotic products to be consumed. This process of "eating the other" objectifies the otherness and difference of minority cultures as objects of desire that add spice to the dull dish of mainstream white culture.[160] Far from being empowered in their particularity, the difference and otherness of minority cultures are celebrated in such a way that particularities are rendered invisible and palatable to the majority culture.

Hughes draws on hooks' work to explore disabled ontology in consumer society. Disabled ontology remains pathologized within contemporary culture. People with disabilities are the Other which is not desired nor "eaten." "[Non-disabled] people do not desire a 'bit of the disabled other' and impairment is seldom, if ever, constructed or represented as exotic."[161] The identity markers of disabled ontology are frailty, limitation, dependency, and vulnerability, and these are not desired by people without disabilities. Instead, they are the stuff of Kierkegaardian dread in

155. Bauman, *Liquid Modernity*, 99.
156. Bauman, *Liquid Modernity*, 99–100.
157. Bauman, *Liquid Modernity*, 103.
158. Bauman, *Liquid Modernity*, 105.
159. Bauman, *Liquid Modernity*, 103.
160. bell hooks, *Black Looks: Race and Representation* (Boston: South End Press, 1992), 21.
161. Bill Hughes, "Being Disabled: Towards a Critical Social Ontology for Disability Studies," *Disability and Society*, 22 (2007): 680.

an ableist culture, and constitute a risk to their sense of ontological security.¹⁶² Disabled ontology throws into question the consumerist ideals of autonomous freedom and self-determination which form the basis of empty spaces.

From the Church as an Empty Space to the Church as Meaningful Community

In the society of consumers, diversity and otherness are un-excludable, and churches are faced with the gospel's demand for communities of difference united in Christ in new ways. Yet, consumerism's process of silent silencing absorbs voices of dissent and objection and, without notice, dissipates and dissolves them into the prevailing system.¹⁶³ The culture of civility that typifies empty places is prominent in many contemporary Church contexts, and enables the silent silencing of otherness and difference. The Church as empty space is primarily empty of meaning because in pursuit of the balance between freedom and security, the particularities of personhood have been left at the door. Such neutered and neutral zones may enable togetherness in worship, after-church coffee, and pot-luck lunches, but they do little to address the renewal of the church's sociality, polity, and ethics.

John Swinton, a disability theologian, observes that the Church is marked by a culture of thin inclusion for people with disabilities. His description of thin inclusion typifies Bauman's account of non-spaces.¹⁶⁴ Churches often welcome the presence of people with disabilities to add to their kaleidoscopic diversity, but they also ensure the particularity of their disabled ontology does not disturb the happy balance of freedom and security that shapes the community life. Churches that are empty spaces may ensure people with disabilities are included by the pervasive culture of civility, but such civility does little to ensure people with disabilities belong in the fullness of their disabled particularity.¹⁶⁵

Whilst some are quick to celebrate instances of the Church's diversity and togetherness, they often refuse to reflect on the Church's collusion with the cult of normalcy.¹⁶⁶ Bauman's critique of the language of multiculturalism may well

---

162. Hughes, "Being Disabled," 680.

163. Bauman, *Consuming Life*, 48.

164. John Swinton, "From Inclusion to Belonging: A Practical Theology of Community, Disability and Humanness," *Journal of Religion, Disability and Health*, 16 (2012): 181. Swinton recounts the story of Elaine, an elderly woman with intellectual disabilities. Elaine's experience of Church is for ninety minutes on a Sunday and no more. She experiences thin inclusion and is not invited into the homes of her religious friends, despite desiring this. Swinton argues that Elaine is included, but she does not belong. Her co-worshippers have little desire "to thicken their understanding of her or to invite her to *belong* with them and too [sic] them."

165. Swinton, "From Inclusion to Belonging," 182–5.

166. For an extended analysis of the Church's cult of normalcy, see Thomas E. Reynolds, *Vulnerable Communion: A Theology of Disability and Hospitality* (Grand Rapids: Brazos, 2008).

extend to the cult of normalcy. Multiculturalism, Bauman argues, is often used as a socially conservative term used in bourgeois discourse to blunt discussions about unjust systems of social inequality and turn them into politically neutral celebrations of cultural diversity.[167] Within the Church, Eiesland is similarly critical of the "disabling theology that functionally denies inclusion and justice for many of God's children."[168]

What is required, Swinton argues, is a shift from a culture of inclusion for people with disabilities to a culture of belonging. To be included "you only need to be present," but to belong, "you need to be missed."[169] If you belong, the community is different because you are not there; the body is not whole and it feels empty without you. "Only when your absence stimulates feelings of emptiness will you know that you truly belong. Only when your gifts are longed for can community truly be community."[170] The emptiness that Swinton speaks of is the anti-thesis of empty spaces because it is an emptiness that arises from the church as a meaningful space where disabled particularities make the community whole. Manuele Teofilo, a Samoan person who lives with cerebral palsy, suggests that "if we are to build a connection between people with special needs and a 'normal' person, we must drop all assumptions we have about the other person. We must all play a part in making a world of difference."[171]

The ableist assumptions of modernity's ontology confuse the categories of creator and created. Disabled ontology captures the fundamental nature of createdness—humans are inherently limited, dependent, vulnerable, and in need of relationships to constitute our being. Stanley Hauerwas maintains that people with disabilities reveal the true nature of our creaturely being and the fact that we are constituted by narratives which we do not choose.[172] The hallmarks of disabled ontology, such as dependency, vulnerability, and limitation, are not problems to overcome, but the vital centre of our shared finite humanity. Vulnerability and frailty are universal realities for all human beings. Being able-bodied is at best only temporary as all humans are heading towards impairment. "Impairment, it seems, is destiny."[173] As Hughes rightly states, "the refusal to recognise – and, indeed, celebrate – frailty and imperfection makes each of us a stranger to ourselves."[174]

---

167. Bauman, *Culture in a Liquid Modern World*, 46.
168. Eiesland, "Encountering the Disabled God," 10.
169. Swinton, "From Inclusion to Belonging," 184.
170. Swinton, "From Inclusion to Belonging," 183.
171. Manuele Teofilo, "'He's My Mate': Cerebral Palsy, Church, and the Gift of Friendship," in *Theology and the Experience of Disability: Interdisciplinary Perspectives from Down Under*, ed. Andrew Picard and Myk Habets (Abingdon: Routledge, 2016), 85.
172. Stanley Hauerwas, "Timeful Friends: Living with the Handicapped," in *Critical Reflections on Stanley Hauerwas' Theology of Disability: Disabling Society, Enabling Theology*, ed. John Swinton (Binghamton: Harworth Pastoral Press, 2004), 16.
173. Hughes, "Being Disabled," 675.
174. Hughes, "Bauman's Strangers," 581.

In a vulnerable communion, as Thomas Reynolds outlines it, there is no simplistic dualism between ability and disability, only "a nexus of reciprocity that is based in our vulnerable humanity."[175]

Whilst the emphasis upon vulnerability and universal impairment rightly problematizes the mastery of the non-disabled body, it risks subsuming the particular social and political exclusions of people with disabilities under a biological universal. The ubiquity of impairment creates an abstract universal that, if taken to the extreme, is emptied of the necessary political content required to address the ongoing oppression of people with disabilities.[176] Normalizing vulnerability is an important reminder of our shared human personhood, but, Hughes argues, it offers a fairly hollow scholastic victory for people with disabilities struggling against systemic discrimination.[177] Impairment is the experience and destination of all humanity, but not all humanity share the experience of exclusion, prejudice, and disablement that people with disabilities face. "[Because] we are all impaired or will all become impaired does not mean that we are all treated in the same way."[178] An account of vulnerable ontology may remove the negativity from the categories of impairment and disability, but it does remove the injustices people with disabilities face.[179] The risk with universalizing vulnerability, limitation, and impairment is that it can departicularize the concept of disability and strip it of the necessary political teeth required to confront the injustices, prejudices, and exclusions that many people with disabilities unnecessarily face.

Any account of the Church as a community of belonging for people with disabilities must, as Eiesland contends, engage with the Church's body politics and its hidden forms of oppression.[180] It is the mythologies of ableism and its body politics that need to be problematized, acknowledged, repented of, and dismantled for the Church's right habitation of creation. "This liberating mission is only possible when sisters and brothers with disabilities are integral to the life of the community—when our voices are heard, our experiences honoured, and our gifts allowed to flourish."[181]

The shift from ecclesiologies of inclusion for people with disabilities to ecclesiologies of belonging is motivated by a desire for faithfulness rather than mere moral or political expediency.[182] For Swinton, it is not simply that if the vulnerable are excluded from community the Church must rise up and agitate for political change, even though that should not be excluded. It is that "if the weak

---

175. Thomas E. Reynolds, *Vulnerable Communion: A Theology of Disability and Hospitality* (Grand Rapids: Brazos, 2008), 14.
176. Hughes, "Being Disabled," 677.
177. Hughes, "Being Disabled," 677.
178. Hughes, "Being Disabled," 678.
179. Hughes, "Being Disabled," 680.
180. Eiesland, "Encountering the Disabled God," 10–12.
181. Eiesland, "Encountering the Disabled God," 15.
182. Swinton, "From Inclusion to Belonging," 187.

and vulnerable are excluded from Christian community there is no community. It may look and feel like community but it is no community at all because people are not looking to Jesus."[183] Reflecting on Paul's image of the Church as a body in 1 Cor 12, Swinton highlights that in Paul's thought "it is in the diversity of bodies within the Body that we find unity."[184] The Church is a meaningful community of belonging that is established by the grace of God to be a community of the different. Through the action of the Spirit, the Church embodies God's grace in its common life. The Spirit conforms the Church to the ways of Christ and enables the Church as a meaningful community to offer its paradoxical life in Christ as a living sacrifice of praise. The Church's experience of life in Christ, and in the Spirit, makes a world of difference.[185]

The Church's identity as Christ's body is displayed through its distinct sociality, polity, and ethics that is formed from the cross of Christ. Christ's cross dismantles established powers, such as ableism, and the Spirit empowers the Church, as Christ's body, to attend to the unjust hegemonies that are embedded within its common life. The dismantling of hegemonies such as whiteness, sexism, and ableism in the Church gives witness to the power of the cross and its foolish wisdom. By attending to the politics of belonging in community, the Church not only gathers for the better, but offers its common cultural life together in the Spirit as a sacrifice of praise to God for God's universal purposes in all creation. The Church's sacrifice of praise does not baptize the sedimented structures and powers of society, but offers a way of being in community in which they are dismantled and overcome through the power of Christ's sacrifice.

The preceding exegesis of 1 Corinthians and examination of disability theology builds upon Gunton's account of the Church's elect calling as God's redemptive community who the Spirit enables, from time to time, to display God's purposes in the world. The right human habitation of the world involves the Spirit conforming the Church's politics of belonging in community to the politics of the cross. A socio-political and socio-historical examination of the Lord's Supper at Corinth offers a more concrete account of the politics of belonging which enriches Gunton's theology of community.

183. Swinton, "From Inclusion to Belonging," 187.
184. John Swinton, "From Inclusion to Belonging: Why 'Disabled' Bodies Are Necessary for the Faithfulness of the Church," in *Theology and the Experience of Disability: Interdisciplinary Perspectives from Voices Down Under*, ed. Andrew Picard and Myk Habets (Abingdon: Routledge, 2016), 173.
185. See Roy McCloughry and Wayne Morris, eds., *Making a World of Difference: Christian Reflections on Disability* (London: SPCK, 2002).

Conclusion: The Church's Sociological Politics as Her Sacrifice of Praise

This chapter builds upon Gunton's account of the culmination of human culture in the Church's celebration of the Lord's Supper through an engagement with the cultural sciences. In particular, insights from socio-political and socio-historical readings of 1 Cor 11:17-34 support and extend Gunton's claims. The findings of this exegesis uphold the broad contours of Gunton's communal reading of 1 Cor 11:17-34 and his celebration of the Church's culture and life in communion with God, one another, and creation as a sacrifice of praise. At the same time, these exegetical insights extend Gunton's account of the Lord's Supper by an exploration of the politics of belonging in community. Historical, cultural, and social scientific insights highlight the politics of togetherness that are fundamental to an interpretation of the text. Gunton focuses his work primarily upon resisting the incursion of the legacy of the Enlightenment, as he views it, and he offers little reflection on the politics of inclusion and belonging in community. This chapter, and its exploration of disability theology, shows that Gunton's insights on the theology of culture can be enriched and extended by engagement with the cultural sciences, which illuminate the centrality of the politics of belonging to the Church's sociality and polity.

The Church's elect calling to the right human habitation of the created order in relationship with God, one another, and creation bears witness to Christ's overcoming of the powers of privilege and domination through its redeemed sociality, polity, and ethics—its culture. The Church's embodiment of the foolishness of the cross in its body politic demands that oppressive sedimented structures, such as ableism, are dismantled and overcome by the power of Christ's cross in order that the Church's life is offered as a living sacrifice of praise. This discussion of the Eucharist provides just one example of how Gunton's theology of culture helps us to understand the transformative work of the Spirit in bringing human culture and sociality to its intended goal. While further explorations lie beyond the scope of this book, I have explored some examples in publications elsewhere.[186] In this book, I have sought to explore the fruitfulness of Gunton's theology of culture; this chapter shows the potential for building upon his thought through engagement with the cultural sciences.

---

186. See Picard, "No Longer Strangers," 53-72; Picard, "From Whiteness Towards Witness," 241-68; Andrew Picard, "'On the Way' and 'In the Fray' in Aotearoa: A Pākehā's Covenantal Reflections from the Context of a Treaty People," *Pacific Journal of Baptist Research*, 11 (2016): 44-58; Andrew Picard and Andrew Clark-Howard, "The Christian Settler Imaginary: Repentant Remembrances of Christianity's Entanglement with Settler Colonialism in Aotearoa New Zealand," *Practical Theology*, 15 (2022): 78-91; Andrew Picard and Jordyn Rapana, "'Let Justice Roll Down': Confronting Injustice in Theological Education for Māori Flourishing," *Studies in Christian Ethics*, 36 no. 4 (2023): 783-800; and Andrew Picard, "Unsettling Providential Partnership: A Critical Examination of Robert Maunsell's and George Grey's Partnership in Māori Education," in *Unsettling Theologies: Memory, Identity, and Place*, ed. Michael Mawson and Brian Kolia (Cham: Palgrave Macmillan, 2024), 109-36.

Chapter 7

CONCLUSION

The overarching aim of this book has been to examine Colin Gunton's trinitarian theology of culture and enquire into its ongoing fruitfulness for today. Gunton believes that theology must engage with the pressing intellectual and cultural challenges of its day, and that trinitarian theology provides the necessary resources to address these challenges and offer healing remedies. In Gunton's reckoning, Western culture and philosophy bequeathed a range of abstractive issues that are deeply enmeshed in society, culture, and theology. Gunton outlines the contours of these enmeshments, the details of which can be summarized as a drive to disembodiment and individualism, and its deleterious effects upon human life and theology, especially the doctrine of creation and createdness. His trinitarian theology of culture and its constructive proposals progress over time and take shape in his quest for a more concrete trinitarianism that arises from divine action in the economy. The most significant contributions of Gunton's quest for a more concrete trinitarianism are not, as I have argued, his *analysis* of culture, but his trinitarian *theology* of culture.

Gunton's trinitarian theology of culture is the outcome of his wider trinitarian project and draws especially from his accounts of mediation, creation, Christology, pneumatology, and ecclesiology. Importantly, each of these theological *foci* is enriched by the progression in Gunton's theology from trinitarian analogies to a trinitarian theology of mediation. I contend that it is Gunton's later writings that express his most developed trinitarian theology of culture. In and of themselves, the progressions in his thought, which have been explored in detail, are important, yet it is the combination and constellation of progressions that coalesce to inform Gunton's trinitarian theology of culture. I have sought in this book to fill an important gap in Gunton research, an examination of his trinitarian theology of culture, whilst also correcting what I consider to be some misinterpretations of the heart of Gunton's trinitarian project. Gunton's quest for a more concrete trinitarianism that arises from a sustained engagement with divine action in the economy remains a fruitful resource for the study of a trinitarian theology of culture and its engagement with contemporary cultural concerns.

Gunton's work is concerned with theological engagements and analyses of culture, as well as proffering an account of trinitarian theology. His analysis of Western culture is outlined in his magisterial work, *The One, the Three and the*

Many, which traces a range of modern cultural ailments through developments in philosophy, theology, and culture to their ancient roots. The details of Gunton's analysis are certainly debated, and yet he identifies legitimate trajectories towards disembodiment and individualism that remain persistent in Western culture and undermine the goodness of life within the created order. Likewise, his constructive relational trinitarian ontology has come under criticism in the contemporary purging of social approaches to the Trinity, yet this book suggests that his desire for a relational trinitarian ontology remains significant for our day. Moreover, some of the shortcomings of his analogical deployment of trinitarian theology are addressed by the progressions in Gunton's trinitarian theology, which are largely unrecognized by his critics. The demand by some of Gunton's critics for a defensible version of his trinitarian project is answered in some ways by Gunton himself in the revised trinitarian articulations of his later writings.

I have sought to utilize under-examined areas of Gunton's theology that rise to prominence in his later writings and shape his trinitarian theology of culture. I maintain that the *Hauptbriefe* in much of Gunton's reception results in scholars giving undue prominence to his major works from the early 1990s.[1] This results in a lack of engagement with his full corpus and a lack of recognition of the progressions in his trinitarian articulations. Future critical engagements with Gunton's work need to engage his full corpus and observe the developments in his work. There are progressions in Gunton's trinitarian articulations that result in the decline of previous sources, methods, and metaphysical conceptions. Of particular significance are the open transcendentals that, along with Coleridgean *ideas*, dominated the constructive proposals of *The One, the Three and the Many* but cease to be used after this work. Likewise, Gunton's use of philosophical sources to buttress and extend analogical insights between divine and created being recedes from usage. Instead, Gunton's work progresses to a trinitarian theology of mediation that is focused on divine action in the economy and its creaturely fruit as it is revealed in the biblical witness. Whilst some have observed the progression in Gunton's thought, this book offers more explanation of the development of his trinitarian theology of mediation that is formed from Irenaeus's account of the Son and the Spirit as the Father's two hands. I attempt to show that the methodological focus on the personal action of the Son and the Spirit in the economy results in more sustained engagements with biblical and theological sources which in turn birth new and revised articulations of trinitarian theology that strengthen and extend his trinitarian theology of culture.

The under-acknowledged progressions in Gunton's thought precipitate new theological articulations that form the basis of his trinitarian theology of culture. Firstly, his doctrine of creation is enriched by a sustained exegesis of Genesis that provides the impetus for understanding creation as a project. Whilst not without its issues, Gunton's theological interpretation of the creation narratives in Genesis forms his doctrine of creation, which he develops through an engagement with

---

1. For a definition of *Hauptbriefe* ("main letters"), see p. 3, fn 5.

contemporary biblical scholarship. Gunton's theological account of the *imago Dei* and humanity's cultural mandate are not widely explored, and nor is his affirmation of human cultural action as sub-agency in the divine redemption and perfection of creation. The emphasis upon the importance of creation and its redemption and perfection leads some to conclude incorrectly that Gunton holds to a creational soteriology. This book disputes such analysis and shows that there is, in Gunton's thought, no perfection without redemption because of the universal effects of the fall. Far from having an under-developed hamartiology, Gunton's understanding of the *imago Dei* and humanity's cultural calling is conditioned by Christology, as it is only in Christ that the image of God faithfully subsists.

Secondly, Gunton's later writings in Christology utilize greater biblical exegesis to emphasize the central significance of Christ's humanity in reaction to docetic tendencies in the tradition. As a result, Gunton stresses Christ's Jewish particularity and gives increased attention to the importance of Israel and the continuity between Israel and the Church. The role of Israel in Gunton's thought is not well recognized. Yet, his later articulations hold that Christ recapitulates not only Adam's fallen humanity but also Israel's calling. As the faithful Israelite, Christ is the one in whom Israel's story is concentrated and brought to fulfilment. Israel's threefold offices of prophet, priest, and king are concentrated in Christ. Furthermore, it is Christ who is the *telos* of the law and the Torah. The Torah and the law, Gunton maintains, are given to hold Israel in its holy calling as God's distinct and representative community of redemption who rightly inhabit the creation. In his faithful humanity that the Spirit enables, Christ takes up this calling, as well as humanity's ministerial calling, and fulfils it in his faithful human career. The law and the right human habitation of creation are vital in Gunton's theological account of culture, as they provide important frames from which to comprehend the Church's elect calling.

Thirdly, whilst it is recognized that Gunton is a theologian of the Spirit, the reach of his pneumatology in some areas related to the theology of culture has not been adequately examined. In Gunton's theology, the Spirit is the perfecting cause whose universal action sets creation free to finitely anticipate its divinely appointed end. Wherever human culture instantiates the goodness, truth, and beauty revealed through Christ, there is the perfecting work of the Spirit. The Spirit's action is universal, but it is particularly concentrated in the community of the Spirit, the Church. Holmes observes that much Gunton scholarship is unaware of the rise in Gunton's interest in ecclesiology, which is developed through his reading of 1 Corinthians.[2] Drawing from Holmes' insight, I have sought to show the centrality of ecclesiology to Gunton's theology of culture, especially his later articulations. Particularly important to Gunton's ecclesiology and trinitarian theology of culture is his pneumatological reworking of the doctrine of election. Despite receiving little scholarly attention, Gunton's pneumatological revision of election stresses its temporal dimensions and the Church's elect calling within the

---

2. Holmes, "Foreword," in *Father, Son and Holy Spirit*, x.

world. The Church, with Israel, is an elect community that is called to represent God's universal purposes in its particular life and culture which is reoriented by divine action to anticipate the end for which the world was created: the worship of God. The Church's offering of worship is its embodied life that is redeemed by Christ and constituted anew by the Spirit as life in communion with God, one another, and the creation—the right human habitation of creation. The Church's life in community is the fruit of reconciliation and the fulfilment of the law. The Spirit enables it to anticipate, from time to time, God's universal eschatological purposes.

Fourthly, Gunton's account of the Church as a distinctive form of redeemed human culture is derived primarily from his exegesis of 1 Corinthians and culminates in his account of the Church's common life as a sacrifice of praise. Gunton's exegetical engagements with 1 Corinthians and their theological fruits are not well recognized in Gunton scholarship, despite their centrality to his ecclesiology and his account of Church as a form of eschatological human culture. It is the Church's distinctive sociality, polity, and ethics, which the Spirit forms to make God's people into Christ's body, that anticipate the eschatological redemption of all things in Christ. Paul's concern with holiness in the Corinthian Church's corporate life demands that the Church exercise its calling as a distinctive community that rightly inhabits creation. The schisms that mar the Church's life together undermine its eschatological identity as Christ's community of reconciled people. Paul's correctives call the Church to become who God has made them to be in Christ by the Spirit's transforming power. For Gunton, life and worship are interrelated realms and the Church's concrete life in community is its embodied worship; the Church's right social embodiment of the gospel is a living sacrifice of praise.

Discussions of the Church's sacrifice of praise find their culmination in the Church's celebration of the Lord's Supper, another vital aspect of Gunton's theology that has been largely overlooked. Worship and thanksgiving in 1 Corinthians are primarily worship and thanksgiving for Christ's sacrifice. This life lived sacrificially, in fulfilment of humanity and Israel's calling, is the perfect sacrifice and the means for all other sacrifices of praise. At the Supper, the Church's reconciled and embodied life together is united by the Spirit with Christ's perfect sacrifice and offered as praise to the Father for God's wise purposes in the beginning. Importantly for Gunton the Supper takes up the created order, and humanity's cultural calling to steward the creation, into the Church's representative worship. The bread and wine are the fruits of creation (grain and grape) manufactured by human cultural action and witness to the created order being representatively taken up in the Church's offering of a sacrifice of praise. At the Supper, through Christ's sacrifice and as the Spirit enables, the Church offers a representative sample of humanity and creation redeemed to God and each other through the right human habitation of creation. Such a rightly ordered form of human life in communion with God, one another, and creation is a living sacrifice of praise to God for God's wise purposes in creation—a form of praise that contributes to the perfecting of God's project of creation.

In the final analysis, each of these revised trinitarian articulations is important and displays the enrichments that arise from Gunton's progression to a trinitarian theology of mediation. Yet, taken together they form the vital basis of Gunton's trinitarian theology of culture and offer original insights into his trinitarian project, which future Gunton research will need to take into account. Moreover, they provide the basis from which future work can build upon Gunton's insights and engage theologically with the key intellectual and cultural currents of our day. The final chapter takes the Lord's Supper as an example of the ongoing fruitfulness of Gunton's trinitarian theology of culture. The chapter brings Gunton's work into conversation with the contemporary rise of the cultural sciences and the intellectual challenges they raise about the sedimented structures of power in Church and society. For all the importance of the Church's concrete life together, the cultural sciences demand that we consider the politics of the Church's togetherness and address intendent issues of privilege and hegemonic power bequeathed embedded in the Church's life and ministries. Following Gunton's use of exegetical insights for theological reflection on divine action in the economy, this chapter explores contemporary socio-political and socio-cultural accounts of the divisions at the Lord's Supper in Corinth to extend Gunton's insights.

As Chapter 6 shows, reflections on the Church's politics of belonging in community are set under the politics of the cross to develop a distinct form of human life in relation to God, one another, and the wider created world. I utilize the example of disability theology to raise important questions about the Church's politics of belonging in community, and draw from Gunton's insights to argue for the Church's need to dismantle ableism to be a meaningful community where particularity bulks large. It is by way of embodying Christ's dismantling of the powers of privilege and domination that the Spirit enables the Church to offer its redeemed human culture as a living sacrifice of praise in and through Christ's sacrifice. The result, as Gunton's work and Chapter 6 exhibit, is a more concrete trinitarianism, ecclesiology, and theology of culture. Gunton's relentless pursuit of an embodied theology results in a rich and insightful trinitarian theology of culture, the fruitfulness of which invites further explorations in the ongoing conversation on a trinitarian theology of Church and culture.

To conclude, this book has shown that Gunton's trinitarian theology of culture provides rich resources for theological accounts of culture and theological engagements with culture. These engagements are not simply the Church's assessment of whether aspects of the modern world adhere to the gospel; they invite reflection on the Church's embodiment of the gospel and its contributions to the divine redemption and perfection of creation. As Holmes notes, Gunton's last words in what was to be his final book before his sudden death capture his deep passion for the gospel and the renewal of creation, and they also underscore much of the focus of this book.[3] "In the interim, Christ's presence in all its manifold forms is realised only through anticipation, and that means through the mediation of the

---

3. Holmes, "Foreword," in *Father, Son and Holy Spirit*, xi.

eschatological Spirit, as anticipated eschatology. Our eschatological membership of the body and bride of Christ belongs in that period of fulfilment and promise, in sure hope of the resurrection of the dead."[4] The Church's living sacrifice of praise is an eschatological offering of its embodied life and ethics in and through the sacrifice of Christ as the Spirit enables.

Questions and debates regarding Gunton's trinitarian theology remain. However, a study of Gunton's trinitarian theology of culture offers new insights into Gunton's articulations of trinitarian theology in general and his theology of culture in particular. While questions remain, Gunton helpfully directs our attention to divine action in the economy and its creaturely fruit and urges us to consider God's embrace of the goodness of creation and desire for human cultural contributions to the redemption and perfection of the project of creation. Human culture, redeemed in Christ and enabled by the Spirit, is a living sacrifice of praise that contributes to God's redemption and perfection of the project of creation.

---

4. Gunton, *Father, Son and Holy Spirit*, 234.

BIBLIOGRAPHY

Adams, Edward. "First-Century Models for Paul's Churches: Selected Scholarly Developments Since Meeks." Pages 60–78 in *After the First Urban Christians: The Social-Scientific Study of Pauline Christianity Twenty-Five Years Later*. Edited by Todd D. Still and David G. Horrell. London: T&T Clark, 2009.

Adams, Edward. *The Earliest Christian Meeting Places: Almost Exclusively Houses?* London: T&T Clark, 2013.

Adams, Edward. "The Shape of the Pauline Churches." Pages 119–46 in *The Oxford Handbook of Ecclesiology*. Edited by Paul Avis. Oxford: Oxford University Press, 2018.

Allen, Leslie C. *A Theological Approach to the Old Testament: Major Themes and New Testament Connections*. Eugene: Wipf and Stock, 2014.

Anatolios, Khaled. "Yes and No: Reflections on Lewis Ayres, *Nicaea and Its Legacy*." *Harvard Theological Review* 100 (2007): 153–8.

Anatolios, Khaled. *Retrieving Nicaea: The Development and Meaning of Trinitarian Doctrine*. Grand Rapids: Baker, 2011.

Anatolios, Khaled. "Personhood, Communion, and the Trinity in Some Patristic Texts." Pages 147–64 in *The Holy Trinity in the Life of the Church*. Edited by Khaled Anatolios. Grand Rapids: Baker, 2014.

Anizor, Uche. "A Spirited Humanity: The Trinitarian Ecclesiology of Colin Gunton." *Themelios* 36 (2011): 26–41.

Anizor, Uche. *Trinity and Humanity: An Introduction to the Theology of Colin Gunton*. Milton Keynes: Paternoster, 2016.

Anizor, Uche. "Gunton on Ecclesiology." Pages 151–68 in *T&T Clark Handbook of Colin Gunton*. Edited by Andrew Picard, Myk Habets and Murray Rae. London: T&T Clark, 2021.

Aristotle, *Metaphysics*. Edited and translated by John Warrington. London: Everyman's Library, 1961.

Arnold, Bill T. *Genesis*. NCBC. Cambridge: Cambridge University Press, 2009.

Ayres, Lewis. "Augustine, the Trinity and Modernity." *Augustinian Studies* 26 (1995): 127–33.

Ayres, Lewis. "Recent Books in … Systematic Theology." *Reviews in Religion & Theology* 4 (1997): 74–8.

Ayres, Lewis. "On Not Three People: The Fundamental Themes of Gregory of Nyssa's Trinitarian Theology as Seen in *To Ablabius: On Not Three Gods*." *Modern Theology* 18 (2002): 445–74.

Ayres, Lewis. *Nicaea and Its Legacy: An Approach to Fourth-Century Trinitarian Theology*. Oxford: Oxford University Press, 2004.

Ayres, Lewis. "*Nicaea and Its Legacy*: An Introduction." *Harvard Theological Review* 100 (2007): 141–4.

Ayres, Lewis. *Augustine and the Trinity*. Cambridge: Cambridge University Press, 2010.

Badiou, Alain. *Being and Event*. Translated by Oliver Feltham. London: Continuum, 2005.

Bailey, Kenneth E. *Paul through Mediterranean Eyes: Cultural Studies in 1 Corinthians*. London: SPCK, 2011.

Ballard, C. Andrew. "Tongue-tied and Taunted: Paul, Poor Rhetoric and Paltry Leadership in 2 Corinthians 5:13." *Journal for the Study of the New Testament* 37 (2014): 50–70.
Barnes, Michel René. "Rereading Augustine's Theology of the Trinity." Pages 145–78 in *The Trinity: An Interdisciplinary Symposium on the Trinity*. Edited by Stephen T. Davis, Daniel Kendall SJ and Gerald O'Collins SJ. Oxford: Oxford University Press, 1999.
Barrett, C. K. *The First Epistle to the Corinthians*. Black's New Testament Commentaries. New York: Harper and Row, 1968.
Barth, Karl. *Church Dogmatics I/1: The Doctrine of the Word of God*. Edited by G. W. Bromiley and T. F. Torrance. Translated by G. W. Bromiley. Edinburgh: T&T Clark, 1936.
Barth, Karl. *Church Dogmatics IV/1: The Doctrine of Reconciliation*. Edited by G. W. Bromiley and T. F. Torrance. Translated by G. W. Bromiley. Edinburgh: T&T Clark, 1956.
Barth, Karl. *The Holy Spirit and the Christian Life: The Theological Basis of Ethics*. Translated by R. Birch Hoyle. Louisville: Westminster John Knox Press, 1993.
Bartholomew, Craig. "The Healing of Modernity: A Trinitarian Remedy? A Critical Dialogue with Colin Gunton's *the One, the Three and the Many: God, Creation and the Culture of Modernity*." *European Journal of Theology* 6 (1997): 111–30.
Bartholomew, Craig G. *The God Who Acts in History: The Significance of Sinai*. Grand Rapids: Eerdmans, 2020.
Basil of Caesarea, *On the Holy Spirit*. In vol. 8 of *The Nicene and Post-Nicene Fathers*. Series 2. Edited by Philip Schaff and Henry Wace. 1886–9. 14 vols. New York: The Christian Literature Company, 1895.
Bathrellos, Demetrios. "Gunton and the Cappadocians." Pages 253–68 in *T&T Clark Handbook of Colin Gunton*. Edited by Andrew Picard, Myk Habets and Murray Rae. London: T&T Clark, 2021.
Bauckham, Richard. *The Jewish World around the New Testament*. Grand Rapids: Baker, 2008.
Bauman, Zygmunt. *Modernity and Ambivalence*. Cambridge: Polity Press, 1991.
Bauman, Zygmunt. *Postmodernity and Its Discontents*. Cambridge: Polity Press, 1997.
Bauman, Zygmunt. *Liquid Modernity*. Cambridge: Polity Press, 2000.
Bauman, Zygmunt. *Community: Seeking Safety in an Insecure World*. Cambridge: Polity Press, 2001.
Bauman, Zygmunt. *Consuming Life*. Cambridge: Polity Press, 2007.
Bauman, Zygmunt. *Does Ethics Have a Chance in a World of Consumers?*. Cambridge, Massachusetts and London: Harvard University Press, 2008.
Bauman, Zygmunt. *The Art of Life*. Cambridge: Polity Press, 2008.
Bauman, Zygmunt. *Collateral Damage: Social Inequalities in a Global Age*. Cambridge: Polity Press, 2011.
Bauman, Zygmunt. *Culture in a Liquid Modern World*. Cambridge: Polity Press, 2011.
Bauman, Zygmunt and Leonidas Donskis. *Moral Blindness: The Loss of Sensitivity in Liquid Modernity*. Cambridge: Polity Press, 2013.
Beers, Holly. *The Followers of Jesus as the "Servant": Luke's Model from Isaiah for the Disciples in Luke-Acts*. London: Bloomsbury/T&T Clark, 2015.
British Council of Churches Study Commission on Trinitarian Doctrine Today. *The Forgotten Trinity: 1. The Report of the BCC Study Commission on Trinitarian Doctrine Today*. London: BCC, 1989.
British Council of Churches Study Commission on Trinitarian Doctrine Today. *The Forgotten Trinity: 2. A Study Guide on Issues Contained in the Report of the BCC Study Commission on Trinitarian Doctrine Today*. London: BCC, 1989.

Brittain, Christopher Craig. "Why Ecclesiology Cannot Live by Doctrine Alone: A Reply to John Webster's 'In the Society of God.'" *Ecclesial Practices* 1 (2014): 5–30.

Brock, Brian and John Swinton, eds. *Disability in the Christian Tradition: A Reader*. Grand Rapids: Eerdmans, 2012.

Brueggemann, Walter. *Genesis*. Interpretation. Atlanta: John Knox, 1982.

Byers, Andrew. "The One Body of the Shema in 1 Corinthians: An Ecclesiology of Christological Monotheism." *New Testament Studies* 62 (2016): 517–32.

Calvin, John. *The Epistle of Paul the Apostle to the Hebrews and the First and Second Epistles of Peter*. Translated by W. B. Johnson. Grand Rapids: Eerdmans, 1963.

Charry, Ellen. "The Crisis of Modernity and the Christian Self." Pages 89–112 in *A Passion for God's Reign: Theology, Christian Learning and the Christian Self*. Edited by Miroslav Volf. Grand Rapids: Eerdmans, 1998.

Cheer, Tony, Sheila Maxey, and Charles Steynor. "Foreword." Pages ix–x in Colin E. Gunton, *The Theologian as Preacher: Further Sermons from Colin E. Gunton*. Edited by Sarah J. Gunton and John E. Colwell. London: T&T Clark, 2007.

Chia, Roland. "Trinity and Ontology: Colin Gunton's Ecclesiology." *International Journal of Systematic Theology* 9 (2007): 452–68.

Chow, John K. *Patronage and Power: A Study of Social Networks in Corinth*. Sheffield: Sheffield Academic Press, 1992.

Clement. *The First Epistle of Clement to the Corinthians*. In vol. 1 of *The Ante-Nicene Fathers*. Edited by Alexander Roberts and James Donaldson. 1885–7. 10 vols. Buffalo: The Christian Literature Company, 1885.

Coakley, Sarah. "'Persons' in the 'Social' Doctrine of the Trinity: A Critique of Current Analytical Discussion." Pages 123–44 in *The Trinity: An Interdisciplinary Symposium on the Trinity*. Edited by Stephen T. Davis, Daniel Kendall SJ and Gerald O'Collins SJ. Oxford: Oxford University Press, 1999.

Coakley, Sarah. "Re-thinking Gregory of Nyssa: Introduction—Gender, Trinitarian Analogies, and the Pedagogy of *the Song*." *Modern Theology* 18 (2002): 431–3.

Coakley, Sarah. "Afterword: 'Relational Ontology,' Trinity, and Science." Pages 184–99 in *The Trinity and an Entangled World: Relationality in Physical Science and Theology*. Edited by John Polkinghorne. Grand Rapids: Eerdmans, 2010.

Coakley, Sarah. *God, Sexuality, and the Self: An Essay "On the Trinity."* Cambridge: Cambridge University Press, 2013.

Coakley, Sarah. "Knowing in the Dark: Sin, Race and the Quest for Salvation. Part 1: Transforming Theological Anthropology in a Théologie Totale." *The Princeton Seminary Bulletin* 32 (2015): 108–22.

Coleridge, Samuel Taylor. *On the Constitution of the Church and State According to the Idea of Each*. 3rd ed. London: William Pickering, 1839.

Colgan, Emily. "Reading the Bible as Waters Rise: Ecological Interpretation of Scripture." Pages 115–34 in *Science, Faith and the Climate Crisis*. Edited by Sally Myers, Sarah Hemstock and Edward Hanna. Bingley: Emerald Publishing, 2020.

Colgan, Emily. "*Kaitiaki*: The Human Vocation to Till and to Keep." Pages 28–32 in *The Earth Our Parish*. Edited by George Zachariah and Te Aroha Rountree. Auckland: Trinity Methodist Theological College, 2023.

Colwell, John. "Provisionality and Promise: Avoiding Ecclesiastical Nestorianism?." Pages 100–15 in *The Theology of Colin Gunton*. Edited by Lincoln Harvey. London: T&T Clark, 2010.

Colwell, John. "A Conversation Overheard: Reflecting on the Trinitarian Grammar of Intimacy and Substance." *Evangelical Quarterly* 86 (2014): 63–76.

Colwell, John. "A Conversation Overheard: Reflecting on the Trinitarian Grammar of Intimacy and Substance." Pages 97–109 in *The Holy Trinity Revisited: Essays in Response to Stephen R. Holmes*. Edited by Thomas A. Noble and Jason S. Sexton. Milton Keynes: Paternoster, 2015.

Crisp, Oliver. "Gunton on Christology." Pages 77–90 in *T&T Clark Handbook of Colin Gunton*. Edited by Andrew Picard, Myk Habets and Murray Rae. London: T&T Clark, 2021.

Cross, Richard. "*Quid Tres*? On What Precisely Augustine Professes Not to Understand in de Trinitate 5 and 7." *Harvard Theological Review* 100 (2007): 215–32.

Cumin, Paul. "The Taste of Cake: Relation and Otherness with Colin Gunton and the Strong Second Hand of God." Pages 65–85 in *The Theology of Colin Gunton*. Edited by Lincoln Harvey. London: T&T Clark, 2010.

Cumin, Paul. *Christ at the Crux: The Mediation of God and Creation in Christological Perspective*. Eugene: Wipf and Stock, 2014.

Cyprian. *The Epistles of Cyprian*. In vol. 5 of *The Ante-Nicene Fathers*. Edited by Alexander Roberts and James Donaldson. 1885–7. 10 vols. Buffalo: The Christian Literature Company, 1886.

Daggett, Arthur Gregory. "Metaphysicians of Modernity: Colin Gunton and George P. Grant Confront the *Zeitgeist*." MA diss., Acadia University, 2013.

Davidson, Ivor. "Gunton on Jüngel." Pages 403–18 in *T&T Clark Handbook of Colin Gunton*. Edited by Andrew Picard, Myk Habets and Murray Rae. London: T&T Clark, 2021.

Downs, David J. *The Offering of the Gentiles: Paul's Collection for Jerusalem in Its Chronological, Cultural and Cultic Contexts*. Tübingen: Mohr Siebeck, 2008.

Downs, David J. "Physical Weakness, Illness and Death in 1 Corinthians 11:30: Deprivation and Overconsumption in Pauline and Early Christianity." *New Testament Studies* 65 (2019): 572–88.

Eiesland, Nancy L. *The Disabled God: Toward a Liberatory Theology of Disability*. Nashville: Abingdon, 1994.

Eiesland, Nancy L. "Encountering the Disabled God." *The Other Side* 38 (2002): 10–15.

Farrow, Douglas. "Ascension and Ecclesia: On the Significance of the Doctrine of Ascension for Ecclesiology and Christian Cosmology." PhD diss., King's College, London, 1994.

Farrow, Douglas. *Ascension and Ecclesia: On the Significance of the Doctrine of Ascension for Ecclesiology and Christian Cosmology*. Edinburgh: T&T Clark, 1999.

Farrow, Douglas. "Gunton and Irenaeus." Pages 239–52 in *T&T Clark Handbook of Colin Gunton*. Edited by Andrew Picard, Myk Habets and Murray Rae. London: T&T Clark, 2021.

Fermer, Richard M. "The Limits of Trinitarian Theology as a Methodological Paradigm." *Neue Zeitschrift Für Systematische Theologie Aund Religionsphilosophie* 41 (1999): 158–86.

Fiddes, Paul S. *Participating in God: A Pastoral Doctrine of the Trinity*. Louisville: Westminster John Knox Press, 2000.

Fiddes, Paul S. *Seeing the World and Knowing God: Hebrew Wisdom and Christian Doctrine in a Late-Modern Context*. Oxford: Oxford University Press, 2013.

Fiddes, Paul S. "Relational Trinity: Radical Perspective." Pages 159–85 in *Two Views on the Doctrine of the Trinity*. Edited by Jason S. Sexton. Grand Rapids: Zondervan, 2014.

Fitzmyer, Joseph A. *First Corinthians: A New Translation and Commentary*. Anchor. New Haven: Yale University Press, 2008.

Ford, David F. *Meaning and Truth in 2 Corinthians*. London: SPCK, 1987.
Fretheim, Terence E. "The Book of Genesis: Introduction, Commentary, and Reflections." Pages 321–674 in *The New Interpreter's Bible Commentary*, vol. 1. Edited by Leander E. Keck et al. Nashville: Abingdon, 1994.
Friesen, Steven J. *Imperial Cults and the Apocalypse of John: Reading Revelation in the Ruins*. Oxford: Oxford University Press, 2001.
Friesen, Steven J. "Paul and Economics: The Jerusalem Collection as an Alternative to Patronage." Pages 27–54 in *Paul Unbound: Other Perspectives on the Apostle*. Edited by Mark D. Given. Peabody: Hendrickson, 2010.
Fuller, Michael E. *The Restoration of Israel: Israel's Re-gathering and the Fate of the Nations in Early Jewish Literature and Luke-Acts*. Berlin: De Gruyter, 2006.
Furnish, Victor Paul. *II Corinthians: Translated with Introduction, Notes, and Commentary*. Anchor. New York: Doubleday, 1984.
Gardner, Gregg. "Jewish Leadership and Hellenistic Civic Benefaction in the Second Century BCE." *Journal of Biblical Literature* 126 (2007): 327–43.
Green, Bradley G. *Colin Gunton and the Failure of Augustine: The Theology of Colin Gunton in Light of Augustine*. Eugene: Wipf and Stock, 2011.
Green, Julie Kaye. "The Worldly Church: The Relationship between Church and Culture as Perichoretic Necessity with Particular Reference to Colin Gunton." PhD diss., University of Aberdeen, Scotland, 2014.
Greggs, Tom. "Proportion and Topography in Ecclesiology: A Working Paper on the Dogmatic Location of the Doctrine of the Church." Pages 89–106 in *Theological Theology: Essays in Honour of John Webster*. Edited by R. David Nelson, Darren Sarisky and Justin Stratis. London: T&T Clark, 2015.
Gregory of Nazianzen. *To Cledonius the Priest Against Apollinaris*. In vol. 7 of *The Nicene and Post-Nicene Fathers*. Series 2. Edited by Philip Schaff and Henry Wace. 1886-9. 14 vols. New York: The Christian Literature Company, 1884.
Grenz, Stanley J. *Rediscovering the Triune God: The Trinity in Contemporary Theology*. Minneapolis: Augsburg Press, 2014.
Gunton, Colin E. "Karl Barth and the Development of Christian Doctrine." *Scottish Journal of Theology* 25 (1972): 171–80.
Gunton, Colin E. "Rudolf Bultmann and the Location of Language about God." *Theology* 75 (1972): 535–9.
Gunton, Colin E. "Process Theology's Concept of God: An Outline and Assessment." *Expository Times* 84 (1973): 292–6.
Gunton, Colin E. "Karl Barth's Doctrine of Election as Part of His Doctrine of God." *Journal of Theological Studies* 25 (1974): 381–92.
Gunton, Colin E. "The Remaking of Christian Doctrine." *Theology* 77 (1974): 619–24.
Gunton, Colin E. "The Theologian and the Biologist." *Theology* 77 (1974): 526–8.
Gunton, Colin E. "Christian Belief Today: God, Creation and the Future." *New Fire III* (1975): 434–41.
Gunton, Colin E. "The Knowledge of God according to Two Process Theologians: A Twentieth Century Gnosticism." *Religious Studies* 11 (1975): 87–97.
Gunton, Colin E. "Rejection, Influence, and Development: Charles Hartshorne and the History of Philosophy." *Process Studies* 6 (1976): 33–42.
Gunton, Colin E. "The Biblical Understanding of Reconciliation: Paul and Jacob before God." *Free Church Chronicle* 32 (1977): 17–22.
Gunton, Colin E. *Becoming and Being: The Doctrine of God in Charles Hartshorne and Karl Barth*. Oxford: Oxford University Press, 1978.

Gunton, Colin E. "The Political Christ: Some Reflections on Mr Cupitt's Thesis." *Scottish Journal of Theology* 32 (1979): 521–40.
Gunton, Colin E. "Transcendence, Metaphor, and the Knowability of God." *Journal of Theological Studies* 31 (1980): 503–16.
Gunton, Colin E. "The Truth of Christology." Pages 91–107 in *Belief in Science and in Christian Life: The Relevance of Michael Polanyi's Thought for Christian Faith and Life*. Edited by T. F. Torrance. Edinburgh: Handsel Press, 1980.
Gunton, Colin E. "Time, Eternity and the Doctrine of the Incarnation." *Dialog* 21 (1982): 263–8.
Gunton, Colin E. *Yesterday and Today: A Study of Continuities in Christology*. London: Darton, Longman and Todd, 1983.
Gunton, Colin E. "David Ford: Barth and God's Story." *Scottish Journal of Theology* 37 (1984): 375–80.
Gunton, Colin E. "Christus Victor Revisited: A Study of Metaphor and the Transformation of Meaning." *Journal of Theological Studies* 36 (1985): 129–45.
Gunton, Colin E. "Creation and Recreation: An Exploration of Some Themes in Aesthetics and Theology." *Modern Theology* 2 (1985): 1–19.
Gunton, Colin E. *Enlightenment and Alienation: An Essay Towards a Trinitarian Theology*. London: Marshall, Morgan and Scott, 1985.
Gunton, Colin E. "The Justice of God." *Free Church Chronicle* 40 (1985): 13–19.
Gunton, Colin E. *The One, the Three, and the Many: An Inaugural Lecture in the Chair of Christian Doctrine*. King's College, London: Pamphlet, limited publication, Given on May 14, 1985.
Gunton, Colin E. "Barth, the Trinity, and Human Freedom." *Theology Today* 43 (1986): 316–30.
Gunton, Colin E. "Barth and the Western Intellectual Tradition: Towards a Theology After Christendom." Pages 285–301 in *Theology Beyond Christendom: Essays on the Centenary of the Birth of Karl Barth, May 10, 1886*. Edited by John Thompson. Allison Park, PA: Pickwick Press, 1986.
Gunton, Colin E. "The Christian Doctrine of God: Opposition and Convergence." Pages 11–22 in *Heaven and Earth: Essex Essays in Theology and Ethics*. Edited by Andrew Linzey and Peter J. Wexler. Worthing: Churchman Publishing, 1986.
Gunton, Colin E. "Christ the Sacrifice: Aspects of the Language and Imagery of the Bible." Pages 229–38 in *The Glory of Christ in the New Testament: Essays in Memory of George Bradford Caird*. Edited by L. D. Hurst and N. T. Wright. Oxford: Clarendon Press, 1987.
Gunton, Colin E. "The Playwright as Theologian: Peter Shaffer's *Amadeus*." *King's Theological Review* 10, (1987): 1–5.
Gunton, Colin E. "Reinhold Niebuhr: A Treatise of Human Nature." *Modern Theology* 4 (1987): 71–81.
Gunton, Colin E. "Revelation." Pages 240–1 in *A Dictionary of Pastoral Care*. Edited by Alastair V. Campbell. London: SPCK, 1987.
Gunton, Colin E. *The Actuality of Atonement: A Study of Metaphor, Rationality and the Christian Tradition*. Edinburgh: T&T Clark, 1988.
Gunton, Colin E. "Christianity among the Religions in the Encyclopaedia of Religion." *Religious Studies* 24 (1988): 11–18.
Gunton, Colin E. "No Other Foundation: One Englishman's Reading of Church Dogmatics, Chapter V." Pages 61–79 in *Reckoning with Barth: Essays in Commemoration of the Centenary of Karl Barth's Birth*. Edited by Nigel Biggar. London: Mowbray, 1988.

Gunton, Colin E. "The Spirit as Lord: Christianity, Modernity and Freedom." Pages 169–82 in *Different Gospels: Christian Orthodoxy and Modern Theologies*. Edited by Andrew Walker. London: Hodder and Stoughton for the C.S. Lewis Centre, 1988.

Gunton, Colin E. *The Transcendent Lord: The Spirit and the Church in Calvinist and Cappadocian*. The 1988 Congregational Lecture. London: Congregational Memorial Hall Trust, 1988.

Gunton, Colin E. "Two Dogmas Revisited: Edward Irving's Christology." *Scottish Journal of Theology* 41 (1988): 359–76.

Gunton, Colin E. "A Far-Off Gleam of the Gospel: Salvation in Tolkien's *Lord of the Rings*." *King's Theological Review* 12 (1989): 6–10.

Gunton, Colin E. "The Church on Earth: The Roots of Community." Pages 48–80 in *On Being the Church: Essays on the Christian Community*. Edited by Colin E. Gunton and Daniel W. Hardy. Edinburgh: T&T Clark, 1989.

Gunton, Colin E. "The Sacrifice and the Sacrifices: From Metaphor to Transcendental?" Pages 210–29 in *Trinity, Incarnation, and Atonement*. Edited by Ronald J. Fenstra and Cornelius Plantinga. Indiana: University of Notre Dame Press, 1989.

Gunton, Colin E. "The Triune God and the Freedom of the Creature." Pages 46–68 in *Karl Barth: Centenary Essays*. Edited by S. W. Sykes. Cambridge: Cambridge University Press, 1989.

Gunton, Colin E. "When the Gates of Hell Fall Down: Towards a Modern Theology of the Justice of God." *New Blackfriars* 69 (1989): 488–96.

Gunton, Colin E. "Augustine, the Trinity and the Theological Crisis of the West." *Scottish Journal of Theology* 43, (1990): 33–58.

Gunton, Colin E. "Baptism and the Christian Community." Pages 98–109 in *Incarnational Ministry: The Presence of Christ in Church, Society, and Family. Essays in Honor of Ray S. Anderson*. Edited by Christian D. Kettler and Todd H. Speidell. Colorado Springs: Helmers and Howard, 1990.

Gunton, Colin E. "The Idea of Dissent and the Character of Christianity." *Reformed Quarterly* 1 (1990): 2–6.

Gunton, Colin E. "Newman's Dialectic: Dogma and Reason in the 73rd Tract for the Times." Pages 309–22 in *Newman After a Hundred Years*. Edited by Alan G. Hill and Ian Ker. Oxford: Oxford University Press, 1990.

Gunton, Colin E. "Used and Being Used: Scripture and Systematic Theology." *Theology Today* 47 (1990): 248–59.

Gunton, Colin E. "Immanence and Otherness: Divine Sovereignty and Human Freedom in the Theology of Robert W. Jenson." *Dialog* 30 (1991): 17–26.

Gunton, Colin E. "Mozart the Theologian." *Theology* 94 (1991): 346–9.

Gunton, Colin E. *The Promise of Trinitarian Theology*. Edinburgh: T&T Clark, 1991.

Gunton, Colin E. "The Spirit in the Trinity." Pages 123–35 in *The Forgotten Trinity, 3. A Selection of Papers Presented to the BCC Study Commission on Trinitarian Doctrine Today*. Edited by Alastair I. C. Heron. London: BCC/CCBI, 1991.

Gunton, Colin E. *Christ and Creation: The 1990 Didsbury Lectures*. Carlisle: Paternoster Press, 1992.

Gunton, Colin E. "Knowledge and Culture: Towards an Epistemology of the Concrete." Pages 84–102 in *The Gospel and Contemporary Culture*. Edited by Hugh Montefiore. London: Mowbray, 1992.

Gunton, Colin E. "Proteus and Procrustes: A Study of the Dialectic of Language in Disagreement with Sallie McFague." Pages 65–80 in *Speaking the Christian God: The Holy Trinity and the Challenge of Feminism*. Edited by Alvin F. Kimel Jr. Grand Rapids: Eerdmans, 1992.

Gunton, Colin E. "Trinity, Ontology and Anthropology: Towards a Renewal of the Doctrine of the Imago Dei." Pages 47–61 in *Persons, Divine and Human: King's College Essays in Theological Anthropology*. Edited by Christoph Schwöbel and Colin E. Gunton. Edinburgh: T&T Clark, 1992.

Gunton, Colin E. "Universal and Particular in Atonement Theology." *Religious Studies* 28 (1992): 453–66.

Gunton, Colin E. "An English Systematic Theology?" *Scottish Journal of Theology* 46 (1993): 479–96.

Gunton, Colin E. "All Scripture Is Inspired?" *The Princeton Seminary Bulletin* 14 (1993): 240–53.

Gunton, Colin E. "Foreword." Pages ix–xi in Thomas Weinandy, *In the Likeness of Sinful Flesh: An Essay on the Humanity of Christ*. Edinburgh: T&T Clark, 1993.

Gunton, Colin E. *The One, the Three and the Many: God, Creation and the Culture of Modernity. The 1992 Bampton Lectures*. Cambridge: Cambridge University Press, 1993.

Gunton, Colin E. "Marriage Address." Pages 148–51 in *As Man and Woman Made: Theological Reflections on Marriage*. Edited by Susan Durber. London: United Reformed Church, 1994.

Gunton, Colin E. *A Brief Theology of Revelation: The 1993 Warfield Lectures*. Edinburgh: T&T Clark, 1995.

Gunton, Colin E. "The Being and Attributes of God: Eberhard Jüngel's Dispute with the Classical Philosophical Tradition." Pages 7–22 in *The Possibilities of Theology: Studies in the Theology of Eberhard Jüngel*. Edited by John Webster. Edinburgh: T&T Clark, 1995.

Gunton, Colin E. "The Community of the Church in Communion with God." Pages 38–41 in *The Church in the Reformed Tradition: Discussion Papers Prepared by a Working Party of the European Committee*. Edited by Colin E. Gunton, Páraic Réamonn and Alan P. F. Sell. Geneva: World Alliance of Reformed Churches, 1995.

Gunton, Colin E. "Editorial Introduction." Pages 1–12 in *God and Freedom: Essays in Historical and Systematic Theology*. Edited by Colin E. Gunton. Edinburgh: T&T Clark, 1995.

Gunton, Colin E., ed. *God and Freedom: Essays in Historical and Systematic Theology*. Edinburgh: T&T Clark, 1995.

Gunton, Colin E. "God, Grace and Freedom." Pages 119–33 in *God and Freedom: Essays in Historical and Systematic Theology*. Edited by Colin E. Gunton. Edinburgh: T&T Clark, 1995.

Gunton, Colin E. "The Real as the Redemptive: P. T. Forsyth on Authority and Freedom." Pages 37–59 in *Justice the True and Only Mercy: Essays on the Life and Theology of P. T. Forsyth*. Edited by Trevor Hart. Edinburgh: T&T Clark, 1995.

Gunton, Colin E. "Relation and Relativity: The Trinity and the Created World." Pages 92–112 in *Trinitarian Theology Today: Essays on Divine Being and Act*. Edited by Christoph Schwöbel. Edinburgh: T&T Clark, 1995.

Gunton, Colin E. "The Trinity." Pages 937–57 in *A Companion Encyclopaedia of Theology*. Edited by Peter Byrne and Leslie Houlden. London: Routledge, 1995.

Gunton, Colin E. "Universal and Particular in Atonement Theology." Pages 147–62 in *Readings in Modern Theology*. Edited by Robin Gill. London: SPCK, 1995.

Gunton, Colin E. "All Flesh Is as Grass: Towards an Eschatology of the Human Person." Pages 22–37 in *Beyond Mere Health: Theology and Health Care in a Secular Society*. Edited by Hilary Regan, Rod Horsfield and Gabrielle McMullen. Kew, Australia: Australian Theological Forum, 1996.

Gunton, Colin E. "Article Review. Bruce L. McCormack's *Karl Barth's Critically Realistic Dialectical Theology: Its Genesis and Development 1909–1936*." *Scottish Journal of Theology* 48 (1996): 483–91.

Gunton, Colin E. "Atonement and the Project of Creation: An Interpretation of Colossians 1:15–23." *Dialog* 35 (1996): 35–41.
Gunton, Colin E. "Foreword." Pages ix–x in Graham McFarlane, *Christ and the Spirit: The Doctrine of the Incarnation According to Edward Irving*. Cumbria: Paternoster Press, 1996.
Gunton, Colin E. "The Indispensable God? The Sovereignty of God and the Problem of Modern Social Order." Pages 1–21 in *Beyond Mere Health: Theology and Health Care in a Secular Society*. Edited by Hilary Regan, Rod Horsfield and Gabrielle McMullen. Kew: Australian Theological Forum, 1996.
Gunton, Colin E. "The Indispensability of Theological Understanding: Theology in the University." Pages 266–77 in *Essentials of Christian Community: Essays for Daniel W. Hardy*. Edited by David Ford and Dennis Stamps. Edinburgh: T&T Clark, 1996.
Gunton, Colin E. "Indispensable Opponent: The Relations of Systematic Theology and the Philosophy of Religion." *Neue Zeitschrift für Systematische Theologie und Religionsphilosophie* 38 (1996): 298–306.
Gunton, Colin E. "Christology." Pages 133–7 in *Dictionary of Ethics, Theology and Society*. Edited by Paul B. Clarke and Andrew Linzey. London: Routledge, 1996.
Gunton, Colin E. "Persons." Pages 638–41 in *Dictionary of Ethics, Theology and Society*. Edited by Paul B. Clarke and Andrew Linzey. London: Routledge, 1996.
Gunton, Colin E. "Pneumatology." Pages 644–7 in *Dictionary of Ethics, Theology and Society*. Edited by Paul B. Clarke and Andrew Linzey. London: Routledge, 1996.
Gunton, Colin E. *Theology Through the Theologians: Selected Papers 1975–1995*. Edinburgh: T&T Clark, 1996.
Gunton, Colin E. "Toleration." Pages 826–9 in *Dictionary of Ethics, Theology and Society*. Edited by Paul B. Clarke and Andrew Linzey. London: Routledge, 1996.
Gunton, Colin E. "The Trinity, Natural Theology and a Theology of Nature." Pages 88–103 in *Trinity in a Pluralistic Age: Theological Essays on Culture and Religion*. Edited by Kevin Vanhoozer. Grand Rapids: Eerdmans, 1996.
Gunton, Colin E. "Between Allegory and Myth: The Legacy of Spiritualising of Genesis." Pages 47–62 in *The Doctrine of Creation: Essays in Dogmatics, History and Philosophy*. Edited by Colin E. Gunton. Edinburgh: T&T Clark, 1997.
Gunton, Colin E. *The Cambridge Companion to Christian Doctrine*. Cambridge: Cambridge University Press, 1997.
Gunton, Colin E. "The Doctrine of Creation." Pages 141–57 in *The Cambridge Companion to Christian Doctrine*. Edited by Colin E. Gunton. Cambridge: Cambridge University Press, 1997.
Gunton, Colin E., ed. *The Doctrine of Creation: Essays in Dogmatics, History and Philosophy*. Edinburgh: T&T Clark, 1997.
Gunton, Colin E. "The End of Causality? The Reformers and Their Predecessors." Pages 63–82 in *The Doctrine of Creation: Essays in Dogmatics, History and Philosophy*. Edited by Colin E. Gunton. Edinburgh: T&T Clark, 1997.
Gunton, Colin E. "The God of Jesus Christ." *Theology Today* 54 (1997): 325–34.
Gunton, Colin E. "Historical and Systematic Theology." Pages 3–20 in *The Cambridge Companion to Christian Doctrine*. Edited by Colin E. Gunton. Cambridge: Cambridge University Press, 1997.
Gunton, Colin E. "Introduction." Pages 1–16 in *The Doctrine of Creation: Essays in Dogmatics, History and Philosophy*. Edited by Colin E. Gunton. Edinburgh: T&T Clark, 1997.
Gunton, Colin E. *The Promise of Trinitarian Theology*. 2nd and enl. ed. Edinburgh: T&T Clark, 1997.

Gunton, Colin E. *Yesterday and Today: A Study of Continuities in Christology*. 2nd ed. London: Darton, Longman and Todd, 1997.

Gunton, Colin E. "The Atonement." Pages 536-41 in *Routledge Encyclopaedia of Philosophy*. Edited by Edward Craig. London: Routledge, 1998.

Gunton, Colin E. "Martin Kahler Revisited: Variations on Hebrews 4.15." *Ex Auditu* 14 (1998): 21-30.

Gunton, Colin E. *The Triune Creator: A Historical and Systematic Study*. Edinburgh: Edinburgh University Press, 1998.

Gunton, Colin E. "A Far-off Gleam of the Gospel: Salvation in Tolkien's *The Lord of the Rings*." Pages 124-40 in *Tolkien: A Celebration. Collected Writings on a Literary Legacy*. Edited by Joseph Pearce. San Francisco: Ignatius Press, 1999.

Gunton, Colin E. "A Rose by Any Other Name? From 'Christian Doctrine' to 'Systematic Theology.'" *International Journal of Systematic Theology* 1 (1999): 4-23.

Gunton, Colin E. "Aspects of Salvation: Some Unscholastic Themes from Calvin's Institutes." *International Journal of Systematic Theology* 1 (1999): 113-18.

Gunton, Colin E. "Christ the Wisdom of God: A Study in Divine and Human Action." Pages 249-61 in *Where Shall Wisdom Be Found? Wisdom in the Bible, the Church and the Contemporary World*. Edited by Stephen C. Barton. Edinburgh: T&T Clark, 1999.

Gunton, Colin E. "The Cross and the City: R.W. Dale and the Doctrine of the Atonement." Pages 1-13 in *The Cross and the City: Essays in Commemoration of Robert William Dale*. Supplement to the *Journal of the United Reformed Church History Society* vol. 6; Supplement to the *Congregational History Circle Magazine* vol. 4. Edited by Clyde Binfield. Cambridge: United Reformed Church History Society, 1999.

Gunton, Colin E. "Dogma, the Church and the Task of Theology." Pages 1-22 in *The Task of Theology Today: Doctrines and Dogmas*. Edited by Victor Pfitzner and Hilary Regan. Edinburgh: T&T Clark, 1999.

Gunton, Colin E. "Editorial: Orthodoxy." *International Journal of Systematic Theology* 1 (1999): 113-18.

Gunton, Colin E. *Incarnation and Imagery: Words, the World and the Triune God*. Volume 4 of *Farmington Papers; Philosophy of Religion*. Oxford: Farmington Institute for Christian Studies, 1999.

Gunton, Colin E. "Authority." Pages 55-6 in *The Oxford Companion to Christian Thought*. Edited by Adrian Hastings, Hugh Pyper and Alistair Mason. Oxford: Oxford University Press, 2000.

Gunton, Colin E. "The Atonement and the Triune God." Pages 113-31 in *Theology After Liberalism: A Reader*. Edited by George P. Schner and John B. Webster. Oxford: Blackwell, 2000.

Gunton, Colin E. "The Church as a School of Virtue? Human Formation in Trinitarian Framework, Faithfulness and Fortitude." Pages 211-21 in *Faithfulness and Fortitude: In Conversation with the Theological Ethics of Stanley Hauerwas*. Edited by Mark Thiessen Nation and Samuel Wells. Edinburgh: T&T Clark, 2000.

Gunton, Colin E. "Creation and Mediation in the Theology of Robert W. Jenson: An Encounter and Convergence." Pages 80-93 in *Trinity, Time and Church: A Response to the Theology of Robert W. Jenson*. Edited by Colin E. Gunton. Grand Rapids: Eerdmans, 2000.

Gunton, Colin E. "Dogmatic Theses on Eschatology: Conference Response." Pages 139-44 in *The Future as God's Gift: Explorations in Christian Eschatology*. Edited by David Fergusson and Marcel Sarot. Edinburgh: T&T Clark, 2000.

Gunton, Colin E. "Election and Eschatology in the Post-Constantinian Church." *Scottish Journal of Theology* 53 (2000): 212-27.

Gunton, Colin E. "Holy Spirit." Pages 304–6 in *The Oxford Companion to Christian Thought*. Edited by Adrian Hastings, Hugh Pyper and Alistair Mason. Oxford: Oxford University Press, 2000.

Gunton, Colin E. *Intellect and Action: Elucidations on Christian Theology and the Life of Faith*. Edinburgh: T&T Clark, 2000.

Gunton, Colin E. "Protestantism." Pages 571–4 in *The Oxford Companion to Christian Thought*. Edited by Adrian Hastings, Hugh Pyper and Alistair Mason. Oxford: Oxford University Press, 2000.

Gunton, Colin E. "'Response' to 'Are You Saved? Receiving the Full Benefits of Grace,' by Cynthia L. Rigby." *Insights: The Faculty Journal of Austin Seminary* 115 (2000): 27–9.

Gunton, Colin E. "Salvation." Pages 143–58 in *The Cambridge Companion to Karl Barth*. Edited by John Webster. Cambridge: Cambridge University Press, 2000.

Gunton, Colin E. *Theology through Preaching: Sermons for Brentwood*. Edinburgh: T&T Clark, 2001.

Gunton, Colin E. "Three Pitfalls in Preaching Creation." *Living Pulpit* 9 (2000): 14–15.

Gunton, Colin E., ed. *Trinity, Time and Church: A Response to the Theology of Robert W. Jenson*. Grand Rapids: Eerdmans, 2000.

Gunton, Colin E. "And in One Lord Jesus Christ ... Begotten Not Made." *Pro Ecclesia* 10 (2001): 261–74.

Gunton, Colin E. "And in One Lord, Jesus Christ ... Begotten, Not Made." Pages 35–48 in *Nicene Christianity: The Future for a New Ecumenism*. Edited by Christopher R. Seitz. Grand Rapids: Brazos Press, 2001.

Gunton, Colin E. *Becoming and Being: The Doctrine of God in Charles Hartshorne and Karl Barth*. 2nd ed. London: SCM Press, 2001.

Gunton, Colin E. "Being and Person: T. F. Torrance's Doctrine of God." Pages 115–38 in *The Promise of Trinitarian Theology: Theologians in Dialogue with T. F. Torrance*. Edited by Elmer M. Colyer. Lanham, MD: Rowman & Littlefield, 2001.

Gunton, Colin E. "Can We Know Anything about God Anyway?." Pages 219–23 in *The Practice of Theology: A Reader*. Edited by Colin E. Gunton, Stephen R. Holmes and Murray A. Rae. London: SCM Press, 2001.

Gunton, Colin E. *Commentary on the Lectionary*. 3 vols. London: Continuum, 2001.

Gunton, Colin E. "Creeds and Confessions." Pages 101–5 in *The Practice of Theology: A Reader*, edited by Colin E. Gunton, Stephen R. Holmes and Murray A. Rae. London: SCM Press, 2001.

Gunton, Colin E. "Doing Theology in the University Today." Pages 441–55 in *The Practice of Theology: A Reader*. Edited by Colin E. Gunton, Stephen R. Holmes and Murray A. Rae. London: SCM Press, 2001.

Gunton, Colin E. "Introduction." Pages xv–xx in Karl Barth, *Protestant Theology in the Nineteenth Century*. New ed. London: SCM Press, 2001.

Gunton, Colin E. "The Place of Reason in Theology." Pages 149–53 in *The Practice of Theology: A Reader*. Edited by Colin E. Gunton, Stephen R. Holmes and Murray A. Rae. London: SCM Press, 2001.

Gunton, Colin E. "Preface." Pages vii–xi in Karl Barth, *Dogmatics in Outline*. Translated by G. T. Thompson. English Translation with Preface. London: SCM Press, 2001.

Gunton, Colin E. "'Until He Comes': Towards an Eschatology of Church Membership." *International Journal of Systematic Theology* 3 (2001): 187–200.

Gunton, Colin E. *Act and Being: Towards a Theology of the Divine Attributes*. London: SCM Press, 2002.

Gunton, Colin E. *The Christian Faith: An Introduction to Christian Doctrine*. Oxford: Blackwell, 2002.

Gunton, Colin E. "The Spirit Moved Over the Face of the Waters: The Holy Spirit and the Created Order." *International Journal of Systematic Theology* 4 (2002): 190–204.

Gunton, Colin E. "Theology in Communion." Pages 31–44 in *Shaping a Theological Mind: Theological Context and Methodology*. Edited by Darren C. Marks. Burlington, VT: Ashgate, 2002.

Gunton, Colin E. "Trinity and Trustworthiness." Pages 275–84 in *The Trustworthiness of God: Perspectives on the Nature of Scripture*. Edited by Paul Helm and Carl R. Trueman. Grand Rapids: Eerdmans, 2002.

Gunton, Colin E. "We Believe in … the Holy Spirit, Who with the Father and Son Is Worshiped and Glorified." Pages 21–36 in *Fire and Wind: The Holy Spirit in the Church Today*. Edited by Joseph D. Small. Louisville, KY: Geneva Press, 2002.

Gunton, Colin E. *Father, Son & Holy Spirit: Toward a Fully Trinitarian Theology*. London: T&T Clark, 2003.

Gunton, Colin E. "Introduction." Pages 1–11 in *The Theology of Reconciliation*. Edited by Colin E. Gunton. London: T&T Clark, 2003.

Gunton, Colin E., ed. *The Theology of Reconciliation*. London: T&T Clark, 2003.

Gunton, Colin E. "Towards a Theology of Reconciliation." Pages 167–74 in *The Theology of Reconciliation*. Edited by Colin E. Gunton. London: T&T Clark, 2003.

Gunton, Colin E. "A Sermon: The Almighty God." Pages 33–7 in *Exploring and Proclaiming the Apostles' Creed: Vol. 1*. Edited by Roger Van Harn. Grand Rapids: Eerdmans, 2004.

Gunton, Colin E. "Election and Eschatology in the Post-Constantinian Church." Pages 97–110 in *Reformed Theology: Identity and Ecumenicity*. Edited by Wallace M. Alston Jr. and Michael J. Welker. Grand Rapids: Eerdmans, 2004.

Gunton, Colin E. "Preaching from the Letters." Pages 621–6 in *Exploring and Proclaiming the Apostles' Creed: Vol 2*. Edited by Roger Van Harn. Grand Rapids: Eerdmans, 2004.

Gunton, Colin E. "Sermon: 1 Corinthians 15:51–8." Pages 228–31 in *Exploring and Proclaiming the Apostles' Creed: Vol 2*. Edited by Roger Van Harn. Grand Rapids: Eerdmans, 2004.

Gunton, Colin E. "The Truth … and the Spirit of Truth: The Trinitarian Shape of Christian Theology." Pages 341–51 in *Loving God with Our Minds: The Pastor as Theologian: Essays in Honor of Wallace M. Alston*. Edited by Michael Welker and Cynthia A. Jarvis. Grand Rapids: Eerdmans, 2004.

Gunton, Colin E. "Towards a Trinitarian Reading of the Tradition: The Relevance of the 'Eternal' Trinity." Pages 63–72 in *Trinitarian Soundings in Systematic Theology*. Edited by Paul Louis Metzger. London: T&T Clark, 2005.

Gunton, Colin E. "Confessions, Dogmas and Doctrine: An Exploration or Some Interactions." Pages 215–17 in *Reformed Theology in Contemporary Perspective: Westminster: Yesterday, Today—and Tomorrow?* Edited by Lynn Quigley. Edinburgh: Rutherford House, 2006.

Gunton, Colin E. "Persons and Particularity." Pages 97–108 in *The Theology of John Zizioulas*. Edited by Douglas Knight. Aldershot: Ashgate, 2006.

Gunton, Colin E. *The Barth Lectures*. Edited by Paul Brazier. London: T&T Clark, 2007.

Gunton, Colin E. "Revelation: Do Christians Know Something No One Else Knows?" Pages 1–19 in *Tolerance and Truth: The Spirit of the Age or the Spirit of Christ?* Edited by Angus Morrison. Edinburgh: Rutherford House, 2007.

Gunton, Colin E. "The Spirit Moved Over the Face of the Waters: The Holy Spirit and the Created Order." Pages 56–73 in *Spirit of Truth and Power: Studies in Christian Doctrine and Experience*. Edited by David F. Wright. Edinburgh: Rutherford House, 2007.

Gunton, Colin E. *The Theologian as Preacher. Further Sermons from Colin E. Gunton*. Edited by Sarah J. Gunton and John E. Colwell. London: T&T Clark, 2007.

Gunton, Colin E. "Reformation Accounts of the Church's Response to Human Culture." Pages 79–93 in *Public Theology in Cultural Engagement*. Edited by Stephen R. Holmes. Milton Keynes: Paternoster, 2008.
Gunton, Colin E. *Revelation and Reason*. Edited by Paul Brazier. London: T&T Clark, 2008.
Gunton, Colin E. and Daniel W. Hardy, eds. *On Being the Church: Essays on the Christian Community*. Edinburgh: T&T Clark, 1989.
Gunton, Colin E., Stephen R. Holmes, and Murray A. Rae, eds. *The Practice of Theology: A Reader*. London: SCM Press, 2001.
Gunton, Colin E. and Robert Jenson. "The *Logos Ensarkos* and Reason." Pages 78–85 in *Reason and the Reasons of Faith*. Edited by Paul J. Griffiths and Reinhard Hütter. London: T&T Clark, 2005.
Gunton, Colin E., Páraic Réamonn, and Alan P. F. Sell, eds. *The Church in the Reformed Tradition: Discussion Papers Prepared by a Working Party of the European Committee*. Geneva: World Alliance of Reformed Churches, 1995.
Gunton, Colin E. and Christoph Schwöbel, eds. *Persons, Divine and Human: King's College Essays in Theological Anthropology*. Edinburgh: T&T Clark, 1992.
Habets, Myk. "Gunton on Pneumatology." Pages 121–36 in *T&T Clark Handbook of Colin Gunton*. Edited by Andrew Picard, Myk Habets and Murray Rae. London: T&T Clark, 2021.
Han, Youngsung. "Trinity and Ontology: Towards a Theology of Being as Space in Colin Gunton." PhD diss., Middlesex University, 2017.
Hardy, Daniel W. "Created and Redeemed Sociality." Pages 21–47 in *On Being the Church: Essays on the Christian Community*. Edited by Colin E. Gunton and Daniel W. Hardy. Edinburgh: T&T Clark, 1989.
Harland, Philip A. *Associations, Synagogues, and Congregations: Claiming a Place in Ancient Mediterranean Society*. Minneapolis: Fortress Press, 2003.
Harnack, Adolf. *History of Dogma*. Translated by Neil Buchanan. 7 vols. New York: Dover Publications, 1961.
Harris, Leon L. "Holy Spirit as Communion: Colin Gunton's Pneumatology of Communion and Frank Macchia's Pneumatology of Koinonia." PhD diss., University of Aberdeen, Scotland, 2014.
Harris, Leon L. *The Holy Spirit as Communion: Colin Gunton's Pneumatology of Communion and Frank Macchia's Pneumatology of Koinonia*. Eugene: Wipf and Stock, 2017.
Harvey, Lincoln. "Introduction." Pages 1–7 in *The Theology of Colin Gunton*. Edited by Lincoln Harvey. London: T&T Clark, 2010.
Harvey, Lincoln. "The Theological Promise of Michael Polanyi's Project: An Examination within the Contemporary Context of Atheism and the Constructivist Critique of the Natural Sciences." Pages 56–73 in *Critical Conversations: Michael Polanyi and Christian Theology*. Edited by Murray A. Rae. Eugene: Wipf and Stock, 2012.
Harvey, Lincoln. "Essays on the Trinity: Introduction." Pages 1–13 in *Essays on the Trinity*. Edited by Lincoln Harvey. Eugene: Wipf and Stock, 2018.
Hauerwas, Stanley. "Timeful Friends: Living with the Handicapped." Pages 11–27 in *Critical Reflections on Stanley Hauerwas' Theology of Disability: Disabling Society, Enabling Theology*. Edited by John Swinton. Binghamton: Harworth Pastoral Press, 2004.
Hays, Richard B. *First Corinthians*. Interpretation. Louisville: John Knox Press, 1997.
Hennessy, Kristen. "An Answer to de Régnon's Accusers: Why We Should Not Speak of 'His' Paradigm." *Harvard Theological Review* 100 (2007): 179–97.

Heron, Alasdair I. C., ed. *The Forgotten Trinity: A Selection of Papers Presented to the BCC Study Commission on Trinitarian Doctrine Today*. London: BCC/CCBI, 1991.
Hill, Wesley. *Paul and the Trinity: Persons, Relations, and the Pauline Letters*. Grand Rapids: Eerdmans, 2015.
Höhne, David A. *Spirit and Sonship: Colin Gunton's Theology of Particularity and the Holy Spirit*. Farnham, UK and Burlington, VT: Ashgate, 2010.
Holmes, Stephen R. "'Something Much Too Plain to Say': Towards a Defence of the Doctrine of Divine Simplicity." *Neue Zeitschrift für Systematische Theologie und Religionsphilosophie* 43 (2001): 137–54.
Holmes, Stephen R. "Foreword." Pages ix–xii in Colin E. Gunton, *Father, Son and Holy Spirit: Essays Toward a Fully Trinitarian Theology*. London: T&T Clark, 2003.
Holmes, Stephen R. "Obituary: Rev. Professor Colin E. Gunton." *Guardian*, June 3, 2003. http://www.theguardian.com/news/2003/jun/03/guardianobituaries.highereducation.
Holmes, Stephen R. "Triune Creativity: Trinity, Creation, Art and Science." Pages 73–86 in Pages 63–72 in *Trinitarian Soundings in Systematic Theology*. Edited by Paul Louis Metzger. London: T&T Clark, 2005.
Holmes, Stephen R. "Introduction: The Theologian as Preacher, the Preacher as Theologian." Pages xi–xxiii in Colin E. Gunton. *The Theologian as Preacher: Further Sermons from Colin E. Gunton*. Edited by Sarah J. Gunton and John E. Colwell. London: T&T Clark, 2007.
Holmes, Stephen R. "Can Theology Engage with Culture?." Pages 1–19 in *Public Theology in Cultural Engagement*. Edited by Stephen R. Holmes. Milton Keynes: Paternoster, 2008.
Holmes, Stephen R. "Three versus One? Some Problems of Social Trinitarianism." *The Journal of Reformed Theology* 3 (2009): 77–89.
Holmes, Stephen R. "Towards the *Analogia Personae et Relationis*: Developments in Gunton's Trinitarian Thinking." Pages 32–48 in *The Theology of Colin Gunton*. Edited by Lincoln Harvey. London: T&T Clark, 2010.
Holmes, Stephen R. *The Quest for the Trinity: The Doctrine of God in Scripture, History and Modernity*. Downers Grove: IVP, 2012.
Holmes, Stephen R. "In Memoriam: Colin Gunton." *Shored Fragments*, May 6, 2013. http://steverholmes.org.uk/blog/?p=6973.
Holmes, Stephen R. "Classical Trinity: Evangelical Perspective." Pages 25–48 in *Two Views on the Doctrine of the Trinity*. Edited by Jason S. Sexton. Grand Rapids: Zondervan, 2014.
Holmes, Stephen R. "Trinitarian Action and Inseparable Operations: Some Historical and Dogmatic Reflections." Pages 60–74 in *Advancing Trinitarian Theology: Explorations in Constructive Dogmatics*. Edited by Oliver D. Crisp and Fred Sanders. Grand Rapids: Zondervan, 2014.
Holmes, Stephen R. "Response: In Praise of Being Criticized." Pages 137–55 in *The Holy Trinity Revisited: Essays in Response to Stephen R. Holmes*. Edited by Thomas A. Noble and Jason S. Sexton. Milton Keynes: Paternoster, 2015.
Holmes, Stephen R. "Gunton, Colin Ewart (1941–2003)." Pages 385–6 in *New Dictionary of Theology: Historical and Systematic*. 2nd ed. Edited by Martin Davie, Tim Grass, Stephen R. Holmes, John C. McDowell and T. A. Noble. Downers Grove: IVP, 2016.
Holmes, Stephen R. "The Rise and Fall of Social Trinitarianism." *Mission Catalyst* 4 (2016): 4–6.
Holmes, Stephen R. "Gunton and Coleridge." Pages 315–26 in *T&T Clark Handbook of Colin Gunton*. Edited by Andrew Picard, Myk Habets and Murray Rae. London: T&T Clark, 2021.

hooks, bell. *Black Looks: Race and Representation*. Boston: South End Press, 1992.
Horsley, Richard A. "The First and Second Letters to the Corinthians." Pages 220–45 in *A Postcolonial Commentary on the New Testament Writings*. Edited by Fernando F. Segovia and R. S. Sugirtharajah. London: T&T Clark, 2007.
Hughes, Bill. "Bauman's Strangers: Impairment and the Invalidation of Disabled People in Modern and Postmodern Cultures." *Disability and Society* 17 (2002): 571–84.
Hughes, Bill. "Being Disabled: Towards a Critical Social Ontology for Disability Studies." *Disability and Society* 22 (2007): 673–84.
Hughes, Bill. "Civilising Modernity and the Ontological Invalidation of Disabled People." Pages 17–32 in *Disability and Social Theory: New Developments and Directions*. Edited by Dan Goodley, Bill Hughes and Lennard Davis. London: Palgrave Macmillan, 2012.
Hughes, Bill. "Disabled People as Counterfeit Citizens: The Politics of Resentment Past and Present." *Disability and Society* 30 (2015): 991–1004.
Hughes, Bill. "Impairment on the Move: The Disabled Incomer and Other Invalidating Intersections." *Disability and Society* 32 (2017): 467–82.
Hughes, Bill. "Invalidating Emotions in the Non-Disabled Imaginary: Fear, Pity and Disgust." Pages 89–101 in *Routledge Handbook of Disability Studies*. 2nd ed. Edited by Nick Watson and Simo Vehmas. London: Routledge, 2019.
Hughes, Bill. *A Historical Sociology of Disability: Human Validity and Invalidity from Antiquity to Early Modernity*. London: Routledge, 2020.
Jenson, Robert W. "Christ as Culture 1: Christ as Polity." *International Journal of Systematic Theology* 5 (2003): 323–9.
Jenson, Robert W. "Christ as Culture 2: Christ as Art." *International Journal of Systematic Theology* 6 (2004): 69–76.
Jenson, Robert W. "Christ as Culture 3: Christ as Drama." *International Journal of Systematic Theology* 6 (2004): 194–201.
Jenson, Robert W. "Afterword." Pages 217–20 in *Trinitarian Soundings in Systematic Theology*. Edited by Paul Louis Metzger. London: T&T Clark, 2005.
Jenson, Robert W. "A Decision Tree of Colin Gunton's Thinking." Pages 8–16 in *The Theology of Colin Gunton*. Edited by Lincoln Harvey. London: T&T Clark, 2010.
Jinkins, Michael. *The Church Faces Death: Ecclesiology in a Post-Modern Context*. Oxford: Oxford University Press, 1999.
Johnson, Keith E. *Rethinking the Trinity and Religious Pluralism: An Augustinian Assessment*. Downers Grove: IVP, 2011.
Kapic, Kelly M. "Gunton and Owen." Pages 339–58 in *T&T Clark Handbook of Colin Gunton*. Edited by Andrew Picard, Myk Habets and Murray Rae. London: T&T Clark, 2021.
Kilby, Karen. "*Perichoresis* and Projection: Problems with Social Doctrines of the Trinity." *New Blackfriars* 81 (2000): 432–45.
Kilby, Karen. "Is an Apophatic Trinitarianism Possible?." *International Journal of Systematic Theology* 12 (2010): 65–77.
Kilby, Karen. "Trinity, Tradition and Politics." Pages 73–86 in *Recent Developments in Trinitarian Theology: An International Symposium*. Edited by Christophe Chalamet and Mark Vial. Minneapolis: Fortress Press, 2014.
Kilby, Karen. "Negative Theology and Meaningless Suffering." *Modern Theology* 36 (2019): 92–104.
Kim, Yung Suk. *Christ's Body in Corinth: The Politics of a Metaphor*. Minneapolis: Fortress Press, 2008.
Kim, Yung Suk. "Reclaiming Christ's Body (*Soma Chrisou*): Embodiment of God's Gospel in Paul's Letters." *Interpretation* 67 (2013): 20–9.

Kittel, Gerard and Gerhard Friedrich, eds. *Theological Dictionary of the New Testament*. Translated by Geoffrey W. Bromiley. 10 vols. Grand Rapids: Eerdmans, 1964–1976.

Klinghardt, Matthias. *Gemeinschaftsmahl Und Mahlgemeinschaft: Soziologie Und Liturgie Frühchristlicher Mahlfeiern*. TANZ 13. Tübingen: Francke, 1996.

Klinghardt, Matthias. "A Typology of the Communal Meal." Pages 9–22 in *Meals in the Early Christian World: Social Formation, Experimentation, and Conflict at the Table*. Edited by Dennis E. Smith and Hal Taussig. New York: Palgrave Macmillan, 2012.

Kloppenborg, John S. "Precedence at the Communal Meal in Corinth." *Novum Testamentum* 58 (2016): 167–203.

Kloppenborg, John S. "Associations, Christ Groups, and Their Place in the *Polis*." *Zeitschrift Für Die Neutestamentliche Wissenschaft* 108 (2017): 1–56.

Kloppenborg, John S. *Christ's Associations: Connecting and Belonging in the Ancient City*. New Haven: Yale University Press, 2019.

Koester, Craig. *Revelation: A New Translation with Introduction and Commentary*. Anchor. New Haven: Yale University Press, 2014.

Lashier, Jackson. *Irenaeus on the Trinity*. Supplements to Vigiliae Christianae 127. Leiden: Brill, 2014.

Last, Richard. *The Pauline Church and the Corinthian* Ekklēsia: *Greco-Roman Associations in Comparative Context*. Cambridge: Cambridge University Press, 2016.

Last, Richard. "*Ekklēsia* outside the Septuagint and the *Dēmos*: The Titles of Greco-Roman Associations and Christ-Followers' Groups." *Journal of Biblical Literature* 137 (2018): 959–80.

Lawrence, Louise J. *Sense and Stigma in the Gospels: Depictions of Sensory-Disabled Characters*. Oxford: Oxford University Press, 2013.

Lee, Jin Hwan. *The Lord's Supper in Corinth in the Context of Greco-Roman Private Associations*. Lanham: Lexington Books/Fortress Academic, 2018.

Lossky, Vladimir. *The Mystical Theology of the Eastern Church*. London: James Clarke & Co. Ltd, 1957.

Lyle, Randal C. "Social Trinitarianism as an Option for 21st Century Theology: A Systematic Analysis of Colin Gunton's Trinitarian Paradigm." PhD diss., SouthWestern Baptist Theological Seminary, 2003.

Maier, Harry O. *Picturing Paul in Empire: Imperial Image, Text and Persuasion in Colossians, Ephesians and the Pastoral Epistles*. London: T&T Clark, 2013.

Martin, Dale B. *The Corinthian Body*. New Haven: Yale University Press, 1995.

Matera, Frank J. *II Corinthians: A Commentary*. New Testament Library. Louisville: Westminster John Knox Press, 2003.

Matthews, Gareth B. and S. Marc Cohen. "The One and the Many." *The Review of Metaphysics* 21 (1968): 630–55.

Mawson, Michael. *Christ Existing as Community: Bonhoeffer's Ecclesiology*. Oxford: Oxford University Press, 2018.

McCloughry, Roy and Wayne Morris, eds. *Making a World of Difference: Christian Reflections on Disability*. London: SPCK, 2002.

McCormack, Bruce L. "Foreword." Pages 1–4 in *Trinitarian Soundings in Systematic Theology*. Edited by Paul Louis Metzger. London: T&T Clark, 2005.

McCormack, Bruce L. "*The One, the Three and the Many*: In Memory of Colin Gunton." *Cultural Encounters* 1 (2005): 7–17.

MacDonald, Nathan. *Deuteronomy and the Meaning of "Monotheism"*. 2nd ed. Tübingen: Mohr Siebeck, 2012.

McDowell, John C. "Gunton on Modernity." Pages 169–86 in *T&T Clark Handbook of Colin Gunton*. Edited by Andrew Picard, Myk Habets and Murray Rae. London: T&T Clark, 2021.

McFadyen, Alistair I. *The Call to Personhood: A Christian Theory of the Individual in Social Relationships*. Cambridge: Cambridge University Press, 1990.

McFarlane, Graham W. P. *Christ and the Spirit: The Doctrine of the Incarnation According to Edward Irving*. Carlisle: Paternoster, 1997.

McFarlane, Graham W. P. "Gunton and Irving." Pages 327–38 in *T&T Clark Handbook of Colin Gunton*. Edited by Andrew Picard, Myk Habets and Murray Rae. London: T&T Clark, 2021.

McGrath, Alister E. *A Scientific Theology: Reality*. Grand Rapids: Eerdmans, 2002.

McKewon, James. *Genesis*. Grand Rapids: Eerdmans, 2008.

McNall, Joshua. *A Free Corrector: Colin Gunton and the Legacy of Augustine*. Minneapolis: Fortress Press, 2015.

McNall, Joshua. "Gunton and Augustine." Pages 269–84 in *T&T Clark Handbook of Colin Gunton*. Edited by Andrew Picard, Myk Habets and Murray Rae. London: T&T Clark, 2021.

McRae, Rachel M. "Eating with Honor: The Corinthian Lord's Supper in Light of Voluntary Association Meal Practices." *Journal of Biblical Literature* 130 (2011): 165–81.

Metzger, Paul Louis. *The Word of God and the World of Culture: Sacred and Secular through the Theology of Karl Barth*. Grand Rapids: Eerdmans, 2003.

Metzger, Paul Louis. "Introduction: What Difference Does the Trinity Make?" Pages 5–8 in *Trinitarian Soundings in Systematic Theology*. Edited by Paul Louis Metzger. London: T&T Clark, 2005.

Metzger, Paul Louis. "Response to Bruce L. McCormack's Tribute." *Cultural Encounters* 1 (2005): 18–22.

Metzger, Paul Louis. "Gunton on Revelation." Pages 9–24 in *T&T Clark Handbook of Colin Gunton*. Edited by Andrew Picard, Myk Habets and Murray Rae. London: T&T Clark, 2021.

Middleton, J. Richard. *The Liberating Image: The* Imago Dei *in Genesis 1*. Grand Rapids: Brazos, 2005.

Milgrom, Jacob. *Leviticus 1–16*. Anchor. New York: Doubleday, 1991.

Moberly, R. W. L. *Old Testament Theology: Reading the Hebrew Bible as Christian Scripture*. Grand Rapids: Baker Academic, 2013.

Moberly, R. W. L. *The God of the Old Testament: Encountering the Divine in Christian Scripture*. Grand Rapids: Baker Academic, 2020.

Molnar, Paul D. "Review of 'Father, Son and Holy Spirit: Toward a Fully Trinitarian Theology' by Colin E. Gunton." *Pro Ecclesia* 14 (2005): 494–7.

Molnar, Paul D. "Classic Trinity: Catholic Perspective." Pages 69–95 in *Two Views on the Doctrine of the Trinity*. Edited by Jason S. Sexton. Grand Rapids: Zondervan, 2014.

Molnar, Paul D. "Response to Stephen R. Holmes." Pages 49–54 in *Two Views on the Doctrine of the Trinity*. Edited by Jason S. Sexton. Grand Rapids: Zondervan, 2014.

Molnar, Paul D. *Divine Freedom and the Doctrine of the Immanent Trinity*. 2nd ed. London: T&T Clark, 2017.

Molnar, Paul D. "Gunton on the Trinity." Pages 41–58 in *T&T Clark Handbook of Colin Gunton*. Edited by Andrew Picard, Myk Habets and Murray Rae. London: T&T Clark, 2021.

Morris, Helen. "The City as Foil (Not Friend nor Foe): Conformity and Subversion in 1 Corinthians 12:12–31." Pages 141–59 in *The Urban World of the First Christians*. Edited by Steve Walton, Paul R. Trebilco and David W. J. Gill. Grand Rapids: Eerdmans, 2017.
Nausner, Bernhard. "Human Experience and Triune God: Theological Exploration of the Relevance of Human Experience for Trinitarian Theology." PhD diss., University of Durham, Durham, 2007.
Nausner, Bernhard. "The Failure of a Laudable Project: Gunton, the Trinity and Human Self-Understanding." *Scottish Journal of Theology* 62 (2009): 403–20.
Officer, Alana and Tom Shakespeare. "The World Report on Disability and People with Intellectual Disabilities." *Journal of Policy and Practice in Intellectual Disabilities* 10 (2013): 86–8.
Oliver, Issac W. *Luke's Jewish Eschatology: The National Restoration of Israel in Luke-Acts*. New York: OUP, 2021.
Ormerod, Neil. "Augustine and the Trinity: Whose Crisis?" *Pacifica* 16 (2003): 17–32.
Palmer, Clare. "Stewardship: A Case Study in Environmental Ethics." Pages 63–75 in *Environmental Stewardship: Critical Perspectives—Past and Present*. Edited by R. J. Berry. London: T&T Clark International, 2006.
Pao, David W. *Acts and the Isaianic New Exodus*. Grand Rapids: Baker, 2000.
Papanikolaou, Aristotle. "Is John Zizioulas an Existentialist in Disguise? Response to Lucian Turcescu." *Modern Theology* 20 (2004): 601–7.
Papanikolaou, Aristotle. "The Necessity for *Theologia*: Thinking the Immanent Trinity in Orthodox Theology." Pages 87–106 in *Recent Developments in Trinitarian Theology: An International Symposium*. Edited by Christophe Chalamet and Marc Vial. Minneapolis: Fortress, 2014.
Park, Young-Ho. *Paul's Ekklesia as a Civic Assembly: Understanding the People of God in Their Politico-Social World*. Tübingen: Mohr Siebeck, 2015.
Patterson, Jane Lancaster. *Keeping the Feast: Metaphors of Sacrifice in 1 Corinthians and Philippians*. Atlanta: SBL Press, 2015.
Peppiatt, Lucy. *Women and Worship at Corinth*. Eugene: Wipf and Stock, 2015.
Peppiatt, Lucy. "Gunton on Community." Pages 205–20 in *T&T Clark Handbook of Colin Gunton*. Edited by Andrew Picard, Myk Habets and Murray Rae. London: T&T Clark, 2021.
Perkins, Pheme. *First Corinthians*. Paideia. Grand Rapids: Baker, 2012.
Picard, Andrew. "No Longer Strangers: Disabled Ontology and the Church as Meaningful Community in Liquid Modernity." Pages 53–72 in *Theology and the Experience of Disability: Interdisciplinary Perspectives from Voices Down Under*. Edited by Andrew Picard and Myk Habets. London: Routledge, 2016.
Picard, Andrew. "'On the Way' and 'in the Fray' in Aotearoa: A Pākehā's Covenantal Reflections from the Context of a Treaty People." *Pacific Journal of Baptist Research* 11 (2016): 44–58.
Picard, Andrew. "Colin Gunton." Pages 527–32 in *T&T Clark Companion to the Atonement*. Edited by Adam J. Johnson. London: Bloomsbury T&T Clark, 2017.
Picard, Andrew. "From Whiteness towards Witness: Revelation and Repentance as Unbelonging to Empire." Pages 241–68 in *The Art of Forgiveness*. Edited by Philip Halstead and Myk Habets. Lanham: Lexington Books/Fortress Academic, 2018.
Picard, Andrew. "Gunton on Culture." Pages 187–204 in *T&T Clark Handbook of Colin Gunton*. Edited by Andrew Picard, Myk Habets and Murray Rae. London: T&T Clark, 2021.

Picard, Andrew. "Unsettling Providential Partnership: A Critical Examination of Robert Maunsell and George Grey's Partnership in Māori Education." Pages 109–136 in *Unsettling Theologies: Memory, Identity, Place*. Edited by Brian Fiu Kolia and Michael Mawson. Cham: Palgrave Macmillan, 2024.

Picard, Andrew, and Jordyn Rapana. "'Let Justice Roll Down': Confronting Injustice in Theological Education for Māori Flourishing." *Studies in Christian Ethics* 36 (2023): 783–800.

Plato, *The Republic*. Translated by A. D. Lindsay. London: J. M. Dent, 1907.

Polanyi, Michael. *Science, Faith and Society*. Chicago: Chicago University Press, 1946.

Polanyi, Michael. *Personal Knowledge: Towards a Post-Critical Philosophy*. Chicago: Chicago University Press, 1962.

Polanyi, Michael. *The Tacit Dimension*. Chicago: Chicago University Press, 1966.

Rae, Murray. "The Travail of God." *International Journal of Systematic Theology* 5 (2003): 47–61.

Rae, Murray. "Introduction." Pages 1–12 in *The Person of Christ*. Edited by Stephen R. Holmes and Murray A. Rae. London: T&T Clark, 2005.

Rae, Murray. "Prolegomena." Pages 9–20 in *Trinitarian Soundings in Systematic Theology*. Edited by Paul Louis Metzger. London: T&T Clark, 2005.

Rae, Murray. "The Liturgical Shape of Christian Life." *Knox Centre for Ministry and Leadership*. Inaugural Lecture, 2008. http://knoxcentre.ac.nz/wp-content/uploads/2012/11/The-Liturgical-Shape-of-Christian-Life.pdf.

Rae, Murray. "The War on Terror in Ruatoki" *International Journal of Public Theology* 2 (2008): 277–91.

Rae, Murray. *Christian Theology: The Basics*. London: Routledge, 2015.

Rae, Murray. *Theology and Architecture: The Art of Place*. Waco: Baylor University Press, 2017.

Rae, Murray. "Colin E. Gunton (1941–2003): The Triune God, Scientific Endeavour, and God's Creation Project." Pages 205–29 in *Science and the Doctrine of Creation: The Approaches of Ten Modern Theologians*. Edited by Geoffrey H. Fulkerson and Joel Thomas Chopp. Downers Grove: InterVarsity Press, 2021.

Rae, Murray. "Gunton on Atonement." Pages 91–104 in *T&T Clark Handbook of Colin Gunton*. Edited by Andrew Picard, Myk Habets and Murray Rae. London: T&T Clark, 2021.

Rae, Murray. "Introduction." Pages 1–6 in *T&T Clark Handbook of Colin Gunton*. Edited by Andrew Picard, Myk Habets and Murray Rae. London: T&T Clark, 2021.

Rahner, Karl. *The Trinity*. Translated by Joseph Donceel. Tunbridge Wells: Burns & Oates, 1970.

Rauser, Randal. "Gunton and Western Philosophy." Pages 285–300 in *T&T Clark Handbook of Colin Gunton*. Edited by Andrew Picard, Myk Habets and Murray Rae. London: T&T Clark, 2021.

Reese, Naomi Noguchi. "Seeking the Welfare of the City: Toward an Evangelical Appropriation of the Pneumatology of Colin Gunton for Public Theology with Special Reference to U.S.A Context." PhD diss., Trinity Evangelical Divinity School, 2016.

Reese, Naomi Noguchi. "Colin E. Gunton and Public Theologians: Toward a Trinitarian Public Theology." *Evangelical Review of Theology* 41 (2017): 150–65.

Reynolds, Thomas E. *Vulnerable Communion: A Theology of Disability and Hospitality*. Grand Rapids: Brazos, 2008.

Rhodes, Michael J. "'Forward unto Virtue': Formative Practices and 1 Corinthians 11:17–34." *Journal of Theological Interpretation* 11 (2017): 119–38.

Rhodes, Michael J. "Formative Feasting: Practices and Economic Ethics in Deuteronomy's Tithe Meal and the Corinthian Lord's Supper." PhD diss., University of Aberdeen, Scotland, 2019.

Rhodes, Michael J. "Arranging the Chairs in the Beloved Community: The Politics, Problems, and Prospects of Multi-Racial Congregations in I Corinthians and Today." *Studies in Christian Ethics* 33 (2020): 510–28.

Roetzel, Calvin J. "The Language of War (2 Cor. 10:1–6) and the Language of Weakness (2 Cor. 11:21b–13:10)." *Biblical Interpretation* 17 (2009): 77–99.

Rumford, Chris. *The Globalization of Strangeness.* New York: Palgrave Macmillan, 2013.

Santmire, H. Paul. "So That He Might Fill All Things: Comprehending the Cosmic Love of Christ." *Dialog* 42 (2003): 257–78.

Schaeffer, Hans. *Createdness and Ethics: The Doctrine of Creation and Theological Ethics in the Theology of Colin E. Gunton and Oswald Bayer.* Berlin: Walter de Gruyter, 2006.

Schüssler Fiorenza, Elizabeth. *Ephesians.* Wisdom Commentary. Collegeville: Liturgical Press: 2017.

Schwöbel, Christoph. "Introduction." Pages 5–8 in *Trinitarian Theology Today: Essays on Divine Being and Act.* Edited by Christoph Schwöbel. Edinburgh: T&T Clark, 1995.

Schwöbel, Christoph. "God, Creation and the Christian Community: The Dogmatic Basis of a Christian Ethic of Createdness." Pages 149–76 in *The Doctrine of Creation: Essays in Dogmatics, History and Philosophy.* Edited by Colin E. Gunton. London: T&T Clark, 1997.

Schwöbel, Christoph. "Radical Monotheism and the Trinity." *Neue Zeitschrift für Systematische Theologie und Religionsphilosophie* 43 (2001): 54–74.

Schwöbel, Christoph. "A Tribute to Colin Gunton." Pages 13–18 in *The Person of Christ.* Edited by Stephen R. Holmes and Murray A. Rae. London: T&T Clark, 2005.

Schwöbel, Christoph. "The Shape of Colin Gunton's Theology: On the Way towards a Fully Trinitarian Theology." Pages 182–208 in *The Theology of Colin Gunton.* Edited by Lincoln Harvey. London: T&T Clark, 2010.

Schwöbel, Christoph. "Where Do We Stand in Trinitarian Theology?" Pages 9–71 in *Recent Developments in Trinitarian Theology: An International Symposium.* Edited by Christophe Chalamet and Mark Vial. Minneapolis: Fortress Press, 2014.

Schwöbel, Christoph. "Europa ohne Gott? Ansichten eines säkularen Zeitalters." Pages 106–19 in *Christentum und Europa: XVI. Europäischer Kongress für Theologie.* Edited by Michael Meyer-Blanck. Leipzig: Evangelische Verlagsanstalt GmbH, 2019.

Schwöbel, Christoph. "Gunton on Creation." Pages 59–76 in *T&T Clark Handbook of Colin Gunton.* Edited by Andrew Picard, Myk Habets and Murray Rae. London: T&T Clark, 2021.

Sexton, Jason S. "Beyond Social Trinitarianism: Stanley J. Grenz's Baptist, Trinitarian Innovation." *Baptist Quarterly* 44 (2012): 473–86.

Sexton, Jason S. *The Trinitarian Theology of Stanley J. Grenz.* London: T&T Clark, 2013.

Sexton, Jason S. "Introduction." Pages 13–24 in *Two Views on the Doctrine of the Trinity.* Edited by Jason S. Sexton. Grand Rapids: Zondervan, 2014.

Smith, Barry D. "The Problem with the Observance of the Lord's Supper in the Corinthian Church." *Bulletin for Biblical Research* 20 (2010): 517–43.

Smith, Dennis E. *From Symposium to Eucharist: The Banquet in the Early Christian World.* Minneapolis: Fortress Press, 2003.

Smith, Dennis E. and Hal E. Taussig, eds. *Meals in the Early Christian World: Social Formation, Experimentation, and Conflict at the Table.* New York: Palgrave and Macmillan, 2012.

Sonderegger, Katherine. *Systematic Theology: Volume 1, The Doctrine of God*. Minneapolis: Fortress Press, 2015.

Spence, Alan. "Incarnation and Inspiration: John Owen and the Coherence of Christology." PhD diss., King's College, London, 1989.

Spence, Alan. *Incarnation and Inspiration: John Owen and the Coherence of Christology*. London: T&T Clark, 2007.

Spence, Alan. "The Person as Willing Agent: Classifying Gunton's Christology." Pages 49–64 in *The Theology of Colin Gunton*. Edited by Lincoln Harvey. London: T&T Clark, 2010.

Stratis, Justin. "A Person's a Person, No Matter How Divine? The Question of Univocity and Personhood in Richard of St Victor's *De Trinitate*." *Scottish Journal of Theology* 70 (2017): 377–89.

Stringer, Michael D. "The Lord and Giver of Life: The Person and Work of the Holy Spirit in the Trinitarian Theology of Colin E. Gunton." PhD diss., University of Notre Dame, Australia, 2008.

Suda, Nathaniel. "Aspects of Colin Gunton's Reading of Genesis 1 and 2." *Colin Gunton Research Blog*, March 14, 2006. http://guntonresearch.blogspot.co.nz/2006/03/gunton-on-genesis-1-and-2.html.

Sutherland, Martin. "Pine Trees and Paradigms: Rethinking Mission in the West." Pages 131–48 in *Mission without Christendom: Exploring the Site. Essays for Brian Smith*. Edited by Martin Sutherland. Auckland: Carey Baptist College, 2000.

Swinton, John. "From Inclusion to Belonging: A Practical Theology of Community, Disability and Humanness." *Journal of Religion, Disability and Health* 16 (2012): 172–90.

Swinton, John. "From Inclusion to Belonging: Why 'Disabled' Bodies Are Necessary for the Faithfulness of the Church." Pages 171–82 in *Theology and the Experience of Disability: Interdisciplinary Perspectives from Voices Down Under*. Edited by Andrew Picard and Myk Habets. Abingdon: Routledge, 2016.

Tapper, Michael A. *Canadian Pentecostals, the Trinity and Contemporary Worship Music: The Things We Sing*. Leiden: Brill, 2017.

Taussig, Hal. *In the Beginning Was the Meal: Social Experimentation and Early Christian Identity*. Minneapolis: Fortress Press, 2009.

Taussig, Hal. "Introduction." Pages 1–8 in *Meals in the Early Christian World: Social Formation, Experimentation, and Conflict at the Table*. Edited by Dennis E. Smith and Hal E. Taussig. New York: Palgrave and Macmillan, 2012.

Taylor, Charles. *Sources of the Self: The Making of Modern Identity*. Harvard: Harvard University Press, 1989.

Taylor, Charles. *A Secular Age*. Cambridge, MA: The Belknap Press of Harvard University Press, 2007.

Teofilo, Manuele. "'He's My Mate': Cerebral Palsy, Church, and the Gift of Friendship." Pages 78–86 in *Theology and the Experience of Disability: Interdisciplinary Perspectives from Down Under*. Edited by Andrew Picard and Myk Habets. Abingdon: Routledge, 2016.

Terry, Justyn. "Colin Gunton's Doctrine of the Atonement: Transcending Rationalism by Metaphor." Pages 130–45 in *The Theology of Colin Gunton*. Edited by Lincoln Harvey. London: T&T Clark, 2010.

Theissen, Gerd. *The Social Setting of Pauline Christianity*. Edited and translated by John H. Schütz. Edinburgh: T&T Clark, 1982.

Thiselton, Anthony C. *The First Epistle to the Corinthians: A Commentary on the Greek Text*. NIGTC. Grand Rapids: Eerdmans, 2000.

Thompson, Mark D. "Has Colin Gunton's Theological Project Really Failed?." *Theological Theology*, December 2, 2009. http://markdthompson.blogspot.com/2009/12/has-colin-guntons-theological-project.html.

Thompson, Mark D. "Gunton and Calvin." Pages 301–14 in *T&T Clark Handbook of Colin Gunton*. Edited by Andrew Picard, Myk Habets and Murray Rae. London: T&T Clark, 2021.

Tibbs, Eve M. "East Meets West: Trinity, Truth and Communion in John Zizioulas and Colin Gunton." PhD diss., Fuller Theological Seminary, 2006.

Tibbs, Eve M. "Gunton and Zizioulas." Pages 387–402 in *T&T Clark Handbook of Colin Gunton*. Edited by Andrew Picard, Myk Habets and Murray Rae. London: T&T Clark, 2021.

Tilling, Chris. "Paul, the Trinity, and Contemporary Trinitarian Debates." *Pacific Journal of Baptist Research* 11 (2016): 19–43.

Tilling, Chris. "Paul the Trinitarian." Pages 36–62 in *Essays on the Trinity*. Edited by Lincoln Harvey. Eugene: Wipf and Stock, 2018.

Torrance, Alan. "Welcome to Participants at the *Logos Conference*, 2019." *Pogos: A Logos Institute Podcast*, Episode 35, 2019. https://soundcloud.com/user-931091141/eleonore-stump-on-aquinas-understanding-of-a-life-in-grace.

Torrance, Thomas F. *Theology in Reconciliation: Essays towards Evangelical and Catholic Unity in East and West*. Grand Rapids: Eerdmans, 1976.

Towner, Philip H. "Pauline Theology or Pauline Tradition in the Pastoral Epistles: The Question of Method." *Tyndale Bulletin* 46 (1995): 287–314.

Trebilco, Paul. "Why Did the Early Christians Call Themselves ἡ ἐκκλησία?." *New Testament Studies* 57 (2011): 440–60.

Turcescu, Lucian. "'Person' versus 'Individual', and Other Modern Misreadings of Gregory of Nyssa." *Modern Theology* 18 (2002): 527–39.

van den Brink, Gijsbert. "Social Trinitarianism: A Discussion of Some Recent Theological Criticisms." *International Journal of Systematic Theology* 16 (2014): 331–50.

Van Kooten, George H. "'Ἐκκλησία τοῦ θεοῦ: The 'Church of God' and the Civic Assemblies (ἐκκλησίαι) of the Greek Cities in the Roman Empire: A Response to Paul Trebilco and Richard A. Horsley." *New Testament Studies* 58 (2012): 522–48.

Van Kuiken, E. Jerome. *Christ's Humanity in Current and Ancient Controversy: Fallen or Not?* London: T&T Clark, 2017.

Waaler, Erik. *The Shema and the First Commandment in First Corinthians: An Intertextual Approach to Paul's Re-Reading of Deuteronomy*. Tübingen: Mohr Siebeck, 2008.

Walton, Steve. "Paul, Patronage and Pay: What Do We Know about the Apostle's Financial Support?" Pages 220–33 in *Paul as Missionary: Identity, Activity, Theology, and Practice*. Edited by Trevor J. Burke and Brian S. Rosner. London: T&T Clark, 2011.

Watson, Francis. *Text, Church and Word: Biblical Interpretation in Theological Perspective*. Edinburgh: T&T Clark, 1994.

Webster, John. "Systematic Theology after Barth: Jüngel, Jenson, and Gunton." Pages 249–64 in *The Modern Theologians: An Introduction to Christian Theology Since 1918*. 3rd ed. Edited by David F. Ford. Malden: Blackwell, 2005.

Webster, John. "Gunton and Barth." Pages 17–32 in *The Theology of Colin Gunton*. Edited by Lincoln Harvey. London: T&T Clark, 2010.

Webster, John. "'In the Society of God': Some Principles of Ecclesiology." Pages 200–23 in *Perspectives on Ecclesiology and Ethnography*. Edited by Pete Ward. Grand Rapids: Eerdmans, 2012.

Welborn, Laurence L. "The Runaway Paul." *The Harvard Theological Review* 92 (1999): 115–63.

Welborn, Laurence L. "Μωρός γένεσθω: Paul's Appropriation of the Role of the Fool in 1 Corinthians 1–4." *Biblical Interpretation* 10 (2002): 420–35.
Welborn, Laurence L. *Paul, the Fool of Christ: A Study of 1 Corinthians 1–4 in the Comic-Philosophic Tradition*. London: T&T Clark, 2005.
Welborn, Laurence L. "The Corinthian Correspondence." Pages 205–42 in *All Things to All Cultures: Paul Among Jews, Greeks, and Romans*. Edited by Mark Harding and Alanna Nobbs. Grand Rapids: Eerdmans, 2013.
Welborn, Laurence L. "Inequality in Roman Corinth: Evidence from Diverse Sources Evaluated by a Neo-Ricardian Model." Pages 47–84 in *The First Urban Churches 2: Roman Corinth*. Edited by James R. Harrison and Laurence L. Welborn. Atlanta: SBL Press, 2016.
Welborn, Laurence L. "How 'Democratic' Was the Pauline *Ekklēsia*? an Assessment with Special Reference to the Christ Groups of Roman Corinth." *New Testament Studies* 65 (2019): 289–309.
Whitney, William B. "The Correlation Between Creation and Culture in the Theology of Abraham Kuyper and Colin E. Gunton." Pages 76–93 in *The Kuyper Center Review. Volume 3: Calvinism and Culture*. Edited by Gordon Graham. Grand Rapids: Eerdmans, 2013.
Whitney, William B. *Problem and Promise in Colin E. Gunton's Doctrine of Creation*. Leiden: Brill, 2013.
Winter, Bruce W. *After Paul Left Corinth: The Influence of Secular Ethics and Social Change*. Grand Rapids: Eerdmans, 2001.
Witherington III, Ben. *Torah Old and New: Exegesis, Intertextuality, and Hermeneutics*. Minneapolis: Fortress Press, 2018.
Wittgenstein, Ludwig. *Philosophical Investigations*. Translated by G. E. M. Anscombe. 2nd ed. Oxford: Basil Books, 1958.
Wright, N. T. *Paul and the Faithfulness of God*. Minneapolis: Fortress Press, 2013.
Wright, Terry J. "Colin Gunton on Providence: Critical Commentaries." Pages 146–65 in *The Theology of Colin Gunton*. Edited by Lincoln Harvey. London: T&T Clark, 2010.
Wright, Terry J. "Colin Gunton: An Introduction." *Theology and Religion Online*. https://www.theologyandreligiononline.com/article?docid=b-9781350996595&tocid=b-9781350996595-002.
Wright, Terry J. "Gunton on Eschatology." Pages 137–50 in *T&T Clark Handbook of Colin Gunton*. Edited by Andrew Picard, Myk Habets and Murray Rae. London: T&T Clark, 2021.
Zizioulas, John D. *Being as Communion: Studies in Personhood and the Church*. London: Darton, Longman and Todd, 1985.
Zizioulas, John D. "On Being a Person: Towards an Ontology of Personhood." Pages 33–46 in *Persons, Divine and Human: King's College Essays in Theological Anthropology*. Edited by Christoph Schwöbel and Colin E. Gunton. Edinburgh: T&T Clark, 1991.
Zizioulas, John D. *Communion and Otherness: Further Studies in Personhood and Church*. Edited by Paul McPartlan. London: T&T Clark, 2006.

INDEX

ableism 14, 247, 250, 268, 277–9, 284
abstraction 10, 19, 37, 42, 44, 46–7, 51, 54–5, 66, 93, 103–4, 108–9, 159, 173, 200, 212, 228–30
Adam 13, 117, 128, 138, 155–6, 158, 167–72, 174, 177–8, 185, 189–92, 194, 197–8, 200–1, 208–9, 282
alienation 19–20, 22, 38, 43, 136, 179
analogy 12, 31, 34, 56, 59, 62, 63, 80, 95, 97, 101, 114–15, 126, 152, 208, 211, 215–17, 219, 224, 226
Anatolios, Khaled 94–7, 99, 101–2, 105, 217
Anizor, Uche 107, 183, 199, 200, 216, 224–7, 229
Aquinas, Thomas 31–2, 69, 77
Aristotle 25
ascension 52, 159, 176, 177, 179, 190–4, 198
aseity 32, 40, 91, 97, 131, 145–6, 200
atonement 126, 167, 170, 177, 182, 184–5, 237
Augustine 27, 30, 36–7, 48–9, 69, 77–80, 82–6, 96, 104, 107, 125, 140–2, 196–7, 212
Ayres, Lewis 76–8, 81, 94

Babel 21, 181
Barth, Karl 2, 4–5, 11–2, 29, 31–2, 66, 72–3, 84, 102, 104, 149, 155, 169, 186, 196, 198–9, 206, 221, 230
Basil of Caesarea 53, 81, 90, 94, 194
Bauman, Zygmunt 270, 272–3, 275–6
body politic 14, 240, 243, 260, 266–8, 277, 279
Brentwood United Reformed Church 7–8, 227
British theology 5–6, 74

Chia, Roland 107, 224
chiasm, chiastic 18, 34, 58, 64, 108

Christ
  as judge 186, 209
  as king 176, 193, 236, 282
  as priest 176–8, 185, 187–91, 193, 198, 208, 231, 236
  as prophet 176, 193, 198, 236, 282
Christendom 17, 19, 21–2, 28, 34–5, 41, 135, 203, 210–13, 234
Coakley, Sarah 70–4, 81–2, 87–8, 107, 249–50
Coleridge, Samuel Taylor 18, 23–4, 31–2, 39, 40, 52–3, 61–2, 65–6, 108, 114, 116, 281
communion x, 6–8, 12, 53–4, 58–62, 64, 72, 74, 80, 88, 93, 95–9, 108–9, 122–42, 131–2, 137, 193–4, 197, 199, 211, 215, 217–19, 220, 229, 246, 268–9, 277, 279, 283
community ix–x, 6–8, 52, 54, 59–61, 82, 88, 96–7, 100, 109–10, 139, 145, 157, 174, 178, 189–90, 193–4, 201–2, 207, 209–12, 214–47, 256–60, 262–3, 265–8, 273–9, 282–4
concrete, concreteness 4, 11, 14, 23, 33–4, 47–8, 54–5, 57, 60, 66, 72, 77, 109, 112, 117, 121–2, 125, 133, 139, 166, 169, 172, 183, 192, 202, 209–10, 212, 214–15, 217–18, 222–3, 227–9, 230–1, 236–7, 242, 246, 251, 265, 278, 280, 283–4
consumerism 19, 49, 270–5
continuity 94–6, 105, 146, 186, 204, 231, 251, 282
createdness 4, 32, 36, 40, 55, 60, 97, 116, 121–2, 130, 134, 137, 145–6, 148, 162, 164, 218, 236, 276, 280
creation
  and history 36, 159
  as project 4, 13–14, 58, 116, 121, 123, 125, 128, 138, 140, 142, 146–51, 155, 157–60, 164–5, 170, 178–9,

182–4, 189, 193, 202–3, 205–6, 223, 245, 281, 283
Crisp, Oliver 199–200
cross 150, 164, 167, 170, 172, 176, 178–9, 181–9, 191, 208, 249, 261–8, 278–9, 284
crucifixion 176, 241, 262–4
culture (as sub-agency) 4, 116, 142, 153, 155, 158, 282
Cumin, Paul 124, 130, 200

Davidson, Ivor 113
deism 5, 22, 52, 74, 247
difference 21, 24, 32, 47–8, 51, 94–6, 98, 115, 156, 164, 232, 238, 260, 269–70, 274–5
   between creator and creation 32, 94, 115, 156, 232
disability 14, 268–70, 275, 277–9, 284
disability theology 275, 278–9, 284
disengagement 19–20, 22
dissent, dissenting 9–10, 23, 60, 133, 195, 209, 214, 217–18, 275
divine attributes 91, 103–5
dualism 4, 129–31, 142–3, 145, 165, 200, 212, 236, 277

Eastern Orthodoxy 74
ecclesiastical 21, 25, 100
ecclesiology 11, 13, 18, 58–9, 61, 67, 92, 108–9, 116–18, 125–8, 139, 172–3, 193, 202, 209–36, 242, 247, 250, 268, 280–4
ecological crisis 49
Eiesland, Nancy L. 269, 276–7
election 125, 139, 173, 174, 198, 220–1, 225–6, 228–31, 244, 265–7, 282
embodiment 4, 13, 19, 46, 49, 66, 129, 141, 165, 227, 234–5, 238–40, 248–52, 261–2
empire 221, 252–5
Enlightenment 4–5, 21, 23, 25–6, 29, 73–4, 114–15, 136, 155, 157, 168, 179, 219, 279
eschatology 37, 150, 156, 173, 178, 182–4, 204, 210, 213, 226, 228, 230, 234–9, 285

Eucharist, eucharistic *see also* Lord's Supper 240–2, 269, 279

Fiddes, Paul S. 111–12
flourishing 19, 21, 39, 44, 76
fool, foolish 263–8, 278–9
fragmentation 19, 25–8, 34, 43, 45
freedom 19, 22–8, 35, 38–42, 45, 47–50, 97, 102, 124, 130–1, 138–8, 142, 145–6, 150, 154, 159, 167, 169–70, 179–81, 191, 193, 199, 204, 214, 218, 220–1, 232, 239, 271–5

gardening 1
gender 60, 156–7, 249, 268–9
Gnostic, Gnosticism 27, 30, 36, 38, 40, 121, 128–31, 136, 141, 162
goodness 1, 4, 19, 26, 28, 30, 32–3, 36, 42, 50, 63, 104, 122, 130–1, 135, 137, 141, 153, 160, 164, 175, 183, 205, 281–2, 285

Harnack, Adolf 211, 219
Harris, Leon 107, 224
Harvey, Lincoln 68–9, 85–6
Hauerwas, Stanley 276
Hauptbriefe 2–3, 12, 66, 70, 106, 113, 117, 183, 210, 223–4, 246, 281
Hegel, G. W. F. 33, 37, 52, 196
heteronomies 19, 45, 135
history 11–12, 25, 35–6, 40, 48, 60, 65, 68, 70, 76–7, 82–5, 87, 105, 125, 134–5, 159, 183, 192, 196, 198, 206, 213–14, 230, 269
   Church 60, 213, 269
   human 135, 159, 183, 192, 196
   intellectual/theological 12, 25, 48, 65, 68, 70, 76–7, 82–5, 87, 134
   salvation 11, 105, 125, 214
Höhne, David 172–3
Holmes, Stephen R. 2, 7, 18, 45, 66, 69, 74, 81, 83, 86–90, 93, 97, 101, 103–4, 108, 113–14, 125, 158–9, 206, 227, 248, 282, 284
Holy Spirit (as perfecting cause) 13, 36, 41, 53–4, 57, 116, 138, 159, 172, 178, 191, 193–6, 199, 202–7, 216, 222, 228, 246, 282

homogeneity 19, 22, 36, 43, 45–8, 51–2, 54, 145
hooks, bell 274
Hughes, Bill 269–70, 274, 276–7
humanity (as priests) 137, 140, 151, 157, 159–60, 175–8, 203, 231–2, 238
hypostasis 18, 45, 54–7, 81, 93–4, 99, 108, 218

idol, idolatry 11, 63, 73, 82, 100, 105, 126, 158, 170, 180–2, 239
imago Dei 13, 25, 48, 50, 109–10, 117, 122, 128, 153, 155, 159, 168–9, 201, 209, 236, 282
immanence 22, 45, 193, 195
individualism 6, 22, 46–7, 50, 73, 81, 87, 100, 106, 155, 280–1
Irenaeus 27–8, 36, 40, 49, 116, 125, 127–33, 145, 149–50, 160, 162, 168, 281

Jenson, Robert 11, 75, 79, 82, 84, 111, 145, 177, 192–3, 200, 231, 235, 237–8, 240

Kant, Immanuel 26–7, 37, 47
Kilby, Karen 81–2, 87, 89, 100–2, 107, 217
King's College, London 5, 7, 69–70, 75, 126
koinōnia 58–9, 81, 215, 222–3, 226–7

Lord's Supper *see also* Eucharist 17, 92, 118, 139, 190, 192, 202, 222, 225–8, 238–47, 251–2, 255–6, 258–65, 268, 278–9, 283–4

McCormack, Bruce 7, 32
meal 92, 226, 239, 241, 243, 253, 255–65, 268
metaphysics 5, 10, 20, 28, 73, 79, 97, 133
modernity 17, 18–28, 34–8, 40, 42–3, 45, 47–50, 56, 58, 63, 65, 87, 134, 179–81, 247, 269–74, 276
    liquid 270–4
    solid 270–2, 274
Molnar, Paul 97, 104, 199–200
monad, monadic 21–2, 30, 32, 41, 54, 77–9, 89, 161, 164, 212, 214

monotheism 89–91
myth, mythology 26, 62, 136, 145, 181, 233, 277

Nausner, Bernhard 3, 70–1, 106–10, 117–18, 224

open transcendentals 3, 13, 18, 20, 23, 28–34, 52, 58, 61, 64–6, 71, 107–8, 113–14, 116, 187, 208, 210, 223–5, 281
oppression 25, 277
otherness 20–3, 31–2, 48, 50–2, 56–7, 60–3, 95, 97, 99, 109, 124, 131, 146, 214, 221, 268, 270–1, 274–5
    between creator and creation 31–2, 95, 97, 99, 124, 131, 214
    in-relation 21, 48, 51–2, 57, 63, 124, 131
ousia 54, 57, 81, 108–9
Owen, John 77, 195, 210, 214, 217–20

panentheism 146
pantheism 27, 37
Papanikolaou, Aristotle 98–9
particularity 18, 28–9, 33, 42–3, 45–58, 61–4, 78–9, 88, 145, 172–4, 191–3, 213, 268, 273–5, 282, 284
perfection (divine) 53, 93, 95, 97, 105, 130
perfection (of creation) 1, 4, 14, 33, 37, 41, 49, 57, 64, 116, 121–2, 124, 128, 130, 133–4, 138, 140–1, 147–50, 153, 157–60, 165, 168–9, 178–9, 183, 189, 191, 193, 196–8, 200, 202–9, 233–4, 244–82, 284
perichoresis 13, 18, 39–45, 52, 57–9, 64, 88, 100, 108–9, 114–15
personhood 2, 47, 54–6, 58, 74, 81, 87, 93, 95–101, 105, 108–10, 155, 169, 272, 275, 277
philosophy of religion 5, 12, 66, 112
Plato 20, 25, 30, 35, 47–8
Platonic, Platonism 36–7, 46–7, 49, 77–9, 141, 161, 221
plurality 21–6, 28, 30–4, 36, 39, 41, 48, 50, 52, 54, 244
Polanyi, Michael 29, 46, 115

politics 1, 14, 134, 139, 203, 206, 243, 247, 249, 251–2, 256, 258, 263, 265–6, 268, 271, 277–9, 284
  of belonging 243, 247, 249, 252, 265–6, 268, 278–9, 284
postmodernity 22–5, 28, 45, 56, 58, 134, 270
practice 10, 23, 26, 28, 47, 236, 243, 253, 255–8, 262, 269
preaching 8, 185, 236
prophet 175–6, 178, 193, 198, 236, 282

Rae, Murray ix, 1, 5, 8–10, 104, 149, 158, 243
rationality 23, 26, 29, 32, 35, 43–4, 58, 72, 104, 135
reason 20–1, 26, 29, 35, 48, 58, 102, 128, 135, 144, 168
recapitulation 13, 36, 40, 62, 117, 128, 138, 150, 167–8, 170–4, 184, 189, 200, 238, 244, 282
relationality 18, 23, 28, 33, 35, 48, 55, 57–8, 61–4, 72–3, 82, 93, 100, 115, 117, 157, 224
resurrection 38, 56, 92, 128, 150, 159–60, 165, 167, 176, 178–9, 184–5, 188, 190–4, 198, 208, 213, 233, 236, 239, 241, 245, 285
revelation 6, 10–11, 29, 32, 40–1, 53, 58, 64, 72–3, 95, 97, 102–5, 113, 125–6, 133, 136–7, 160, 251
Rhodes, Michael J. 256, 265, 268
Roman associations 243, 252–3, 258–60, 262
Roman Empire 211, 252–3, 255–6, 258, 262–5

sacrament, sacramental 8, 157, 193, 222, 226, 235–7, 240–3, 245, 269
sacrifice, 62, 175, 178, 184–92, 203, 220, 233–5, 241, 244–6
sacrifice of praise, 4, 13, 14, 58, 63, 64, 139, 159, 175–7, 184–5, 188–92, 201, 203, 207–8, 226–8, 240, 242, 244–6, 247, 249, 278–9, 283–5
Schwöbel, Christoph 6, 8, 34, 51, 72, 74–6, 78, 83, 85, 91–4, 111, 113, 122–5, 187
Selbständigkeit 130, 142, 146, 193, 200
Sexton, Jason S. 69
simplicity 78, 80, 88, 91–3, 96

social trinitarianism 12, 18, 53, 58–9, 65–6, 69–70, 76, 81–2, 86–7, 101–2, 110–12, 210
sociality 44, 58–64, 113, 118, 218, 225–8, 234, 237–8, 240–7, 249, 251–2, 257, 259–60, 263, 265, 267, 275, 278–9, 283
Sonderegger, Katherine 89–90
sports 1
stranger 270–1, 273–4, 276
substantiality 25, 51, 54–9, 64
Swinton, John 275–8
systematic theology 5, 10, 75, 105, 133, 249

Taylor, Charles 19–20
telos 64, 101, 136, 163, 170, 186, 190, 193, 207, 219, 233, 256, 282
temporal 31, 33, 35–46, 55, 63, 68, 121, 123, 125, 130–1, 139, 141, 145–51, 160–4, 171, 183–4, 198, 213, 220–1, 228–30, 259–60, 265, 282
Torah 92, 175, 186, 225, 234, 238–40, 244, 282
Torrance, Thomas F. 84, 86, 111, 114
totalitarianism 19, 21
transcendence 22–3, 34, 38, 63, 161, 195, 214, 218–19
Trinity, trinitarian
  analogies 2, 11–12, 14, 31–4, 41–2, 53, 56–66, 79–80, 93, 95–8, 101, 103, 105–6, 109–17, 125–6, 133, 152, 153, 208, 210–11, 215–19, 223–4, 226, 280–1
  Eastern and Western 6, 72–4, 77–8, 82, 86, 93–4
  economic 73, 79, 103–5, 125, 127
  immanent 40, 53, 73, 89, 103–4, 111, 114, 122–3, 125, 127, 132–3, 217
  more concrete 4, 11, 14, 72, 77, 109, 112, 117, 125, 133, 166, 169, 202, 246, 280, 284

Webster, John 5, 7, 115, 124, 140, 198–201, 216
Welborn, Laurence L. 264, 266
Western culture 1, 4, 13–14, 17–20, 45–6, 55, 64–6, 115, 121–2, 129, 133, 161, 247, 280–1

Whitney, William B. 124, 179, 183
wisdom 149–50, 164, 178, 197, 208, 249, 263–4, 278
Wittgenstein, Ludwig 29, 136
worship 4, 22, 62, 86, 89, 100, 139, 156–7, 168, 175, 179–81, 185, 188–93, 202–4, 207, 209, 222, 225–9, 232, 236–8, 240–7, 252, 258, 275, 283
Wright, Terry J. 173, 225

Zizioulas, John 6, 54, 59, 73–4, 80–2, 85–8, 97–9, 110–11, 214–15